Connie Wood

**Principles of
LIFE INSURANCE
Volume I**

JANICE E. GREIDER LL.B., FLMI, CLU
Counsel
State Farm Life and Accident Assurance Company

WILLIAM T. BEADLES D.B.A., CLU
Professor of Insurance, Emeritus
Illinois Wesleyan University
National Insurance Education Adviser
State Farm Insurance Companies

Volume I
Principles of
LIFE INSURANCE

1972 • Revised Edition

Published for

LIFE OFFICE MANAGEMENT ASSOCIATION
100 Colony Square, Atlanta, Georgia 30361

By

Richard D. Irwin, Inc.   Homewood, Illinois   60430

© LIFE OFFICE MANAGEMENT ASSOCIATION, 1964 and 1972

All rights reserved. No part of this publication may be reproduced, stored in a retrieval system, or transmitted, in any form or by any means, electronic, mechanical, photocopying, recording, or otherwise, without the prior written permission of the copyright holder.

Revised Edition
0 11 12 13 SD 5 4 3 2

ISBN 0-256-01396-9
Library of Congress Catalog Card No. 72–86621
Printed in the United States of America

To GRACE and LETA

PREFACE

This is the first revision of Volume I of a two-volume series of textbooks originally developed in 1964, for use in the Life Office Management Association Education Program. These books are intended especially for use by home and field office employees in the life insurance industry and have been designed generally to meet the needs of any beginning student of life insurance.

This book is primarily concerned with principles of life insurance, basic life insurance plans, and the most widely used types of individual life insurance contracts. However, it also includes single chapter surveys of industrial life insurance, individual health insurance, group life insurance, and group health and retirement plans. It thus constitutes a brief, general survey of the major personal insurance coverages.

For the majority of students who will use this book, it will be a true introduction to life insurance. For that reason, we have tried to present fundamental insurance principles in a context that will show the relationship of life and health insurance to insurance generally, and give the student some idea of the economic function of insurance as a means of handling risk. The areas covered are broad, and it has not been possible to discuss any aspects of the subject matter as fully as we would have liked. It is hoped, however, that the treatment has been sufficiently detailed to stimulate the student to complete the Life Office Management Association Insurance Education Program and perhaps undertake other related insurance courses.

We have tried to present this material as nontechnically as possible. For that reason, footnotes have been used sparingly, and as technical terms have been introduced, every effort has been made to define them in nontechnical language. All statistics concerning life insurance have been taken from the Life Insurance Fact Book, 1971 edition; and those relating to health insurance are based on statistics given in the 1971–1972 edition of the Source Book of Health Insurance, published by the Health Insurance Institute.

The authors are deeply indebted to many people, company reviewers as well as members of the LOMA educational staff. The former include Messrs. Henry DeMena, John F. Briggs, Jr., and Robert F. Muller, who read revisions as early as the fall of 1969 and made many helpful comments. Later reviewers were Mr. Eugene C. Foge and Miss Normagene Gillespie, and most recently, Messrs. Dean B. Carlson and Wendell Halvorson. We are especially indebted to Mr. Halvorson, whose detailed review of, and assistance with, chapters 15 and 16 were invaluable. Canadian reviewers include Mrs. Agnes Hepburn and Mr. William Lomax. To all of these people we express our sincerest thanks.

Members of the LOMA staff have worked closely with us at every stage of this revision, and it would be impossible to designate them all individually or thank them adequately. We do, however, want to express our special thanks to Messrs. Lynn G. Merritt and R. Werner Lederer, Mrs. Helen H. Wachsman, Mrs. Margaret L. Ferrara, and more recently, Messrs. Frederick H. Antil and Gene A. Morton, and Mrs. Linda L. Lagerroos. Each has helped in ways that were invaluable.

September 1972　　　　　　　　　　JANICE E. GREIDER
　　　　　　　　　　　　　　　　　　WILLIAM T. BEADLES

CONTENTS

1. WHY WE HAVE INSURANCE   1

The Problem of Economic Loss. Life Insurance Companies and Economic Loss: *Death. Loss of Health. Old Age.* How Economic Losses May Be Met: *Losses May Be Transferred. Losses May Be Assumed. Losses May Be Shared.* How Insurance Began: *The Earliest Years. Later Developments.* Insurance Means Loss-Sharing. Risk and Insurance: *The Meaning of Risk. How Insurance Reduces Risk.* How Losses Are Predicted: *Probability. The Law of Large Numbers.* How Modern Life Insurance Came About: *The Statistical Records. Insurable Interest.* The Insurable Risk: *Common to Large Numbers of People. The Loss Must Be Definite. The Loss Must Be Unexpected. No Undue Exposure to Catastrophic Loss. The Loss Should Not Be Trivial. The Chance of Loss Must Be Calculable. The Cost Should Be Feasible.* The Life Insurance Risk.

2. BASIC LIFE INSURANCE PLANS   20

Ordinary, Industrial, and Group Life Insurance. Term Life Insurance: *Term Life Insurance Policies. The Renewal Privilege. The Conversion Privilege. Automatic Renewal or Conversion. Term Life Insurance Policies Classified. Level or Varying Amounts of Coverage.* Whole Life Insurance: *Continuous-Premium, Whole Life Insurance. Limited-Payment, Whole Life Policies. The Single-Premium Policy.* Endowment Life Insurance: *Makeup of Endowment Insurance.* Uses of the Basic Plans: *Whole Life Plans. Term Life Insurance. Endowment Plans.* "Buy Term and Invest the Difference."

3. HOW LIFE INSURANCE IS PAID FOR   47

The Increasing Probability of Death. What the Level Premium Means: *The Assessment Principle. Inadequacies of the Assessment Plans. Fraternal Benefit Associations. Pay-as-You-Go Insurance. The Level Premium.* How Premiums Are Computed: *General Objectives. Mortality. Interest.*

The Net Single Premium. The Net Level Annual Premium. The Gross Annual Premium. The Early Life Insurance Companies: *In England. In the United States. The Beginning of Regulation.* The Legal Reserve: *The Amount of the Reserve.* Nonforfeiture Benefits. Notes on Canadian Practices.

4. HOW CONTRACTS ARE FORMED — 73

Insurance as a Contract. The Law of Informal Contracts: *Competent Parties. Assent to the Promise. Consideration. Form. Statutes Concerning Validity.* The Nature of the Life Insurance Contract: *The Contract Described.* The Law of Agency: *The Agency System. Agents and Their Authority.* Notes on Canadian Practices.

5. HOW PEOPLE BECOME INSURED — 90

The Life Insurance Application: *Contractual Information. Risk Appraisal Information. Agent's Authority and Effective Date of Insurance. Signatures. The Agent's Statement. The Initial Premium.* The Risk Appraisal Process. Offer and Acceptance in Life Insurance: *The Application Only Is Submitted. The Initial Premium Is Paid, but No Premium Receipt Is Given. A Premium Receipt Is Given.* The Policy Is Issued and Delivered: *Policy Forms. Settlement Arrangements. The "Entire" Contract. When the Insurance Is Effective.*

6. BENEFICIARY DESIGNATIONS AND THE SETTLEMENT OPTIONS — 109

The Right to Designate the Beneficiary. Beneficiaries in the Order of Their Rights: *The Primary Beneficiary. Contingent Beneficiaries. The Final Beneficiary.* Revocable and Irrevocable Beneficiaries. Minor Beneficiaries. How Beneficiary Designations May Be Changed: *The Endorsement Method. The Recording Method.* The Optional Modes of Settlement: *Election of the Options. The Interest Option. The Fixed-Period Option. The Fixed-Amount Option. The Life Income Options.* The Spendthrift Trust Provision. Settlement Option Agreements. Notes on Canadian Practices.

7. WHILE THE CONTRACT IS IN FORCE — 129

The Premium Provisions: *When Premiums Are Payable. Modes of Premium Payment. Deferring or Waiving Premium Payment.* Policy Loans: *The Request Loan. The Automatic Premium Loan.* Policyowner Dividends: *Premiums and Participation. The Dividend Options. The One-Year Term Dividend Option. Dividends in General. Other Policy Provisions Relating to Dividends.* The Nonforfeiture Benefits: *If the Policy Lapses. The Cash Surrender Benefit. Reduced Paid-up Insurance. Extended Term Insurance. The Automatic Option. Continued Privilege of Cash Surrender.* Notes on Canadian Practices: *Premiums. Nonforfeiture Benefits.*

8. OTHER OWNERSHIP RIGHTS   152

The Life Insurance Contract as Property. Assignments: *The Absolute Assignment. The Collateral Assignment. Conflicts under Collateral Assignments.* Transfer of Ownership by Endorsement: *Endorsement Method versus Assignment.* Change of Plan. Reinstatement. Notes on Canadian Practices: *Assignments.*

9. THE PAYMENT OF BENEFITS   164

Living Benefits: *Matured Endowments. Cash Surrenders.* Death Benefits: *The Policy Provisions. The Liability of the Company. The Risks Not Assumed. The Suicide Clause. The Accidental Death Benefit.* Contestable Claims: *The Incontestable Clause.* Claimants and Their Rights: *Problems Created by Assignment. Incomplete Beneficiary Changes. Interpleader. Loss of Rights by Law. Common Disasters and Short-Term Survivorship.* Settlement of the Proceeds: *The Amount Payable. One-Sum Settlement. The Settlement Agreement. Supplementary Contracts.* How Life Insurance Benefits Are Taxed: *Death Taxes. The Federal Income Tax.* Notes on Canadian Practices: *Taxation.*

10. SPECIAL WHOLE LIFE POLICIES AND ADDED BENEFITS   190

Variations of the Whole Life Plan: *Policies with Varying Premium Rates. Policies with Adjustments in Amount of Insurance.* Benefits That May Be Added by Riders. Disability Benefits: *The Waiver-of-Premium Benefit. Limitations. The Waiver-of-Premium Benefit in Term Policies. The Disability Income Benefit.* The Accidental Death Benefit: *Accidental Means. Risks Not Assumed under the Accidental Death Coverage. Value of the Coverage.* Term Life Insurance by Rider. The Guaranteed Insurability Benefit. The Additional Deposit Privilege.

11. SPECIAL POLICIES FOR FAMILY NEEDS   211

Insurance on the Husband's Life: *The Family Income Coverage. The Family Maintenance Coverage. Double Protection Policies.* Insurance on the Lives of Children (Juvenile Insurance): *Statutory Limitations on Amount. Ownership Arrangements. The Payor Benefit. The Guaranteed Insurability Coverage. Typical Juvenile Plans.* The Family Policies: *The Family Life Policy. Other Policy Provisions. Variations of the Family Life Policy. Other Family Plan Coverages.* The Joint Whole Life Policy.

12. INDUSTRIAL LIFE INSURANCE AND THE DEBIT SYSTEM   237

Historical Background. Distinctive Characteristics: *Marketing. Fewer Plans. Higher Premium Rates.* The Industrial Life Insurance Policy:

xii ▪ Contents

Option to Surrender. Premium Payment. The Grace Period. Dividend Provisions. Assignment. Settlement Provisions. Benefit for Loss of Eyesight or Limbs. The Accidental Death Benefit. Industrial Insurance for Children. Industrial Life Insurance—an Evaluation.

13. HEALTH INSURANCE 250

Health and Insurance: *The Development of Health Insurance.* Health Insurance Benefits. Disability Income Benefits: *The Amount of Income. When the Income Becomes Payable. How Long the Income Will Be Paid. Related Benefits. Excluded Risks. Business Overhead Expense Benefits.* Accidental Death and Dismemberment Benefits. Expense Reimbursement Benefits: *Hospital Expense Benefits. Surgical Expense Benefits. Regular Medical Expense Benefits. Major Medical Expense Benefits.* Family Coverages. Limited Policies. Risk Appraisal in Health Insurance: *General Objectives. Sources of Risk Appraisal Information. Antiselection. Factors of Insurability. Amount of Benefit.* Contractual Safeguards: *The Deductible Amount. Percentage Participation. Waiting Periods. Exclusions. Preexisting Conditions. The Policyowner's Right to Renew.* The Individual Health Insurance Contract: *Approval of Policy Forms. The Face Page. The Policy Schedule. The Benefit Provisions. Exceptions and Exclusions. The General Section.* The Uniform Policy Provisions Law: *Required Policy Provisions. Optional Policy Provisions.* The NAIC Advertising Code. Notes on Canadian Practices.

14. ANNUITIES 286

What an Annuity Is: *A Series of Payments. The Applicants Has Many Choices.* How the Applicant Will Pay: *Single-Premium Annuities. Annual-Premium Annuities.* Choices as to Minimum Guarantees: *The Annuity with Period Certain. Refund Annuities.* When Income Payments Begin: *The Annuity Due.* Annuities on More than One Life. The Survivorship Annuity. Annuities and the Settlement Options. How Annuity Payments Are Calculated: *Annuity Tables.* Retirement Annuities: *The Annual-Premium Deferred Annuity. The Retirement Income Contract. The Flexible-Premium Annuity.* The Variable Annuity: *Operation of the Variable Annuity.* Tax-Sheltered Annuities: *Eligible Organizations. Requirements. The "Tax Shelter."* How Annuity Income Is Taxed. Notes on Canadian Practices.

15. GROUP LIFE INSURANCE 314

Origin and Development: *The Earliest Group Plans. The NAIC Model Group Insurance Bill.* Insurance for Employer-Employee Groups: *Legal Requirements. The Selection Process. General Characteristics of Employee Group Plans. The Amount of Insurance.* Group Life Insurance Premiums: *Minimum Premium Rates. General Principles. Dividends and Experience Rating. Reserves.* The Group Life Insurance Policy: *The Grace Period. The Incontestable Clause. The Beneficiary. Conversion Provisions. Assign-

Contents • xiii

ment of Group Life Insurance. Individual Certificates. Administration of the Plan. Permanent Life Insurance for Employee Groups: *Level-Premium Group Permanent Life Insurance. Group Paid-Up Insurance. Group/Ordinary Life Insurance.* Accidental Death and Dismemberment Insurance. Creditor Group Life Insurance: *Makeup of the Group. Premium Payment.* Notes on Canadian Practices: *Group Life Insurance. Creditor's Group Life Insurance.*

16. GROUP HEALTH INSURANCE AND RETIREMENT PLANS   343

Group Health Insurance: *Disability Income Benefits. Medical Expense Benefits. The Major Medical Plans. Other Health Coverages.* Blue Cross and Blue Shield Plans: *Blue Cross Plans. Blue Shield Plans.* Group Coverages and Retirement Plans: *A "Qualified" Retirement Plan. Definitely Determinable Benefits. How Retirement Plans Are Funded. Trusteed Retirement Plans. Group Deferred Annuities. Deposit Administration Plans. Combination Plans.* Retirement Plans for Self-Employed. Notes on Canadian Practices: *Health Insurance Plans. Group Coverages and Retirement Plans.*

GLOSSARY OF COMMON LIFE INSURANCE TERMS   364

INDEX   377

1 WHY WE HAVE INSURANCE

For one reason or another, insurance is important to almost everyone in countries such as the United States and Canada. Homes and furnishings are routinely insured against loss by fire. Insurance is essential if one owns or drives a car. Life insurance is so important to the public generally that United States and Canadian residents alone purchase more than $200 billion of life insurance every year.

Traditionally, different kinds of insurance have been discussed and studied separately. However, the basic insurance principles are common to all lines; and in recent years, there has been a noticeable trend among insurance companies to write more than one kind of insurance. Therefore, although this book will be concerned primarily with life insurance, it will begin with a brief consideration of insurance generally.

■ THE PROBLEM OF ECONOMIC LOSS

Fundamentally, we have insurance to protect ourselves against the possibility of economic loss. Webster defines loss as the "unintentional parting with something of value." Economic loss, therefore, may be defined as the unintentional parting with something of monetary value. Insurance is concerned primarily with possible losses involving monetary value.

Economic losses are of many kinds and vary widely as to severity. Some are small and relatively unimportant. A neglected cigarette causes a fire in an apartment, damaging a few draperies and an easy chair. A driver swerves his automobile sharply to avoid a bicyclist and damages another car. Other losses are more extensive, often making headlines. A trusted employee disappears, taking with him many thousands of dollars in marketable securities. A commercial plane crashes. A raging tropical storm destroys millions of dollars in property values.

These examples, illustrating different kinds and amounts of loss, have two characteristics in common. First, each loss is unexpected. Second, the loss or losses in each instance are measurable in money. Each example, therefore, illustrates loss in the insurance sense of the word—an unintentional parting with something of monetary value.

■ LIFE INSURANCE COMPANIES AND ECONOMIC LOSS

Some kinds of economic losses have been recognized and dealt with for centuries. Loss of property transported in trade, for instance, was recognized as a potential economic loss at a very early date. Agreements specifying how and by whom such losses should be borne have been traced as far back as 2250 B.C. and were the earliest forerunners of insurance. By contrast, the idea of death as a cause of economic loss did not attain much significance until after the Industrial Revolution. Thus, life insurance as we know it today has had the major part of its development since 1800.

Life insurance companies are concerned with three basic kinds of economic loss: economic loss resulting from death, economic loss resulting from accident or sickness, and economic problems resulting from old age.

Death

Few people would question the fact that death is a frequent cause of economic loss. Last illness and burial expenses clearly mean financial obligations for someone, regardless of when an individual's death may occur. Much greater, however, is the loss of future earnings that may result from death during a person's earning years.

The continued life of a wage earner may have economic significance to many people. Certainly it is important to any dependents he may have. It is important also to his employer and to his creditors, if any. If the individual is in business for himself or as a partner, his life may be economically significant to his employees, to his partner or partners, and to other business associates as well.

Often the continued life of a single individual may have a potential economic value—sometimes referred to as the "human life value"—of many tens of thousands of dollars. This value is lost at his death. Aside from any other considerations, therefore, death during one's earning years (often referred to as "early death") may mean extensive economic losses to many people. Life insurance offers a way of reducing the impact of such losses, no matter how large they may be or when death may occur.

Loss of Health

The expenses of medical care and treatment and the loss of income resulting from disabling accidents and sickness are measured in billions of dollars every year. Insurance plans which provide protection against such losses are generally classified as health insurance. A great deal of health insurance is sold by insurance companies that do not offer life insurance, but life insurance companies are by far the largest writers of health insurance today.

Old Age

The financial problems of old age and the possibility that even a relatively well-to-do person may outlive his financial resources constitute the third area of possible economic loss with which life insurance companies are concerned. Protection against this possibility is provided by the annuity.

An annuity is an agreement under which an insurance company will pay an income at regular intervals to a person called the annuitant. There are many different kinds of annuities. Under some versions, payments are made as long as the annuitant lives; under others, payments are made only for a specified number of years. As it is most commonly understood, however, an annuity means a guaranteed income paid by an insurance company, at regular intervals, for the lifetime of the annuitant, no matter how long the annuitant may live. An agreement of this kind clearly offers guaranteed protection against the possibility of outliving one's financial resources.

■ HOW ECONOMIC LOSSES MAY BE MET

Often a cause of economic loss can be prevented. Development of the Salk polio vaccine, for example, made it possible to prevent a significant cause of economic loss. Obviously, when prevention is possible, and economically feasible, it is the most desirable approach to the problem.

Even if a cause of loss cannot be prevented, the effects of loss may be reduced or minimized. The use of fire-resistant materials in building construction may reduce both the number and the amount of fire losses. Safety campaigns and safety devices in factories have succeeded in preventing and reducing the serious results of many industrial accidents. Discoveries in medical science have brought about significant reductions in death rates, particularly at the lower ages and from communicable diseases. In spite of the best efforts of everyone concerned, however, some economic losses will occur. Consequently, several ways of meeting them have been developed.

Losses May be Transferred

One of the traditional ways for individuals to meet economic losses that are caused by the negligence of others is to sue the person or persons responsible for causing them. If John Miller negligently causes injury to Richard Smith, Smith may sue Miller and recover money damages. It should be apparent, however, that this merely transfers, or shifts, the loss from one person to another. If the loss would have been an economic burden to Smith, there is no reason to believe that it will not also be a burden to Miller. Shifting an economic loss from one individual to another, therefore, obviously benefits the person who wins the lawsuit, but it does not furnish a completely satisfactory solution, socially, to the basic problem.

Losses May be Assumed

Many economic losses, particularly small ones, are simply borne by the persons on whom they originally fall. If one's umbrella is stolen, he buys another. If one is ill and must purchase medicine, he pays the doctor and the pharmacist out of current income. Similarly, many losses incurred by business firms are paid in the normal course of business. A business machine is accidentally damaged and is repaired at the owner's expense. Even relatively large losses are often met out of current earnings by many businesses.

Beyond a certain point, however, economic losses can present a serious problem to almost any individual or business firm. Illness for several months or longer can mean serious financial loss to an individual. Losses caused by embezzlement, extensive fires, or liability for property damage or loss of life can easily exceed the financial capacity even of large businesses. Without some practical means of reducing the impact of such losses, therefore, the fear of incurring them could have a highly inhibiting effect on individuals and business firms alike.

Losses May be Shared

For the average person and the average business, insurance furnishes the most practical means of protection against the possibility of serious economic loss from such hazards as fire, liability for personal injuries, illness, and death. Insurance is the most feasible way of handling such losses because it is essentially a loss-sharing arrangement. In other words, people who are subject to any one of many possible economic losses can, through insurance, join with others who are subject to similar losses in such a way that the losses experienced by any members of the group are shared by all members.

People and businesses become insured by entering into insuring agreements with an insurance company and by making regular payments (called "premiums") to the company. In exchange for these payments, the insurance company agrees to reimburse the insured person or business, as provided in the contract, for the losses actually experienced. To summarize, therefore, insurance may be defined as a systematic plan for protection against economic losses, in which large numbers of people agree to make regular payments to an insurance organization in exchange for the assurance that they will be reimbursed for losses they may suffer from such hazards as fire, windstorm, accident, and death. Without the assurance such agreements provide, many business enterprises would not be launched and many personal ventures would never be undertaken.

■ HOW INSURANCE BEGAN

The Earliest Years

Agreements resembling insurance were used in Babylon several thousand years ago. At that time, traders were traveling throughout the known world, selling merchandise of Babylon; and they were exposed to many dangers in their travels. To protect themselves against losses from marauders in their journeys, these traders made agreements with the owners of the goods they sold that the traders would not be held responsible if the goods were stolen from them. The Romans later adopted this practice and developed agreements strongly resembling what was later to be known as marine insurance.

Practices similar to life insurance also had their beginnings in the distant past. The early Egyptians (and later the Greeks) had religious societies whose members made regular contributions to provide burials for themselves, in accordance with the religious rites of the society. The Romans adopted this practice also, but made the benefits available without respect to religion.

It is probable that the Romans used such plans to provide funds in excess of those needed merely for funeral expenses. In fact, there is evidence that in the early centuries of the Christian era the Romans were deciding legal questions relating to contracts that provided for money to be paid "if he dies" and "when he shall die," suggesting agreements strongly resembling life insurance contracts. The Romans also developed a table of values for annuities, which was used for many centuries. With the fall of Rome, however, these practices disappeared; and they did not reappear for many years.

Later Developments

Insurance of Ships and Cargoes. In the 11th century, trade began to thrive again, and with it came the development of marine insurance—that is, insurance of ships and cargoes. By the middle of the 15th century, special marine insurance laws were in force in Barcelona and Florence; and by the time England became an important commercial nation, marine insurance practices were well established. Insuring agreements of this kind were so important during the Elizabethan era that a special court was established in 1601 to hear and decide marine insurance cases.

As the business of insurance grew, some people began to devote their full time to making insurance agreements. They became known as "underwriters," because of their practice of writing their names under the insurance proposals, together with the amount of the insurance they were willing to assume.

During the 17th century, these underwriters frequented the London coffeehouses, where information was available concerning ships, tides, and other factors relating to the seagoing trade. Edward Lloyd, the proprietor of one of the coffeehouses of the day, was especially cooperative in making shipping information available to his underwriter-customers. As a result, his coffeehouse gradually became better known than any other as a center where underwriters gathered. From that time to the present, "Lloyd's of London" has been an important name in the insurance world.

Insurance Against Fire Losses. Fire insurance also had its modern beginnings during this period. Plans for sharing fire losses among groups of people had been known for many years. As early as the 13th century, organizations of craftsmen and merchants (guilds) had plans for sharing the fire losses of their members. Following the great London fire of 1666, however, there was more serious concern about the problem of fire, and several fire insurance societies were organized during the next half century. One of these, the Sun Fire Office, formed in 1710, has continued in business to the present time.

Agreements Insuring Lives. Specific references to contracts concerning loss of life date back as early as the 13th century. Most of these were agreements to "insure" the lives of ship captains and traveling merchants, and they were made in connection with marine insurance agreements covering the ships in which these persons traveled. As a result, such "life insurance" was limited to the period of the particular voyage concerned; and the rates were based on little more than rough estimates of chance happenings. As a matter of fact, chance played such an important part in agreements of this kind that in the Netherlands and in France as late as the 1790's, all life insurance was considered illegal, as mere wagering.

England, however, had no laws against agreements concerning human lives, and wagering life insurance contracts were openly made during the reign of Elizabeth I. Such agreements reached the height of their popularity during the 18th century, when people freely made "life insurance" contracts based solely on the dates well-known persons might die. With good reason, this has been called the speculative period in the history of life insurance.

Even during these years, however, there was some awareness of a need for life insurance in the sense in which the term is used today —that is, as protection against economic loss resulting from death. During these years, also, developments were taking place that would make life insurance possible on a scientific basis, rather than on the basis of mere chance. To realize the significance of these developments, it is necessary to understand the basic operation of insurance as a loss-sharing plan.

■ INSURANCE MEANS LOSS-SHARING

The effect of insurance so far as loss is concerned is most simply illustrated in fire insurance. Suppose a person owns a home valued at $40,000, subject to a mortgage indebtedness of $25,000. If the

8 ▪ Principles of Life Insurance

house is completely destroyed by fire, he will have lost what he has invested in the property and yet he will still owe the amount of the unpaid debt. With adequate fire insurance, however, he could collect the value of the home ($40,000), pay the mortgage, and have his $15,000 equity in cash. This would enable him to buy or build another home, whichever he preferred. In other words, with adequate insurance, an otherwise serious financial loss can be so effectively cushioned that the insured person can go on, in an economic sense, very much as if the loss had not occurred.

Insurance furnishes this protection by applying a very simple principle: if the economic losses that actually result from a given hazard such as fire can be shared by large numbers of people subject to such losses, the cost to each person will be relatively small. Consider how this principle applies in fire insurance.

Large numbers of persons who own or have an interest in property have fire insurance, for all are subject to a possible economic loss if their property burns. Not everyone, in fact very few of these insured people, will suffer a fire loss during any given period of time. Nevertheless, all of them pay premiums; and these premiums are so calculated that they will enable the company to pay the losses experienced by members of the group, as well as the costs of administering the insuring plan. If enough people are insured in a group of this kind, the premium for each member can be kept to a relatively small amount.

In this way, insurance spreads among large numbers of people the economic losses actually experienced by some members of the group from such hazards as fire, automobile collisions, and early death. People become members of such groups because they are aware that they themselves could experience such a loss or losses—that is, they know they have a "risk" of loss.

▪ RISK AND INSURANCE

The Meaning of Risk

Although the word "risk" has a variety of meanings, in the economic sense it always conveys the ideas of the *possibility* of loss and of *uncertainty* with respect to its occurrence. Each of these ideas is important. For instance, the homeowner does not expect to have a fire loss, but he knows that he could have one. Similarly, the applicant for life insurance does not really expect to die during his earning years, leaving his dependents without support, but he knows that this could happen. It is this possibility of loss that prompts people to obtain insurance.

The idea of uncertainty is equally important. The person whose house has just burned cannot obtain insurance against its loss. For him, there is no uncertainty with respect to fire loss. His loss is an accomplished fact. In the insurance sense, therefore, risk of loss implies not only exposure to loss but also uncertainty with respect to its occurrence.

Even this does not define the term adequately. As a second step, therefore, the concept of risk may be divided into *speculative* and *pure* risk.

Speculative risk involves uncertainty as to the happening of an event which may result in loss but which may, on the other hand, result in gain. For instance, people speculate on the stock market, knowing that they may lose but hoping that they will gain. Others may invest in an untried corporation, hoping that it will succeed and produce a profit for them, but knowing that it may fail and cause them loss. A speculator is willing to face this possibility of loss because of the chance that he may profit. The possibility of gain may at times be remote, but in a speculative venture it is always there.

With pure risk, the situation is quite different. Pure risk involves uncertainty as to the happening of an event which may produce a loss but which involves no possibility of gain. The homeowner, for example, has a risk of loss by fire. A fire would mean an economic loss to him, with no legitimate possibility of gain. Similarly, the death of a husband and father will result in economic loss to his widow and children who were dependent upon his income-producing abilities. This possibility of economic loss, unaccompanied by any possibility of gain—pure risk—is the only kind of risk with which insurance is concerned.

Pure and speculative risks may be closely related. For example: Edward Long builds a factory, equips it, hires workers, and takes the risk of starting a manufacturing business. He has a chance of failing and thus a risk of loss. He also has a chance of making a profit, and therefore he has a chance of gain. Thus, the business venture itself involves a speculative risk. However, as the owner of property, Long has another risk of loss—loss of the factory building and its contents by fire. That risk of loss is unaccompanied by any possibility of gain. It is a pure risk, therefore, and a proper subject for insurance.

How Insurance Reduces Risk

It is frequently said that insurance reduces risk—that is, that it reduces uncertainty. This idea, however, requires some explanation. For example, if a possible fire loss is uncertain to the individual insured, why is it not equally uncertain to the insurance company? If the individual cannot know when he will die, why is the position of the life insurance company any more certain? The answer is found in the fact that insurance companies are always considering risk with respect to groups of people rather than individuals.

To the individual, losses of the kind we have been discussing will always be uncertain. Edward Long's factory, for instance, may or may not be destroyed by fire this year, next year, or any other year. He has no way of knowing when or if a fire will occur, and insurance does not change his position in that respect.

The insurance company, however, is in a different situation. True, it cannot know, any more certainly than Long can, whether fire will destroy that particular factory during any given year. With adequate statistics concerning fire losses, however, the company knows the number of similar buildings (out of every thousand, for instance) that are destroyed by fire each year. And, unlike the individual insured, the insurance company is in a position to apply that knowledge.

A fire insurance company insures hundreds of buildings similar to Long's, and there is little reason to believe that the proportion of fire losses in future years among such buildings will be significantly different from the number of losses that have been experienced in prior years. Under these circumstances, the insurance company is not considering uncertain losses. On the contrary, it can predict future losses with a considerable degree of accuracy, but only because its predictions are made with respect to groups. The insurance company does not know whether Long, Smith, or Jones will have a fire loss in any given year, but it does know approximately how many losses it must be prepared to pay among the buildings it has insured, and that is all the certainty it needs.

■ HOW LOSSES ARE PREDICTED

An individual who has adequate fire insurance is said to have transferred his risk of loss by fire to his fire insurance company. The insurance company, on its part, reduces the risk for everyone it insures because it is able to make predictions of future losses on a group basis. In arriving at these predictions, the company relies primarily on the principles of probability and appropriate statistics. It is important, therefore, to have some understanding of these subjects.

Probability

Probability is the mathematics of chance. As a study, it is said to have had its beginning when a French count became interested in his chances of winning at roulette. He asked the famous French mathematician Blaise Pascal to consider the problem, and Pascal developed the theory of probability.

In simplified terms, probability, as it is used in insurance, concerns the mathematical expression of how many incidents of a certain kind may be expected to occur in a given number of trials or exposures. For example, how many tosses of a coin will be heads, if you toss it 10,000 times? How many deaths may be expected this year among a group of 10,000 insureds, all 35 years of age?

Probability can be expressed as a fraction or as a percentage. Thus, one chance in 100 would be expressed as 1/100 or 1 percent or .01. The denominator indicates the number of times the event in question *could* happen. (All tosses could be heads; all insureds age 35 *could* die this year.) The numerator expresses the number of times the event is expected to happen. Thus, if a coin is expected to land heads up 500 times out of 1,000 tosses, the probability of its landing heads up is expressed as 500/1000 or ½ or 50 percent.

Insurance companies use the principles of probability, together with statistics of past losses, to estimate the number of losses that may be expected to occur in the future among the members of a specified group. Premium rates can then be computed that will produce sufficient funds to pay the predicted losses within the group.

To use a very simple example, assume that one out of every 100 insured homes burned last year and that the average loss from each fire was $10,000. A company insuring 100 similar homes might reasonably expect one fire loss in the next year, requiring a payment of $10,000. The probability of loss would be one in 100 or 1/100. Multiplying this fraction by the average loss of $10,000, we have $100, the premium each insured would have to pay in order to meet the expected losses.

In actual premium computation, other factors have to be taken into consideration, such as the expenses of operating the business and allowances for possible variations in losses actually experienced. The example used, however, suggests one additional point—that a small number of exposures will probably not produce a very reliable result. In a group of 100 insured houses, there could easily be no fire losses whatever for a year. On the other hand, there might be several. And variations of this kind would have a significant effect on the adequacy of the premium rate. In considering the matter of probability, therefore, the law of large numbers is of the utmost importance.

The Law of Large Numbers

The law of large numbers assumes that events which happen seemingly by chance, actually will be found to follow a predictable pattern, if enough such happenings are observed. In accordance with this law, the greater the number of happenings one observes, the more nearly will the actual results approach those indicated by the mathematics of probability.

For example, if there are 50 red balls and 50 white ones mixed in a jar, and if one ball is drawn at random, it seems clear that the chances of withdrawing a red ball on the first try should be 50 in 100, or $\frac{1}{2}$. Suppose 10 of the balls are withdrawn, each being replaced before the next is taken. Theoretically, five of these should be white and five red. Actually, eight may be white and two red, or four may be white and six red. In other words, it is only rarely that the probable results will be obtained in any small scale practical application. As more and more withdrawals and replacements are made, however, the actual results will more and more closely approach the theoretical probabilities.

The principles of probability and the law of large numbers are basic to insurance. The development of these mathematical tools, therefore, was the first essential step in the evolution of life insurance from a generally speculative venture into a scientific process. The second step was the application of these mathematical principles to records of deaths among the populations of England and other countries, so that predictions of expected deaths at various ages became possible. In this way, the foundation was laid for life insurance as we know it today.

■ HOW MODERN LIFE INSURANCE CAME ABOUT

The Statistical Records

In the early 17th century, a series of plagues swept across the city of London. As a means of informing the public, death records called "bills of mortality" were published each week in the various parishes of the city. This custom was continued even after the plagues had subsided; and for the first time, a continuing record of deaths became available.

In 1661, an English mathematician named John Graunt published a scientific study based on these records. This study contained what was probably the first mortality table—that is, a statistical table showing rates of death. The mortality table included in John Graunt's study, however, was of limited usefulness, because the records on which it was based had not reflected the ages of the persons at death.

Some 30 years later, Sir Edmund Halley, the famous astronomer, constructed mortality tables based on statistics he obtained from the city of Breslau, in Silesia. There the death records included the age of each person at death, which, of course, was exactly what was needed. Nevertheless, it was half a century more before these mathematical studies were given application in the field of life insurance.

About the middle of the 1700's, another English mathematician named James Dodson was refused membership in a life insurance association because he was too old (he was past 45). This challenged him to work out a plan under which higher premiums could be paid by older persons upon entrance into an insurance plan. In devising this plan, he took a basic step toward establishing a life insurance premium structure on a scientific basis. In fact, the company he eventually founded, The Society for Equitable Assurance on Lives and Survivorships (later shortened to The Equitable Society), is still in operation in England today.

Insurable Interest

A third significant event in the development of life insurance took place in 1774, when the English Parliament enacted a law against wagering insurance contracts. Specifically, this law stated that an insurance contract would be unlawful unless the person to whom the insurance proceeds would be paid had an insurable interest—that is, a risk of loss if the event insured against should occur.

It is not easy to say in every case exactly what constitutes an insurable interest. In property insurance, for instance, a person has an insurable interest if he would suffer a monetary loss in the event the insured property should be damaged or destroyed by the hazard insured against (fire, windstorm, etc.). Thus, anyone who owns a building has an insurable interest in that building so far as fire insurance is concerned.

In life insurance, as will be discussed in a later chapter, the insurable interest requirement is applied in two different ways, depending on whether the insurance is applied for by the person whose life is insured or by someone else. When the insurable interest requirement is met, however, life insurance may be considered on essentially the same basis as any other kind of insurance—as a plan for sharing losses that result from the event insured against.

■ THE INSURABLE RISK

The basic principles of prediction and of premium computation are essentially the same for life insurance as for any other kind of insurance. In applying these principles, however, some difficulties are encountered in life insurance that are not met in other kinds of insurance. To understand these problems, it is necessary to examine some of the basic characteristics of an insurable risk.

Theoretically, any pure risk could be the subject of insurance. As a practical matter, however, other requirements must be met before a risk can be said to be insurable. Among these requirements are the following: the risk must be common to a fairly large number of people; it must involve a loss that is definite; the loss must be unexpected; there should be no undue exposure to catastrophic loss; the loss should not be trivial; the chance of loss must be reasonably calculable; and the cost should be feasible. These requirements will be discussed in the above order.

Common to Large Numbers of People

One of the most important requirements of an insurable risk is that it must be common to a large number of people. Otherwise, of course, the law of large numbers cannot be applied. With only a few insured persons, the insurance company's position is little better than that of the individual. Under those circumstances, it is impossible to make reliable predictions of future losses, and equitable premium rates cannot be established. However, since every person faces the risk of premature death for a considerable part of his life, finding a large number of people subject to the risk is not a problem in life insurance.

The Loss Must be Definite

A second requirement is that the loss be definite. An insurable risk must concern an event which, if it happens, will produce a loss that can be clearly identified. For example, in disability insurance, it is often difficult to know whether the loss insured against has actually been suffered—that is, whether an injury is as disabling as the insured may contend that it is. For this reason many health insurance contracts define the losses insured against in terms of loss of income or of actual expenses incurred. Such definitions furnish objective standards against which questionable losses can be measured. By contrast, the loss resulting from death is certainly definite, although it is not always easy to measure in an economic sense.

The Loss Must be Unexpected

An insurable risk must involve a loss that is unexpected and, so far as the individual is concerned, unpredictable. In other words, the loss must occur by chance. In most instances, the loss involved in life insurance meets this requirement. Death itself is not unexpected, of course, but most people cannot predict the time their deaths will occur. Those who, for some reason, are in a position to do so are generally suffering from a serious illness or contemplating suicide. In the former situation, their applications will be denied because they are uninsurable. In the second situation, even though a policy may be issued, death by suicide will be excluded during the first two years by the suicide provision of the policy. In other kinds of insurance, also, losses deliberately caused by the insured are frequently excluded by specific policy provisions.

No Undue Exposure to Catastrophic Loss

An insurable risk should not present any undue exposure to catastrophic loss. Insurance is not practicable if catastrophic losses are frequent, and insurance companies take numerous precautions to guard against such possibilities. For instance, fire insurance companies spread their risks over large territories; and insurance companies of all kinds often transfer some of their business to other insurers, if they have unusually large concentrations of risks. (Agreements under which such transfers are made by one insurance company to another are called "reinsurance" agreements.)

In general, the risk of death qualifies very well with respect to this requirement, although catastrophic losses are occasionally experienced as the result of epidemics, such as the influenza epidemic of 1918, and natural catastrophes such as floods, tornadoes, and earthquakes.

The Loss Should Not be Trivial

An insurable risk should concern a loss that is not trivial. Any insurance plan involves some expense—for issuing policies, accounting for premiums, and paying claims, to list only major operations. These expenses must ultimately be borne by the policyowner as a part of the premium he pays. If losses, when they occur, mean a genuine hardship to the policyowner, the expense element in his premium will be well justified, because of the protection he receives. If the losses insured against are relatively small, however, the policyowner may be better advised to assume (that is, not insure) such losses, than to pay premiums which include a disproportionate element for the expense of administering the insuring plan.

The loss with which life insurance is concerned—loss of human life—is never trivial. However, health insurance is frequently concerned with losses that may be relatively small. Medical expense coverages, for example, may involve numerous small claims. In such instances, the costs of claim handling and administration may consume an unreasonably large percentage of the premium. To avoid this, health insurance contracts frequently provide that benefits will be paid only after covered medical expenses have reached and exceeded a stated minimum amount, commonly referred to as a "deductible." This arrangement conserves a larger portion of the premium dollar to meet losses that involve a genuine financial burden.

The Chance of Loss Must be Calculable

To be insurable, a risk must be of such a nature that it is possible to calculate the chance of loss with reasonable accuracy. The risk of premature death meets this requirement satisfactorily, but the statistics and procedures necessary for such calculation were developed only over an extended period of time.

The Cost Should be Feasible

An insurable risk should involve losses of such a nature that those experienced by some members of the insured group can be met at a reasonable cost to everyone. For example, there is no theoretical reason why life insurance could not be provided to a group of 95-year-old persons. However, according to the general population death rates, death benefits would become payable for almost one-third of these people before they reached age 96. Thus the premium rates for life insurance at such an advanced age would be prohibitively high.

Insurance premiums should be small enough that they can be paid without undue hardship by a relatively large number of people. This makes it easier to obtain the large numbers of insureds necessary for reliable predictions and, at the same time, makes the benefits of insurance available to more people.

■ THE LIFE INSURANCE RISK

The risk of premature death meets most of the requirements of an insurable risk. Death is common to everyone; hence, the large numbers requirement presents no problem. Death is definite and usually unexpected; the resulting loss is not trivial; and the chance of loss, based on appropriate statistics, is easily calculated. There is some possibility of catastrophic loss, but safeguards can be used to minimize this possibility. Achieving a feasible premium, however, was a problem for the early insuring plans, because of basic differences in the nature of the life insurance risk as compared to the risk with which other kinds of insurance are concerned. These differences are found primarily in the areas of certainty, totality and value of the loss, and probability.

One of the most significant differences between the risk of loss by death and that of loss by fire, automobile accident, embezzlement, and other similar hazards is the fact that death, unlike the other hazards, is certain to occur. Many buildings are erected, stand for years, and are ultimately torn down, without having suffered damage of any kind from fire. In fact, the majority of insurable risks concern events that may or may not happen to the individual insured. The risk of death is not uncertain in this sense. The uncertainty that makes death an insurable risk is not *whether* it will happen but *when*. In this sense, death is uncertain and thus a proper subject for insurance.

A second difference between the risk of death and the risks involved in other forms of insurance is the fact that when death occurs, the loss is total. Partial losses are frequent in other kinds of insurance. In life insurance, by contrast, the total future income the insured might have earned is lost by reason of his death.

A third difference that characterizes the life insurance risk, as compared with the risk in other forms of insurance, is found in the difficulty of measuring the value of the loss, even approximately, in monetary terms. Losses resulting from fire, theft, tornado, illness, accidents, and so on, can be appraised and valued by objective standards. In health insurance, the amount of loss is frequently established as the expense actually incurred for medical treatment and hospitalization. In most instances, however, there is no similar way to measure loss in life insurance. If death occurs during the insured's earning years, the loss may be measured by his probable future earnings if he had lived; but if death occurs after retirement, this method is inapplicable. For this reason, a life insurance policy states a definite amount of insurance that will be payable at the death of the insured, without regard to the question of economic loss. Most other forms of insurance are designed to pay the amount of the loss suffered, or the amount of the insurance, whichever is less.

The fourth and most significant difference between the risk of death and the risk involved in other forms of insurance is found in the area of probability. Except for the first 10 or 11 years, the probability of death increases relentlessly and progressively with each additional year of life. This characteristic—the increasing probability of death as one grows older—is of major significance in the calculation of life insurance premiums. For example, an annual premium that will be just adequate to pay death claims in the first year of insurance, for a group of 35-year-old insureds, will not be adequate to pay claims among the survivors of the same group (now age 36) the very next year. The premium will be even less adequate the following year, and this inadequacy will increase more and more rapidly with each succeeding year. The full implications of this increasing probability of death were not recognized in connection with the earliest life insurance plans; and, as a result, many early life insuring associations failed. It was not until a level-premium system was devised that life insurance became possible on more than a relatively limited scale.

Under the level-premium system, a premium is established that can be paid in the same amount each year as long as the policy remains in force. Because the rate of death increases from year to year, claim payments will increase similarly under any group of life insurance policies. Consequently, level premiums that will be adequate for the lifetimes of a group of insureds will be more than adequate to pay death claims in the early years and less than adequate in later years. Under the level-premium system, therefore, the amounts not needed to pay claims in the early years are invested so that they will be available to help pay claims that are presented in later years. The level-premium system will be discussed in more detail later, but first, some acquaintance with the basic plans of life insurance is necessary.

■ QUESTIONS FOR REVIEW

1. Define "economic loss" in the insurance sense of the term.
2. What are the losses with which life insurance companies are concerned?
3. List three methods, other than insurance, by which the problem of economic loss may be met.
4. Why is insurance often preferable to other ways of meeting economic loss?
5. Describe the origin of the word "underwriter."
6. Briefly summarize the loss-sharing principle applied in insurance.
7. State the essential difference between pure risk and speculative risk.
8. Briefly discuss (1) the principles of probability and (2) the "law of large numbers" as they are used in insurance.
9. Define "insurable interest."
10. List and explain the basic requirements of an insurable risk. Which of these requirements presented the most serious problems in the development of modern life insurance?
11. List four ways in which the risk of loss in life insurance differs from the risk with which most other kinds of insurance are concerned.

2 BASIC LIFE INSURANCE PLANS

Commercially, life insurance has developed along three different *lines*: ordinary, industrial (or *debit*), and group insurance. Life insurance is available in each of these lines, under many different kinds of policies. In spite of an apparent complexity, however, there are really only three basic life insurance *plans*. They are term, whole life, and endowment plans.

This chapter will discuss the general characteristics of these basic plans and some of the more common situations in which they are most appropriate. First, however, let us take a brief look at the three major lines of life insurance.

■ ORDINARY, INDUSTRIAL, AND GROUP LIFE INSURANCE

This book is primarily concerned with ordinary life insurance—that is, insurance provided under individual policies in amounts of $1,000 or more, with premiums payable annually, semiannually, quarterly, or monthly.

Industrial life insurance is also provided under individual policies, but the amounts are smaller, usually less than $1,000. It is characteristic of industrial life insurance that premiums are payable, traditionally on a weekly basis, to an agent of the company, who calls at the policyowner's home to make the collection.

Group life insurance is insurance on the lives of a number of persons, insured as a group under one master policy. Instead of individual policies, the members of the group receive certificates, which describe the essential details of their coverage. The largest amount of group life insurance is in force on employee groups, but a great deal is also issued to corporate creditors such as banks and finance companies, to insure the lives of their debtors.

The relative significance of these three lines of life insurance is indicated in Figure 2–1. In 1950, ordinary life insurance accounted for almost twice as much insurance in force as industrial and group life insurance combined. During the next 20 years, the amount of group life insurance in force increased more than 10 times and ordinary life insurance increased more than four times, while the amount of industrial life insurance decreased slightly during the last half of that period.

FIGURE 2–1

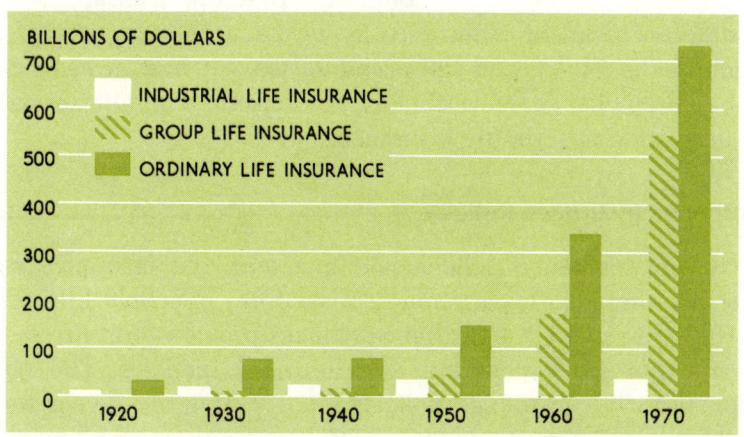

Life Insurance in Force in the United States

In spite of the remarkable increase in the amount of group life insurance in force in the past two decades, ordinary life insurance still accounts for the largest amount of life insurance in force; and it is ordinary life insurance that most people think of when life insurance is mentioned. For these reasons, this chapter will discuss the basic life insurance plans—term, whole life, and endowment—as they are available in ordinary life insurance policies. (Group and industrial life insurance will be discussed more fully later.)

■ TERM LIFE INSURANCE

Term life insurance is insurance provided under an agreement to pay a death benefit if the death of the person whose life is insured occurs during a specified period of time—that is, the term covered by the agreement. This was true of the earliest life insurance agreement about which we have any definite information. A group of marine underwriters made the contract on June 18, 1583, insuring the life of William Gybbons for a period of 12 months. Gybbons died on May 28, 1584, but the underwriters refused to pay, contending that 12 months meant 12 lunar months of 28 days each. In the suit that followed, the court held that 12 months meant 12 calendar months, and the insurers were required to pay.

In a sense, it is regrettable that the first life insurance claim of which we have any knowledge was disputed, but without the court record, it is doubtful that any account of such a contract would have been preserved. It should be noted also that this transaction was quite different from life insurance as we know it today. Only one contract was involved, and the premium was, at best, a mere estimate, based on chance. Nevertheless, the episode is significant as an early illustration of term life insurance.

Term Life Insurance Policies

Some life insurance policies combine term life insurance with another or other plans, particularly some form of whole life insurance. However, many life insurance policies provide term life insurance only and are called term life insurance policies. The more common term life insurance policies are 1-year term, 5-year term, 10-year term, and term to age 65 or 70.

Under any term life insurance policy, if the person whose life is insured dies during the period covered by the policy, the death benefit is payable. If the insured survives to the end of this period, no benefit of any kind is payable, and the policy will terminate (expire) unless there is a provision in the policy permitting it to be continued and the policyowner elects to continue it.

In this respect, term life insurance is very similar to fire insurance. Under either kind of coverage, if there is a loss during the period covered, the claim is paid; if there is no loss, the policyowner will have received what he paid for—the assurance that if there had been a loss, it would have been covered.

Term life insurance policies usually include one or more provisions permitting the owner to continue his insurance beyond the original term of the policy, if specified requirements are met. Typically, these provisions either permit the policy to be renewed, in which case the policy is said to be renewable, or permit it to be converted to a whole life or endowment plan, in which case the policy is said to be convertible. It is very unusual for an individual term life insurance policy not to include at least one of these privileges. Often the same policy will be both renewable *and* convertible.

The Renewal Privilege

If a term life insurance policy is renewable, it includes a provision giving the policyowner the right to renew the contract for at least one additional period. Usually this additional period is the same length as the period for which the policy was originally written. Thus, a 5-year renewable term life insurance policy may be renewed for at least one additional period of five years, and a 10-year renewable term policy may be renewed for at least one additional 10-year period.

Every life insurance company develops the policy forms that seem most appropriate to its own marketing situation and objectives. Thus, renewal provisions, like other policy provisions, differ from one policy to another. However, most renewal provisions state the number of times the policy may be renewed and, in addition, make it clear that (1) a higher premium will be payable at each renewal, and (2) the company will not require evidence of insurability—that is, evidence that the person whose life is insured meets all the risk selection requirements that he would have to meet if he applied for new insurance on his life.

It is relatively standard practice to permit 5-year term policies to be renewed several times, provided that the coverage will not be continued beyond a specified age—typically, the insured's age 65 or 70. In contracts for longer terms, the renewal privilege may or may not be available. Thus, 10-year term policies are often limited to one renewal and, in some instances, may not be renewed at all. Regardless of the length of the term, however, there is always an upper age limit, beyond which a term life insurance policy cannot be extended by renewal.

Because a higher premium will become payable at each renewal, a table of renewal premiums is included in any renewable term policy. The premium is level during each individual term and increases in a pattern similar to that shown in Figure 2–2.

FIGURE 2–2

Premiums Payable—5-Year Renewable Term Life Insurance Policy (Issue age 20; renewed to age 65; amount of insurance $10,000)

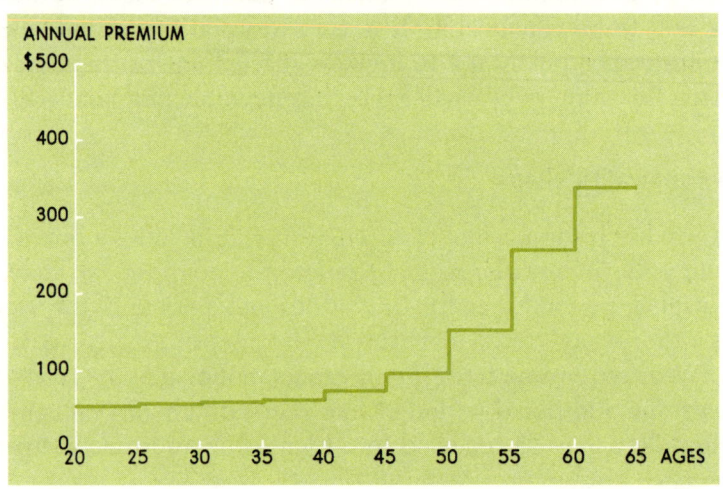

Experience has shown that in the renewal of term life insurance policies, there is a certain amount of what is called "antiselection," sometimes referred to as "adverse selection" or "selection against the company." These are merely different ways of referring to a rather general tendency on the part of persons with health impairments or hazardous occupations to be more interested in obtaining and continuing life insurance than persons without such impairments or hazards.

Antiselection is especially possible in connection with the renewal privilege in term life insurance policies since evidence of insurability, though required when the policy is originally issued, is not required at the time of renewal. As a consequence, an insured whose health is poor will usually be more interested in renewing his policy than an insured who is in good health and would have no problem satisfying the insurability requirements of the company. The probability of some antiselection is taken into consideration in establishing the premium rates for renewable term insurance policies. Such rates, therefore, are somewhat higher than the rates for otherwise comparable term policies that are not renewable.

The Conversion Privilege

If a term life insurance policy is convertible, it contains a provision giving the policyowner the right to exchange it, without evidence of insurability, for a policy on a different plan—usually whole life or endowment insurance. As is true of the renewal privilege, company requirements with respect to conversion of term policies differ, and the policy provisions differ accordingly. However, the following provision is illustrative:

Conversion Privilege. This policy may be converted to any whole life or endowment plan, without evidence of insurability, at any time while this policy is in force, subject to the following conditions:

1. Conversion shall be effective when the company receives at its home office the written request of the owner, the initial premium for the policy to which conversion is made, and this policy for cancellation;
2. The policy to which conversion is made shall be for an amount of insurance equal to or less than the amount of insurance provided by this policy and the policy selected must be one for which the company's minimum size requirements are satisfied;
3. The policy to which conversion is made will be issued upon a form in use on the effective date of conversion at the then premium rate for the attained age of the insured and class of risk in which the insured is placed under this policy. The policy to which conversion is made shall include all limitations of risk applicable to this policy as of the effective date of conversion.

The illustrative provision just quoted permits conversion at any time during the term of the policy, if written request is made, accompanied by the appropriate premium. By contrast, companies sometimes limit the period during which a policy may be converted, so that the owner must convert prior to the last year or so of the term. For example, a 5-year term policy might not be convertible during the last year of coverage, and a 10-year term policy might not be convertible during the last two years. A term-to-age-65 policy might not be convertible beyond age 60.

Limitations of this kind, when used, are intended to reduce antiselection. They require the policyowner to make his decision somewhat earlier than would otherwise be necessary, and antiselection on a last-minute basis is thereby avoided. Under many term policies issued today, however, conversion is permitted at any time while the policy is in force.

Conversion provisions usually state that the policy will be issued on a form the company is offering on the date the conversion is made and that it will be issued at the premium rate for the insured's age on that date. Thus, if John Allen has a 5-year term insurance policy that he purchased when he was age 29, and if he elects at age 32 to convert it to a whole life plan, the premium for his new policy will be the whole life premium for male insureds age 32. Conversion on this basis is known as conversion at the attained age of the insured, or "current-date" conversion.

Companies sometimes permit conversion on an "original-date" basis, if the policyowner prefers. Under this procedure, the new policy is issued at the premium the insured would have paid at his age when the term policy was issued, and the new policy is dated as if it had been issued when the term policy was. On this basis, in the example just given, the premium for John Allen's new policy would be the whole life premium for male insureds age 29, and his new policy would bear the same date as the term policy he converted.

Unlike current-date conversion, original-date conversion usually requires a special financial adjustment. If the new whole life or endowment policy had in fact been issued at the earlier date, the policyowner would have been paying a higher premium during the intervening years; and such a policy, unlike the term policy, might have developed some cash value.[1] To compensate for this, the policyowner may be required to pay an extra charge, in addition to the current applicable premium for the new policy. However, this charge is paid only once, at the time of conversion.

Under the conversion privilege of most term life insurance policies, the amount of insurance for which the new policy may be issued is limited to not more than the amount of the term life insurance in effect at the time of conversion. However, if the policyowner prefers, conversion will usually be permitted for a smaller amount of insurance, subject to company limitations as to the minimum amount that will be issued.

Automatic Renewal or Conversion

For many years, it was customary to permit a term life insurance policy to be renewed or converted only if the policy included the necessary provision and the owner in fact requested renewal or con-

---

[1] This term will be discussed later in this chapter, in connection with whole life and endowment plans.

version and paid the appropriate premium. However, it has become increasingly common to make either or both renewal and conversion automatic under some circumstances and in some plans.

For example, if a term policy includes a provision for waiving (that is, not collecting) premiums that become payable during any period in which the insured is totally disabled, the policy may provide for automatic renewal or conversion. Thus a renewable term policy including the waiver-of-premium provision may specify that if the insured is totally disabled at the end of any period during which renewal is permitted, and if the last premium due before expiration of the policy has been waived because of the total disability, the policy will be automatically renewed, with premiums continuing to be waived so long as the disability continues. Similarly, a convertible term life insurance policy may provide that if the insured is totally disabled at the end of the conversion period, the policy will be automatically converted to a whole life plan. The amount of insurance will be the amount that is then provided by the term policy, and premiums on the new policy will be waived so long as the insured's total disability continues.

Automatic conversion is also provided sometimes under special policies developed for young people who are just getting started in their careers. Such policies operate as term policies for a limited period at the outset (five or ten years, for instance) and on a whole life plan thereafter. The theory is that after five or ten years, the insured will be sufficiently well established in his chosen work that he can afford the higher premium required for permanent coverage.

Term Life Insurance Policies Classified

Term life insurance policies are often grouped into general classes on the basis of the length of the terms for which they are written. On this basis, there are yearly-renewable term policies, short- or intermediate-term policies, and policies for longer terms, or to a specified age of the insured. (It is not customary to issue individual policies of term life insurance for periods shorter than one year.) Term insurance policies may also be differentiated according to whether the same amount of insurance is provided throughout the term, in which case they are said to be level term policies, or whether the amount of insurance increases or decreases during the period for which the policy is written (increasing or decreasing term policies).

Finally, although much term life insurance is available under separate individual policies, it is also provided frequently in the form of riders, which are separate provisions that may be attached to policies providing insurance on a different plan.

1. Yearly-Renewable Term Policies. One-year term life insurance policies issued to individuals usually permit renewal for additional terms of one year each, to a specified upper age limit, typically 65 or 70. Thus, they are referred to as yearly-renewable, or annually-renewable term policies. Each year, as the contract is renewed, the policyowner pays a higher premium, and there are never any cash values.

Yearly-renewable term life insurance is not usually very satisfactory as one's only life insurance protection. At best, if the insured lives into his 60's or 70's, his total outlay for insurance protection under this plan will often exceed the amount he would have paid under a whole life policy if he had purchased it in the first place. At worst, if he lives beyond age 65 or 70, his term life insurance will expire, since conversion at such ages is not usually permitted.

2. Short- or Intermediate-Term Policies. Term life insurance policies written for terms of 5, 10, 15, or 20 years are generally referred to as short- or intermediate-term policies. Policies in this group may or may not be renewable, depending upon the purposes for which the policies were designed and whether a level or decreasing amount of insurance is provided. For decreasing term coverages, renewal is not appropriate. However, many short- or intermediate-term policies are both renewable and convertible.

3. Longer-Term Policies. Term life insurance contracts written for longer terms are often described as term to a certain age, such as "term to age 60" or "term to 65." Sometimes the period is defined as "term to life expectancy." Life expectancy means the average number of years persons of a given age can be expected to live, according to the mortality table currently being used by the insurance company. Thus, the life expectancy of the individual insured depends entirely upon his age when his policy is issued. This is a difficult concept to explain to most policyowners and beneficiaries, and term coverages to a specified age are more frequently offered.

Level or Varying Amounts of Coverage

Term life insurance plans under which the amount of insurance remains level throughout the term are referred to as level term policies. Term policies of this kind are most appropriate for life insurance needs that are relatively temporary and that do not vary appreciably during that temporary period.

Many temporary life insurance needs, however, decrease as the years go by. Indebtedness that one is repaying is a good example. At one's death, there is a very definite need for cash to pay the amount of the unpaid debt. For needs of this kind, decreasing term insurance contracts are especially appropriate. They provide coverage in a stated initial amount at the outset of the period, but this amount decreases each year throughout the term of the policy.

Finally, the continuing inflation of the past several years has prompted many life insurance companies to offer term life insurance on an increasing basis. This increasing term coverage is usually provided in a special provision or rider that may be attached to a basic life insurance contract. The effect is that during the term of the rider, the proceeds payable on the death of the insured are increased by stated amounts each year. Such riders are often designed to coincide roughly with an estimated rate of increase in the cost of living and are called "cost-of-living" riders.

■ WHOLE LIFE INSURANCE

Under a whole life insurance plan, a death benefit is payable at the insured's death, whenever that may be. A whole life policy, therefore, may be kept in force for the insured's entire lifetime, regardless of his age at the time it becomes effective. Premiums, however, may be payable for different periods of time. Whole life contracts are grouped into general classes accordingly.

Under some whole life policies, premiums are payable as long as the insured lives. A policy of this kind is said to be a "straight life policy," a "continuous-premium, whole life policy," or an "ordinary life policy." However, the word "ordinary" is used also to describe a line of business (as distinct from industrial and group). The term "ordinary life policy," therefore, is somewhat confusing, and the other terms are preferable.

If the policyowner wishes, he may pay the equivalent of the entire future cost of his whole life policy in one premium, in which case the policy is a "single-premium, whole life policy."

Between the extremes of the continuous-premium, whole life policy and the single-premium, whole life policy are found a great many limited-payment, whole life policies. These policies provide insurance for the whole of life, but premiums are payable for not longer than a specified period, or until the death of the insured if that occurs prior to the end of the period. The premium-payment period may be described as a certain number of years, such as 10 or 20, or to a stipulated age of the insured. Whether premiums are payable for the entire lifetime of the insured or limited to a specified maximum period, a level premium is used, and the policyowner pays the same amount of premium each year during the premium-payment period. However, the premium will always be somewhat higher under a limited-payment policy than it is for a continuous-premium, whole life policy.

Continuous-Premium, Whole Life Insurance

The continuous-premium, whole life insurance policy has a wide range of possible uses and provides more insurance for a given annual premium than any other whole life policy. Year after year, it accounts for a larger amount of ordinary life insurance in force than any other single kind of policy.

Consider, for instance, the insurance needs of John Barrett, age 25. Like most other young (or even middle-aged) people, John confidently expects to live to a "ripe old age," but he wishes to be sure that funds will be available to meet the expenses of his last illness and burial whenever they are needed. Term insurance is available but not really adequate, since term policies cannot usually be renewed beyond age 65 or 70. A whole life policy, therefore, is indicated, primarily because it will provide a death benefit even though he may be in his 90's when he dies.

Assume that John purchases a whole life policy in the amount of $10,000. This amount, which will be paid in the event of his death while the policy is in force, is often referred to as the "face amount" of the policy. This is because it is customary to print it on the first or "face" page of the policy. Practices differ as to the use of this terminology, however, and many companies use such terms as the "amount of insurance" or the "sum insured."

The death benefit is not the only valuable feature of a whole life insurance plan, however; and in discussing such a plan with John, a life insurance agent is likely to emphasize some of the other advantages. In fact, he may summarize his explanation under three headings: If you live—; if you die—; if you quit.

1. If John Lives—If John Barrett lives, his policy will begin to accumulate a cash value within the first three years, often in the first year. This is characteristic of whole life and endowment insurance, and results directly from the level-premium system, mentioned earlier. In general terms, the level-premium system provides for payment of premiums in level amounts over the entire period covered by a whole life or endowment policy. Such premiums are more than adequate to pay claims in the early policy years, and the amounts not needed for claims and expenses in those years are invested by the insurance company and held until the later policy years, when current premiums are less than current claims.

These amounts, held and invested year after year, will eventually be needed if the policy is kept in force until the death of the insured. If the policyowner ceases paying premiums, however, he is entitled to a refund of part of the values (the reserve) that his level premium has helped to accumulate. The minimum share to which he is entitled is specified by law and is called the "cash value" or "cash surrender value" of the policy.

The cash value of a whole life contract at the end of different policy years must be set forth as a part of the printed policy. For example, assume that John pays an annual premium of $180 for his $10,000 whole life policy. Under one illustrative whole life policy, there will be a cash value of $256.50 at the end of the fifth policy year; a value of $873.40 at the end of the tenth policy year; $1,567.10 at the end of the fifteenth year; and so on, in a pattern as shown in Figure 2–3.

As John continues to pay premiums under his policy, the cash value will continue to increase, as indicated in this figure; and the company reserve for the policy will be increasing in the same way. For instance, the cash value of John's policy when he is age 60 will be $4,808.50. The difference between the reserve of the policy at the end of a year and the amount of insurance that would be payable at the death of the insured is referred to as the "net amount at risk."

As the insurance continues in force, the reserve and cash value continue to increase and the amount at risk diminishes accordingly. Because of this, the whole life policy is frequently described as a combination of decreasing term insurance and an increasing savings or "investment" element. The amount at risk continues to diminish as the policy is kept in force, until finally, if the insured lives long enough, the investment element, or cash value, will equal the amount of insurance provided by the policy (the face amount).

Under most whole life policies issued today, the cash value equals the face amount at the insured's age 100. If the insured reaches that age, it is customary to pay the amount of insurance to the policyowner at that time, although this procedure is not specifically provided for in the contract. Since very few people live to age 100, the payment of the face amount of his policy to an insured who survives to that age is usually considered a newsworthy item when it occurs.

FIGURE 2-3

Analysis of a Continuous-Premium, Whole Life Policy (issue age 25; annual premium $180; amount of insurance $10,000)

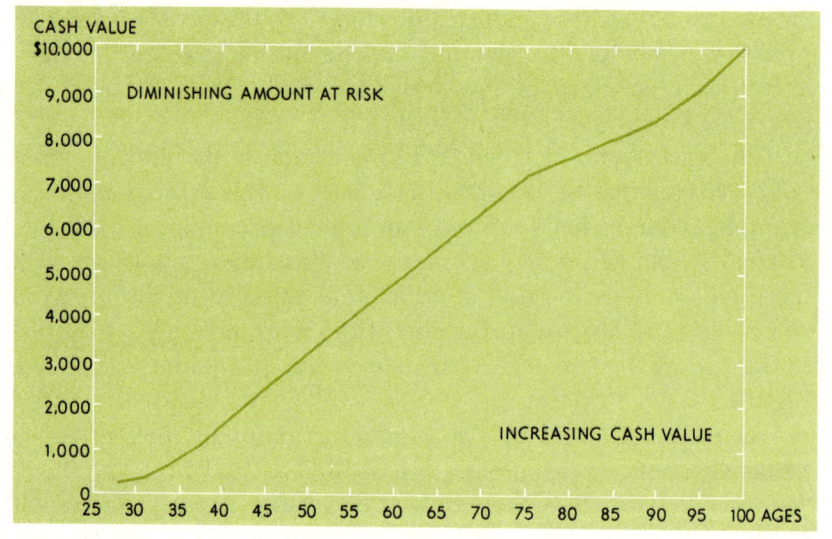

2. If John Dies.—If John Barrett should die at any time after the policy becomes effective (while the policy is in force and before he reaches age 100) the company will pay a death benefit of $10,000 to the person or persons he designates to receive it (his beneficiary or beneficiaries).

3. If John Quits.—If John should decide, whatever the reason, that he no longer wants to continue premium payments under this policy, he can surrender his policy for its cash value. In that event, the insurance company will send him a check for the amount of cash value indicated in the cash value table of the policy, and the insurance coverage will be terminated.

If John prefers, he can leave the cash value with the company and it will be used as a single premium to continue his insurance protection. If he does not elect otherwise, his continued insurance will probably be term insurance in the face amount of the policy, extended (and therefore called *extended term insurance*) for as long as the cash value will provide. Paid-up whole life coverage in a reduced amount (*reduced paid-up insurance*) is usually also available and may be elected by the policyowner.

These benefits—(1) cash value, (2) extended term insurance, and (3) reduced paid-up insurance—are collectively referred to as the "nonforfeiture benefits" of the policy, and become available only if premium payments are discontinued. At that time, the policyowner has a choice as to the nonforfeiture benefits, which, for that reason, are commonly referred to as nonforfeiture "options." Nonforfeiture benefits (or options) are required by law to be provided under every whole life and endowment insurance contract and will be discussed more fully in a later chapter.

Limited-Payment, Whole Life Policies

Life insurance policies that may be kept in force for the whole of life, but under which premiums are payable only for a limited period of time or until the death of the insured, if earlier, are called limited-payment policies. Because all premiums are payable within a shorter period, premium rates are higher for these policies than for

FIGURE 2-4

Premiums and Cash Values for $10,000 of Insurance Continuous-Premium and Limited-Payment Life Policies

Type of Policy	Annual Premium Age 45	Guaranteed Cash Value			
		Age 50	Age 55	Age 60	Age 65
Continuous-Premium Whole Life Policy	$331.15	$ 843.10	$2,010.10	$3,198.20	$4,375.00
30-Payment Whole Life Policy	363.20	942.80	2,242.90	3,604.60	5,028.10
20-Payment Whole Life Policy	452.00	1,252.40	2,966.10	4,866.70	7,056.60

continuous-premium, whole life policies, and the cash values therefore increase more rapidly. Figure 2–4 illustrates these differences.

Policies such as "10-payment life," "20-payment life," and so on have been offered for many years. In addition, it is customary today to offer policies under which premiums are payable for considerably longer periods. Thus policies "paid-up" at ages 65 and 70 are increasingly being used.

Under some circumstances, the policyowner will find the limited-payment policies advantageous in spite of their higher rates; under other circumstances, this will not be true. To illustrate, William Francis, age 45, plans to retire at age 65. Under these circumstances, a 20-payment plan offers two possible advantages. First, he will complete his premium payments by the time he is ready to retire, and he will have a paid-up policy at that time. Second, by paying the higher premium, he will build up the cash value of the policy more rapidly than would be true of a continuous-premium contract. As a result, he will have a larger cash value at age 65. This may be an advantage if he should want to surrender his policy and use the cash value to provide an income for himself, to supplement his Social Security and other retirement income.

The basic disadvantage of limited-payment policies, as compared to the continuous-premium, whole life contract, however, should also be considered. It is true that cash values accumulate more rapidly under the limited-payment contracts, but this is because the premiums are higher. The same premium outlay, therefore, will buy more insurance protection at any given age under the continuous-premium, whole life plan than under a limited-payment plan.

A comparison of illustrative premium rates demonstrates that there may be a significant difference between the amount of insurance available under a continuous-premium policy, for a specified annual premium, and that provided under a limited-payment contract. For example, one company makes $10,000 of whole life insurance available to a male at age 35 for an annual premium of approximately $220 under a continuous-premium policy. The same amount of insurance at the same age under a 20-payment contract would require an annual premium of $340. Thus, the annual premium this policyowner pays for $10,000 of insurance on the 20-payment basis would purchase more than $15,000 of insurance under a continuous-premium policy.

When the premium-payment period is longer, the difference is not so great. Thus, in this same company, a life paid-up at age 65 policy would require an annual premium of $270 for $10,000 of insurance at age 35 (male). This annual premium outlay would purchase about $12,000 of insurance under a continuous-premium policy.

In other words, the limited-payment policies may be advantageous in some instances, but the insured is always giving up the added coverage he could have had under a continuous-premium, whole life policy with the same premium outlay. It should be noted also that the advantage of having a policy paid-up at a specified future date is not confined to the limited-payment policies. Premium payments can be discontinued under a continuous-premium, whole life contract with similar results, at any time after the policy has acquired a cash value. Thus the owner of a continuous-premium, whole life policy may, if he wishes, discontinue paying premiums when he reaches retirement age and continue the policy in a reduced paid-up amount.

The more rapidly increasing cash value of the limited-payment contracts, however, means that a greater emphasis is placed on the savings element of the contract. This is a definite advantage in the minds of persons who feel that they are unlikely to carry out any other systematic savings plan. Perhaps it is a combination of these factors that prompts some people, such as high-salaried professional athletes, to purchase limited-payment policies. They complete their life insurance programs during the period of their highest earnings and at the same time save more than they might otherwise have done.

The Single-Premium Policy

A single-premium, whole life policy provides insurance for the whole of life, in exchange for which the policyowner pays the total premium required, in a single sum at the time of application. For most people, of course, this is neither attractive nor possible. (It is also disadvantageous if the insured should die shortly after the policy is issued, since no part of the premium will be refunded.) However, a single-premium policy is well suited to some needs. For example, it makes an excellent gift. Perhaps a grandfather wishes to make a gift to his grandson. A single-premium policy on the grandson's life is useful and attractive. The premium is relatively low in the early years of life, and a large amount of life insurance can thus be given to the boy for a very moderate cash outlay. For instance, most companies make $10,000 of life insurance available on a boy age eight for a single premium of slightly more than $3,000.

For this reason, and because gifts offer a convenient way for persons in higher tax brackets to reduce their taxable estates, the single-premium policy is frequently used for gift purposes in connection with estate planning for well-to-do persons.

Single-premium policies are sometimes purchased by people who are especially interested in the large investment element of such policies. The savings and investment element is almost free of risk and earns a guaranteed rate of interest. Furthermore, the single-premium policy has a cash value as soon as the policy becomes effective.

■ ENDOWMENT LIFE INSURANCE

Endowment life insurance is provided under an agreement to pay either the face amount if the person whose life is insured is living at the end of the endowment period, or a death benefit of the same amount if he dies within the same period. To illustrate, a 10-year endowment insurance policy in the amount of $5,000 will mature as an endowment 10 years from the issue date if the insured is then living, and $5,000 will be paid at that time to the owner of the policy (or to someone else, at his request). If the insured dies at any time during the 10-year period, a death benefit of $5,000 will be paid to the beneficiary.

Endowment life insurance policies, like those providing term life insurance, are available for periods of different lengths. Thus, there are 10-year endowments, 20-year endowments, endowments at ages 60, 65, and 70, and many others.

An endowment life insurance policy, in its basic makeup, is very similar to a whole life policy. In fact, if the whole life policy is viewed for the entire period contemplated by the mortality table —that is, for the period ending at the insured's age 100—the policies are exactly alike; and the whole life policy is, in effect, an endowment at age 100. The basic difference is that endowment policies are written for much shorter periods than to the insured's age 100. Endowment policies divert a much larger proportion of each premium into the savings and investment element than do whole life contracts. As a consequence, endowment policies provide a smaller amount of insurance protection than would be available under a whole life plan for the same premium, and the maximum period of insurance protection is the endowment period. Thus, the longest period for which a 20-year endowment policy can provide life insurance protection is 20 years. If the insured is living at the end of the period, the maturity value will be paid, and the life insurance protection will be terminated.

Endowment life insurance policies are appropriate for any situation in which a fund needs to be accumulated, since they guarantee that the fund will be completed by the end of the specified period, whether the insured lives or dies. Such policies are most appropriate, however, where the need for life insurance is somewhat incidental—that is, where the policyowner needs life insurance only to assure himself that his savings plan will be completed in the event of his death prior to the end of the specified period. In such cases, the policyowner may be using his premium money more nearly in accordance with his needs by purchasing endowment insurance than by purchasing whole life insurance. For life insurance needs that are expected to continue beyond the end of the endowment period, however, some form of whole life coverage is preferable.

Makeup of Endowment Insurance

Mathematically, endowment life insurance combines two concepts which have long been used in life insurance—level term insurance and the pure endowment. A pure endowment, no longer written as a separate policy, operates in exactly the opposite way from level term life insurance. Term insurance provides for payment of a benefit only if the insured dies within a specified period; the pure endowment provides for payment of a benefit only if the insured lives to the end of a specified period. Thus, a 20-year endowment policy combines a 20-year level term contract with a 20-year pure endowment.

A different, and sometimes more helpful, analysis of the endowment policy emphasizes the economic aspects of the coverage. This economic analysis views the policy as a combination of decreasing term life insurance and an increasing saving and investment element. By use of a diagram similar to that shown in Figure 2–3 on page 32, the cash values of the endowment policy will be seen to increase through the endowment period until they equal the face amount of the contract on the maturity date.

As the policyowner continues to pay premiums under his endowment policy, the saving and investment element increases and

38 ▪ Principles of Life Insurance

the amount at risk diminishes. Therefore, the amount at risk is, in effect, decreasing term insurance. At any point in time, the sum of these elements—the decreasing term insurance plus the saving and investment element—is exactly equal to the face amount of the policy. For example, for the $10,000 policy in Figure 2–5, the cash value (saving and investment element) at the insured's age 30, is $4,430; and the amount at risk, or term insurance, is $5,570. At the end of the endowment period, the entire amount payable is made up of savings and investment.

FIGURE 2–5

Analysis of a 10-Year Endowment Policy (issue age 25; annual premium $1,024.30; amount $10,000)

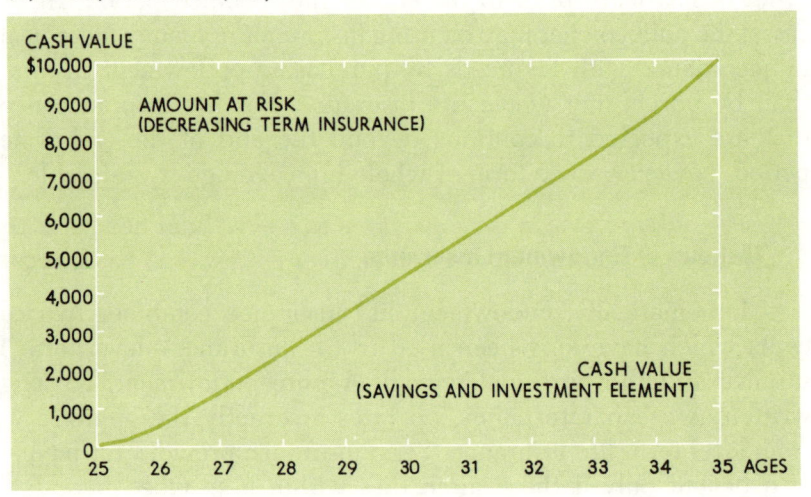

[Graph showing CASH VALUE from $0 to $10,000 on vertical axis and AGES 25 to 35 on horizontal axis. The curve rises from 0 at age 25 to $10,000 at age 35. The area above the curve is labeled "AMOUNT AT RISK (DECREASING TERM INSURANCE)" and the area below the curve is labeled "CASH VALUE (SAVINGS AND INVESTMENT ELEMENT)".]

The resemblance of endowment life insurance to the whole life contract is especially evident when Figures 2–3 and 2–5 are compared. Thus, it will be seen that both contracts have cash values that increase through the years until they equal the face amount at the end of the period for which coverage is provided.

Endowment life insurance also resembles term life insurance in the fact that it provides insurance protection for the term of the policy only. It differs from term coverages in at least three respects, however. First, endowment policies always build cash values; term policies usually do not. In fact, term policies never have cash values at the end of the term and usually do not have such values at any time during the term. Some term policies, however, have cash values for a limited length of time in the middle years, if they are written for relatively long periods of time. Second, endowment contracts always pay a value at the end of the period covered, if a death benefit has not been payable during the term of the policy. Under the same circumstances, term insurance policies expire without value unless they are renewed. Third, once an endowment policy has matured as an endowment, there is no provision for continuing the insurance protection. By contrast, term policies are usually either renewable or convertible, and they often include both privileges.

■ USES OF THE BASIC PLANS

Whole Life Plans

More individual life insurance is in force under whole life plans than under any other plan or combination of plans. The reasons are simple and fundamental. The basic life insurance needs are to provide funds for last illness and funeral expenses and for the support of dependents after one's death. The person in modest circumstances relies heavily on whole life insurance to meet these needs, since it is the only plan that will meet them on a guaranteed basis, regardless of the date of the insured's death.

The wealthy person uses life insurance to provide ready funds for estate and inheritance taxes (succession duties in Canada), funds to provide cash for many other needs that may arise at his death, and funds to provide gifts to favorite charities. These are all permanent objectives, in the sense that funds will be needed to achieve them regardless of when death occurs; and permanent life insurance (that is, whole life insurance) is needed if such goals are to be attained.

Term Life Insurance

In spite of the long-term nature of many life insurance needs, there are numerous needs that are confined to somewhat limited periods of one's life. Money to complete the payments on a mortgage, if the mortgagor should die before it has been paid; money to support children, if the parent dies before they have become financially independent; money to finance a child's higher education, in the event of the parent's death before the education has been completed. These are all needs that will probably not continue beyond a relatively definite date. To meet them, term insurance policies are highly valuable, since they provide a great deal of temporary coverage for the premium dollar.

One of the most common temporary needs for life insurance arises out of personal indebtedness. When a person borrows a sum of money, he usually expects to repay it out of his earnings. His death before the loan is paid thus constitutes a clear possibility of economic loss to the lender (creditor). Often there is no estate from which the creditor can collect the unpaid debt; and even when collection is possible, some delay is unavoidable. The creditor, therefore, has a definite need for insurance on the life of his debtor for the period of the loan.

The debtor, too, has a need for insurance in this instance. If he should die before repaying the loan in full, his family's share of any property he leaves will be reduced by the amount of the indebtedness remaining at his death. For this reason, many borrowers insure their lives for an amount sufficient to repay their loan in the event they die before payment has been completed. Term life insurance is clearly appropriate for either creditor or debtor.

Term life insurance is especially appropriate in connection with a mortgage for the purchase of a home. Here the policyowner has borrowed a relatively large sum of money, usually to be repaid in monthly installments over a period of 15, 20, 25, or 30 years. His death during this period could easily mean the loss of the family home. Term life insurance policies, often called mortgage protection policies, are available from most life insurers for protection in this situation. They may be issued to cover the identical period of the mortgage loan and in amounts that decrease from year to year at approximately the same rate as the unpaid balance of the loan will decrease. In other words, they are decreasing term life insurance policies.

There are many other situations in which life insurance needs, though perhaps not quite so clearly temporary in nature as these, are nevertheless confined to somewhat limited periods of time. This is true, for example, of certain family needs. In almost every family, the period of greatest financial need coincides with the years in which the children are growing up and being educated. Term life insurance on the life of the father is often utilized to provide special protection during these years. On a temporary basis, such plans provide a great deal more life insurance coverage for a given premium outlay than whole life insurance. Decreasing term coverages are so extensively used for family protection that they will be discussed in some detail in Chapter 11.

The longer-term coverages are also appropriate for family protection. Thus, the executive in a company with a liberal retirement plan may use the longer-term plans to provide a maximum amount of protection during the years when his family responsibilities are greatest. Much of this need will terminate when his children are grown; and his retirement benefits, plus Social Security (Government Pension Plan in Canada), may constitute adequate provision for his retirement years. In such cases, the term contracts to ages 60 or 65 may furnish exactly the additional protection he needs. The insurance will terminate at or about the time his major life insurance needs diminish.

Convertible term life insurance plans are especially appropriate during the periods of low income faced by many young people who are just getting started in a business or profession. Their economic prospects are favorable. Eventually, they will no doubt reach significantly higher income brackets, and whole life insurance will be well within their means. However, their present incomes are quite limited.

A young dentist, for example, faces a period in which his income will be considerably lower than he can reasonably expect it to be later. At the same time, his immediate life insurance needs may be very great. Perhaps he is in debt for some of his education; perhaps for office equipment, his home, or his car; perhaps for all of these. Often he is married and has small children. In other words, his life insurance needs are most extensive at a time when his ability to pay premiums is most limited. Convertible term life insurance is the answer in this situation.

For many reasons whole life insurance should be this young man's ultimate goal. If he is self-employed, he has only himself to look to for a retirement plan beyond Social Security. He will, therefore, undoubtedly need a significant amount of permanent life insurance, although he cannot yet afford to pay for it. Thus, the temporary nature of this man's financial limitations, as well as his needs, make term life insurance appropriate for him. If he lives for 10 years, he will have built up his practice, he will probably have repaid most of his indebtedness, and many of his other financial problems will have been resolved.

The solution for this young dentist (and for others similarly situated) is a convertible term life insurance policy. This will furnish the protection he needs at a premium he can afford, during the period in which his income is most limited. Later, when his financial situation has improved, he can convert his policy to whole life insurance without evidence of insurability. He will then have the advantages of protection for the remainder of his life.

Endowment Plans

Because an endowment policy guarantees payment of the face amount of the policy at the end of the endowment period if the insured is then living, endowment plans are appropriate in any situation where a specific sum of money is needed by a definite future date. Two of the most common situations involving needs of this kind arise at or about age 18, for a young person who is entering college, and at age 65, for the person who is retiring. Special endowment policies are available to meet each of these needs.

An endowment-at-age-18 policy is available from most life insurance companies for the purpose of accumulating funds that will be needed by a child for college expenses. However, life insurance on the life of the parent is usually preferable to an endowment contract on the life of a dependent child for this purpose, since the death of the child would eliminate the need for which the policy was purchased. For this reason, most financial counselors recommend the purchase of life insurance on the life of the parent. Their reasoning is that the greatest need is for insurance on the life of the parent, and the cash values of a whole life policy can be used to help pay college expenses, if necessary.

The relative values of an 18-year endowment policy on the life of a child and whole life insurance on the life of the father are illustrated below:

	Annual Premium	Death Benefit	Cash Value at Child's Age 18
$10,000 Endowment-at-Age-18, Issue Age 0	$515	$10,000	$10,000
$31,300 Whole Life Insurance, Parent's Age 25	515	31,300	7,019

As indicated by these figures, $31,300 of whole life insurance on the life of a man age 25 can be purchased for the same annual premium that would be required for a $10,000 endowment-at-age-18 policy for a child age 0. At the same time, this much greater amount of insurance protection is on the life of the father, whose death would result in a vastly greater economic loss than the death of the child. True, the cash value of the whole life insurance policy at the child's age 18 is less than the maturity value of the endowment policy. Nevertheless, it represents a significant saving, that can be used, if needed, for the child's college expense.

For retirement needs, income endowment policies are frequently used. These are endowment policies designed to provide an income for the insured following his retirement. Such policies usually provide a lifetime income beginning at age 65, although the insured may elect a proportionately smaller income beginning at an earlier date. They thus provide a relatively simple way of assuring a specified income following retirement, though many other special policies have been designed for this purpose.

Again, however, it should be mentioned that this same effect can be achieved with the whole life policy. The insured may, if he wishes, surrender it at retirement and use the cash surrender value to provide a life income for himself. In the meanwhile, the whole life policy will have provided considerably more life insurance protection than an endowment policy during years when, presumably, the life insurance needs of the insured were greatest.

■ "BUY TERM AND INVEST THE DIFFERENCE"

Each of the basic life insurance plans serves a useful purpose. Term life insurance furnishes protection for temporary periods. Endowment plans provide specified sums at definite future dates, with insurance to pay the same amount in the event of the prior death of the insured. Whole life insurance provides insurance for the entire lifetime of the insured, and its usefulness for essential life insurance needs is generally recognized. Nevertheless, the argument is sometimes proposed that one is ill-advised to pay the higher premium required for whole life coverage when lower premium term life insurance is available.

Since whole life insurance includes an increasing saving and investment element, the sophisticated insurance buyer, it is said, will purchase a level term life insurance contract in the amount of the protection he wishes and select his own investments for the difference in premium he has "saved." In the event of his death while his life insurance is in force, his beneficiary will receive the full face amount of the term policy, plus whatever is available in the separate investment fund. By contrast, if he had purchased whole life insurance, his beneficiary would have received only the insurance proceeds. After all, this argument goes, since the whole life policy is essentially a combination of decreasing term insurance and an increasing saving and investment fund, why shouldn't the knowledgeable applicant apply for a term life insurance policy and do his own investing?

Basically, the argument assumes that the policyowner can invest the difference between the term life insurance premium and the premium for a whole life insurance contract more effectively than the life insurance company and thus be in a better financial position in his later years than if he had used the entire premium to purchase whole life insurance. In a period of generally rising prices, it is tempting to believe that investments in common stocks would be preferable to the more conservative investments of the life insurer. In such periods, the fixed guarantees of life insurance seem ever to be falling behind the rising costs of living, and it is only natural for the thoughtful life insurance buyer to consider any reasonably attractive alternatives that may be available. Even in a period of rising prices, however, there are a number of reasons why the advice to "buy term and invest the difference" may be of doubtful value so far as basic whole life protection is concerned.

Probably the most persuasive reason is found in the questionable assumption on which the argument is based—that the difference between the term life insurance premium and the premium for an equal amount of whole life insurance will actually be invested by the policyowner, systematically and over a long period of time. As a practical matter, most people find it very difficult to continue an individual program of saving and investment for any appreciable length of time. Sooner or later, no matter how sincere the saver may have been, pressing needs for money will usually cause him to postpone and often to abandon his savings program.

Saving through life insurance is different. The whole life policy combines protection and savings in such a way that the saving element cannot be terminated without terminating the protection. As a consequence, most people make a special effort to pay life insurance premiums as they fall due. This is sometimes referred to as the "semicompulsory" nature of premium payment. It is an important factor in explaining why many people who seem unable to maintain an individual savings program for any extended period can save small amounts, year after year, if they pay them to a life insurance company as premiums on cash value policies.

Another reason why the advice to buy term and invest the difference should not be followed without careful consideration arises out of the ease with which one can liquidate personal investments when he needs ready cash. The policyowner is more likely to hesitate before he surrenders his life insurance for its cash value. He knows that the policy will not be easy to replace. In fact, it will be irreplaceable if he is uninsurable. By contrast, the man who sells his securities can usually purchase others without much trouble when he wishes to invest again.

Another significant consideration is the problem of finding suitable, and reasonably safe, investments when the investor has only relatively small sums to invest on a regular basis. Usually, if such investments are found, the yield, after payment of brokerage commissions, income taxes, and other expenses, does not exceed the net earnings on the investment portion of the life insurance contract by any significant amount, if at all.

Finally, one's personal investments are rarely guaranteed. The death benefit under a whole life insurance contract, by contrast, is payable on a guaranteed basis, as is the cash value; and whole life insurance can be kept in force until the insured dies, no matter how long he may live. For this reason, investment counselors recommend a basic program of life insurance before any investment program is undertaken.

■ QUESTIONS FOR REVIEW

1. Identify the three *lines* of life insurance.
2. Name and describe the three basic life insurance *plans*.
3. Differentiate between a renewable term life insurance policy and one that is convertible. Briefly state the advantages of each privilege to the policyowner; the disadvantages, if any.
4. Briefly distinguish between limited-payment and continuous-premium, whole life policies.
5. What is meant by the statement that the whole life insurance contract is essentially an "endowment at age 100"?
6. For what insurance needs are whole life insurance policies best suited?
7. Describe two life insurance needs for which term life insurance policies would be appropriate.
8. For what purposes are endowment life insurance policies most suitable?

9. How do endowment life insurance policies resemble term life insurance policies? How do they differ from term coverages?
10. Briefly explain the advice to "buy term and invest the difference." What is the principal argument in favor of such a program? What are some arguments against it?

3 HOW LIFE INSURANCE IS PAID FOR

The level-premium system makes it possible to continue a life insurance contract, with no increase in premium, until the death of the insured, even if he lives to an advanced age. This chapter will discuss the level-premium system and the related concepts of the legal reserve and nonforfeiture benefits that together make up the basis of life insurance as we know it today.

■ THE INCREASING PROBABILITY OF DEATH

The increasing probability of death at every age after ages 10 or 11 is of such fundamental significance in a study of life insurance that mortality statistics need to be considered in some detail. It is customary to compile such statistics in tables showing the number of deaths per 1,000 lives at each age from birth to some upper age such as 100, or even ages as high as 109 or 110. Tables of this kind are called mortality tables, and the rates of death at the various ages —1.94 deaths per 1,000 lives at age 25, for example—are called mortality rates.

The pattern of mortality rates at the different ages, according to mortality statistics used by life insurance companies today, may be summarized as follows: High at the beginning (7.08 deaths per 1,000 at age 0), the rate drops quickly during the first year of life to 1.76 per 1,000 at age 1. It continues to decrease slightly from year to year until ages 9 and 10. Thereafter, the rate begins a virtually uninterrupted increase, accelerating rapidly in the later years, until

48 ▪ **Principles of Life Insurance**

FIGURE 3–1

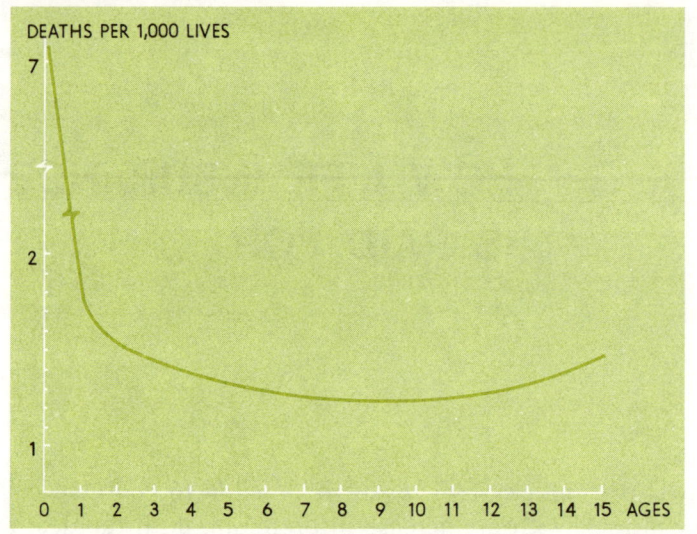

Mortality Rates (ages 0–15)

DEATHS PER 1,000 LIVES

Source: Commissioners' 1958 Standard Ordinary Mortality Table.

FIGURE 3–2

Mortality Rates (ages 50—59)

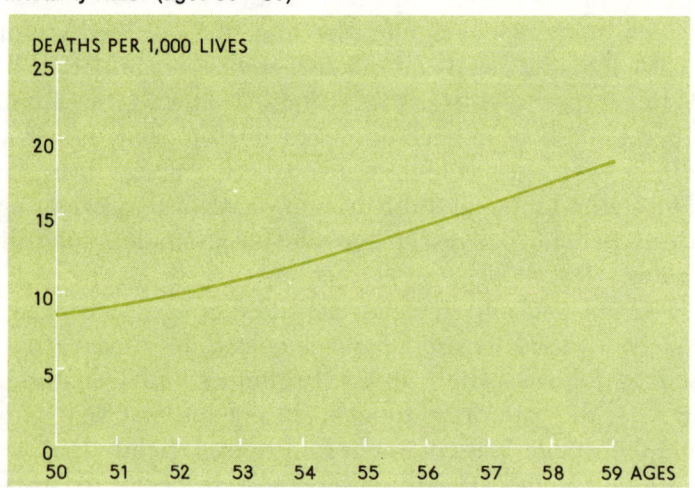

DEATHS PER 1,000 LIVES

3 How Life Insurance Is Paid For ▪ 49

age 99, at which age the last survivors of the large group of persons (who started at age 0) are assumed to die.

Because this pattern is basic to an understanding of life insurance, it is illustrated for various ages in Figures 3–1 through 3–3 and for the whole of life in Figure 3–4. Figure 3–1, for example, illustrates the rates of death per 1,000 persons, beginning with the first year of life (age 0), and shows the declining rates of death between age 0 and ages 9 and 10. The rate then begins to increase slightly from year to year, as illustrated through age 15.

FIGURE 3–3

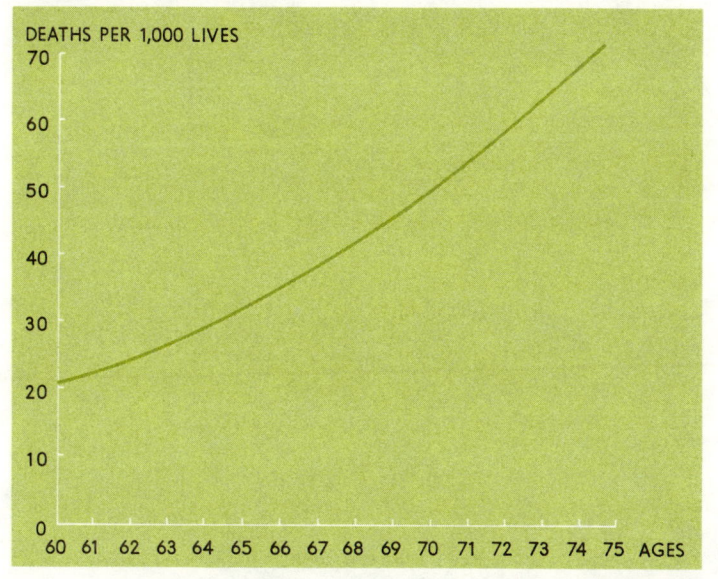

Mortality Rates (ages 60—75)

The mortality rate continues upward through the 20's, the 30's, and the 40's, increasing more rapidly in the 50's, as shown in Figure 3–2.

The mortality rate increases much more rapidly in the 60's and the 70's, as shown in Figure 3–3. Note that if these rates were charted on the same scale as Figure 3–2, we would have to have a chart more than three times as high, to include the rate at age 75.

In the last years of life, mortality rates are very high. At age 95, the mortality rate used by life insurance companies is 351.24 per

50 ▪ Principles of Life Insurance

1,000; at 96 it is 400.56; and at 97 it is 488.42. It is impossible to chart these rates on any of the scales used for the mortality rates in Figures 3–1 through 3–3. In order to convey some idea of the pattern of mortality rates throughout the entire life span, therefore, it is customary to omit the early years and the most advanced ages. The result is a chart such as that shown in Figure 3–4. Note that this is on a scale that is completely different from that used for the previous charts in this chapter.

FIGURE 3–4

The Mortality "Curve"

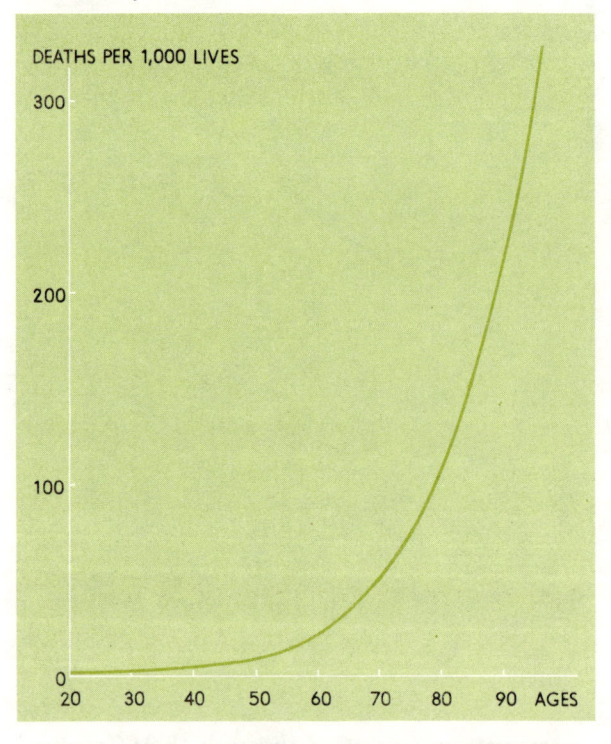

[Graph: DEATHS PER 1,000 LIVES on vertical axis (0, 100, 200, 300), AGES on horizontal axis (20, 30, 40, 50, 60, 70, 80, 90), showing an exponentially rising mortality curve]

Source: Commissioners' 1958 Standard Ordinary Mortality Table.

The significance of the increasing mortality rate, so far as life insurance is concerned, can be demonstrated by considering the death rates at ages 60 and 61. Assume that premiums are collected from 1,000 persons, age 60, in amounts just sufficient to pay a death benefit of $1,000 each for all persons in this group who die during the coming year.

According to the mortality rates charted in Figure 3–3, 20.34

persons per 1,000 are expected to die at age 60. If we treat this as 20 probable death claims (which seems a reasonable assumption), we will need 20 x $1,000, or $20,000, to pay claims during the year. In the very next year, however, there will be 22.24 deaths per 1,000 persons. Clearly, the premium for this year would have to be higher than for the previous year, since there is a larger amount to be paid in death claims and fewer persons left from the original group to pay premiums.

FIGURE 3–5

The Level Premium

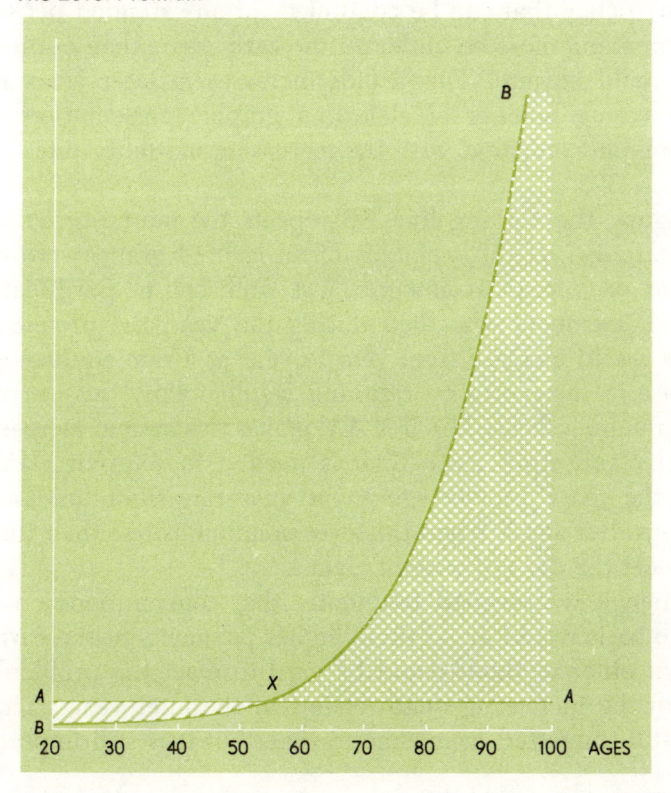

This need for an increasing premium in succeeding years, if death benefits are to be paid on a year-by-year basis, characterizes life insurance for insureds at every age after age 10. Furthermore, the rate of increase accelerates, as the mortality rate accelerates, considerably in the middle years and very rapidly in later years. Yet the incomes of most people show a definite drop by the time they reach 65 or 70 years of age. The result is a double problem so far as life insurance is concerned: premiums are increasing most rapidly at a time when policyowners are least able to pay. The level-premium system resolved those problems, but it was developed only after many other means of funding life insurance plans had failed.

■ WHAT THE LEVEL PREMIUM MEANS

The level premium is exactly what its name suggests—a premium that is level in amount for as long as it is payable. In order to achieve this under any policy that can be continued for an extended period of time, the premium must be higher in the early years than current claim costs would require. This avoids increases in later years to meet the increasing number of claims. A graphic presentation of the level premium, compared with the increasing mortality rates, is shown in Figure 3–5.

In this figure, the curving line BB repeats the mortality curve shown in Figure 3–4. If the members of an insured group were to pay premiums each year in amounts just sufficient to pay death benefits for all members who died during the year, the premium contributions would increase from year to year at a rate equivalent to the increase in the mortality rate and would follow this curve. The level premium, indicated by line AA, makes this annual increase unnecessary by collecting more than is needed for current claim costs during the years prior to age X and investing these amounts for use in years after age X when the level premium is less than that required to meet the costs of current claims.

At one time it was argued frequently that contributions on a pay-as-you-go basis would avoid these higher payments in the early years and that other methods could be used to meet the problems resulting from the increasing death claims in the later years. This approach is still suggested from time to time, but it is still impractical.

It is true that the higher early payments under the level premium system can be avoided if the pay-as-you-go principle is followed, but the history of insuring organizations which have operated on this basis is not encouraging. Sooner or later, regardless of the "other methods" used, the costs of continuing the plan have increased so much that participants who survived to the later years have been unable or unwilling to continue their insurance—often at an age when they could not obtain insurance elsewhere on a permanent basis at any price. The full significance of the level-premium principle, therefore, is more easily understood if the inadequacies of the pay-as-you-go system are recognized.

The Assessment Principle

One of the most common pay-as-you-go arrangements is known as the assessment plan. An insurance group operating on this principle levies a charge on each member for his proportionate share of the benefit payable whenever a loss is experienced by a member of the group. Assessment plans were used by many of the early life insurance associations and by groups organized to provide benefits in the event of loss by fire. Life insurance, however, has always presented a special problem. Two illustrations will help to make this clear.

Assume that a group of 1,000 homeowners in a small community, concerned about the possibility of property loss by fire, agree among themselves that they will share the losses (up to $10,000, for instance) of any member or members whose property is damaged or destroyed by fire. They appoint a secretary to keep the necessary records, notify each member when a contribution is required, receive the contributions, and pay a benefit to any member whose home is damaged or destroyed by fire.

If there are many fire losses among the members in any one year, these people may, of course, have relatively heavy assessments for that year. Barring such a catastrophe, however, there is nothing about the risk of fire that would prevent the group from operating with reasonable success over a long period of time. For instance, assume that one or two fire losses of $10,000 each are experienced the first year. A contribution of only $10 or $20 from each of the members will be sufficient to pay these losses. It would be well worth that amount to know that, if one's own home were to burn, he would be reimbursed for his loss up to the specified limit.

The next year the destroyed homes will probably have been rebuilt. Two or three other fires may be experienced in that same year, but these damaged or destroyed homes, too, will probably be repaired or rebuilt. There is no reason to believe that, on the average, the number of losses will differ significantly from year to year. Associations have been formed to provide fire protection on the assessment basis and have operated successfully for many years.

With life insurance, the situation is different; but, unfortunately, the difference is not usually apparent until an insuring plan has been in operation for a number of years. Assume, for instance, that a group of 1,000 young people, each 20 years of age, agree that on the death of any member of the group a contribution will be made by each survivor in such an amount that a benefit of $1,000 can be paid to the beneficiary of the deceased member.

In a group of 1,000 persons age 20, an arrangement of this kind would be quite practicable for several years. According to mortality statistics used by life insurance companies, only one or two deaths per year would need to be anticipated in a group of this size and age for a period of more than 10 years. Thus, contributions of only a dollar or two per year from each survivor during those years would be sufficient to provide the benefits promised.

As in the fire insurance group, there is some danger of catastrophic loss, since an automobile accident or a plane crash could take several members in one year. Nevertheless, a group starting with 1,000 members could make the relatively small additional contribution to meet death benefits even for several members in one year without undue hardship. It is only in the later years of life that the real problem arises.

Because of the increasing probability of death and the fact that death is certain for everyone eventually, there will ultimately be a death claim for every continuing member of an insured group if the plan operates long enough. This is not true in fire insurance. Fire losses are not usually suffered by any large percentage of an insured group, even over a long period of time. Moreover, the fire losses actually experienced do not necessarily reduce the number of members of the group, since most of the burned houses can be expected to be rebuilt. Finally, the number of fire losses among any particular group does not vary significantly from year to year.

In life insurance, by contrast, a benefit will eventually be payable for every continuing member. Moreover, every benefit paid means a reduction in the number of persons from whom future contributions may be received; and, finally, every succeeding year means an increase in the percentage of members for whom a death claim will be payable.

If the members of the group are relatively young at the outset, these problems will not become evident for several years. The rates of death increase slowly during the twenties and the thirties, and death benefits can be provided for several years by relatively small assessments for a group of this kind. At about age 50, however, the mortality rate begins to show a more rapid increase (see Figure 3-2). Now the secretary of the group will find that he is being notified more frequently that another member of the group has died—or two, or three, or four. Remember, also, that while the group started with approximately 1,000 members, each death has reduced the size of the group by one. Thus each claim has meant an increasing contribution from a decreasing number of contributors.

Eventually, in any group of this kind there will be many more death benefits to pay each year and far fewer persons from whom contributions will be received. At age 70, only slightly more than one-half of the original group will remain, and 25 of these can be expected to die before reaching age 71. The problem now is how to raise $25,000 from about 525 people at an age when some are ill and very few are employed. A contribution of more than $45 in one year at age 70 for a $1,000 policy is not very realistic (though it is not unreasonable under the assumed conditions) and most groups of this kind would have disbanded many years earlier.

Inadequacies of the Assessment Plans

Most life insurance assessment groups planned to, and often did, add new members regularly, to take the place of those who died or withdrew. Thus, the number of persons making contributions was kept more nearly constant than in the illustrative group. Nevertheless, adding new members did not solve the basic problem, as most such groups discovered.

The Average-Age Problem. It was realized that if enough new young members were added to an assessment group each year, a relatively low average age could be maintained for the members of the group. In that case, it was thought, death benefits payable and assessments required would remain reasonably constant. This was not a valid assumption, however, for two basic reasons. First, it was virtually impossible to keep the average age very low; and second, even if it were possible, a low average age would not necessarily mean a comparably low mortality rate for the group. These reasons are most easily explained by illustration.

Assume a group of 1,000 persons 35 years of age in 1972. These people will, of course, be 36 years old in 1973. How many new members, age 30, would be required in 1973 to keep the average age of the group at 35? Exactly 200, if no one has dropped out.

It may not be especially difficult to obtain 200 new members age 30. In that case, in the following year, the original members are 37 years old and the members who joined in 1973 are 31 years old. Now 240 new members, age 30, are required if we are to keep the average age of the group at 35 for the third year. In the fourth year, 288 new members age 30 will be required; and if the average age of the group is to be kept at 35 in the fifth year, more than 345 new members age 30 will have to be added in that one year.

After five years, even though more than 1,000 new members, all age 30, have been brought into the group, the average age of the members will be somewhat higher than when the group was organized. Note also that no allowance has been made for withdrawals for any reason and that it has been assumed that persons 30 years of age will continue to join this group, whose surviving members are, of course, growing older every year. Anyone who has tried to enlist the interest of new people in membership in any organization, no matter how worthy the purpose, will recognize that the membership needs, even for the first year, will probably not be met.

The Average-Age Fallacy. Even if enough new entrants were obtained, however, keeping the average age of the members of the group at a constant level will not keep the death rate at the same level. For instance, according to the mortality table presently used by life insurance companies, the mortality rate at age 50 is 8.32 per 1,000 lives. The rates for ages 40 and 60, however, are 3.53 and 20.34 per 1,000, respectively. A group consisting of 500 persons age 40 and 500 age 60, therefore, would have an average age of 50, but the mortality rate for the group would be found by adding the mortality rates of each group (3.53+20.34) and dividing by two. This gives a rate of 11.94 per 1,000, as contrasted with 8.32 per 1,000 for a group composed entirely of persons age 50.

This difference would be even more marked as some members of the group reached the more advanced ages. Assessments, therefore, would come with greater frequency and the number would increase more rapidly as older members grew still older, even though the average age of the group remained the same. As a consequence, younger people would be even more reluctant to join the group.

Fraternal Benefit Associations

Life insurance on the assessment plan is not common today, but the plan was widely used in the latter part of the 19th century, especially by fraternal benefit associations. These organizations, often called lodges, were especially popular during the period between 1874 and 1920, and many of them made use of the assessment plan to provide a death benefit for their members. For these fraternal associations, as with the illustrative group we have described, the assessment principle usually operated with some success for the first several years. As their members grew older, however, the fraternal benefit associations began to experience the same problems that faced our hypothetical group, and their subsequent history was rarely more favorable.

Several variations of the assessment principle were introduced in attempts to solve the basic problem. Some associations made regular assessments without waiting for deaths to be reported. That is, they made assessments at the beginning of the year, based on the number of estimated deaths for the year. (This might be called a "pre-assessment" plan, as contrasted with the "post-assessment" approach previously discussed.) Other associations used assessments that differed according to the ages of their members when they joined. Nothing proved really effective, however, and the basic problem was not solved for the fraternals until they adopted the level-premium system and established their insurance on the same sound actuarial basis as the commercial life insurers.

Pay-as-You-Go Insurance

The experience of the fraternal organizations offers practical evidence of the inadequacies of the pay-as-you-go principle to provide death benefits for any group of people. Death claims always increase in the later years at such a rate that many surviving members cannot pay the necessary assessments and are forced to drop out, often at a time when they are no longer insurable. The ideal solution, of course, is a premium that is sufficiently high in the early years that it never has to be increased, no matter how long an insured may live. In other words, the ideal solution is a level premium.

The Level Premium

The basic idea of the level premium is simple. The amounts required to pay death benefits on a year-to-year basis under a group of policies are computed on the assumption that deaths will occur in the future at rates that do not differ significantly from those experienced in the past. Then a level premium is calculated which, if paid by the surviving insureds each year, will provide the amounts needed to pay benefits as they fall due. Because the largest number of deaths will occur in later years, a level premium requires higher payments in the early years than are needed to pay current claims. This difference is not so great as might be supposed, however, because of the effect of compound interest.

A portion of each premium collected in the early years under any group of level-premium policies is invested. As interest is earned on these invested sums, the interest too is invested and interest continues to be earned on the total amount. Interest computed in this way is called compound interest. Some idea of the importance of compound interest may be obtained when one considers that any given amount, invested at 5 percent per year, with interest compounded, will more than double itself in 15 years.

The effect of compound interest in the level-premium system is indicated in Figure 3–5, which shows the relationship of the level premium to the increasing premium that would be necessary if premiums were collected each year in exactly the amount necessary to meet the claim costs of that year. The two lines, AA and BB, intersect at the year in which the level premium is exactly equal to the cost of death claims for that year. An amount in excess of the claim costs (shaded in the diagram) has thus been collected in all earlier years. In each of the later years, the premium will be less than the mortality cost for that year. Thus, the shaded area represents the total excess premium collected in the early years under the level premium system, and the dotted area indicates the amount by which the total of death claims payable in later years will exceed the premiums actually collected in those years. Under the level premium system, the dotted area will always be greater than the shaded area because the amounts indicated by the shaded area are invested and earn compound interest.

The practical effect of the level premium, therefore, is twofold. First, it enables the policyowner to pay a large share of the total premiums for his policy during the years in which his earning power is usually highest. Second, because of the interest element, it reduces the total premiums required. Interest, therefore, is one of the basic factors of premium computation. Two other factors are (1) the number and timing of death claims to be expected and (2) the costs of administering the insurance plan.

■ HOW PREMIUMS ARE COMPUTED

General Objectives

Premiums for any kind of insurance must be adequate, reasonable, and equitable. In some lines of insurance, these are legal as well as practical requirements. Premiums for life insurance must be adequate in the sense that they must be sufficient, with interest, to pay the benefits promised, as well as the expenses of administering the plan. They must also be reasonable. Insurance is a highly competitive business, and premiums must be sufficiently competitive that other companies cannot offer substantially the same benefits at a significantly lower premium. Even if there were no competition, however, good business sense suggests that a company would not sell very much insurance if its premiums were unreasonably high.

Life insurance premiums must also be equitable. Thus, consideration must be given to such factors as the age, sex, health, and occupation of the persons whose lives are to be insured. This means that premiums must be fair. The same or very similar benefits cannot ethically be offered to one policyowner at one premium rate and to another at a different rate unless there are variations in risk or expenses to justify the difference. Most companies would follow this principle as a matter of good business practice alone, but discrimination among insureds of the same class or classes is prohibited by law in most states and provinces.

The procedures involved in computing life insurance premium rates, therefore, are governed by practical considerations and legal requirements as well as by technical requirements. However, the following discussion will be confined to the technical factors of mortality, interest, and expenses.

Mortality

The first factor in premium computation concerns the number and timing of the claims the insurance company must be prepared to pay. If an adequate fund is to be accumulated for the payment of claims as they arise, it is first necessary to estimate the number of expected losses and when they will probably occur. In most lines of insurance, these estimates are based on statistics of past experience.

60 ▪ Principles of Life Insurance

In life insurance, such statistics concern the mortality rates at the various ages and, as previously noted, these statistics are compiled in mortality tables.

Mortality Tables. A mortality table is a statistical device which starts with an arbitrarily selected number of persons who are assumed to have been born in a given year. The table then lists the number of persons still living and the number dying at each successive age as the group grows older, terminating with the year in which the last survivors are assumed to have died. The result is a table like the following, but for all ages:

The Commissioners' 1958 Standard Ordinary Mortality Table (ages 0–5)

Age	Number Living	Number Dying	Deaths per 1,000	Expectation of Life (years)
0	10,000,000	70,800	7.08	68.30
1	9,929,200	17,475	1.76	67.78
2	9,911,725	15,066	1.52	66.90
3	9,896,659	14,449	1.46	66.00
4	9,882,210	13,835	1.40	65.10
5	9,868,375	13,322	1.35	64.19

Note: The key figures in this table are found in the column titled "Deaths per 1,000." The "Number Living" and "Number Dying" columns are used to develop these figures. The "Expectation of Life (years)" column, by contrast, usually appears in mortality tables, but it is not significant in the development of premium rates.

Mortality is the basic consideration in establishing the premium rates for any group of life insurance contracts because it is the basis for estimating the number and the timing of future claims. Mortality statistics, therefore, constitute an area of continuing concern for every life insurance company. Obviously, if death rates are seriously overestimated, higher premiums will be charged than would be necessary. Similarly, if the mortality rates are underestimated, premiums will be inadequate.

Interest

The second basic factor in premium computation is interest. As mentioned earlier, the investment of the excess portion of each premium paid in the early policy years is essential if the level-premium system is to operate successfully. When the level premium is calculated, therefore, it is presumed that a part of the premium collected in the early years will be invested as it is received and that it will earn interest at an assumed rate. The length of time these funds will remain invested can be estimated in exactly the same way that death claims can be estimated—by using a mortality table.

The Rate of Interest. The fundamental objective in establishing a premium rate is to accumulate a fund adequate to meet future claims as they are presented. Obviously, if money is invested at 6 or 7 percent as it is received, a larger fund will be accumulated over the years than would be the case if the same amount were invested at 4 or 5 percent. Consequently, if the funds are invested at a higher rate of interest, a lower premium will produce a fund sufficient to meet future claims. Obviously, also, the interest rate actually earned will depend, among other things, upon economic conditions, which are extremely difficult to predict.

Reliable estimates of future interest earnings are highly important in life insurance premium computation. Many policies issued today will be kept in force 50, 60, even 70 or more years. It would be very easy, therefore, for a company to establish low premium rates by assuming that a high rate of interest would be earned. If the assumed rate were higher than the rate actually realized, however, the premium rates would prove inadequate. On the other hand, assuming a rate substantially lower than that reasonably to be expected would produce an unduly high premium rate and place the company at a competitive disadvantage.

The usual practice is to make a conservative estimate of the probable future interest rates. An interest rate is selected which the officers believe the company will earn, on the average, during the lifetimes of the insureds under any group of policies. This decision represents the best judgment of the officers, based upon past company experience and their most reliable estimate of future economic conditions.

The calculation of premium rates for life insurance contracts involves mathematical processes that are beyond the scope of this book. Some acquaintance with the procedure in a general sense, however, is essential to an understanding of many aspects of the life insurance business. For that reason, the principles of premium computation will be outlined here, beginning with those applicable to the net single premium.

The Net Single Premium

The net single premium can best be explained by using a hypothetical example. Assume that a life insurance company issues a group of life insurance policies, all of which become effective on January 1 of a given year. Assume, also, that on that day the company collects premiums under all the policies in exactly the amount that, with interest, will enable it to pay all expected death claims under the policies whenever those deaths occur. The total of the premiums so collected would be the "net single premium" for that group of policies. The net single premium may be defined, therefore, as the amount which, with interest, will be sufficient to pay all benefits promised under a block of policies, as the benefits (claims) become payable. (Note, therefore, that the net premium is just sufficient to pay all claims. It does not include any allowance to cover expenses.)

The net single premium for an *individual* policy equals the net single premium that has been calculated for a group of policies, divided by the number of life insurance policies in the group. For example, if the figure of 10,000 life insurance policies is used in the computation, and the total net single premium for the group is $11,562,100, the net single premium for an *individual* policy will be $1,156.21.

In computing the net single premium, it is only necessary to predict the number and timing of claims to be expected under the policies and to estimate the rate of interest that may be earned by the insurance company on its invested funds. Thus, in calculating the net single premium, only two factors are of concern: mortality and interest. The way these factors are used may be illustrated by a hypothetical case.

Assume that a company officer is discussing the calculation of the net single premium. From the mortality table to be used, he shows how it is possible to estimate the number of death claims the company must be prepared to pay in each year for every 1,000 policies issued to insureds of any given age. If a $1,000 benefit is payable at each death, the exact amount needed in any given future year is found by multiplying the number of assumed deaths by $1,000.

It takes only a moment's thought to realize that somewhat less than the total amount so calculated will be sufficient if the money is collected now and invested at interest until it is needed. Furthermore, if a definite interest rate is assumed, the exact amount the insurer needs to collect today to pay claims in any given future year can be computed. This amount is called the "present value" of the sums needed in the future.

The present value of a sum due on a given future date is the amount which, if invested at a specified rate of interest, will produce the sum needed on the date it is due. The idea of "present value" always concerns money due in the future and a specified rate of interest. Thus, at 4 percent interest, the present value of $1 one year from now is a little more than $.96. That is, an amount slightly larger than $.96 today, invested at 4 percent interest, will equal $1 one year from today.

The net single premium for any group of life insurance policies is computed by calculating the present value of the benefit (claim) payments that will be made in every year during which the policies will remain in force. The total of these present values is the amount which, if received by the company on the date the policies become effective, and invested at the specified rate of interest, would be sufficient to pay all benefits under the policies as those benefits become payable. (This is the definition of the net single premium given on page 62.) Thus, the net single premium for any group of policies is the present value of all future benefits to be paid under those policies.

The Net Level Annual Premium

If life insurance premiums were payable only in single sums at the time the policies were issued, the amount of life insurance purchased would be seriously limited. Most people cannot afford to pay a very large single premium for life insurance, but they can and do pay the equivalent in smaller annual premiums. To make this possible, therefore, it is necessary to find the level annual amount that will produce the mathematical equivalent of the net single premium. This level annual amount is called the net level annual premium.

The net level annual premium is developed as follows: First, it is assumed that each policyowner will make a payment of 1 at the time the policies are issued and that continuing payments of 1 each year will be made by each surviving policyowner as long as any policies remain in force. The present values of these future payments are then computed, and the total of these present values is divided into the total of the present values of all future benefits payable under the policies (the net single premium). The result is the net level annual premium—the actual amount that must be paid annually by surviving policyowners to equal the net single premium. To summarize:

THE PRESENT VALUE OF = THE PRESENT VALUE OF
FUTURE ANNUAL NET PREMIUMS   FUTURE BENEFITS
                                OR
                        THE NET SINGLE PREMIUM

This formula is equally true for a group of policies or for an individual life insurance policy.

The Gross Annual Premium

Net level annual premiums are computed to produce sufficient amounts to pay all death claims as they are presented, if deaths occur in accordance with the mortality table used and if interest is earned at the rate assumed. The net premium makes no allowance for such factors as the expenses of running the company, the possibility that there could be more deaths in some years than those shown by the table, or that a lower rate of interest might actually be earned. To provide for these, as well as other factors, an addition known as the "loading" is made to the net premium. The result is the gross premium, which is the amount the policyowner actually pays.

The level-premium system made it possible to offer life insurance for the whole of life at a realistic premium. At the same time, however, it presented other problems. One of these was an accounting problem, concerning the accumulation of assets that results from the level-premium system. It was essential to account for those assets in such a way that they could not be considered profit even though they were not currently needed to pay claims. A second problem concerned the equitable treatment of policyowners who paid a level premium for several, often many years, and then withdrew from the insuring plan. Must such policyowners forfeit the amounts they had paid in excess of current insurance costs during those years?

As the business of life insurance grew, many life insurance companies voluntarily developed accounting practices which reflected the fact that a part of the premium collected in the early years would be needed in later years and would be used then. Many companies also introduced the practice, at a fairly early date, of making some benefit available to policyowners who withdrew after having paid a level premium for a specified length of time. Later, the various states enacted legislation requiring uniform practices in these respects. These developments took place over a period of approximately 100 years from the date the level-premium system was first used.

The following section will discuss the history of life insurance during that period.

■ THE EARLY LIFE INSURANCE COMPANIES

In England

The level premium was first used by the life insurance association established by James Dodson and Thomas Simpson in 1762—The Society for Equitable Assurance on Lives and Survivorships. A number of associations for life insurance purposes had preceded this company, though little is known about most of them. The Hand-in-Hand, established in 1696, is thought to have been the first insurance office in England.

Another association, The Society of Assurance for Widows and Orphans, was organized in 1699, as a mutual assessment company. Each member was to pay five shillings (about $\frac{1}{4}$ of a pound) when he joined and five shillings whenever a claim was presented. A benefit of £500 was to be paid at the death of each member, and membership was limited to 2,000 persons. However, the later history of the association is not known, not even how long it survived.

More is known about the Amicable Society for a Perpetual Assurance Office, which was established in 1706. No one was accepted if he was over 45 years of age (though no other age distinctions were made). Members paid a specified amount each year, and the total contributions were divided, in accordance with a predetermined formula, to provide death benefits. The association continued to operate on that basis for 160 years.

A great many companies were organized in succeeding years, many of them on a highly speculative basis; but it was not until James Dodson was refused insurance with the Amicable (because he was more than 45 years of age) that a really sound system was devised. In collaboration with Thomas Simpson, an insurance authority, Dodson worked out a plan under which insurance for the whole of life could be offered to older applicants who would pay higher premiums in a level amount for the duration of their policies. The company they established, The Equitable Society, operated on this principle, requiring a specified premium and paying a stated amount of insurance on the death of the insured. Thus, the level-premium, whole life concept of life insurance was introduced.

In the United States

The little life insurance that was written in the earliest days of the North American colonies was written by English companies. Later, a few life insurance contracts were written here and there by marine insurers, but almost no American life insurance companies were formed before 1800.

Two significant organizations had their beginnings in this pre-1800 era, however. One was the Corporation for the Relief of Poor and Distressed Presbyterian Ministers and of the Poor and Distressed Widows and Children of Presbyterian Ministers. Chartered in 1759, this organization was established for the purpose expressed so completely in its name, although it did not operate as a true life insurance company at first. It has been called The Presbyterian Ministers' Fund since 1888, and it is still in operation as a commercial insurance company.

The second organization dating from the 18th century was the Insurance Company of North America. This company was chartered in 1794 and authorized to do a life insurance business, but it issued only a small number of life insurance policies and withdrew from the life insurance business a few years later. (It is interesting to note that this company reentered the life insurance business in 1956 and organized a new company—Life Insurance Company of North America—for that purpose.)

Between 1800 and 1840, several stock [1] life insurance companies were organized. One of these, The Pennsylvania Company for Insurance on Lives and Granting Annuities, organized in 1809, was the first commercial company organized in the United States for the sole purpose of writing life insurance. Other stock life insurers organized in this period were The Massachusetts Hospital Life Insurance Company and two companies chartered in 1830, The New York Life Insurance and Trust Company, and The Baltimore Life Insurance Company.

The concept of mutual [2] life insurance gained impetus in the 1840's. Many mutual companies organized during this period are

---

[1] A stock company is a company with stockholder-owners, such as General Electric or General Motors. A stock life insurance company is a stock company formed for the purpose of doing a life insurance business.

[2] A mutual life insurance company is a life insurance company that is owned by its policyowners, by contrast with a stock life insurance company, which is owned by its stockholders.

still among the leaders in the industry. Examples are: New England Mutual Life Insurance Company, State Mutual Life Assurance Company, Mutual Life Insurance Company of New York, Mutual Benefit Life Insurance Company, Connecticut Mutual Life Insurance Company, and Penn Mutual Life Insurance Company.

The decade of the 1840's was a dynamic time for life insurance growth. Life insurance in force in the United States increased over 2,000 percent during those years, more than in any other similar period in the history of life insurance. However, competition for new business increased markedly with the emergence of many new companies during this period and brought with it practices that led to widespread criticism and suspicion of the industry, as well as a number of company failures. This criticism, together with the depression of 1857, caused a temporary slowing of the rate of increase in new business, but soon records were again being broken. At the beginning of the Civil War, life insurance in force had risen more than 3,000 percent in the preceding 20 years.

The Beginning of Regulation

During these years, life insurers had rather generally determined for themselves the financial safeguards they thought necessary to assure that they could pay the future claims under outstanding policies, and they had not yet developed any standard practices for treatment of withdrawing policyowners. As a result, the period was characterized by numerous company failures and a notable lack of uniformity in connection with benefits, if any, for persons who could not, or for other reasons did not, continue premium payments to keep their insurance in force.

One of the persons who became especially concerned about the solvency of life insurers and the rights of withdrawing policyowners was Elizur Wright, one of the most important single figures in the history of life insurance in the United States. Wright was born in 1804 and was graduated from Yale University in 1823. He taught mathematics at Western Reserve University for a brief time and then went to New York to edit antislavery journals. A few years later, while on a trip to England, he undertook to obtain some insurance information for the Massachusetts Hospital Life Insurance Company and had occasion to visit the Royal Exchange in London. There, he witnessed the sale of several life insurance policies by insureds who, old and ill, were unable to continue their premium payments. Their policies were purchased by persons who had no insurable interest in the lives of the insureds, and who purchased the policies solely as speculative investments—that is, to make a profit on the death of the insured. This practice seemed so reprehensible to Wright that he returned home determined that similar practices would not be followed in the United States if he could do anything to prevent it.

With the same zeal that had made him effective in the antislavery movement, Wright undertook his insurance activities. In 1858, he became one of the first insurance commissioners in Massachusetts, and in the next few years he succeeded in obtaining the enactment of laws in that state to require insurance companies to follow uniform practices in two significant respects. First, they were required to estimate their liabilities for future claims in accordance with standard legal requirements (called legal reserve laws); and second, they were required to grant some benefits to policyowners who had paid a level premium for a specified length of time and then permitted their policies to lapse (that is, to expire) for failure to pay further premiums. These benefits were required to prevent the forfeiture of whole life policies under which the policyowners had paid premiums for the specified length of time and thus are called "nonforfeiture" benefits. These two concepts—the legal reserve and the nonforfeiture benefits—will be briefly discussed in the following pages.

■ THE LEGAL RESERVE

It is doubtful that any other single life insurance concept lends itself more readily to misunderstanding than the idea of the policy reserve. The word "reserve" is not too well chosen because it is used in several different ways in accounting and finance, where it may mean an asset, a reduction from an asset, or a liability. In life insurance, the policy reserves (the legal reserves) are liabilities. They are established as a way of determining or measuring the assets the company must maintain in order to be able to meet its future commitments under the policies it has issued.

The level-premium system contemplates the investment of that part of every net premium which exceeds the current cost of protection. It is frequently said that these amounts are "held" and invested, to be used in the payment of claims in later years. However, these amounts are not really held or invested as a separate fund and, indeed, the "reserve" itself is not a fund—that is, it is not money, not assets of any kind. Thus, the reserve cannot be "invested," and it is not "used" in later years, when current premiums received by the company are not sufficient to meet current claims.

In other words, a life insurance company does not have special funds earmarked for any group of policies "out of which" it pays claims in later policy years. On the contrary, premiums are collected in large amounts daily, and current funds are used for the payment of current company obligations (including current claims). In short, the life insurance company collects premiums, pays claims, and meets its other obligations on a much more general and much less rigid basis than the theoretical description of the level-premium system would suggest. Some financial safeguards, therefore, are essential if the company is to be certain that it will have sufficient assets to pay its claims and other commitments when they fall due. These financial safeguards are established in the form of reserve liabilities.

Every life insurance company is required to compute its future liabilities under all policies in force, in accordance with detailed legal requirements, and to show the net total of these liabilities as a "policy reserve" liability figure in the financial report (the "Annual Statement") it submits each year to the insurance departments of all the states in which it operates. The company must, therefore, have assets in an amount equal to this reserve liability, or it will be considered insolvent. Life insurance companies that operate in this way, complying with the legal reserve requirements established by the state insurance laws, are known as legal reserve life insurance companies.

The Amount of the Reserve

The policy reserve liability that must be reported by a life insurance company in its Annual Statement is defined in technical detail in the insurance laws of the various states. In general, these laws specify minimum requirements. Thus, the reserve must be not less than the reserve that would be produced if estimates of future claims were based on a specified mortality table and if not more than a specified interest rate were assumed. For policies issued currently, the specified mortality table is the 1958 Commissioners' Standard Ordinary (C.S.O.) Mortality Table.

There are several different ways of arriving at the reserve liability figure for a group of policies as of any given date. Assume, for instance, that you wish to calculate the reserve as of December 31,

1972, for a group of continuous-premium, whole life policies issued in 1965 to male insureds, age 25. One of the simplest ways to calculate the reserve is to compute the present value of all future expected claims under these policies as of December 31, 1972 and the present value of all future net premiums payable under them. The present value of the future net premiums is then subtracted from the present value of the future claims. The difference is the reserve liability for that particular group of policies—that is, the amount the company must hold in assets as of that date if it is to be able to pay future claims when they fall due. This is known as the "prospective" method of computing the reserve, because it is based on future (prospective) claims and future net premiums.

PRESENT VALUE OF FUTURE CLAIMS − PRESENT VALUE OF FUTURE NET PREMIUMS = AMOUNT OF POLICY RESERVE LIABILITY

There are other methods of calculating policy reserves, but the resulting liability will be the same regardless of which method is used. Under one such alternative method, the reserve is computed by accumulating, at the assumed rate of interest, all net premiums that have been paid under the policies to the specified date and subtracting all *tabular* claims—that is, all claims that would have been presented if deaths had occurred at the rates shown in the mortality table used. This is known as the "retrospective" method of computing the policy reserve.

The practical effect of the policy reserve may be illustrated as follows: Assume that the present value of future claims under a given group of life insurance policies is $1 million as of the date of the Annual Statement. Assume also that the present value of all net premiums that will be payable in the future under those policies is $900,000. In this situation, the potential claim liability of the company is more than the potential premium income. The insurer, therefore, must have additional balancing assets or it can expect to become insolvent before all claims are paid under those policies. By showing a policy reserve of $100,000 as a liability and maintaining assets to match this liability, the company demonstrates its financial ability to meet its long-term commitments. Thus the policy reserve measures the adequacy of company assets by establishing and valuing the liabilities of the company to its policyowners. It thus tests the solvency of the company on a long-term basis and assures that, if premiums are collected as provided by the policies, if interest is earned as assumed, and if claims become payable in accordance with the mortality table on which the rates are based, the company will be able to pay its claims when they fall due.

■ NONFORFEITURE BENEFITS

So long as insureds remain with an insuring plan until their respective deaths, the level-premium system operates with fairness. However, policyowners often discontinue premium payments. In such instances, the policy is said to lapse for failure to pay a premium when due.

In the early days of life insurance, if a policyowner permitted his policy to lapse, even after he had paid a level premium for many years, he had no right under the terms of the policy to receive any part of the premium amounts he had paid in excess of the current cost of his protection. In the 1830's and 40's, some insurance companies were making cash payments to withdrawing policyowners under these circumstances, but they were not required to do so.

As a result of the activities of Elizur Wright, the Massachusetts legislature in 1861 enacted a law requiring insurance companies to continue a limited amount of insurance in force under a policy that lapsed after premiums had been paid for a specified number of years. Legislation enacted later required the company to pay a cash value under these same circumstances if the policyowner wished to surrender his policy.

Today, standard nonforfeiture laws are in effect in all states. They will be more fully discussed in a later chapter. Briefly, however, they require nonforfeiture provisions to be included in whole life policies under which level premiums are paid for a specified length of time. If the policyowner fails to elect one of these benefits, the policy must specify which one will become effective in the event the policy lapses for nonpayment of premiums. Thus, the benefits are truly nonforfeitable—the policyowner cannot lose them even if he does not know of their existence.

■ NOTES ON CANADIAN PRACTICES

In Canada, the law does not require life insurance companies to use specific mortality tables in reserve calculations. However, any mortality table a company wishes to use must be approved by the Federal Department of Insurance. The law does not require nonforfeiture provisions either, but companies voluntarily provide such benefits in order to be competitive, and when they are provided, they *must* be shown in the policy.

■ QUESTIONS FOR REVIEW

1. Briefly explain why the assessment principle operates with greater success in fire insurance than in life insurance plans.
2. Explain in general terms why two groups of persons having the same average age might develop significantly different mortality rates.
3. List three general objectives in determining life insurance premiums.
4. What two factors are basic in the calculation of the net single premium?
5. Define a mortality table.
6. Why is interest important in calculating life insurance premiums?
7. Define "present value."
8. Briefly define:
    a) net single premium
    b) net level annual premium
    c) gross annual premium.
9. What is the purpose of the policy reserve?
10. Briefly explain why the nonforfeiture benefits may be said to be "nonforfeitable."

4 HOW CONTRACTS ARE FORMED

People insure their lives by applying for life insurance from a life insuring organization, usually a life insurance company. If the requirements of the company are met, a policy will be issued; and, if the legal requirements are fulfilled, the applicant will have a life insurance contract with the company that can be enforced in a court of law, if necessary. Thereafter, the rights of the policyowner and the obligations of the insurer are governed by the terms of this contract. The purpose of this chapter is to discuss the most significant legal principles that are involved in the formation of the life insurance contract.

■ INSURANCE AS A CONTRACT

In a basic sense, a life insurance contract operates in essentially the same way as any other contract—a contract to buy a home, a contract to repay a loan, or a contract to furnish janitorial services for a year. In each of these examples, there is an obligation or promise, on the part of one or more persons, to perform an act or acts. These promises are made to other persons in such a way that the latter will have the right to require the promised actions to be performed.

A life insurance contract represents the same kind of binding obligations on the part of the life insurance company and the same kind of legally enforceable rights on the part of the policyowner. In order to have this effect, however, the life insurance must be applied for (by the applicant) and a policy must be issued (by the insurer) in accordance with certain well-defined principles of contract law.

■ THE LAW OF INFORMAL CONTRACTS

A contract has been defined by one authority [1] as "a promise or a set of promises for breach of which the law gives a remedy, or the performance of which the law recognizes as a duty." In other words, a contract involves a promise or promises that are legally enforceable.

There are two basic ways in which promises may be made legally enforceable. One is by using a special form. Negotiable instruments, such as checks and drafts, and promises that were once executed under seal, such as deeds, are all enforceable because of their form. For this reason they are called "formal" contracts.

A much greater number of contracts involve promises that are legally enforceable because of the circumstances under which the promises are made, rather than any particular form in which they may be expressed. These are called "informal" contracts. The life insurance contract is an informal contract.

If an agreement is to be enforceable as an informal contract, it must meet certain legal requirements that may be summarized as follows:

1. The parties who make the agreement must be legally competent to enter into a binding contract.
2. The parties must express definite assent to the terms of the promise or promises involved.
3. There must be legally adequate consideration for the promise.
4. If a special form is required by law, that form must be used (although compliance with such a requirement will not, of itself, mean that the contract will be enforceable).
5. There must be no statute or rule of law declaring such contracts invalid.

Competent Parties

With only a few exceptions, every person is presumed to have the legal capacity to make an enforceable contract. The most notable

---

[1] *Williston on Contracts*, (Mt. Kisco, N.Y.: Baker, Voorhis & Co., Inc., 1957), Vol. I, p. 1.

exceptions, so far as life insurance contracts are concerned, are persons who have not attained the required legal age (minors) and insane persons.

Minors. The age at which a person has the legal capacity to make a contract that can be enforced against him—that is, his age of majority—depends upon the law of the jurisdiction (state or province) in which he resides. If there is no law to the contrary, this age is 21. In recent years, there has been a definite trend toward establishing age 18 as the age of majority, but there are still many variations in state laws. For instance, some states provide that a person 18 years of age or older will be considered an adult for contractual purposes if he or she is married. Other states have established different ages—21 for men and 18 for women. Whenever there is a question as to whether a person has attained the age of majority, it will be decided in accordance with the law of the particular state or province concerned.

The legal effect of a contract made by a minor is commonly summarized by saying that such contracts are "voidable but not void." This difference is important. A void contract has no legal effect whatever. It is as if no contract had ever been made. A voidable contract is a contract which has a legal defect, but which will be binding if the person who has the right to disaffirm it does not exercise that right.

To say that a minor's contracts are voidable, therefore, means that a contract a minor has made with an adult will be enforceable in accordance with its terms unless the minor elects to disaffirm (in legal terms, *avoid*) it. If he disaffirms the contract, he will not have to carry out the promise or promises he has made; and he may request and receive back whatever he has given or paid to the other contracting party.

Assume that Mike Nelson, age 17, makes a contract to purchase a car from Rex Brown, an adult. The contract will be enforceable in accordance with its terms unless Mike elects to disaffirm it. If he wishes, however, he may disaffirm the contract, return the car if he still has it, and require Mr. Brown to return any money he (Mike) has paid him. Mr. Brown will be bound by the contract—that is, it will be enforceable against him. Mike, however, will not be bound, and Mr. Brown cannot require him to carry out his part of the agreement.

A minor may disaffirm most contracts at any time during his minority and within a reasonable length of time after he has attained the age of majority. However, he cannot disaffirm a contract for the sale of real property—land and attached buildings—until he reaches the age of majority.

A minor's contracts to pay for food, shelter, clothing, and similar things that may be held by the courts to be "necessaries" are treated differently. Necessaries may be defined as those things that are reasonably necessary to a minor's well-being and suitable to his particular circumstances. Thus, they may differ according to the financial circumstances and needs of the minor. Contracts for necessaries are not generally enforceable against the minor in strict accordance with their terms, but the minor is usually required to pay what is considered the fair value of the articles purchased. Life insurance, however, is generally held not to be a necessary. In the absence of a special law, therefore, a life insurance contract made with a minor is subject to the general rule and is "voidable but not void."

To illustrate: Larry Williams, a minor, applies for life insurance from the Ajax Life Insurance Company. A policy is issued to him, and he pays the premiums as they become due. Under these circumstances, the contract is enforceable against the life insurance company; and if Larry dies before he reaches age 21, the death benefit will be payable in accordance with the terms of the policy. In other words, the fact that Larry was a minor has no effect on the obligations of the life insurance company.

The fact of his minority is of basic significance to Larry, however; and, if he wishes, he may disaffirm the contract at any time during his minority and for a reasonable period thereafter. In that case, according to the majority of court decisions, he may recover all premiums he has paid. The insurer is released from its obligation, but the right to disaffirm is Larry's and Larry's alone. An adult with whom a minor has made a contract cannot use the minority of the latter to avoid it.

A number of states have enacted special laws that make it possible for minors 15 or 16 years of age, or over, to apply for and exercise all rights granted under life insurance contracts, on the same basis as if they were adults. The wording of these statutes varies. Typically the age is 15. Typically, also, the statutes permit the minor to purchase insurance on his own life or on the life of another person in whose life he has an insurable interest. Frequently, the insurance must be payable to the minor himself (if the insurance is on the life of another) or to a member of his family (if the insurance is on his own life). In states having statutes of this kind, a minor of the specified age or older may purchase life insurance in accordance with the statutory requirements, and he will be treated as an adult so far as that life insurance contract is concerned. That is, he will not have the right to disaffirm such a contract later on the grounds that he was a minor when it was made.

Insane Persons. A contract made by a person who was insane at the time of contracting but whose insanity had not been established as a matter of law is, like the contract of a minor, "voidable but not void." If the person later regains his sanity, he may disaffirm the contract or require that it be carried out, whichever he prefers. As is also true of contracts with a minor, the other contracting party has no right to disaffirm and must carry out the terms of the contract if required to do so. However, contracts made by a person whose insanity has been legally established and for whom a conservator (or guardian) has been appointed are said to be "void" as a matter of law.

Business Organizations. A corporation's capacity to make contracts is governed by the powers set forth in the legal document (*charter*, or *articles of incorporation*) which establishes the corporation. A contract for any purpose that is within those powers may be made in the name of the corporation by an authorized officer of the corporation. This is true of the life insurance company. The kinds of contracts it makes must fall within the kinds authorized by its charter. Thus, a company authorized to write life insurance only may not legally issue contracts of health insurance.

Assent to the Promise

Offer and Acceptance. Every contract requires that two or more legally competent parties reach an agreement. Both or all must agree to the same thing, with a reasonably clear understanding of the terms. This has generally been held to mean that a proposal (or offer) must be made by one person, in a form to which he is willing to be bound if it is accepted by the other. When such a proposal, or offer, is accepted by the other party (assuming all other requirements have been met) a legally binding contract is created.

The person who makes an offer is the *offeror*. The person to whom an offer is made is the *offeree*. The offeree may accept an offer by performing an act or by making a promise.

Suppose Alan Gray offers to sell his car to Edward Dobbs for

$3,500. Dobbs can accept the offer by paying the $3,500 to Gray. In that case, he has accepted by performing an act, and Gray must deliver the car. Alternatively, Dobbs may say he accepts the offer and promises to pay for the car on delivery. In that case, he has accepted by making a promise.

Either method of acceptance creates a binding contract. In the first instance, when Dobbs pays the purchase price, he has no further duties so far as the agreement is concerned. Gray, however, has promised to deliver the car. Thus the resulting contract consists of a promise on the part of one person only—that is, a promise only on one side. Contracts of this kind are called "unilateral" contracts. The life insurance contract is a unilateral contract since the only promises under it are those made by the life insurance company.

In the second example, where Dobbs accepts the offer of Gray and promises to pay for the car when it is delivered, the resulting contract is one under which both parties have made promises. Contracts of this kind are called "bilateral" contracts.

If an offeree rejects an offer, it lapses. The offeree cannot later attempt to accept it and complete a contract. Nor can he say that he accepts an offer but actually add new conditions. If he does so, he has, in effect, rejected the original offer and made a counteroffer. A counteroffer must, in turn, be accepted by the original offeror, if a binding contract is to be completed.

Consideration

Consideration, as the word is used in contract law, is variously explained, but in its simplest form, it may be defined as whatever the promisor asks in exchange for his promise. Consideration always relates to a promise. In the illustration previously used, when Edward Dobbs pays Alan Gray for the car, his payment is consideration for Gray's promise to deliver the car. Similarly, payment of the initial premium by the applicant for life insurance is consideration for the promises of the insurer under the life insurance contract.

In a bilateral contract, each party makes a promise and is, therefore, both promisor and promisee. In that case, each promise is said to be consideration for the other. In general, anything a promisor may bargain for, or ask in exchange for his promise, is consideration for it.

A promise must be supported by adequate consideration, but this only means consideration that is adequate in the legal sense.

A court will not usually substitute its own judgment as to whether the consideration is adequate so far as its value is concerned. Thus, in life insurance, if the required premium has been paid, a court will not attempt to determine whether or not the premium was proper in amount. Courts are interested only in determining that something of value was actually given, not that the price was necessarily adequate.

Most life insurance policies state that they are issued "in consideration of the application and the payment of premiums." They also usually provide that the insurance shall not become effective until the first premium has been paid. Payment of the first premium, therefore, is consideration for the promises of the life insurance company, since this is the premium that puts the insurance in force. It is also what the promisor (the life insurance company) asks in exchange for its promise. Payment of the initial premium, then, satisfies the definition of consideration given above. (Payment of later [renewal] premiums as they fall due are conditions—not consideration. These continuing conditions must be met if the insurance is to be kept in force, but payment of renewal premiums has nothing to do with whether an effective contract of insurance has or has not been made.)

Form

Many contracts are governed by special legal requirements as to form. For instance, some contracts are required to be in writing or they are not enforceable. Others are subject to detailed requirements that cannot effectively be met except in writing. The life insurance contract falls in this latter group. Most states do not expressly require that a life insurance contract be in writing, but all have extensive requirements as to policy provisions. Thus, a written contract is necessary as a practical matter.

Statutes Concerning Validity

Some contracts cannot be enforced because there is a specific law or laws declaring them to be invalid. This is true, for instance, of contracts relating to gambling, contracts that attempt to exact an illegal rate of interest, many contracts in restraint of trade, and contracts made for the purpose of accomplishing anything that is in itself illegal. Similarly, life insurance contracts are invalid if the insurable interest requirement is not met. In other words, the basic statute or rule of law that relates to the validity of the life insurance contract is the law requiring an insurable interest.

The purpose of the insurable interest requirement is to establish that there is a genuine risk of loss and, therefore, a legitimate basis for the insurance. In life insurance, this legal requirement is met in somewhat different ways depending upon the person who applies for the insurance.

Most applicants for life insurance apply for insurance on their own lives. As a matter of law, they are said to have an unlimited insurable interest in their own lives and they may, therefore, name anyone they wish to receive the benefit payable on their death.

When one person applies for insurance on the life of another, a third person is introduced into what would otherwise be a two-party agreement (between applicant-insured and the life insurance company). This situation is commonly referred to as a "third-party ownership case," or simply an "ownership case." It is customary to say that the applicant for life insurance in third-party cases must have an insurable interest in the life to be insured. However, this assumes that the applicant will name himself as beneficiary. It is more nearly correct, therefore, to say that in this situation the benefit of the contract must be payable to someone who has an insurable interest in the life to be insured.

There are two ways in which the insurable interest requirement may be met in life insurance. One is for the beneficiary to be closely related to the person whose life is to be insured, either by blood or marriage. Thus, a parent has an insurable interest in the life of a child, a husband has an insurable interest in the life of a wife, and a wife has an insurable interest in the life of her husband. Any of these people may apply for life insurance on the life of the other and name themselves as beneficiary.

If there is no close relationship of this kind, the beneficiary must have a genuine possibility of economic loss as the result of the death of the person whose life is to be insured. A businessman whose business depends for its services largely upon the skills of one man has an insurable interest in the life of that man. The death of such a skilled person would mean a genuine monetary loss to the businessman for whom he works. A lender has an insurable interest in the life of the person to whom he has lent money, and one partner usually has a risk of economic loss as the result of the death of the other partner or partners.

Most life insurance companies are more strict with respect to the question of insurable interest than the legal requirements alone would suggest. Thus, even when an applicant is applying for insurance on his own life, companies usually require that the designated beneficiary be someone who has an insurable interest in the life of the proposed insured. If this does not appear to be true in any given situation, the circumstances will be carefully inquired into, in order to be sure that the application is not, in reality, an attempt to accomplish indirectly what the beneficiary could not have accomplished directly—that is, obtain insurance by submitting an application in his or her own name. (It is not necessary, however, that the beneficiary still have an insurable interest at the death of the insured. In life insurance, the law requires only that an insurable interest exist at the time the contract is completed. This is in clear contrast to the rule in other kinds of insurance, where the insurable interest requirement must be met at the time of a claim.)

Unless the insurable interest requirement is met, an agreement to pay a sum of money to a specified person on the death of another person would be invalid as a wagering contract. In fact, insurance contracts are included in the same legal class as wagering contracts. Both are legally classified as "aleatory" contracts.

Aleatory contracts may be more clearly understood if they are contrasted with "commutative" contracts. A commutative contract is an agreement that provides for the exchange of relatively equivalent values. For instance, when a person buys a new car, he pays a price that is generally equivalent to the value of the car. A contract of employment operates in much the same way. Services are exchanged for wages in roughly equal values. The contracts most commonly used in the business world, therefore, are commutative contracts, under which generally equivalent values are exchanged.

An aleatory contract, on the other hand, is a contract under which one person may recover a great deal more than he has paid, depending upon the happening of an uncertain event (or "contingency"). This contingency may be the winning of a race by a certain horse, in which case it is a wagering contract. The contingency may be the damage or destruction of one's home by fire (the contingency involved in fire insurance), or it may be the early death of a person whose life is insured (the contingency in life insurance).

Insurance contracts, however, unlike wagering contracts, are favored by the law, if the insurable interest requirement is met. When there is an insurable interest, the certainty of a relatively small premium payment is substituted for the uncertainty (risk) of loss, and the contract is both socially and economically desirable. With a wager, on the other hand, there is no risk either of gain or loss *until* the wager has been made. This introduces uncertainty where it did not previously exist. In most jurisdictions, wagering agreements are held to be against public policy and void.

■ THE NATURE OF THE LIFE INSURANCE CONTRACT

The Contract Described

The life insurance contract is frequently described in ways that emphasize its basic legal characteristics. Thus, as already mentioned, it is an informal, rather than a formal contract, since it is not the form of the contract that is essential but the way the agreement is reached. The contract is unilateral, not bilateral, since promises are made by only one party—that is, the life insurance company. It is also an aleatory contract, though it differs from a wagering contract because of the presence of an insurable interest.

The life insurance contract has other characteristics that are also important. Among these are the facts that it is not a contract of *indemnity*, that it requires the exercise of good faith to a greater extent than many other contracts, and that it is a contract of *adhesion*. Because each of these characteristics is important in understanding the life insurance contract, they will be discussed in some detail.

Not a Contract of Indemnity. Life insurance contracts differ from many other kinds of insurance contracts with respect to the amount which the insurer will pay if the event insured against occurs. In most other lines of insurance, if a loss occurs, the insured is paid the amount of his loss, up to the limits of the contract, but nothing more. For example, if Dan Stuart's home burns, causing a loss of $35,000, and if he has a fire insurance policy with limits of $50,000, only $35,000 would be paid by the insurer. The purpose of a fire insurance policy is to reimburse the insured for his loss, but it cannot, legitimately, provide a financial gain.

There is good reason for this limitation in most lines of insurance. If the full amount of an insurance contract were payable for each loss the insured might incur, regardless of the amount, it would easily benefit some insureds to incur losses. Thus, insurance might well serve as a tacit incentive to bring about automobile accidents, fires, or other events which might be the subjects of insurance. Such a situation could encourage crime in some instances—arson, for example—and certainly it would violate some of the basic principles of insurance.

In life insurance, the problem is more complex. It is impossible to say what the loss of a human life means in monetary terms. There is no question about the fact of loss, but the amount of economic loss cannot accurately be stated in dollars and cents. For this reason, the life insurer simply promises to pay a stated amount on the death of the insured, and no attempt is made to establish the amount of loss. In this sense, the life insurance contract is a "valued" policy and not an indemnity contract. The value of the loss is agreed upon at the time the contract is made; and the full amount is paid at the death of the insured, regardless of his earning power or lack of it at the time of his death.

As a result of this approach, there is a possibility of financial gain under a life insurance contract in some instances, and this could present a temptation to the unscrupulous beneficiary to commit a crime far more serious than arson or fraud. However, the requirement of an insurable interest is considered a reasonable safeguard against this possibility.

Good Faith. The parties to most business contracts are required to deal fairly with one another, but neither owes the other any special duty. Insurance contracts, by contrast, at a very early date, were said to be "contracts of the highest good faith." This meant that the applicant and the insurer were required to exercise the "utmost" good faith in their dealings with each other. In marine insurance, for example, the applicant was required to disclose all information that might have a bearing on the insurability of the ship and cargo to be insured. These strict rules were rather generally modified when they were applied to fire and life insurance, but all insurance involves a higher degree of good faith than would be required in many other contracts. Insurance contracts, therefore, are governed by some rules that differ in some respects from those that govern contracts in general.

In life insurance, the applicant's duty to disclose information concerning his insurability is generally confined to furnishing correct and complete answers to the questions asked in the application for the insurance. When a person applies for life insurance, he completes a printed application form that includes a number of questions about his medical history, his occupation, and similar matters.

The life insurance company is entitled to truthful answers to these questions, and the decision to issue or not to issue a policy is made in reliance upon the truthfulness of such information. If a material question or questions (that is, questions that are essential to an evaluation of the application) have not been answered truthfully, there is said to have been a material misrepresentation in the application. In other words, a material fact has been misstated. In such situations, the insurance company may have the right to avoid the contract and *rescind* (that is, cancel) it on the grounds of material misrepresentation.

There are two basic rules concerning a life insurance company's right to rescind a life insurance contract after it has been issued. The first rule concerns the situation where a question or questions have been asked in the application but have not been answered truthfully by the applicant. In that instance, the insurance company has the legal right to rescind the contract if it would not have issued the policy had the company known the truth at the time the application was being considered.

The second rule concerns the situation where information essential to a consideration of the application (that is, material information) was not inquired about in the application. In that situation, the company may rescind the contract only if this material information was fraudulently withheld. In other words, if the applicant did not volunteer the information and the company did not ask about it, the applicant must have known that it was material to an evaluation of his application and he must have withheld the information intentionally.

In either instance, the right of the insurer to rescind a life insurance contract is generally limited to the first two years following the issuance of the policy because of a special policy provision called the incontestability clause. This clause will be discussed in a later chapter.

A Contract of Adhesion. Life insurance contracts also differ from many other contracts in the way in which their terms are agreed upon. Many contracts are not formed until after a preliminary period of bargaining and are then written to express the wishes of both parties. Insurance contracts are not usually developed in this way. A life insurance contract, for instance, is prepared by the insurance company; and the applicant has no part in writing its provisions. He elects the plan and amount of insurance, and he has some choices as to settlement methods and other options. If he accepts the contract, however, he adheres to it as a whole, as it was prepared by the insurer. Contracts of this kind are known as "contracts of adhesion." This fact becomes important when a legal question arises concerning the meaning of any of the terms of a life insurance contract.

Questions frequently arise as to the meaning of specific words or phrases that have been used in a contract, and it is sometimes necessary to have such questions decided in a court of law. This is especially true when the language used in the contract is ambiguous—that is, when a word or phrase can be interpreted differently by reasonable people. In such situations, the contract may have to be interpreted (*construed*) by the court. This means that the court decides which meaning must be given effect in carrying out the contract.

In reaching a decision on such questions, courts apply *rules of construction,* which have been developed over the years. One of the most common rules of construction is that a contract of adhesion will be interpreted most strictly against the party who drafted it. This rule is based on the theory that the person who drafted the contract had the opportunity to protect his own rights and if he did not do so, any loss should fall on him rather than the other party, who had no choice as to wording.

As this rule is applied to the life insurance contract, it means that any ambiguous words or phrases in the life insurance policy will be interpreted in favor of the policyowner or beneficiary rather than the insurance company, because the latter drafted the policy and, therefore, chose the language. For example, if the language of a policy is unclear as to the date on which a certain coverage terminates, the contract will be interpreted in the way most favorable to the policyowner or beneficiary. Thus, if the policy language is unclear as to whether the insurance terminated on June 2 or June 5, and the insured died on June 4, the interpretation most favorable to the beneficiary will be adopted—that coverage did not terminate until June 5.

■ THE LAW OF AGENCY

The Agency System

Most life insurance companies acquire new business through the agency system. This is a system in which individuals variously called sales representatives, soliciting agents, or field underwriters, represent the company in different parts of the country, for the purpose of soliciting applications for life insurance and accepting initial (first) premiums. The agency system has been an important factor in the growth of life insurance into a major industry, but it has also presented a number of legal problems. It is just as important, therefore, to have a working knowledge of the law concerned with such problems (agency law), as to understand the basic legal principles governing the completion of informal contracts.

Agents and Their Authority

Defined in the legal sense, agency is a relationship under which one person has the authority to represent and act for another person, including a corporation, in the making and modification of contracts. The person who is authorized to act in this way is called an agent; the person for whom he acts is called the principal.

The sales representative of a life insurer, therefore, is an agent in the legal sense of the word, regardless of the title he may actually have. The life insuring organization is his principal, since he is authorized, by his agency contract, to represent and act for that organization in the making of life insurance contracts.

In the most typical situation, the life insurance agent does not have the authority to complete a binding contract on behalf of the company. He is usually authorized only to solicit applications and accept initial premiums. Nevertheless, he may, under some circumstances, commit his principal (the life insurance company) to obligations, in connection with the contract, that were not intended either by the company or the agent. This is because, in his dealings with applicants and policyowners, he is governed by the general principles of agency law. Two of the most important of these principles relate to his actions while he is representing his principal and the knowledge he may acquire in his capacity as an agent. They may be summarized as follows:

1. The actions of the agent, within the scope of his authority, are considered the actions of the principal.
2. The knowledge of the agent, acquired while he is acting within the scope of his authority, is the knowledge of the principal.

To illustrate, assume that a life insurance agent accepts an application and the initial premium for a whole life policy from Herman Andrews, who tells him that he has been taking medication for hypertension (high blood pressure) for the past several months but that "everything is normal now." The agent tells Andrews that, under these circumstances, it is not necessary to mention the treatment on the application. The policy is issued on a standard basis and Andrews dies a few months later. Assume further that the medical treatment was such that if the company had received full and complete answers to the questions on the application, the application would have been declined.

The exact legal position of the insurer in such a situation depends upon many factors, including the precise wording of the application and the provisions of the applicable state laws. In most instances, however, if the questions on the application were not truthfully answered, the insurance company could deny a claim arising within the first two policy years and successfully defend its denial on the basis of misrepresentation of a material fact. In this illustrative case, however, the company may be precluded from denying the claim because its agent had informed Andrews that it was not necessary to report the treatment. The actions of the agent, so long as they are consistent with the authority he has been given (that is, "within the scope of" his authority) are considered to be the actions of the principal (in this instance, the insurance company).

The fact that the agent may have knowledge of matters affecting the insurability of a proposed insured is sometimes just as crucial as his actions, so far as the company's legal position may be concerned. In many situations, the agent's knowledge will be considered to be the knowledge of the company. For example, if the agent knows that the proposed insured has not fully recovered from a recent accident at the time he completes an application for life insurance, the agent's knowledge may be considered knowledge of the company in spite of the fact that the application did not contain full details and, in fact, no one except the agent had such knowledge. Under circumstances of this kind, the legal position of the company, in the event of a subsequent early claim, may be exactly the same as if the information known to the agent had been made available to the home office personnel and considered by them when the policy was issued.

■ NOTES ON CANADIAN PRACTICES

The Revised Uniform Life Insurance Act of Canada, which governs life insurance contracts issued in all of the provinces except Quebec, clarifies the contractual capacity of minors in those provinces and spells out the insurable interest requirement. It provides that a minor 16 years of age or over may make an enforceable life insurance contract on his own life or the life of anyone else as if he were age 21 or older.

This law also provides that a contract shall not be void for lack of an insurable interest if it is a contract of group insurance or if the person whose life is being insured has consented in writing to have the policy issued. The law as to what constitutes an insurable interest is very similar to the law in most of the United States. Thus, a person has an insurable interest in his own life and in the life of a child, grandchild, or a spouse. The law also specifically states that a person has an insurable interest in the life of anyone on whom he is dependent for support or education, his employee, and anyone in "the duration of whose life he has a pecuniary interest."

In Quebec, a minor 15 years of age or older may insure his life in his own favor, or in favor of "his heirs" or any one or more of them. However, he cannot exercise any of the rights or privileges under the contract or give a valid receipt for any sum paid under it without the consent of a "family council."

■ QUESTIONS FOR REVIEW

1. Briefly define a formal contract, an informal contract. Which term applies to the life insurance contract?
2. List five legal requirements that must be met if an informal agreement is to create a legally enforceable obligation.
3. Summarize the general rule as to a minor's right to disaffirm a contract he has made. In what way have some of the states modified this rule as it applies to the life insurance contract?
4. In the legal sense, what constitutes "consideration" for the life insurance contract?
5. Briefly explain how the insurable interest requirement applies in the following instances:
    a) Charles Farrell applies for life insurance on his own life, payable to his wife, Elizabeth.
    b) Charles Farrell applies for life insurance on Elizabeth's life, payable to himself.
6. What is meant by the statement that a life insurance contract is not a contract of indemnity?
7. Briefly define a contract of adhesion. What rule of construction is based upon the fact that a life insurance contract is a contract of adhesion?

8. Briefly define the term "agency" in its legal sense.
9. What is meant by the term "agency system" as it is used in life insurance?
10. Briefly summarize two principles of agency law which apply to the life insurance agent.

5 HOW PEOPLE BECOME INSURED

Life insurance is applied for and life insurance policies are issued in accordance with procedures designed to establish legally effective insuring agreements between the company and the applicants for insurance. In this way, people insure their own lives and the lives of others; and life insurance companies issue the many insuring agreements that are necessary if the law of large numbers is to operate.

This chapter will outline the application and policy issue procedures in which the principles of insurance are combined with principles of contract and agency law so that legally effective life insurance contracts are established.

■ THE LIFE INSURANCE APPLICATION

Typically, a life insurance agent is equipped with a life insurance rate manual and a supply of life insurance application forms. The rate manual contains descriptions and the applicable rates for the various plans of insurance his company offers. When a life insurance agent discusses life insurance with a prospective insured, he uses the information in the rate manual as a basis for his recommendations and suggests the insurance plan he feels is most appropriate. If his recommendations are accepted, an application must be completed, signed by the applicant, and submitted to the company before the policy can be issued.

A life insurance application is a detailed form, designed to give the insurance company two general kinds of information. First, it must provide identifying data concerning the applicant, and describe the insurance applied for. Second, it must provide the company with much (often all) of the information that will be needed to decide whether the person whose life is to be insured (the *proposed insured*) meets the company's standards of insurability. Thus, for convenience, the application may be considered as consisting of two general sections. One of these sections furnishes general contractual information. The other section contains risk appraisal information—that is, information relating to the insurability of the proposed insured.

Contractual Information

The first blanks on the application form usually concern the name and address of the proposed insured. In most instances, this person is also the applicant. For instance, if Roger Dorfman applies for insurance on his own life, he is the applicant and he is also the proposed insured. The contract, when completed, will be between him (as the applicant) and the insurance company. In this type of situation, the same person will be both policyowner and insured.

In other situations, however, insurance is applied for by one person on the life of another. If a policy is issued, the policyowner and the insured will be different persons. Thus, the name and address of the applicant as well as of the proposed insured are needed in this situation. Figure 5-1 shows the name and address section of an illustrative life insurance application.

Applications are often submitted by corporations for insurance on the lives of especially valuable employees (key men) or officers of the company. In such instances, the application is signed by an officer, acting for the corporation, and the corporation itself is a party to the resulting contract.

The situation is somewhat different where an unincorporated business is concerned. Such businesses are customarily conducted either as partnerships or sole proprietorships. A partnership is owned and usually operated by two or more persons; a sole proprietorship is owned by one only. Life insurance for partnership needs is usually applied for by the partners as individuals (although applications may also be made in the name of the firm by one of the partners). If the business is owned and operated by one person (a sole pro-

92 ▪ **Principles of Life Insurance**

prietorship), the proprietor acts as an individual and applies for life insurance in that capacity.

Suppose James Michaels operates a business as a sole proprietor. He has a valuable employee, Joseph Blake, whose life he wishes to insure. If Blake were to die suddenly, it would cost the firm a considerable amount of money to replace him and train his successor.

FIGURE 5–1

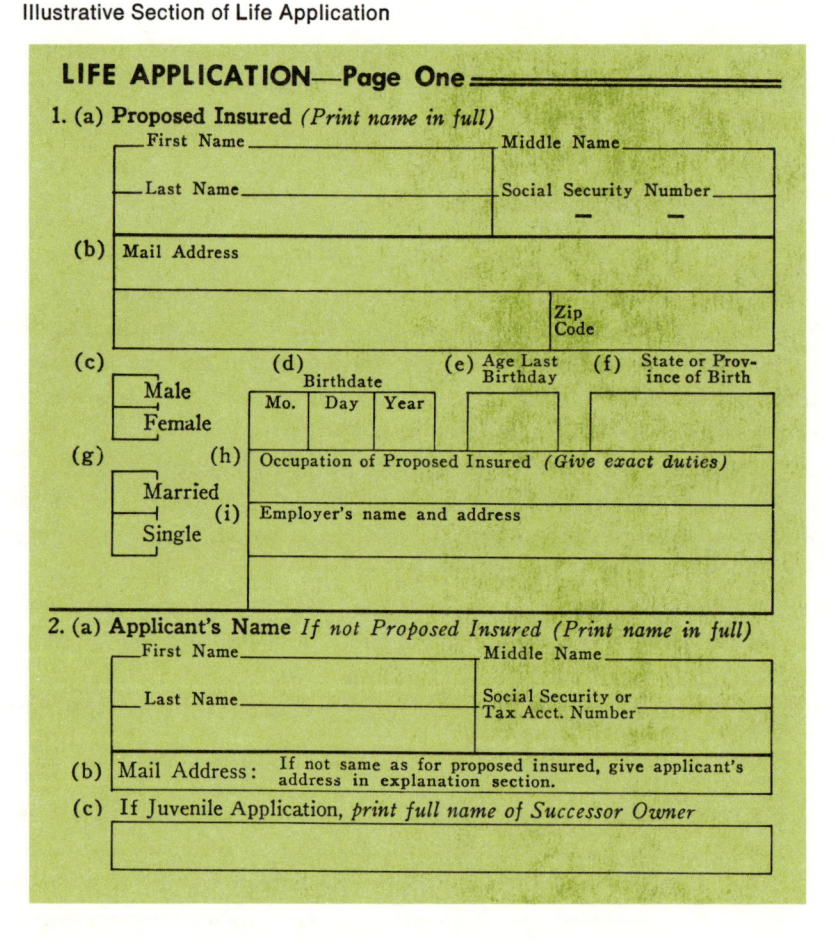

Illustrative Section of Life Application

LIFE APPLICATION—Page One

1. (a) **Proposed Insured** *(Print name in full)*
   - First Name
   - Middle Name
   - Last Name
   - Social Security Number

   (b) Mail Address
   - Zip Code

   (c) Male / Female
   (d) Birthdate — Mo. Day Year
   (e) Age Last Birthday
   (f) State or Province of Birth

   (g) Married / Single
   (h) Occupation of Proposed Insured *(Give exact duties)*
   (i) Employer's name and address

2. (a) **Applicant's Name** *If not Proposed Insured (Print name in full)*
   - First Name
   - Middle Name
   - Last Name
   - Social Security or Tax Acct. Number

   (b) Mail Address: If not same as for proposed insured, give applicant's address in explanation section.

   (c) If Juvenile Application, *print full name of Successor Owner*

Michaels wishes to protect the firm against this particular economic loss. He therefore insures Blake's life for an amount that he estimates will offset the reduction in profits that would result in the event of Blake's death and provide funds to enable the firm to find and train a successor. If his application is accepted and a policy is issued, the contract will be between Michaels and the insurance company, but the insurance will be on the life of Blake.

Other blanks in this section of the application relate to the plan and amount of insurance being applied for. The plan may be whole life, term, or endowment, or any of a number of variations of these basic plans. All are described in the agent's rate manual, together with the applicable premium rates per $1,000 of insurance at the various ages at which the company is willing to issue them. Usually, also, the rate manual specifies minimum and maximum amounts of insurance the company is willing to issue at the various ages.

The applicant for life insurance usually has a choice with respect to some of the provisions and privileges that will be included in the policy he will receive. Typically, these choices concern one or more of the following:

1. How frequently he wishes to pay the premiums.
2. How he wishes policy dividends, if any, to be used.
3. How, and to whom, the policy proceeds are to be paid.

Under most life insurance policies issued today, premiums may be paid annually, semi-annually, quarterly, or monthly. The life insurance application includes a blank where the applicant's wishes may be indicated.

If the life insurance applied for is participating life insurance, the applicant also has a choice as to the use of his policy dividends. Under a participating life insurance policy, the policyowner pays a premium in a specified amount that is calculated by the company to be somewhat in excess of the amount that will actually be needed for policies on that plan during the period the policies are expected to remain in force. This practice provides a margin of safety in the event that claim expense and the costs of administering the plan are higher than expected, or interest earnings are lower. Nevertheless, it is anticipated that after the first year or so a portion of the premium for participating life insurance can be returned to the policyowner, annually, as a policy dividend. In applications for participating life insurance, therefore, the applicant indicates whether he wishes his policy dividends to be paid to him as they become payable, or used in other ways as provided in the policy. In general, policy dividends may usually be (1) applied to reduce future premiums, (2) paid to the policyowner, (3) left with the company to accumulate at interest, or (4) used to purchase additional insurance. These various choices, called dividend options, will be discussed more fully in a later chapter.

Finally, the application contains an area in which the applicant specifies the person or persons (beneficiaries) whom he wishes to receive the benefit payable on his death. The subject of beneficiary designations will be discussed in some detail in a later chapter.

Risk Appraisal Information

In most instances, the largest amount of information requested in the life insurance application concerns risk appraisal information —that is, information the company needs in order to decide whether the proposed insured is insurable in accordance with the company's underwriting or risk appraisal standards. This process of evaluating the insurability of the proposed insured is variously called underwriting, risk appraisal, or selection of risks. Probably the most descriptive term is "risk appraisal."

The age and birthdate of the proposed insured are always required, as well as his occupation. Other questions concern his military status, flying activities, and hazardous avocations. In fact, if he flies his own plane, he may be required to complete a special aviation questionnaire. During the past several years, life insurance companies have also begun to inquire into possible avocations of a hazardous nature, such as scuba and skindiving, parachuting, and gocart racing.

The Medical Examination. A great deal of life insurance is issued today without a medical examination. At one time, however, it was customary to require a medical examination in connection with most applications, and medical examinations are still required when large amounts of insurance are applied for. Usually, a medical examination is required, also, for any amount of insurance, if the proposed insured is 40 or 45 years of age or older.

When a medical examination is required, a local physician (usually one who has been approved by the company for this purpose) examines the proposed insured and completes a medical examination blank which the life insurance company has furnished him. These blanks include fairly detailed questions as to the proposed insured's present health and personal medical history. The examiner is asked to measure and weigh the proposed insured, take his blood pressure and pulse rate, check his heart sounds, and in general perform a relatively complete physical examination. When larger amounts of insurance are applied for, more detailed information is required, and additional examinations by other physicians may be requested before a decision is made. In every instance, however, the basic information, such as height, weight, blood pressure, and pulse rate is required. The doctor then signs the medical report, as does the proposed insured.

Incidentally, the medical examiner is acting as the insurance company's agent in the legal sense of the word when he makes this insurance examination. His statements and activities, therefore, are governed by the general principles of agency law, just as are the statements and activities of the soliciting agent.

Nonmedical Business. Most life insurance companies issue some nonmedical business, although it is usually limited as to the amounts that will be issued and the ages of the proposed insureds who will be considered for such coverage. Thus, a company might issue, on a nonmedical basis, policies up to $20,000 to proposed insureds of not more than 40 years of age. However, such limits vary from company to company.

For nonmedical business, detailed medical questions are included in the regular application blank. These questions are asked by the agent and the answers recorded by him. General questions are asked concerning possible impairments of eyes, hearing, or limbs; and more specific questions inquire into the applicant's medical history for evidence of heart disease, ailments of brain or nervous system, and other serious conditions. Figure 5–2 shows a portion of a typical medical-history section of a life insurance application for nonmedical business.

Although detailed medical questions are asked in the application for nonmedical business, the risk appraisal department may nevertheless require that the proposed insured be medically examined if the answers given to any of the questions in the application indicate the possibility of a serious health impairment. In other words, the fact that an application is submitted on a nonmedical basis does not rule out the possibility that a medical examination may be required before a policy will be issued.

Agent's Authority and Effective Date of Insurance

Most life insurance applications contain a section that explains in some detail the agent's authority and summarizes the legal effect of the completed application. If the authority of the agent is limited in any way, the details of such limitations are set forth in this section of the application. For example, life insurance companies fre-

FIGURE 5-2

Illustrative Section of Life Insurance Application for Nonmedical Business

8. To the best of your knowledge and belief do you have, or have you ever had, or been treated for: *(Circle applicable items and give details)*   Yes   No
   (a) Dizziness, fainting, convulsions, frequent headache; paralysis or stroke; mental or nervous disorder?   ☐ ☐
   (b) Shortness of breath, asthma, emphysema, tuberculosis, or other disorder of the respiratory system?   ☐ ☐
   (c) Chest pain, palpitation, high blood pressure, rheumatic fever, heart murmur, heart attack or other disorder of the heart or blood vessels?   ☐ ☐
   (d) Recurrent indigestion, jaundice, any type of ulcer, colitis, or other disorder of the stomach, intestines, liver or gall bladder?   ☐ ☐
   (e) Sugar, albumin, blood or pus in urine; stone or other disorder of kidney, bladder, or reproductive organs?   ☐ ☐
   (f) Sugar diabetes; arthritis or gout?   ☐ ☐
   (g) Cyst, tumor, cancer or disorder of skin or lymph glands?   ☐ ☐
   (h) Allergies; anemia or other disorder of the blood?   ☐ ☐
   (i) Excessive use of alcohol or any habit-forming drugs?   ☐ ☐
   (j) Any other mental or physical disorder not listed above?   ☐ ☐

9. Give your exact height and weight. | feet | inches | | pounds |

10. Give names and addresses of all doctors consulted by or for **you**, for any reason, including hospitalizations, during the past five years, with full details of treatment and results. *(If none, so state)*

Names and Addresses of Doctors and Hospitals	Disease or Disorder	Date, Treatment and Result

11. **Explanations:** *Show question number as reference. If space is insufficient, use reverse side or additional sheets, which shall be a part of this application.*

quently state in the application that the agent cannot waive any of the requirements of the company.

Generally, in the absence of either a conditional or a binding receipt, insurance will not become effective until the application has been approved, the first premium has been paid, and a policy has been issued and delivered "during the lifetime and continued insurability of the insured." These conditions are usually set forth specifically in the application. (This will be discussed later.)

Signatures

The application is signed by the applicant and, if the insurance is to be on the life of someone else, that person must also sign. Thus, in the example given earlier, if James Michaels is applying for insurance on the life of Joseph Blake, both men must sign the application, though for different reasons. The applicant's signature affirms the truth of the information set forth in the application. The proposed insured signs to indicate that he consents to the issuance of insurance on his life, under a policy to be owned and controlled by someone else. The consent of the proposed insured in situations of this kind is required as a matter of public policy. This prevents unscrupulous persons from securing insurance on the lives of others against their wishes or without their knowledge.

The Agent's Statement

In the process of completing a life application, the agent is compiling information which the home office will use in making its decision concerning the insurability of the proposed insured. The agent is not authorized to approve the application in any sense of the word, nor to make statements concerning the probable risk appraisal decision of the company. Nevertheless, he is often one of the best sources of information about the proposed insured. It is he who has solicited the insurance and who has talked with the applicant during the course of the sale. Often the agent's personal acquaintance with the applicant extends back several years. His knowledge and judgment, therefore, can be of great benefit to the company in evaluating the proposed insured's fitness for insurance.

For these reasons, most insurers request some information based on the agent's own knowledge. This is supplied in what is called the agent's statement. Generally speaking, the questions in the agent's statement relate to how long and how well the agent has known the applicant, details of any business arrangements—partnerships, key man situations, and so on—that may be involved in connection with the insurance being applied for, and arrangements for the payment of premiums. If there are other significant circumstances that might affect the risk appraisal process, the agent is asked to mention them, also. In many instances, he will write a separate note, explaining in detail the purposes for which the insurance is to be used and mentioning other pertinent factors that may be helpful in the risk appraisal process.

The Initial Premium

Although the agent is authorized, and even encouraged, to accept the initial premium in connection with each application for life insurance, it is not essential that he do so before the application is sent to the home office. The applicant is always free to wait until a policy is issued and delivered to him before he pays the premium. If he waits, however, there is always the possibility that he may become uninsurable or die before the insurance becomes effective. It is possible, also, that he may change his mind about his need for insurance and decide not to accept the policy when it is delivered to him.

Experience has shown that if the initial premium is paid when the application is completed, the applicant is much more likely to accept the policy when it is issued. For this reason, life insurance companies have, for a long time, been issuing a form of premium receipt—variously called a conditional receipt, binding receipt, or conditional binding receipt—designed to encourage payment of the premium with the application. The purpose of such receipts is to acknowledge receipt of the premium and, in addition, provide insurance coverage at an earlier date than would otherwise be true, usually on condition that the proposed insured is found to be insurable.

Premium receipts—whether conditional or binding—differ widely in wording as well as contractual intent. Conditional receipts are the more widely used and, in most instances, are intended to provide insurance only if the proposed insured is found to have been insurable as of a date specified in the receipt. Usually, this is the later of the date of the receipt or the date of the medical examination, if an examination is required. For this reason, and because risk appraisal is basic in the formation of a life insurance contract, a brief examination of the risk appraisal process is necessary before the receipts or the completion of the contract itself can be discussed in any meaningful way.

■ THE RISK APPRAISAL PROCESS

Premium rates for life insurance are established on the assumption that mortality rates among insured persons will be generally comparable to the mortality rates of the past, as reflected in the mortality tables used. To assure that this will be true and that premium rates will be adequate, some standards of insurability must be established and procedures followed to select persons whose insurability is within limits the company has established as acceptable. When a life insurance application reaches the home office (or issue office) of a life insurance company, therefore, it is directed to the desk of a risk appraiser. Risk appraisers (sometimes called "underwriters") are employees whose responsibility it is to evaluate the insurability of persons whose lives are proposed for insurance.

Risk appraisers, in general, view their responsibilities constructively rather than negatively and usually attempt to qualify as many proposed insureds as possible for some kind of life insurance, if they cannot issue the policy applied for. Nevertheless, risk appraisal is necessary, basically, because persons whose health is impaired or whose occupations are hazardous are more likely to apply for life insurance than those in better health or less hazardous work. The tendency for persons in such circumstances to apply for life insurance in greater numbers than persons whose prospects are more favorable is an example of what has previously been noted as antiselection. If an insurance company took no precautions to identify and guard against antiselection, an undue number of persons with less favorable mortality prospects would be insured, and premium rates would eventually prove inadequate.

Life insurance companies establish their standards of insurability in such a way that a broad range of health and occupational classes will be acceptable at standard premium rates. Most insurance companies also offer insurance under most of their insurance plans, and for a wide range of ages, at higher than standard premiums, to the much smaller percentage of persons who do not meet the insurability requirements for standard rates. These people are insurable but at what are called "substandard rates." Substandard premium rates range from slightly to very much higher than standard rates and policies for which those premium rates are payable are said to be "rated." The vast majority—approximately 97 percent—of all applications received for insurance on the ordinary life plans are accepted on some basis, either standard or rated.

Risk selection is the process of deciding where, within the range of acceptable health and occupational classes, the proposed insured may be properly fitted. In this way, the person who is accepted for insurance will be charged a premium rate commensurate with the risk presented by his health, occupation, habits, finances, and environmental situation.

The risk appraiser makes his decision as to insurability on the basis of information gained from the application form, the agent's statement, the medical examiner's report (if a medical examination is required), and sometimes a so-called "inspection report" concerning the proposed insured's environment and habits, obtained from a commercial inspection company.

Using the information available to him, the risk appraiser evaluates many aspects of the proposed insured's insurability. The most significant information concerns the age and sex of the proposed insured; his physical condition, medical history, and family history; his build; and his habits, occupation, and finances.

After each of these factors has been considered and evaluated, the risk appraiser decides whether insurance should be issued or the application should be declined. If the insurance cannot be issued as applied for, it may be issued on a rated basis; or a different plan of insurance may be offered. For example, term life insurance may not be issued to some applicants, and some plans of insurance may not be available at every age.

There are always some applications that cannot be accepted for insurance even at a greatly increased premium. If the risk of early death is very great, the proposed insured may be uninsurable on any basis. In those instances (about 3 percent), the applicant is notified that his application has been disapproved, and any premium he has paid is returned to him.

■ OFFER AND ACCEPTANCE IN LIFE INSURANCE

A life insurance contract is completed in the same way as any other informal contract—that is, through an offer made by one party and accepted by another. The requirements for life insurance are technical, however, and risk appraisal is essential. The offer and acceptance procedures in life insurance usually fall into one of three situations.

First, there is the situation where the initial premium is not submitted with the application. Second, there is the situation where the initial premium is submitted with the application but a premium receipt is not given. (This should be an unusual occurrence.) Third, the initial premium and the application are submitted together, and the agent gives the applicant either a conditional or a binding premium receipt. These situations will be discussed in that order.

The Application Only Is Submitted

If the initial premium is not paid when the application is submitted, the applicant is considered merely to have invited an offer from the life insurance company. If the application is approved, the company makes the offer, in the contractual sense of the word, when it issues a policy and sends it to the agent for delivery to the applicant. The applicant accepts this offer when he accepts the policy and pays the initial premium. The contract is completed at that time; and the insurance becomes effective.

The Initial Premium Is Paid, but No Premium Receipt Is Given

When the application and the initial premium are submitted together, but no premium receipt has been given, the applicant has made a valid offer in the contractual sense. (As previously noted, this should be an unusual occurrence, since life insurance agents are customarily authorized to give either a binding or a conditional receipt, if they collect the premium with the application.) If the risk appraiser approves the application in accordance with its terms and a policy is issued, the company has accepted the offer and a contract of insurance is completed. The terms and conditions of the contract are expressed in the policy; and the insurance becomes effective in accordance with the policy provisions—usually when the policy has been delivered to the applicant.

A Premium Receipt Is Given

In the third and most common situation, the applicant pays the initial premium at the time the application is submitted, and the agent gives him a conditional or, in some instances, a binding receipt.

A conditional receipt (which is more common than the binding receipt) is a printed form which contains an acknowledgment by the company that the initial premium (or a specified part of it) has been paid, in connection with an application for life insurance. In addition, conditional premium receipts state that insurance will become effective prior to the date a policy is issued, subject to conditions specified in the receipt. Premium receipts are often attached to the application form, to be detached by the agent and given to the applicant when he pays the premium.

The legal effect of premium receipts depends upon many factors. In general, however, they fall into two distinct classes—conditional or binding—depending upon when and under what circumstances the insurance provided under them is intended to take effect.

Conditional Receipts. If the company does not want to make insurance effective until the application has been evaluated, but will then grant coverage as of an earlier date than would have been true in the absence of the receipt, it uses a conditional receipt. This name is derived from the fact that insurance is provided by the receipt if a condition or conditions expressed in the receipt are met. Usually, the effective date of the insurance provided under such receipts is the date of the application or the date of any required medical examination, if later. Usually, also, the proposed insured must be found to be insurable in accordance with the company's standards of insurability for the plan and amount of insurance applied for. Often the amount of insurance provided under a conditional receipt is limited to a specified maximum such as $50,000 or $100,000. Conditional receipts which require only a determination of insurability are called "insurability" type receipts.

The operation of an insurability type of conditional receipt may be illustrated as follows. Assume that John Stevenson applies for a $10,000 whole life policy on September 15, 1972. He pays the initial premium, and the soliciting agent, Bill Novick, issues a conditional receipt of the insurability type. Novick mails the application and premium to the home office on September 16, and Stevenson is struck by an automobile and killed while crossing the street that evening.

The receipt provides that if the proposed insured is found to be insurable as of the date of the receipt (or of the medical, if one is required), the insurance will be effective as of that date. Assume that this is a nonmedical case and that the home office risk appraiser, after considering the application and other risk appraisal information, finds that Stevenson was insurable on September 15, the date of the application. In this event, the condition specified by the receipt will have been met, and the claim will be paid.

A second type of conditional receipt, which is less often used, resembles the insurability type in most respects, but requires that the application be approved by the insurance company before insurance becomes effective. These receipts are called "approval" type conditional receipts.

Given the same set of facts outlined above but an approval type of conditional premium receipt, it could be contended that since the application had not been approved prior to Stevenson's death, no insurance was in force on the date of his death. Because questions of this kind are more likely to arise in connection with the approval type of conditional receipt, such receipts are not so widely used today as the insurability type. Under the latter, the insurability of a proposed insured as of a particular date is generally considered to be a fact that can be determined after his death.

Binding Receipts. Some companies are willing to make insurance effective as of the application date, subject to their right to terminate the coverage later if the application is disapproved. In that case, the company uses a binding receipt. This terminology is borrowed from other lines of insurance, most notably fire insurance, where agents have long had the authority to "bind" the risk—that is, the authority to grant immediate coverage.

A binding premium receipt serves essentially the same basic purposes as a conditional premium receipt. That is, it acknowledges receipt of the initial premium, or a portion of it, and makes insurance effective prior to the date a policy is issued. Unlike the conditional receipt, however, the binding receipt makes insurance effective immediately—that is, as of the date of the receipt—even though the proposed insured may later be found to be uninsurable. It thus provides *interim* insurance, that remains in effect until a policy is issued or the application is disapproved.

Exactly how the conditional and binding receipts affect the offer and acceptance process depends primarily upon the wording and intent of the receipts. The basic purpose of the receipts, however, is to encourage payment of the initial premium with the application. When a life insurance company uses either a conditional or a binding receipt, therefore, it is offering to make insurance effective on some basis, at an earlier date than the usual risk appraisal and policy issue procedures would accomplish, *if* the applicant pays the initial premium with the application. The applicant accepts that offer by paying the premium, and an agreement is reached. The amount of life insurance that becomes effective under such receipts, as well as the date the insurance becomes effective, are governed by the terms of the particular receipt that is used.

■ THE POLICY IS ISSUED AND DELIVERED

When the risk appraiser approves a life insurance application, he specifies the amount and plan of insurance for which it is approved, any additional benefits that are to be included, and the appropriate premium rate. The next step is the preparation of the policy itself.

Policy Forms

After policy forms have been developed, they are submitted to the insurance departments of the various states for approval. The company then prints them in large numbers in the approved form. When the risk appraiser has accepted an application, therefore, a policy form is selected which provides the kind of insurance to be granted. If the plan is one providing cash values, the policy form must include a section setting forth the appropriate cash and other nonforfeiture values for the first 20 years following the insured's age at issue.

Many life insurance companies use computers in the preparation of their policies, in which case the appropriate values and other applicable data are printed automatically. (Computer preparation has the additional advantage of permitting both the policy form and the policy records to be prepared from the same basic data, so that errors and inconsistencies are reduced to a minimum.)

Even if some of the details in the policy forms are individually typed, however, policy preparation is not usually an elaborate procedure. Generally, only a few items need to be typed. (The remainder of the policy form is preprinted.) The typed items include the name of the insured, name of the policyowner, the amount of insurance, the amount of the premium and the frequency with which it is to be paid, the age and sex of the insured, the policy (or effective) date, and the date the policy is issued. Often this information is given in a panel on the face page of the policy, in a format similar to that shown in Figure 5–3.

Settlement Arrangements

Most life insurance contracts provide that the amount of insurance payable on the death of the insured (the policy proceeds) will be paid to the designated beneficiary in one sum. Other methods of settlement (modes of settlement, or settlement options) are available and may be elected by the owner, either in the application or later, in accordance with the provisions of the policy. (If a one-sum settlement is provided at the death of the insured, the beneficiary usually has the right to elect another settlement method, if he or she wishes.)

FIGURE 5–3

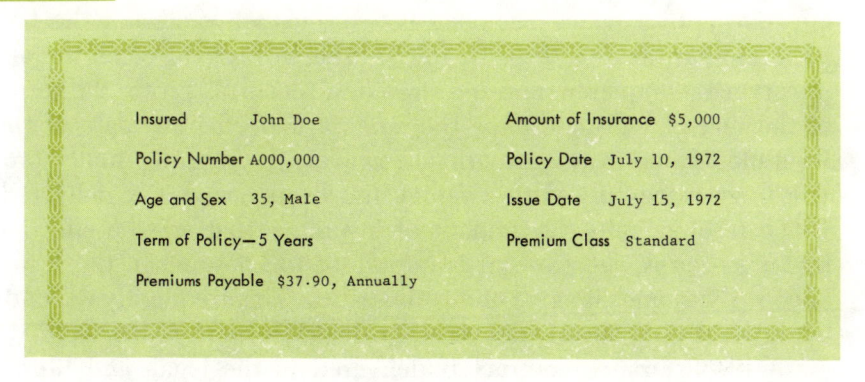

Insured John Doe	Amount of Insurance $5,000
Policy Number A000,000	Policy Date July 10, 1972
Age and Sex 35, Male	Issue Date July 15, 1972
Term of Policy—5 Years	Premium Class Standard
Premiums Payable $37.90, Annually	

From the policyowner's point of view, the settlement section is one of the most important sections of the policy, since it will govern the distribution of the insurance proceeds at his death. This section is also important to the life insurance company. In a very real sense, it defines the obligation of the insurer at the death of the insured, and settlement in accordance with the policy's provisions terminates the liability of the company. Because of their basic importance, therefore, beneficiary designations and the most typical settlement options will be discussed in chapter 6.

The "Entire" Contract

When a life insurance policy has been issued and is ready to be sent to the agent for delivery to the applicant, it usually includes a copy of the application. Together, the application and the policy constitute the contract between the applicant and the life insurance company. In fact, the laws of many of the states require a life insurance company to include in the policy a provision to this effect, as follows:

This policy and the application, a copy of which is attached, when issued, constitute the entire contract.

This policy provision makes it clear that no other documents can be used to diminish the rights or privileges of the policyowner or beneficiary.

When the Insurance Is Effective

Most life insurance applications specify that, except as any conditional or binding receipt may provide, no insurance will become effective until a policy has been issued and delivered and the first premium has been paid. If the initial premium is paid when the application is completed, and if a premium receipt is given, the terms of the receipt will determine the amount and effective date of the insurance. Even in this situation, however, the receipt usually provides insurance only until a policy has been issued and delivered. If the receipt limits the amount of insurance that will be effective under its terms, therefore, it is important to know when the insurance will become effective under the policy. This frequently depends upon when the policy is delivered in the legal sense of the word.

A life insurance contract is delivered in the legal, and literal, sense of the word when it is manually handed to the applicant by the agent, with the intention of completing a contract between the applicant and the life insurance company. This is actual, or manual, delivery. There are other actions, however, which may be "construed" as meeting the legal requirements of delivery and thus to constitute "constructive" delivery. For example, if the initial premium has been paid and the application approved for the plan of insurance applied for, the policy is often mailed to the agent for unconditional delivery to the applicant. That is, nothing remains to be done by the agent except to hand the policy to the owner. In such instances, the act of mailing the policy to the agent is construed to be delivery of the policy to the owner, since the insurance company has parted with possession with the intention of completing the contract.

A policy is also delivered, in the legal sense of the word, if it is left at the residence of the applicant or at his regular place of business, with someone who represents him. It is basic in agency law that delivery to an agent of the applicant (his wife, for example, or his secretary, or anyone else who may represent him for this purpose) is the legal equivalent of delivery to the applicant himself.

Delivery for Inspection. When a policy has been issued other than as applied for (that is, on a different plan of insurance or at a different premium rate), the applicant has the choice of either accepting the insurance or rejecting it. (In the latter instance, any premium he has paid will be refunded to him.) In such situations, the applicant may wish to think the matter over carefully before making up his mind; and the agent sometimes permits him to keep the policy for a few days "for inspection." In fact, the agent may leave a policy with an applicant in other situations as well—for instance, when the initial premium has not been paid but the applicant wishes to review the policy and decide whether he really wants the insurance.

Under circumstances such as these, the agent has not delivered the policy in the legal sense of the word, since there was no intention to complete the contract at that point. Nevertheless, if the applicant dies while the policy is in his possession, regardless of the reason, it may be extremely difficult for the insurer to prove that the policy was not "delivered" in the legal sense of the word. For example, assume that a policy is issued on a rated basis and that the applicant refuses to accept it and pay the higher-than-standard premium. Assume further that the agent attempts to persuade the applicant to accept the policy and suggests that he leave it with the applicant so that the latter can "think it over." Before a decision is reached, the proposed insured is killed in an accident. The wife (and beneficiary) of the proposed insured knows nothing of the circumstances surrounding the agent's attempted delivery of the policy. The agent knows that the premium was not paid, but the wife knows only that the policy was in her husband's possession at the time of his death. This situation may present a difficult question, both as a matter of law and of public relations. To avoid such problems, therefore, life insurance agents are usually instructed to request the person with whom a policy is left to sign an "inspection receipt." The receipt makes it clear that the policy is left for inspection only and that the insurance will not be in force until the premium is paid.

Backdating. Occasionally an applicant wishes to have his policy issued with a date earlier than the date it would ordinarily be given, in order that the insured's age on the effective date will be lower and he will have the benefit of a lower premium. In insurance terminology, this is a "date-back to save age." Backdating always results in the payment of a premium for a period in which there was no actual insurance coverage. For example, Paul Berg applies for insurance on June 1, requesting that the policy be issued with an effective date of March 1. This earlier date precedes his birthday and thus qualifies him for a premium payable by a person one year younger than Berg is at the time he applies. By paying the premium from March 1, however, he is paying a premium for a period—March 1 to June 1—during which he had no coverage.

For this reason, many states limit the length of time for which a policy may be dated back. Typically, this limit is six months. Subject to limits of this kind, however, life insurance companies customarily honor requests to issue policies with dates earlier than the date of application.

■ QUESTIONS FOR REVIEW

1. What are the two basic purposes served by the life insurance application?
2. Briefly distinguish between medical and nonmedical life insurance applications.
3. If an application is submitted by someone other than the proposed insured, what is the legal significance of the signature of the proposed insured?
4. Define "antiselection."
5. What is meant by a "rated" life insurance policy?
6. Assuming that the policy is issued as applied for in each of the following instances, when will the insurance become effective?
    a) The application is submitted, but the initial premium is not paid until the policy is delivered.
    b) The initial premium is paid at the time the application is submitted, and a conditional receipt is issued.
    c) The initial premium is paid at the time the application is submitted, and a binding receipt is issued.
7. Differentiate between conditional premium receipts of the insurability type and those of the approval type.
8. Under what conditions and for what purpose is an inspection receipt used?
9. What is meant by a "date-back to save age"?

6 BENEFICIARY DESIGNATIONS AND THE SETTLEMENT OPTIONS

The basic purpose of life insurance is to provide a benefit payable to someone at the death of the insured. When the applicant designates the beneficiary, therefore, and decides how the proceeds are to be paid, he is making some of the most important decisions he will ever make in connection with his life insurance contract. The purpose of this chapter is to discuss the policy provisions and some of the more significant company practices concerning beneficiary designations and the optional modes of settlement available under most individual life insurance contracts.

■ THE RIGHT TO DESIGNATE THE BENEFICIARY

In one way or another, the applicant always designates a beneficiary at the time an application for life insurance is completed. If he does not name a specific individual at that time, the policy will be payable to his estate. Under most life insurance policies issued today, the beneficiary designation may be changed by the policyowner at any time while the insured is living, and as often as the policyowner may wish. These rights are granted in a policy provision which usually also spells out the procedure for making an effective beneficiary change.

Although the right to designate the beneficiary is often referred to as an "ownership right"—that is, a right belonging to the owner of property—it is more closely related to a "power to appoint." This is a legal phrase that means the power to designate a person or persons to whom specified property will pass at an ascertainable date in the future, even though the person who has the power does not own the property. Kevin Murray, for instance, may leave his property at his death in trust, for the benefit of his wife. The trust instrument may give her the full use of the property for her lifetime and the "power to appoint" those among their children who will inherit the property at her death. Mrs. Murray does not own the property after Mr. Murray's death, but she has the power under the trust instrument to say who is to own it after her death.

Life insurance presents a similar situation. The owner of a life insurance contract does not own the death benefit. Thus, when he designates the person or persons to whom it is to be paid, he is not disposing of his own property but rather exercising a "power to appoint." It is helpful to bear this in mind, since the right to designate and change the beneficiary of a life insurance contract may, in some instances, be treated differently from other rights of the policyowner. For instance, the guardian of a minor policyowner or of an incompetent adult policyowner is generally held not to have the power to designate or change the beneficiary on behalf of his ward, although he may have the authority to exercise other ownership rights under the policy.

BENEFICIARIES IN THE ORDER OF THEIR RIGHTS

The Primary Beneficiary

In its basic form, the beneficiary designation simply names the person or persons to whom the amount of insurance provided by the policy is to be paid on the death of the insured. The person who has the first, or primary, right to receive the insurance proceeds is called the "primary" beneficiary. There is nothing to prevent the applicant (or policyowner, after a policy is issued) from naming more than one person as primary beneficiary, if he wishes. In fact, children or sisters and brothers of the insured are frequently designated to share the insurance proceeds, in equal or unequal shares. It is customary also for the policy to provide that the insurance will be payable only to those beneficiaries who survive the insured. Therefore, if two or more primary beneficiaries are named, the proceeds will be payable only to those who are living on the date of the insured's death.

Contingent Beneficiaries

Since there is always the possibility that no primary beneficiary will be living on the date of the insured's death, it is customary, and usually very desirable, to designate another person or persons to whom the insurance shall be paid if no primary beneficiary survives the insured. This substitute beneficiary is generally called a "contingent" beneficiary, since his or her right to receive the insurance is subject to a contingency—the death of the primary beneficiary prior to the death of the insured. Sometimes the contingent beneficiary is called a "secondary" beneficiary and sometimes he is called a "first contingent" beneficiary. A second contingent beneficiary may also be named, to receive the insurance proceeds in the event that there is neither a primary nor a first contingent beneficiary living at the death of the insured. Company practices differ as to the number of contingent beneficiaries the applicant or policyowner may name.

The Final Beneficiary

Most policies specifically provide that if no beneficiary is designated, or if there is no designated beneficiary living at the death of the insured, the proceeds will be payable to the executor or administrator of the insured's estate. The use of these words reflects the fact that if the insured leaves a valid will at his death, his property will be handled differently than if he dies without a will. If he leaves a valid will, he is said to have died "testate," and a court appointed *executor* will take charge of his property and distribute it according to the provisions of his will. If he dies without a valid will, he is said to have died "intestate," and an *administrator* will be appointed (also by a court) to distribute his property in accordance with the provisions of the applicable state law. The policy, therefore, provides that if there is no living beneficiary to receive the proceeds, the money will be paid to the executor or the administrator, who will distribute it in accordance with the insured's will or the provisions of the applicable law.

■ REVOCABLE AND IRREVOCABLE BENEFICIARIES

The earliest life insurance contracts were relatively simple insuring agreements and contained no provisions giving the owner the right to revoke or change the beneficiary designation. Under these agreements, the beneficiary, once named, could not, without his or her consent, be deprived of the right to receive the proceeds of the insurance by a subsequent change of beneficiary. In the language of life insurance, the beneficiary designation could not be revoked without the consent of the beneficiary. Therefore, the beneficiary designation was *irrevocable*.

Later, companies began to include in their application and policy forms provisions permitting the applicant to reserve the right to change the beneficiary if he wished, without obtaining the consent of the person or persons previously named. This created a *revocable* designation, and the person so named was called a revocable beneficiary. Most life insurance policies issued today provide that unless a beneficiary is designated irrevocably, the beneficiary designation can be revoked and changed as frequently as the policyowner wishes.

Nevertheless, an applicant or policyowner still, on occasion, wishes to designate a beneficiary irrevocably; and most insurers will comply with such requests. In those cases, the designation will usually read as follows:

The beneficiary shall be Mary Doe, wife of the insured, irrevocably.

An irrevocable beneficiary designation, unlike the revocable designation, is said to give the beneficiary a "vested" interest in the proceeds of the policy. This means that the irrevocable beneficiary cannot be deprived of the right to receive the death benefit without his or her consent. Since the revocable beneficiary can be deprived of his or her interest whenever the policyowner wishes to revoke or change the designation, the interest of a revocable beneficiary is generally said to be a "mere expectancy" until the death of the insured. At that time, it is said to be vested, since beneficiary changes are not usually possible after the insured's death.

Once a policyowner has designated a beneficiary irrevocably, he cannot thereafter revoke or change the designation, nor can he obtain a loan under the policy or surrender it for cash, unless the beneficiary consents. An irrevocable beneficiary, therefore, has a kind of veto power over any action the owner may wish to take with respect to the exercise of the various ownership rights provided under the policy. However, most policies contain a provision terminating the interest of an irrevocable beneficiary, like that of a revocable beneficiary, if he dies prior to the death of the insured. The following is illustrative of this type of policy provision:

The interest of any beneficiary who dies during the insured's lifetime will vest in the owner unless otherwise provided.

■ MINOR BENEFICIARIES

A minor's right to disaffirm a contract was discussed in connection with the law of contracts generally. This right is also important when a claim is paid under a life insurance contract made by an adult but payable to a minor beneficiary. In the absence of a special state law to the contrary, it is legally impossible for a minor to give a receipt for insurance proceeds that he cannot later disaffirm. For this reason, whenever a sum of money becomes payable to a minor, whether as a claim or otherwise, the insurer has a problem. If payment is made directly to the minor, there is always the possibility that the company might have to pay a second time, should the minor later choose to disaffirm the receipt he has given.

Even under the special statutes previously mentioned (which permit minors of a specified age or older to complete life insurance contracts as if they were adults), the minor cannot give a binding receipt for insurance proceeds unless they are paid under a policy he himself has applied for. A few states have special laws that make it possible for life insurance companies to pay limited insurance benefits to, and receive a binding release (that is, a receipt that he cannot later disaffirm on the basis of his minority) from any minor beneficiary of a specified minimum age even though the insurance was applied for and owned by someone other than the minor. In one state, for instance, a special law of this kind permits a minor to give a binding release for any single sum payment or for installments totaling up to $3,000 in any one year, if the minor is at least 18 years old and the insurance company has not, at the time of payment, received written notice that a guardian of the estate of the minor has been appointed.

Except in the limited number of states having laws of this kind, insurance proceeds becoming payable to a minor, under policies applied for and issued to an adult, cannot safely be paid except to the court-appointed guardian of the minor's estate. Payment is made to that person in his legal capacity as guardian. In that capacity, the guardian can do what the minor cannot do—give a binding receipt or release; and the insurance proceeds can then be used under the supervision of the court for the benefit of the child. This provides a satisfactory procedure from the insurer's point of view, but it may involve some delay in making payment. The appointment of a guardian usually involves some expense to the beneficiary also, that would have been avoided if an adult beneficiary had been named.

If these possible complications are understood, however, and if the policyowner still wishes to designate a minor child or minor children as beneficiaries, there is no reason why he should not do so. In fact, most life insurers will permit a policyowner or applicant to designate his children as a class, although class beneficiary designations are not generally favored by life insurance companies.

A class beneficiary designation is a designation that names the members of a class collectively, rather than as individuals. For instance, a class designation would read "children of the insured," rather than "Sandra, Brian, and Christopher Morris, children of the insured."

Class designations may create problems for the life insurance company at the time a claim is settled, since every surviving member of the class must then be identified and located. This can be a difficult and time-consuming procedure, yet it must be done, since the sum payable to each depends upon the number who survive the insured. For this reason, life insurance companies customarily limit the class designations they are willing to accept to persons closely related to the insured. Thus, the insured's children, or the brothers and sisters of a minor insured, constitute the most usual examples of permissible class designations.

In probably the most common situation, the members of the class will be designated as contingent beneficiaries, as in the following example:

To Barbara L. Crawford, wife of the insured, if living; otherwise to the children born of this marriage, equally or to the survivor.

One of the advantages of this type of designation is that it automatically includes any children who are born after the designation has been made (after-born children). Under the class designation quoted above, all the children of the insured born of his marriage to Barbara, who are living at the time of his death, will share in the proceeds of his insurance if his wife does not survive him. Thus, if any of them becomes entitled to a share of the proceeds, all will share. To achieve this result if each child were named individually, the designation would have to be changed each time an additional child was born. It is very easy to neglect to do this, in which case one or more of the children born after the date of the application might easily be omitted and hence not share in the proceeds.

■ HOW BENEFICIARY DESIGNATIONS MAY BE CHANGED

Most policies provide that the policyowner may revoke and change the beneficiary designation as often as he wishes (though he relinquishes this right if he designates a beneficiary irrevocably). The only requirement is that the procedure outlined in the policy must be followed.

There are two principal methods of making beneficiary changes. One method requires the policy to be submitted to the company for endorsement of the change and is therefore called the "endorsement" method. The other method requires only that a written request signed by the policyowner be filed with and recorded by the company. This method is generally referred to as the "recording" method. Each of these methods has its advantages and each has its disadvantages. However, the trend at the present time is toward the use of the recording method.

The Endorsement Method

For companies using the endorsement method of beneficiary change, a fairly typical change-of-beneficiary policy provision would read as follows:

Change of Beneficiary or Settlement Agreement. Subject to the rights of the assignee of record, if any, and subject to the limitations, if any, in the beneficiary designation or settlement agreement, the owner may as often as desired change the beneficiary, or may change the settlement agreement, to any other method of payment upon which the owner and the company may agree, by filing with the company written request therefor in such form as the company may require. Such change shall be effective only if endorsed on the policy by the company, but when so endorsed shall take effect as of the date the request was signed, subject to any payment made or action taken by the company before such endorsement.

The word "endorsement" comes from two Latin roots—*en* (on) and *dorsum* (back). Originally, an endorsement was any provision or writing on the back of a document, and the idea is retained in this original sense when we speak of endorsing a check. The endorsement method of beneficiary change, therefore, requires that the fact of the change and the name of the new beneficiary must actually be typed on, or firmly fastened to, the policy itself. Obviously, this requires that the policy be submitted to the company, together with the written request for a change of beneficiary.

Change of beneficiary provisions specifying the endorsement method usually state that a beneficiary change will be effective only if endorsed on the policy. In fact, some policies, particularly those that were issued some years ago, require that the endorsement be completed during the lifetime of the insured or it will not be effective. However, many change of beneficiary provisions in policies being issued today provide that when the change of beneficiary has been endorsed, it will be considered to have been made as of the date the request was signed "whether or not the insured is living at the time the change is endorsed." Usually there is a limitation (as in the quoted policy provision) specifically excepting any payment made by the company prior to the endorsement.

The Recording Method

The recording method of beneficiary change is illustrated in the following policy provision:

Change of Beneficiary or Settlement Agreement. Subject to the rights of the assignee of record, if any, and subject to the limitations, if any, in the beneficiary designation or settlement agreement, the owner may, as often as desired, change the beneficiary, or may change the settlement agreement, to any other method of payment upon which the owner and the company may agree. Such change of beneficiary shall be made by filing with the company a written request in a form satisfactory to the company. No such change will be effective unless recorded by the company, but on being so recorded, shall take effect as of the date the request was signed, provided that any interest created thereby shall be subject to any payment made or other action taken by the company before such recording.

This is known as the recording method of changing the beneficiary, because the request needs only to be recorded at the home office to be effective. Usually, as in the policy from which this provision is quoted, the change is effective as of the date of the request, if it is recorded by the company. Usually, also, the company is protected (by wording similar to that used in the last sentence of the quoted provision) against loss resulting from actions it may take or payments it may make before it receives the new beneficiary designation.

If the policy includes this type of provision, the request for a change of beneficiary usually needs only to be signed and mailed to the company to be effective. The policy does not need to be submitted. Even though several days may elapse before the request reaches the home office of the company, the new beneficiary will be entitled to the proceeds of the policy from the date the request was signed, if the claim has not already been paid to the beneficiary previously named. In the latter instance, if the company has made settlement without knowledge of the policyowner's actions, it will not ordinarily be required to pay the proceeds again to the new beneficiary.

An Illustration. Let us say that Martin Clark is the owner of a life insurance policy that he bought shortly after he finished college. At that time, he was unmarried, and he designated his parents as primary beneficiaries, to receive the death benefit in equal shares if they were living at his death. Three years later, Martin marries. He writes to the company for forms to change the beneficiary,[1] and on March 2 he completes a form naming his wife, Susan, as beneficiary. He mails the request for beneficiary change to the company the same day, but it doesn't reach the home office until March 5. On Wednesday, March 4, driving home at dusk, Martin is killed in an automobile accident. Because Martin's policy includes a "recording" change of beneficiary provision, the change he requested became effective as of the date he signed it. (The only requirement was that the request be received and recorded by the company; and "recording" is a routine act that can be performed after the insured's death.) As a result, Susan, not Martin's parents, would be entitled to the proceeds of Martin's policy.

This same result would be achieved also under most policies providing for the endorsement method of beneficiary change. However, as previously mentioned, some policies require the endorsement to be made "during the lifetime of the insured." If Martin Clark's policy had contained a change of beneficiary provision with this requirement, his attempt to designate his wife as beneficiary would not have been effective. Under those circumstances, his parents, not his wife, would have been entitled to receive the death benefit, as "beneficiaries of record."

---

[1] This is the usual procedure, but for simple beneficiary changes, if the details of the change are sufficiently clear, a letter alone may be sufficient.

The endorsement method of beneficiary change is often inconvenient for the policyowner, since the policy must be submitted with the request for beneficiary change. Sometimes, as when an estranged wife has possession of the policy, this may be impossible. However, if the endorsement procedure is used, there is less likelihood that the company will overlook a beneficiary change when a claim is settled. If the policy is endorsed, the most recently designated beneficiary (the beneficiary of record) can always be ascertained from the policy itself. Under the recording method, the successive beneficiary changes do not appear on the policy but are on separate documents, one of which could be overlooked at the time settlement is being made.

The recording method is more convenient to the policyowner, however, since the policy does not have to be submitted when a beneficiary change is made. It is also less expensive, since it reduces the cost of handling the policies when they are submitted, as well as postage costs. For these reasons, the majority of companies have adopted the recording method of making beneficiary changes.

■ THE OPTIONAL MODES OF SETTLEMENT

Most life insurance contracts provide that unless there is an agreement to the contrary, the benefit payable on the death of the insured will be paid in one sum "on receipt of due proof" of the death of the insured. (A one-sum or lump-sum settlement means that the entire proceeds of the policy will be paid to the beneficiary in one check.) Frequently, under a one-sum settlement, a relatively large sum will be payable to a person who has had only limited experience in handling financial responsibilities. Usually, also, the beneficiary of a life insurance contract is under a heavy emotional strain at the time of settlement, and it is unrealistic to expect a person in such circumstances to make wise decisions as to the investment of a large sum of money. As early as the 1860's, therefore, life insurance companies began making periodic payments (income settlements) available at the death of the insured, as an alternative to one-sum settlements.

Income settlements for life insurance proceeds first became popular in the 1930's, a period marked by the failure of many other kinds of investments. By contrast, the security of life insurance seemed particularly attractive. Today, under the optional modes of settlement, companies offer several ways in which the proceeds of life insurance can be retained by the company, to be withdrawn as needed or paid in regular payments until the proceeds plus interest are exhausted. The applicant or policyowner can thus elect the settlement method he believes will be most suitable for his family, with complete assurance that the settlement elected will be carried out by the company in accordance with his wishes.

At least four optional modes of settlement are provided under most life insurance policies today. Modifications of these methods are frequently included, but most such modifications are only variations of the following:

1. An interest option, under which the proceeds are retained by the company at interest, with interest payable annually, or more frequently, if preferred.
2. A fixed-period (fixed-years) option, under which the proceeds, together with interest, are paid out in regular installments over a specified period of time.
3. A fixed-amount option, under which the proceeds are paid out in regular installments of a fixed amount until both proceeds and interest are exhausted.
4. A life income option, under which the proceeds and interest are paid out in equal installments for the remainder of a designated payee's life.

Election of the Options

Under most policies, the applicant may elect an optional mode of settlement when he designates the beneficiary; and later, as a policyowner, he may elect or change the mode of settlement whenever he wishes. Most policies also permit the beneficiary to elect an optional mode or modes at the time the insurance becomes payable, if the proceeds are payable in a lump sum.

The policy specifies the circumstances under which such elections may be made and the conditions under which they may be changed. As a general rule, the requirements of the insurer are relatively flexible. Usually, the policyowner (or beneficiary) may elect to have settlement made partly under one mode and partly under another, if he wishes, provided that not less than a specified minimum—such as $1,000—will be applied under each option. He may also elect settlement under one option for the first few years of the settlement period, with an automatic or elective change provided at a specified future date. Thus, it is usually possible to elect both concurrent and consecutive options in connection with settlement of the proceeds of a given policy.

If the policyowner elects an optional mode of settlement, he may specify that any applicable rights provided by the policy—the right of withdrawal, the right to change to another option, and so on—be granted to or withheld from the beneficiary, either entirely or for a specified period. If the beneficiary elects the settlement method, all applicable rights granted by the policy will be available to him (or her, as the case may be). These rights differ from one option to another and will be discussed more specifically in connection with the options to which they apply.

The Interest Option

Under the interest option, the insurance proceeds are left with the company; and interest on those proceeds is paid to the beneficiary at regular intervals. Usually, this interest is paid annually unless the company is requested to pay at more frequent intervals. Usually also a minimum amount, such as $20, must be payable, or payment will be made at less frequent intervals.

Because life insurance contracts often remain in effect for many years, the rate of interest specified under this option may compare more favorably with other investment opportunities in some years and less favorably in others. However, it is customary to provide that interest will be paid at "not less than" a specified rate. This means that the rate of interest is guaranteed never to be lower than that stated; but if the investment experience of the company warrants it, additional interest may be paid. This additional interest is variously referred to as "excess interest," or "surplus interest," and it is usually paid at the end of the year.

Because insurers are legally prohibited from retaining policy proceeds indefinitely, companies frequently limit the period of retention under this option to the lifetime of the primary beneficiary or 30 years, whichever is longer. Usually the beneficiary may be given the right to withdraw all or any part of the principal at any time. However, if the policyowner wishes, he may direct that the payee be given no withdrawal rights or that such rights shall be limited to the withdrawal of not more than a stated amount—$6,000, for example, or $10,000—in any given period, such as a year, or not more than, say, $2,000 at any one time.

The rules and practices of most companies permit a considerable amount of flexibility with respect to changes from the interest option to a different option at a later date, with the possible exception of a later change to the life income option. Some companies require that any change to the life income option be made within a specified period such as one or two years following the date of the insured's death. This practice tends to reduce antiselection.

The right to change to a different option at a later date makes the interest option especially useful. Settlement arrangements are frequently requested under which insurance proceeds are to be held at interest until a specified future date and then applied under an income option. For instance, assume that Richard Anderson purchased a $20,000 ten-year term insurance policy on his own life, naming his son, Stephen, as beneficiary. He intends the proceeds of this policy to be used for Stephen's college education in the event of his death. He may, therefore, specify that if he dies prior to Stephen's 18th birthday, the proceeds are to be held under the interest option until Stephen reaches age 18, and then paid out in installments, to be used for Stephen's college education.

Settlement agreements of this kind often provide that on receipt of proof of the child's enrollment in an institution of higher learning, the insurer will apply the proceeds under the fixed-period option and pay them out in equal installments for four years. Such settlement agreements usually provide that the beneficiary shall have full withdrawal rights on reaching a specified age, such as age 25, in the event that the child does not attend college.

Uses of the Interest Option. The interest option is the simplest and most flexible way of meeting the problem of what to do with the insurance proceeds immediately following the death of the insured. It is often elected by the policyowner when he does not wish to make a final decision concerning the disposition of the insurance. For instance, he may wish his wife to elect the optional mode or modes under which the proceeds are ultimately to be paid but not wish to place on her shoulders the burden of immediate choice at the time of his death, when she will have the responsibility of making many other serious and far-reaching family decisions. The interest option permits the proceeds to be retained by the company and interest to be paid to the beneficiary while she has the time to consider the family circumstances and make her final decision.

The interest option is also a good choice for proceeds that will probably be needed in the first few months after the insured's death for the payment of last illness and funeral expenses. Amounts intended for this purpose are often referred to as "clean-up" funds because they are intended to be used to pay any outstanding debts. If this fund is large enough that it will not be immediately exhausted, it can be left with the company under the interest option, with full right of withdrawal and the right to change to another option later if any amount remains after all debts have been paid. In this way the money will be available when needed and yet some of it will continue to earn interest.

The Fixed-Period Option

The fixed-period option, sometimes called the fixed-years option, is appropriate for the policyowner who wishes to provide an income for the beneficiary for a specified period of time after his death. Under this method of settlement, the company retains the proceeds after the death of the insured and pays the money, both proceeds and interest, to the named beneficiary in equal installments, usually

FIGURE 6-1

Fixed-Period Installments Table (monthly installments that $1,000 will obtain for number of years elected)

No. of Years Elected	Monthly Installments	No. of Years Elected	Monthly Installments
1	$84.90	16	$6.78
2	43.18	17	6.48
3	29.28	18	6.22
4	22.33	19	5.98
5	18.17	20	5.77
6	15.39	21	5.58
7	13.41	22	5.41
8	11.93	23	5.25
9	10.78	24	5.11
10	9.86	25	4.98
11	9.11	26	4.86
12	8.49	27	4.75
13	7.96	28	4.64
14	7.51	29	4.55
15	7.12	30	4.46

monthly, for the exact period selected by the policyowner. The monthly installments that can be provided for each $1,000 of insurance proceeds for various periods of time are set forth in a table in the policy, similar to that shown in Figure 6-1.

According to this table, if the length of time over which payments are to be made is 20 years, payments of $5.77 per month will be made for each $1,000 of insurance proceeds applied under this option. To find the amount of each installment for the total proceeds of a specific policy, therefore, this amount is multiplied by the number of thousands of dollars of the proceeds. Thus, a $10,000 policy would provide payments in the amount of $57.70 per month for a period of 20 years.

As is true under the interest option, excess interest may be paid if the investment experience of the company justifies it. Excess interest is either paid in one sum at the end of the year or used to increase the amount of the payments otherwise provided in succeeding years.

The amount of the individual payments under this option depends upon the total amount of proceeds, the period over which payments are to be made, the frequency of payments, and the rate of interest guaranteed. A change in any of these factors, therefore, would require recomputation of the installments over the remaining period. For this reason, partial withdrawals are not usually permitted under this option, although the right to withdraw the present value of all remaining unpaid installments may be granted. (This right is referred to as the "right of commutation," since the present value of future guaranteed payments is the commuted value of those payments.)

Uses of the Fixed-Period Option. The fixed-period option is most useful in circumstances where income is needed for a definite time. For instance, it may be used to provide an income for a child during his college years, or to provide an income for the family for a limited period after the death of the insured, to permit readjustment to a more permanent financial plan. In fact, the fixed-period option is appropriate for any situation where the income needs will terminate or change at the end of a definite period.

The Fixed-Amount Option

Under the fixed-amount option, the insurance company retains the insurance proceeds and pays the money out in installments of a specified amount until the proceeds plus interest are exhausted.

In a sense, the fixed-amount option is essentially the same as the fixed-period option. Both use the insurance proceeds and guaranteed interest to provide installments over a period of time. The fixed-amount option, however, is considerably the more flexible of the two. Thus, installments of different amounts may be provided for different periods, as for example, $500 per month for 24 months and $250 per month thereafter until the proceeds are exhausted. Usually, also, the beneficiary may be given the right to make partial withdrawals (not usually available under the fixed-period option), as well as the right to withdraw the commuted value of all unpaid installments.

Since installments are payable in the specified amount under the fixed-amount option, any excess interest payable will extend the period during which the payments will be made, rather than increase the amount of the payments. This, of course, is in contrast with the effect of excess interest under the fixed-period option. (Under that option, as previously mentioned, excess interest is paid at the end of the year or is used to increase the amount of the individual payments.)

Policies usually specify that a minimum amount, such as 5 percent of the total proceeds, must be paid each year under this option, in order that the total proceeds will be paid out within a reasonable length of time.

Uses of the Fixed-Amount Option. The fixed-amount option is appropriate in any situation where it is more important that payments be made in a specified amount than for any particular length of time. This may be especially true when the amount of the insurance is limited and would not provide an adequate income for the insured's family for very long. For instance, $2,000 of life insurance would provide only $36.34 per month if payments were spread over a period of five years. This income would be guaranteed for that period of time; but if it were the only income available to a family, it would be almost meaningless. In situations of this kind, therefore, the fixed-amount option is usually more appropriate. Under this option, installments in the amount selected—$500, $600, or whatever monthly income seems necessary—will be paid to the beneficiary until the last penny of the insurance proceeds, plus interest, has been paid out. Even if these payments cannot be continued very long, they will help a widow while she finds employment or makes other arrangements for the support of the family. Under these circumstances, election of this option may prove to be the wisest choice.

The Life Income Options

Life income options provide exactly what the names suggest—a fixed income for the lifetime of the beneficiaries. In technical language, this is an annuity. When a life income option is elected, therefore, the insurance proceeds will be used as a net single premium to provide an annuity for the beneficiary. The life income options are probably the most valuable of all the optional methods of settlement, for similar benefits cannot be purchased commercially from any other institution.

When life insurance proceeds are settled under a life income option, the income payments are calculated in such a way that the policy proceeds, plus interest, will be paid out (liquidated) over the lifetime of the beneficiary. These payments are guaranteed to be made until the death of the beneficiary, who is thus assured that he will not "outlive his income." This fact—that the payee will receive an income as long as he lives—is the basic advantage of the life income option.

Payments under this option are made in an amount determined at the time the option goes into effect, and are based upon the age of the beneficiary at that time, as well as the sex of the beneficiary, the rate of interest provided in the policy, the type of life income selected, and the total amount of proceeds applied under the option. Larger income payments can be provided for older beneficiaries than would be made to younger ones, since the income will not be paid to them over as many years. Larger payments can also be provided for men than for women beneficiaries, because statistics show that women have a longer life expectancy than men.

The life income options provided in individual life insurance contracts are commonly of two kinds:

1. The straight life income option, under which installments are payable for the lifetime of the payee, but no longer.
2. The life income with "period certain," under which payments are guaranteed to be made to someone for a specified period, even if the designated payee does not live that long, and for the remainder of the payee's life, if that is longer than the specified period.

Other variations of the life income option are sometimes offered and are frequently available by company practice, even when they are not specifically provided by the policy. Since all these life income options are essentially annuities, they will be discussed more fully in the chapter devoted entirely to the subject of annuities.

■ THE SPENDTHRIFT TRUST PROVISION

Most insurance companies take advantage of the statutes, enacted by a number of the states, which permit the inclusion of a special provision in the policy or the settlement option agreement to protect the policy proceeds from the claims of creditors of the beneficiary before those proceeds are actually paid to him or her. Such provisions are commonly referred to as "spendthrift trust" clauses. The following is illustrative:

Except as otherwise prescribed by law, no payment of interest or of principal shall, in advance of actual payment by the company, be subject to the debts, contracts, or engagements of any person entitled to payment, nor to any judicial process to levy upon or attach the same for payment thereof.

The effect of a provision such as this is to prevent persons to whom the beneficiary owes money from taking legal action against the insurance company to require the company to pay directly to them any proceeds to which the beneficiary is entitled. The spendthrift trust clause provides no further protection to the beneficiary after the proceeds have been paid by the company.

The phrase "except as otherwise prescribed by law" is included because spendthrift trust provisions are considered to be contrary to public policy in a few states. These states are in the decided minority, however, and the courts of most states will uphold a provision of this kind. Many life insurance companies include a spendthrift trust provision in every settlement agreement.

■ SETTLEMENT OPTION AGREEMENTS

When a settlement option is elected by the applicant or policyowner, his designation of beneficiaries and his choice of the option or options under which settlement is to be made to each beneficiary are usually incorporated in a document called a settlement option agreement or settlement agreement. This is customarily included in and made a part of the policy if the election is made at the time of application.

Company practices differ, however, as to whether later changes in the settlement agreement will, by endorsement, be made a part of the policy itself. The present-day trend toward the recording method of beneficiary designations has been accompanied by a similar trend toward recording changes of settlement option agreements. If the recording method is used, the settlement agreement will be recorded in the home office and a copy sent to the policyowner to be kept with his policy; the policy does not need to be submitted to the company.

■ NOTES ON CANADIAN PRACTICES

In Canada, the insurance legislation sets out the insured's right to name and change the beneficiaries for his insurance, and the ways in which this may be done. In Canada, therefore, by contrast with the situation in the United States, it is not necessary for these rights to be spelled out in the policy itself.

The Revised Uniform Life Insurance Act (in force in all Provinces except Quebec) permits a beneficiary to be designated or revoked either in a contract or by a declaration. A declaration is a document—that is, a written statement—signed by the policyowner, and (1) requiring endorsement on the policy, or (2) identifying the contract, or (3) describing all or a part of the insurance fund. A will is considered a "declaration" within the terms of this provision, and thus a beneficiary may be designated by will. This is in contrast to the prevailing law in the United States, where it is usually held that the policy requirements concerning beneficiary designations and changes must be complied with. A designation or change of beneficiary by will does not constitute compliance, and attempted beneficiary designations by will are not usually given effect in the United States. (United States Government Life Insurance policies and National Service Life Insurance policies issued to members of the armed services and veterans constitute exceptions to this rule and specifically provide for beneficiary designations and changes by will.)

The insured may designate a beneficiary irrevocably, but the necessary document must be filed at the insurer's home office during the insured's lifetime; and an irrevocable designation cannot be made by will. If the insured attempts to designate a beneficiary irrevocably by will, the effect is to designate a beneficiary revocably.

In the Province of Quebec, the naming of beneficiaries, and their rights, are governed by the Quebec Civil Code and the Husbands' and Parents' Life Insurance Act.

It should be noted that in Canada, many beneficiaries under policies issued prior to 1962 have a vested interest in the policy, conferred upon them by the insurance legislation in effect at the time they were appointed. Prior to 1962, the Uniform Life Insurance Act provided that all beneficiaries closely related to the insured—spouse, children, parents, and grandchildren—had a "preferred trust" interest in the policy. The insured could not surrender the policy or borrow against or assign it without the consent of any beneficiary he had designated within this class. The insured could make changes of beneficiary from one member to another within the preferred class (for instance, from mother to wife), but he could not change to a beneficiary outside the preferred class without the consent of the preferred beneficiary. When the Uniform Life Insurance Act was revised in 1962, specific provision was made to carry forward the vested interest of preferred beneficiaries who had been appointed prior to that date, but the "preferred trust" status was abolished for all beneficiaries designated after that date.

In Quebec, beneficiaries appointed under the Husbands' and Parents' Life Insurance Act (wife and children) acquire a similar vested interest in the policy.

The Uniform Life Insurance Act provides that a beneficiary who has attained the age of 18 years has the capacity of a person 21 years of age to receive insurance money payable to him and to give a binding discharge for it. There is no similar provision in the law of Quebec.

■ QUESTIONS FOR REVIEW

1. Briefly define the following:
   a) primary beneficiary
   b) contingent beneficiary
   c) final beneficiary
2. How do the rights of an irrevocable beneficiary differ from those of a revocable beneficiary?
3. Describe the basic problem involved in connection with settlement of life insurance proceeds payable to minor beneficiaries.
4. What is a class beneficiary designation? What principal problem may be encountered in settling a claim payable to beneficiaries as a class?
5. What are the two principal methods of making beneficiary changes under life insurance policies? Summarize each method.
6. Describe the basic optional modes of settlement commonly offered under life insurance contracts.
7. List three rights or privileges that may be granted to the beneficiary under the interest option.
8. How is the payment of excess interest handled under the fixed-years option? Under the fixed-amount option? Give reasons for the difference.
9. Describe two forms of life income options that are commonly offered as settlement options under life insurance contracts.
10. Summarize the purpose of the spendthrift trust provision.

7 WHILE THE CONTRACT IS IN FORCE

Most life insurance contracts involve a great deal more than just the payment of premiums to the insurer during the lifetime of the insured, and the payment of the policy proceeds to the beneficiary at the time of the insured's death. Often additional benefits are available to the policyowner during the insured's lifetime; and, after a few years, whole life or endowment insurance contracts may represent significant cash values, which the policyowner is free to use in many ways.

This chapter will discuss the various provisions of the life insurance contract that govern the relationship between the life insurance company and the policyowner during the insured's lifetime. The whole life policy will be used as a basis for the discussion, but where significant differences exist, other plans will also be discussed.

■ THE PREMIUM PROVISIONS

It has been customary to state the amount of the applicable premium on the first or "face" page of the life insurance policy (although information of this kind is frequently included now on a separate computer-prepared page). Many policies also state on the face page that the insurance is granted "in consideration of the application and the payment of premiums." This statement makes it clear that the legal requirement of consideration has been fulfilled. However, this phrase is frequently omitted today in the interest of simplicity.

While payment of the initial premium is "consideration" for the contract, payment of renewal premiums (all premiums except the first) constitutes a continuing condition that must be met if the insurance is to be kept in full force. The following discussion will be concerned with payment of renewal premiums only.

When Premiums are Payable

Many of the states require that a provision be included in the life insurance contract specifically stating that all premiums after the first must be paid at the home office of the company, or to an authorized agent in exchange for an official receipt signed by an authorized officer of the company and countersigned by the agent. It is not customary to give a receipt, except upon request, if the premium is mailed to the home office. Since most soliciting agents for ordinary life insurance are not authorized to accept renewal premiums, an official receipt is provided for those situations where an agent is so authorized.

Questions sometimes arise at the time of a death claim as to whether the most recent premium was or was not paid on the date it was due, or within the grace period. Perhaps the premium was mailed to the home office but not received until after the end of the grace period. Perhaps the policyowner paid the premium to the agent, who failed to send it in to the home office promptly.

If the envelope containing the premium payment is postmarked within the grace period, it is customary to consider that the premium was paid within the grace period. However, if payment was made to an agent who was not authorized to accept renewal premiums, and if the premium did not reach the home office until after the expiration of the grace period, there may be a question as to whether the policyowner was justified in relying upon the agent's appearance of authority to accept renewal premiums. In any event, if the policy provision regarding renewal premiums is complied with, such problems will rarely arise.

Modes of Premium Payment

It is important for the policyowner to know where and to whom his life insurance premiums are payable. It is also important for him to know that he may, if he wishes, pay the premiums more frequently than annually. Life insurance premiums are customarily expressed on an annual basis, payable at the beginning of each succeeding policy year. (In fact, this was one of the early assumptions established by life insurance actuaries as a basis for premium computation.) For a slight additional amount, most policies permit payment on a semiannual, quarterly, or monthly basis, if the policyowner prefers. These various frequencies are referred to as "modes" of premium payment.

Typically, a semiannual premium is 51 percent of the annual premium, a quarterly premium is 26 percent of it, and a monthly premium is 8.8 percent of it. The policy usually specifies that a minimum amount, such as $10, must be payable. Thus, if the premium payable on a monthly basis is not at least that large, payment must be made on a quarterly or less frequent basis.

It is customary to permit the policyowner to change from one mode of premium payment to another. Policies often permit this change without notice to the insurer, specifying only that payment of the premium for a different interval will constitute an election to change the frequency of premium payment. The following policy provision illustrates this privilege:

> Premiums may be paid at annual, semi-annual, quarterly, or monthly intervals at the company's applicable premium rate for the mode of payment requested, subject to the company's approval. Payment to and acceptance by the company of a premium on a new mode of payment shall constitute a change in mode for subsequent premiums.

Deferring or Waiving Premium Payment

Regardless of how completely convinced one may be of the value of life insurance, the fact remains that premium payments may extend over a very long period of time. Economic conditions generally, and the financial situation of the policyowner specifically, may vary significantly during that time. As a result, payment of premiums may be particularly difficult from time to time. In recognition of these facts, several policy provisions or benefits have been developed to alleviate special hardships that may arise in situations where it may be difficult or impossible to pay the premium on time. Among these are the grace period provision, the automatic premium loan provision, and the waiver-of-premium-for-disability benefit. Each of these has as its purpose the modification or alleviation of the strict requirement of premium payment on or before the premium due date.

The Grace Period Provision. In 1909 the state legislature of New York enacted a Standard Policy Provisions Law, requiring certain provisions to be included in every life insurance policy issued in that state. Other states passed similar laws in subsequent years, with the result that several policy provisions are uniformly found in all life insurance policies and are correctly referred to as "required" provisions. Even before these state laws were passed, however, most of these provisions were already being included voluntarily by life insurance companies, simply because they represented good business practices. This was especially true of the grace period provision, which was used voluntarily by many insurers long before it became a required provision. Most companies use a provision similar to the following:

Grace Period. A grace period of thirty-one days shall be allowed for payment of a premium in default. This policy shall continue in full force during the grace period. If the insured dies during the grace period, the premium in default shall be paid from the proceeds of this policy.

The gist of this provision is that if the policyowner fails to make a premium payment on or before the due date, he will have a period of 31 days of grace in which to pay it. The grace period is measured from the due date of the premium, and the insurance always remains in force to the end of the period. Thus, the death benefit is payable if the insured dies during the grace period, even though the premium was not paid before his death. However, the premium will still be due and is deductible from the policy proceeds.

The Automatic Premium Loan. Whole life and endowment policies frequently include a special provision permitting the company to establish a policy loan to pay a premium in default, if the policyowner wishes, and if the loan value of the policy is sufficient. The details of this automatic premium loan provision will be discussed later in the section dealing with policy loans. Electing the automatic premium loan, however, is one way the policyowner may help to assure that his whole life or endowment policy will be kept in force in spite of his failure to pay a premium when due.

Waiver-of-Premium-for-Disability Benefit. A frequent concern of applicants for life insurance is that they may have a long period away from work because of illness or injury, and for that reason find it difficult, if not impossible, to continue premium payments. As a protection against this risk of loss, many life insurance contracts include a special section that provides for continuation of the insurance coverage in the event the insured becomes totally disabled and remains so disabled for a specified period, usually six months. Total disability is usually defined in the policy as inability, as the result of illness or injury to "engage in any occupation for remuneration or profit." This provision will be discussed in greater detail in chapter 10. The subject is significant at this point, however, because, if the waiver-of-premium-for-disability coverage is included, the company will waive, (that is, it will give up its right to require) payment of all premiums falling due during any period of total disability of the insured, if the disability continues for the required length of time.

■ POLICY LOANS

The practice of making a policy loan available to the individual policyowner, secured by the cash value of his policy, was started on a voluntary basis by life insurance companies themselves at a relatively early date. It proved so valuable that the laws of most states now require most cash value policies to include a policy loan provision.

There are two kinds of policy loans: the request loan and the automatic premium loan, mentioned above. The request loan provision gives the policyowner the right to receive an advance from the life insurance company, secured by the cash value of his policy, any time he requests it. The automatic premium loan is a policy loan which the life insurance company is authorized by the policyowner to establish for the sole purpose of paying a premium that the policyowner has not paid at the end of the grace period.

The Request Loan

The request loan policy provision defines the amount of the policy loan available, specifies the rate of interest that will be charged until the loan is repaid, and lists the conditions relating to repayment. The life insurance company is required by law to reserve the right in the policy to defer the granting of any request loan for a period of six months. However, this provision is required solely as a protection to the insurer in the remote possibility of extreme financial stress upon the company. The policy loan is one of the best sources of ready cash available to the average policyowner, since he has the right to request the loan at any time he wishes.

In one sense, a policy loan is treated as a true loan, since interest is charged and is added to the principal if the policyowner does not pay it. However, policy loans are always limited to an amount which, plus interest, will not exceed the cash value of the policy. Since the cash value will always be adequate security for the loan, there is no requirement that the "borrower" repay the loan. In fact, he does not promise to repay it or to pay interest on it. For these reasons, a policy loan does not have the legal characteristics of a true loan and is more properly termed an "advance." This terminology is often used in the wording of the policy loan provision, where the "loan" is referred to as an "advance."

Should Interest be Charged? Occasionally, it is contended that policyowners should not be charged interest on their policy loans. However, if one understands the operation of the level-premium, legal reserve system, the necessity for charging interest becomes apparent.

It will be recalled that the calculation of the level premium is based on two assumptions: (1) that death claims will be presented at a rate not to exceed the rate shown in the mortality table adopted, and (2) that interest at not less than a specified rate will be earned on the accumulating values of the policy. If the company should make any appreciable portion of these accumulating values available without interest, even to policyowners, the interest that the company would otherwise have earned on those funds would have to be made up from some other source. The most equitable way to meet this problem is to charge interest on policy loans. Exactly what rate of interest should be charged, however, presents a question.

It is sometimes contended that the interest rate for policy loans should be roughly equivalent to the average rate of interest earned on all the other invested assets of the company. After all, if interest is charged only because the insurance company must have assets invested and earning a minimum return in order to meet the commitments of the company, why should not the policy loan interest rate reflect the investment earnings of the company generally? In periods when the prevailing interest rates are lower than the rates currently charged on policy loans, it would be advantageous from the policyowner's point of view if policy loan rates followed the prevailing interest rates more closely. From the insurer's viewpoint, however, the problem is not so easily resolved, for at least three reasons.

The first consideration is that the rate of interest for policy loans must be guaranteed for the lifetime of the policy. Thus it will frequently apply to loans which may not be made until 40 or 50 years after the policy is issued. Who can say at the time a policy is issued what interest may be earned on the invested assets of the company at such future dates?

A second point to consider is the fact that policy loans frequently seem to be a contributing cause when policies are permitted to lapse. So long as cash values are unimpaired, a policyowner seems to feel that he has an investment in his contract. He tends to protect this investment by continuing to pay premiums as they fall due. If payment of the current premium proves difficult, however, the fact that there is a large or maximum loan against the policy seems to lessen the value of the contract in the eyes of the owner; and it is thought that he is more likely to permit the contract to lapse. Most insurers, therefore, do not want to encourage the making of policy loans. An interest rate much below the prevailing rate at any given time might have that effect.

A third significant consideration is the expense of administering policy loans. The administrative costs of handling the typically small loan transactions would alone justify charging a rate of interest on policy loans that is higher than the rate earned on the invested assets generally. However, some state statutes specify a maximum rate of interest for policy loans. Thus, an insurer cannot charge a higher rate in those states, even if it wished to do so.

The rate of policy loan interest specified by most policies currently being issued is 5, 5.5, or 6 percent. These rates are believed to be high enough that, during most periods, policy loans will not seem overly attractive and yet low enough that the privilege will constitute a genuine benefit to the policyowner when he needs it. Nevertheless, some prominent life insurance authorities favor legislation that would permit life insurance companies to adopt a flexible rate of interest for policy loans. Under one such proposal, life companies could change the policy loan interest rate on an annual basis, provided they did not exceed a specified maximum rate.

The Policy Loan Provision. The wording of most policy loan provisions makes it clear that obtaining a policy loan is an ownership right and that a loan will be granted on the request of the policyowner. In some instances, the policy is required to be submitted to the insurer for endorsement. Practices differ on this point, and frequently the insurer merely reserves the right to require submission of the policy, if any question as to the policyowner's rights needs to be clarified.

Loan Repayment. A policy loan may be repaid, with interest, any time the policyowner wishes, so long as the policy remains in force and the insured is living. Nevertheless, the policy loan is an advance rather than a true loan, and the company does not require that it be repaid. If, during the insured's lifetime, the principal of the loan, together with any unpaid interest, reaches the point where the total equals or exceeds the maximum loan value, the policy will terminate. If a loan remains unpaid at the insured's death, most life insurance companies deduct the amount of the loan, plus any accrued interest, from the proceeds payable to the beneficiary.

This practice of deducting an unpaid policy loan from the sum payable on the insured's death may work an unnecessary hardship on the beneficiary in some situations. For instance, if the loan is of a significant size, it may seriously distort the settlement plan the policyowner has carefully worked out. For this reason, some insurers permit policy loans to be repaid after the insured's death. This makes the full death benefit available for any settlement the policyowner planned or the beneficiary may wish. Usually this privilege, when available, is limited to a specified period, such as 30 or 60 days following the insured's death.

The Automatic Premium Loan

The automatic premium loan provision has been referred to previously in connection with the payment of premiums. The effect of the provision is to authorize the life insurance company, when a premium is unpaid at the end of the grace period (and if the policy has an adequate loan value), to establish a policy loan in an amount sufficient to pay that premium. When this is done, the premium is paid in exactly the same sense as if the policyowner had paid it personally, but a policy loan has been established or an existing policy loan has been increased.

A provision of this kind is included in some policy forms by many companies, but usually it does not become operative unless the policyowner specifically elects it. He may make this election when he applies for the insurance, usually by checking the appropriate box in the application; or he may elect it later, in writing. Once elected, the provision remains in effect until it is revoked.

When the automatic premium loan provision is elected, the company makes this a matter of record. Thereafter, whenever a premium falls due and is not paid by the end of the grace period, the company establishes a policy loan and pays it.[1] If the available loan value is not sufficient to pay the entire premium then due, the company is not legally obliged to apply the amount available to pay a part of the premium. However, since this could cause the policy to lapse for nonpayment of that premium, many companies will voluntarily change the premium mode—for instance, from an annual mode to semiannual—if the loan value is not sufficient to pay the annual premium but is enough to pay a semiannual or quarterly premium.

After a loan has been established to pay a premium, the automatic premium loan operates in exactly the same way as the request loan. The loan does not have to be repaid, but the policyowner may repay it. In fact, most companies encourage him to repay it, since any unpaid loan, plus accrued interest, will reduce the benefit payable at his death.

■ POLICYOWNER DIVIDENDS

Premiums and Participation

All life insurance premiums are based on estimates of mortality, interest, and expenses. The insurer, therefore, cannot be certain that premiums under any group of policies will always be adequate. Life insurance contracts often remain in force for many years. Economic conditions change; investment returns vary; epidemics and war deaths may result in claims considerably in excess of those anticipated. For these reasons, life insurance companies make use of numerous margins of safety in establishing their premium rates. For instance, mortality tables are so constructed that the death rates are deliberately overstated, and the assumed interest rate is always established on a conservative (relatively low) basis, to guard against periods of unusually low interest earnings. In addition, many life insurance companies issue what are called "participating" policies.

Participating life insurance policies are policies for which the premiums are established with reasonably generous margins of safety. The policy then gives the policyowner the right to "participate" in distributions of surplus, by receiving policy dividends if

---

[1] Policies sometimes provide that successive premiums will be paid by automatic premium loan only for a specified period, such as a year, and then the automatic premium loan must be re-elected by the policyowner. This prevents the exhaustion of the total loan value for the payment of premiums unless the policyowner specifically wishes it to be so used.

actual company experience is sufficiently favorable. (Nonparticipating policies do not include this right.)

Most mutual life insurance companies issue participating policies. In fact, mutual companies organized and operating under the laws of New York are required by law to issue participating policies. Stock life insurance companies, on the other hand, customarily issue nonparticipating policies. There is no set rule to this effect, however, and some stock life insurance companies issue participating policies only, while others issue both participating and nonparticipating policies. Most mutual companies issue only participating policies but a few also issue nonparticipating policies. It is the policy itself rather than the nature of the issuing company that is controlling so far as policy dividends are concerned.

Participating policies usually have higher premiums than comparable nonparticipating policies, but it is anticipated that a net reduction in premium outlay will be achieved as the result of policyowner dividends. Under participating policies, dividends are formally allocated at regular intervals to groups of participating policyowners, by action of the directors or trustees of the company. These dividends are apportioned among the various classes of policies in accordance with the mortality, interest, and cost experience developed by those policies. A typical policy provision relating to dividends reads in part as follows:

Dividends. Annual dividends such as the company may apportion shall be payable while this policy is in force, other than as extended term insurance, without condition as to the payment of any subsequent premium.

The Dividend Options

Policy dividends declared by the company constitute amounts payable to the policyowners. However, this does not necessarily mean that the company issues checks for these amounts each year and mails them to the respective policyowners. Most participating policies provide several ways in which dividends may be used. These choices are called dividend options, and the following options are typically offered: (1) a cash payment option; (2) a premium reduction option; (3) an interest (or accumulation) option; and (4) a dividend additions (or paid-up additions) option.

The policyowner may elect any of these options and later change his election, any time he wishes, to apply to future dividends. The policy states which option will apply if, for some reason, the policyowner makes no election. Usually this automatic option is the dividend additions option.

The relative popularity of these various dividend options is indicated in Figure 7–1.

FIGURE 7–1

Application of Policyowners' Dividends (United States)—1970

Taken in cash	21%
Used to reduce premiums	24
Left to accumulate under the interest option	28
Used to purchase additional insurance	27

1. The Cash Payment Option. If the policyowner elects the cash payment dividend option, dividends will be paid to him annually, by check, as they are declared. This has the effect of reducing the cost of the insurance; but other options, particularly the dividend additions option, may be more valuable to the policyowner in the long run.

2. The Premium Reduction Option. Under the premium reduction option, the dividend is used directly to reduce the current premium. When a premium notice is sent, the company notifies the policyowner of the amount of the premium and the amount of the dividend, and the policyowner pays only the difference. Use of this option always reduces the current cost of the policyowner's insurance.

3. The Interest Option. Under the interest option, the dividends are left with the company to accumulate at interest. This option operates in very much the same way as a deposit in a savings account in a bank, except that the company, not the policyowner, makes the "deposit" with itself, to the policyowner's credit. A minimum rate of interest is guaranteed, and if a higher rate is earned, it will be credited to the "deposit." Each year the new dividend is added to the policyowner's account, together with interest to date on the old amount, and the policyowner is sent a notice, stating the amount of the current dividend, interest earned, and the new total on deposit.

At any time while dividends are thus being accumulated at interest, the policyowner may withdraw the accumulated fund, in whole or in part. Otherwise, the accumulated total, whatever it is, will be added to and made a part of the settlement at the death of the insured, at the surrender of the contract, or at the maturity of any endowment. In other words, whenever final settlement is made under the policy, any accumulated dividends, plus interest, are paid.

4. The Dividend Additions Option. Under the dividend additions option, the policyowner may use each dividend as a net single premium to purchase additional life insurance on a paid-up basis and on the same plan as the basic policy. Even though the amount of additional insurance thus purchased may be relatively small in any given year, the policyowner who uses this option over a long period of years may add a substantial amount of insurance to his basic policy. As an example, under the current dividend scale of one life insurance company, a young man age 22, with a $10,000 continuous-premium, whole life insurance contract, might almost double the amount of insurance in force under his policy by age 65, if he applies all dividends under this option.

The dividend additions option is particularly valuable to the insured who has become uninsurable, since it makes available something he cannot obtain in any other way—additional life insurance. Moreover, the additional insurance is purchased at net premium rates, which make no allowance for the company's operating expenses. The paid-up additions also have cash values, so they can be surrendered for cash separately at any future time, without affecting the basic insurance. As a matter of practical usefulness, therefore, this option is often better than the interest option (since the interest earnings—not the dividends, but the interest on the dividends—under that option are subject to income tax). In any situation where added paid-up insurance is needed, election of the dividend additions option is appropriate.

The One-Year Term Dividend Option

A fairly recent innovation in the use of dividends is what is sometimes called the "fifth" (or term insurance) dividend option. This option, offered by a number of life insurers, permits the dividend to be used to purchase additional insurance on a one-year term insurance basis (as contrasted with paid-up insurance on the same plan as the policy, which is provided by the usual dividend additions option). The one-year term insurance is payable (in addition to the face amount of the policy) if the insured dies during the year following this application of the dividend.

Under this option, the additional insurance always terminates at the end of the policy year; and some policies provide that it will terminate at the end of the grace period of any unpaid premium falling due before the end of the year. Under other policies, the term insurance is permitted to continue to the end of the year, even though the policy itself may lapse earlier for nonpayment of premium. A few policies provide a conversion privilege under this option, so that the term insurance may be converted to insurance on the same plan as the policy itself.

Although some companies permit the purchase of as much one-year term insurance as the dividend will purchase as a single premium, under most companies' policies the amount of one-year term insurance that can be purchased is limited to the cash value of the policy. In some instances, the limitation may be expressed in the form of a percentage, such as 25 percent, of the face amount of the contract. Any portion of the annual dividend not used to provide the amount of term insurance elected (up to the specified maximum) will be paid in cash or applied under one of the other dividend options, as elected by the policyowner.

The following table illustrates the estimated dividends per $1,000, at various ages, for an illustrative continuous-premuim, whole life policy, issued at age 25. Shown also are the cash values at these ages and the amount of one-year term insurance the dividend would purchase.

FIGURE 7–2

One-Year Term Dividend Option, Continuous-Premium, Whole Life Policy (values per $1,000 of insurance, issue age 25)

Insured's Age	Estimated Dividend	Amount of One-Year Term Insurance Dividend Would Purchase	Cash or Loan Value
30	$ 1.89	$ 658.54	$ 38.64
35	4.50	1,363.64	103.64
40	7.20	1,525.42	176.92
45	9.95	1,389.66	257.11
60	13.00	476.89	502.52
65	14.67	344.77	583.79

Since a significant amount of additional insurance may be provided under this option, antiselection is a distinct possibility if the option is elected after the date of the application for the policy. For this reason, evidence of insurability is usually required if this option is elected at any time other than when the policy is applied for.

The one-year term addition option is especially useful when a policyowner wishes to make maximum use of the policy loan privilege. As an illustration, assume that the owner of a $100,000 continuous-premium policy (with values on the same basis as those shown in Figure 7–2) wishes a maximum policy loan at age 30. This would give him a loan of approximately $3,864. His dividend would be $189, which is more than enough to purchase one-year term insurance in the amount of the loan. If the insured dies during a year in which his dividend has been applied under this option, the additional term insurance will be sufficient to offset the amount of the loan plus loan interest. Then the full face amount of the policy will be payable to the beneficiary.

If there is no limitation on the amount of one-year term insurance purchased, this option can often provide a substantial amount of additional insurance. For example, if the owner of the $100,000 policy had been permitted to use the full dividend at age 30 to purchase one-year term insurance, he could have had approximately $65,854 of additional insurance on that basis, in addition to his $100,000 of coverage. It should be kept in mind, however, that the added insurance under this option is temporary and, since it is term insurance, it has no cash value. By contrast, the paid-up additions option provides paid-up insurance, which has a cash value and will remain in effect as long as the policy does (unless it is separately surrendered).

Dividends in General

It is sometimes helpful if the dividend options are considered generally, in terms of what they are intended to accomplish. Viewed in this way, it is clear that the policyowner may elect to have the dividends under his policy used either to reduce his costs or to increase the benefits provided by the policy. Thus, under the cash or premium reduction options, the cost of the insurance is reduced. Under all other dividend options, the benefits payable by the company are increased.

Other Policy Provisions Relating to Dividends

Over a long period of years, the accumulation of dividends left on deposit and the cash surrender value of paid-up additions may reach a fairly large sum. Most participating policies permit the policyowner, in that case, to have these dividend credits used for either of two purposes: to pay up the policy or to mature it as an endowment.

The Paid-Up Policy Privilege. The privilege of using accumulated dividends and the cash surrender value of paid-up additions as a net single premium to pay up the policy is made available in a policy provision reading substantially as follows:

Fully Paid-Up Policy Privilege. This policy will be made fully paid up by application of outstanding dividend credits as of any premium due date on which the tabular cash value of the policy, determined in accordance with the table of cash, loan and nonforfeiture values, together with such dividend credits equals or exceeds the net single premium (calculated on the same basis as the premium for this policy) at the insured's attained age, last birthday, for such fully paid-up, participating policy, if the owner so requests in writing within 31 days of such premium due date.

Assume that at some future date the net single premium for a fully paid-up policy of $10,000 at the insured's attained age is $2,600, and the total dividend credits (accumulated dividends and the cash value of any paid-up additions), plus the cash value of the policy, equal or exceed $2,600. In that case, the insurer will, on request, endorse the policy as fully paid up, and no more premiums will be payable under it. Of course, the dividend accumulations and paid-up additions so used will be cancelled (although future dividends may continue to be paid.)

The Endowment Privilege. The endowment privilege is comparable to the paid-up privilege except that it relates to an amount payable to the owner instead of the beneficiary. Under this provision, when the dividend credits (the total of accumulated dividends and the cash value of any paid-up additions) reach an amount which is sufficient, if added to the cash value of the policy, to equal the face amount of the policy, the owner may, on request, have this amount paid to him as an endowment. This settlement may be made in a lump sum or under one of the optional methods of settlement, as the policyowner may prefer. A typical policy provision follows:

Endowment Privilege. This policy will be matured as an endowment, payable to the owner, by application of outstanding dividend credits if the owner so requests in writing, when its tabular cash value together with such dividend credits equals or exceeds the face amount of the policy.

These paid-up policy and endowment privileges differ from the dividend options in a very basic sense. The dividend options concern the application of individual dividends as they become payable. The paid-up policy and endowment privileges concern the use of dividends that have been left with the company to accumulate at interest over many years, and those that have been used to purchase paid-up additions. Usually, therefore, they are referred to as "privileges" rather than "options."

■ THE NONFORFEITURE BENEFITS

If the Policy Lapses

A policy is generally said to lapse if a premium remains unpaid at the end of the grace period, and this is the sense in which the word is used in this text. However, the word "lapse" may be used to mean different things. Its exact meaning in any specific instance, therefore, will depend upon the context in which it is used. Sometimes a policy is said to lapse when a premium remains unpaid, only if no nonforfeiture benefits are provided by the policy (as, for example, a term policy), or if a cash value policy has not been in force long enough to have developed nonforfeiture values.

Sometimes, if a premium remains unpaid at the end of the grace period, a policy which has developed a cash value is said to have lapsed "except as to any nonforfeiture benefits that may apply." This reflects the fact that any whole life or endowment contract that has been in force for more than a few years will have developed some cash value. If a premium under a policy of this kind is not paid when due or within the grace period, a premium loan will be established if the policyowner has so elected (and if there is sufficient cash value); otherwise, one of the nonforfeiture benefits will go into effect automatically.

There are three nonforfeiture benefits: A cash surrender benefit, a reduced paid-up insurance benefit, and an extended term insurance benefit. The Standard Nonforfeiture Law requires the cash surrender benefit and at least one of the other two benefits to be included in every whole life and endowment policy, as well as in level term contracts for periods longer than 15 years. Most companies include all three benefits—often called options—in all such policies unless they are issued on a rated basis. (In that event, only one option in addition to cash surrender may be provided.)

The Cash Surrender Benefit

The Standard Nonforfeiture Provisions Law specifies a formula for determining minimum cash values for life insurance contracts. Insurers are free to provide higher values, if they wish, and ordinarily they do so. This discussion will present a general overview of the benefits provided.

The purpose of the cash surrender benefit, in general terms, is to return to the withdrawing policyowner a share of the values his premium payments have helped to accumulate. These values, it will be recalled, result from the level-premium system. Under this system, portions of the premiums received in early policy years are invested and held until later years when the level premium alone is not adequate to pay current claims. If a policyowner withdraws from the insured group, therefore, the values attributable to his policy will no longer be needed, since no death benefit will be payable.

The exact amount of cash value that can equitably be paid to a withdrawing policyowner will depend upon company philosophy, and may vary among different plans in the same company. It will not be less than the minimum cash value required by law, but how much more is a matter of company judgment, based on the experience of the company.

The values of each of the nonforfeiture benefits of the policy in each of the first 20 years after issue must be shown in the policy. It is customary to show these values in a table such as the following:

Table of Values—(for each $1,000 of insurance) Whole Life Policy—Issue Age 35

End of Policy Year	Cash or Loan Value	Extended Term Insurance Years	Extended Term Insurance Days	Paid-Up Insurance
1	$ .00	0	0	$ 0
2	15.26	3	328	40
3	30.84	6	280	79
4	46.71	8	341	117
5	62.87	10	212	153
6	79.29	11	314	188
7	95.97	12	314	223
8	112.92	13	236	256
9	130.11	14	96	287
10	147.55	14	270	318
11	165.23	15	37	348
12	183.11	15	132	377
13	201.20	15	199	405
14	219.45	15	240	432
15	237.86	15	260	457
16	256.41	15	260	482
17	275.07	15	242	506
18	293.84	15	210	530
19	312.69	15	164	552
20	331.60	15	107	573
Age 60	426.25	14	81	669
Age 65	518.52	12	325	746

Tables of this kind enable the policyowner to know, in any given policy year, exactly what his contract would be worth on surrender for cash, and what it will be worth in future years if he continues to pay the premiums as they fall due.

The Standard Nonforfeiture Law requires the insurer to include a provision in the life insurance policy reserving the right to defer the payment of any cash surrender value, just as it must reserve the right to defer the making of a policy loan (except for the payment of premiums), for a period of six months after request is received. As is true of the policy loan deferment, this is purely a precautionary measure and would be invoked only in periods of serious financial stress.

Reduced Paid-up Insurance

If the policyowner does not want to continue paying premiums but nevertheless wishes to continue his insurance for the period and on the plan originally provided by the policy, he may elect the reduced paid-up insurance option. If he does this, the cash value of his policy will be used as a net single premium to provide insurance on the same plan as the policy itself, for as large an amount as the cash value will purchase, and no further premiums will be payable. The operation and effect of this nonforfeiture option are most clearly illustrated if two examples are used.

Under a Whole Life Policy. The owner of a continuous-premium, whole life policy who elects the reduced paid-up insurance option will have the insurance under his policy extended for the rest of his life. However, the insurance will be reduced to the amount that the cash surrender value, applied as a net single premium, will purchase at the insured's attained age when the option becomes effective. For example, under the whole life policy illustrated in the previous table, issued at age 35, a cash surrender value of $331.60 per $1,000 of face amount is available at the end of 20 years. This will purchase $573 of paid-up, whole life insurance at age 55, for each $1,000 of insurance. Under a $10,000 policy, therefore, the policyowner who was 35 years of age when the policy was issued could cease paying premiums at age 55, elect the reduced paid-up option, and have a $5,730 paid-up whole life policy.

Under an Endowment Policy. The owner of an endowment life insurance policy who elects the reduced paid-up option will have a reduced paid-up endowment contract. In this case, the amount of the paid-up endowment life insurance will be the amount the cash surrender value will purchase as a net single premium at the insured's attained age. Under one company's 20-year endowment contract, issued at age 35, if premiums have been paid for 10 years, $415 in cash value will be available for each $1,000 of the face amount of the policy. This will purchase $525 of paid-up endowment life insurance per $1,000 for the remaining 10 years. A $10,000 endowment policy would then have a cash value of $4,150, which would buy a 10-year paid-up endowment policy of $5,250.

In short, if the policyowner elects the paid-up insurance option, he will have the same plan of insurance he had before, except that the applicable amounts will be smaller and no further premiums will be payable. Quite literally, the insurance is both "reduced" and "paid-up."

Extended Term Insurance

If the policyowner prefers, he may elect the extended term insurance option. Under this option, the cash surrender value of a whole life contract is also used as a net single premium, but in this case it is used to purchase term insurance in the amount of the death benefit then payable under the policy, for as long a period as the single premium will provide, or for the term of the policy, if shorter.

To illustrate, under the whole life policy referred to in the table on page 145, the cash surrender value available at the end of 20 years is $331.60 for each $1,000. This will extend the death benefit provided by the policy, on a term insurance basis, for 15 years and 107 days. If this insured stopped paying premiums at age 55 and this option became effective, his insurance would continue in force in the full face amount until he was past age 70.

This option has the advantage of continuing the same amount of insurance that was effective on the date of lapse (by contrast with the reduced amount available under the reduced paid-up option). However, it is continued in effect for a limited period only. This period is determined by the amount of cash surrender value available, or the term of the contract, if it is not a whole life contract. For instance, if it is a 20-year endowment policy, the extended insurance will not continue beyond the expiration date of the original contract.

A modification is necessary when a policy loan is in effect at the time the extended term option becomes effective. Since the loan is actually an advance, it must be subtracted from the cash value, and this reduces the cash value available for application under this option. It is standard practice today, also, to reduce the face amount of the insurance by the amount of the loan and to purchase term insurance in the reduced amount for as long as the reduced cash value will permit. This is sometimes erroneously criticized as deducting the policy loan twice.

Actually, once the loan has been deducted from the cash value, the loan has been paid, and no further reduction in values is made. The only question is whether the face amount of the insurance will be purchased for a given length of time (determined by the cash value) or the face amount less the amount of the policy loan will be purchased for a longer period. But note the inequity that will result if the existence of the loan is ignored in establishing the amount of the term insurance to be provided: If a $20,000 policy lapses while a $5,000 loan is in effect, and if the policy is extended in the full face amount for as long as the reduced cash value will permit, the death of the insured soon after lapse would result in a larger death benefit being paid than if he had died while the policy was being continued on a premium-paying basis. This inequity is remedied by extending only the amount of the death benefit that would have been payable immediately prior to lapse. Since that is a smaller amount than the original amount of insurance, it can be extended for a longer period of time.

The operation of the extended term option with respect to endowment contracts presents a special situation. Here, the cash surrender value is also applied as a net single premium to purchase extended term life insurance in the amount of the insurance then payable under the policy. Because of the high cash values of endowment policies, however, the cash surrender value will frequently be more than enough to purchase term insurance for the remainder of the term of the policy.

For example, under one 20-year endowment contract issued at age 35, the cash value at the end of 10 years will be $415 per $1,000. This is more than enough to provide $1,000 of term life insurance for the remaining 10 years if the policy lapses. Since the contract will terminate 20 years from the issue date (and 10 years from the date of lapse), the amount needed to provide ten years of term insurance is deducted from the $415 cash value and the remainder of the cash value is used to purchase a pure endowment [2] of $457. This will be payable if the insured is living on the maturity date. Thus, under this option, the contract will pay $1,000 per $1,000 amount of en-

---

[2] A pure endowment, it will be recalled, is a sum of money that is payable if the policyowner is living on a specified date in the future.

dowment coverage if the insured dies before the maturity date, or it will pay a pure endowment of $457 per $1,000 if the insured is living on that date. This is why the extended term column in an endowment life insurance policy shows both a period of time and a dollar amount in the later years. In the above illustration, it would show for its tenth year—"10 years/$457."

The Automatic Option

Under most policies, the extended term insurance option is the automatic nonforfeiture option. It will go into effect automatically when the policy lapses, if the policyowner does not elect another option. This gives the maximum amount of protection for a limited period and has the advantage, from the company's point of view, of avoiding small amounts of paid-up insurance, which may remain on the records of the company almost indefinitely. Under policies issued on a rated basis, however, it is customary to provide that reduced paid-up insurance shall be the automatic option and, in practice, many companies do not even include the extended term insurance option in substandard policies.

Continued Privilege of Cash Surrender

The Standard Nonforfeiture Law requires that, under the reduced paid-up option, the policy must still provide a cash surrender value. As a matter of company practice, however, it is customary to provide a cash surrender benefit during any period in which the policy is continued under either the reduced paid-up or extended term insurance option.

■ NOTES ON CANADIAN PRACTICES

Premiums

The Uniform Life Insurance Act of Canada contains several provisions relating specifically to the payment of premiums under a life insurance policy. First, it provides that, except in the case of group insurance, an assignee, a beneficiary, or anyone acting on behalf of any of them, may, as a matter of right, pay any premium that the insured might pay. (This is not statutory law in the United States, but United States companies do not usually refuse to accept payments that are made by persons other than the policyowner. In such instances, the payment is considered a gift to the policyowner.)

The Uniform Act also provides that if a premium is paid by check or any other written promise to pay, and if the check or other written promise is not itself paid according to its terms, the premium will be considered not to have been paid. (This is general contract law in the United States, but it is not specifically written into the insurance law.)

The Act also provides a grace period of 30 days—or the number of days provided in the policy—for the payment of a premium. If the insured dies during the grace period, the contract remains in force, but the premium will be deducted from the death benefit. This law, therefore, has the same legal effect as the requirement in the United States that the policy contain a grace period provision. In Canada, however, the law itself provides a period of grace whether such a provision is included in the policy or not. According to the Uniform Life Insurance Act, if a premium is sent by registered letter and is received by the insurer, payment shall be considered to have been made at the time the letter was registered.

The Quebec Insurance Law provides for a grace period of 30 days for payment of premiums, during which the policy remains in force. This act also gives the beneficiary the right to pay premiums.

Nonforfeiture Benefits

In Canada there are no statutory requirements for the inclusion in the policy of surrender values, policy loan provisions, or nonforfeiture options, as is the case in the United States. However, under the Uniform Life Insurance Act, the insured has the right to reinstate his policy; and the policy must set forth any particulars concerning reinstatement, and the options, if any, for surrender, loans, and paid-up or extended insurance. In general, the nonforfeiture practices in Canada are quite similar to those required by law in the United States. However, the usual automatic provision which is effective on default in premium payment is the automatic premium loan.

■ QUESTIONS FOR REVIEW

1. In terms of legal significance, how does payment of the initial premium for a life insurance contract differ from payment of renewal premiums as they fall due?

2. Explain the effect and significance of the following provisions as they concern the payment of life insurance premiums: (1) the grace period; (2) the automatic premium loan; and (3) the waiver of premium for disability.
3. Explain whether each of the following policies would include a policy loan provision: (1) A continuous-premium, whole life policy; (2) a 10-year endowment policy; (3) a 10-year convertible term policy.
4. How is an unpaid policy loan treated in each of the following situations?
   a) When a death claim is settled.
   b) When a policy is surrendered for cash.
   c) When a policy lapses for nonpayment of a premium and the extended term insurance nonforfeiture option becomes effective.
5. List the four dividend options that are usually provided in a participating life insurance policy.
6. How does the one-year term dividend option differ from the paid-up additions option?
7. List and describe three nonforfeiture options.
8. Assume that a $10,000 continuous-premium, whole life policy lapses for nonpayment of a premium and the policy is continued under one of the nonforfeiture options. The insured dies a short while later. If the death benefit is $10,000, which of the nonforfeiture options became effective?
9. Summarize the operation of the extended term insurance option under an endowment policy as compared with its operation under a whole life policy for the same face amount.

8 OTHER OWNERSHIP RIGHTS

Any cash value life insurance contract sooner or later has a value to the owner that does not depend upon the contingency of death. In this respect, contracts of whole life or endowment insurance bear a strong resemblance to noninsurance documents such as bonds and certificates of stock. These documents have no real value in themselves, but they serve as evidence of property rights that are sometimes highly valuable. Documents of this kind are referred to as "intangible personal property," and the life insurance contract may be so classified. This chapter will discuss some of the ways the life insurance contract can be used as property.

■ THE LIFE INSURANCE CONTRACT AS PROPERTY

It is customary today to include in a life insurance contract a provision specifically defining the rights of the policyowner. The following provision is illustrative:

Ownership. Every right, benefit, and privilege available under this policy while the insured is living is vested in the owner and may be exercised without the consent of any revocable beneficiary. However, all rights of the owner are subject to the rights of any assignee of record and of any irrevocable beneficiary.

Some life insurance contracts describe the policyowner's rights in detail. Others only touch upon those rights briefly and in general terms. In every instance, however, the rights granted under the policy are exercisable by the policyowner. The policyowner may also exercise some rights that are not expressly granted by the contract and that are available to him simply because he is the owner of the contract. Among these rights are the rights to sell or give away his property—in this instance, the life insurance contract.

Under present-day life insurance contracts, a policyowner may usually transfer ownership of his policy—give it away or sell it—in either of two ways. He may transfer ownership by assigning the policy or he may transfer it by complying with the requirements set forth in a transfer-of-ownership provision in the policy. Assignment is the traditional way to transfer ownership of a life insurance contract, however, and for that reason will be discussed first.

■ ASSIGNMENTS

The right of an owner of property to sell or give away his ownership rights is basic. No one questions a person's right to sell his house, his car, or any other article of tangible property. Equally accepted is his right to give these articles away if he wishes. In the case of intangible personal property, however, the situation is not so clearly understood. Here the owner is transferring rights instead of things, but the basic principles are the same.

The customary way to transfer rights in intangible personal property is to execute an assignment. The person who transfers such rights—that is, the owner—is called the "assignor." The person to whom the rights are transferred is called the "assignee." If misunderstandings and possible conflicts are to be avoided, an assignment should be in writing, although this is not a legal requirement. An assignment should state the rights transferred, the person to whom they are transferred, the purpose and extent of the transfer, and should include any other explanatory data that might be of help in clarifying the transaction.

Life insurance contracts are generally considered to be freely assignable unless they contain a specific provision to the contrary. For this reason, ordinary life insurance contracts do not usually contain a provision stating that the owner may assign the policy. There is no need for such a provision. The privilege of assignment is inherent in the meaning of ownership of intangible personal property. Therefore, the customary policy provision concerning assignment declares the company's position with respect to any assignment the policyowner may make and explains the effect of an assignment. The following provision is illustrative:

Assignment. The company assumes no responsibility for the validity or effect of any assignment of this policy, and no assignment will be recognized until it has been duly filed with the company. An assignment of this policy shall operate to the extent thereof to transfer to the assignee the interest of any beneficiary whom the assignor has the right to change. Any amount payable to the assignee shall be payable in one sum, notwithstanding any settlement agreement in effect at the time the assignment was executed.

This provision neither grants nor restricts the right to assign the policy. It is assumed that the policy is assignable and that the owner may exercise this right if he wishes. The insurer knows, however, that particular assignments are often ineffective, for one reason or another, to accomplish the purpose the policyowner may have had in mind. Some assignments are poorly drafted and others fail to comply with essential legal requirements. The company has no part in drafting the assignment and therefore assumes no responsibility if the assignment is not valid or if it accomplishes something that the policyowner did not contemplate.

The life insurance company cannot give effect to any assignment if it does not know of the assignment's existence. Therefore, the policy requires that a copy of any assignment must be filed with the company before it will be recognized.

Finally, to clarify the rights of the beneficiary if the policy has been assigned, this provision specifically states that an assignment will transfer to the assignee, to the extent of the assignment, the interest of any revocable beneficiary. Thus, if a $10,000 policy is assigned to secure repayment of a $3,000 debt, that portion ($3,000) of the interest of the beneficiary is transferred to the assignee. In this situation, if the insured should die while the assignment is still in effect, the assignee would receive $3,000 of the proceeds and the beneficiary would receive the remainder.

The Absolute Assignment

If the policyowner transfers all his rights under the policy to another person, unconditionally, the assignment is said to be absolute. For example, suppose Ray Egbert and George West have been partners in an advertising business for several years, and each owns an insurance policy on the life of the other. Now they decide to dissolve their partnership and settle their accounts. Since neither will have further need for the policy he owns on the life of the other, the men decide that each will convey the policy he owns to the other so that, in each case, the insured will own his own policy. To accomplish this, they use absolute assignments, and each assigns the policy he owns to the other (the insured).

Or, let us say Kate Johnson purchased an insurance policy on the life of her grandson when he was two years old. Now she wishes to give the policy to the child's parents as a gift. Here, too, the absolute assignment would be used to transfer all of her ownership rights in the policy, unconditionally, to the parents of her grandson.

When all ownership rights under a life insurance contract are unconditionally assigned in exchange for money or other property (that is, for consideration), the transaction is a sale. When an absolute assignment is made without consideration, it is a gift. In either case, when the absolute assignment has been completed, the assignee will have the power to exercise all ownership rights previously exercisable by the assignor (the former owner).

The Collateral Assignment

Because of the values represented by the life insurance contract, it is an excellent kind of property to use as collateral security in case the owner wishes to borrow money. For example, suppose Gary Cook owns an insurance policy on his life, with a face amount of $10,000. It has a cash surrender value of $5,800. He wishes to borrow $5,000 from the First National Bank and since the policy is worth more than that even during his lifetime, the bank is willing to accept an assignment of the policy as collateral security for the loan.

Assignments made for purposes of this kind are called collateral assignments, and the policy is said to be collaterally assigned. In such situations, an absolute assignment is not appropriate. The creditor needs only to be protected against loss if the borrower fails to pay. Thus the assignee (creditor) needs to be granted enough rights to assure that he can recover the unpaid balance of the loan out of the death benefit, if the loan has not been repaid at the death of the insured. He should also have the right to recover the unpaid balance of the loan out of the cash surrender value of the policy, if payments are not made as they become due during the insured's lifetime. Although no particular wording is required for a collateral assignment, the assignee is usually given one or both of these rights (but by no means all of the ownership rights).

Usually a collateral assignment is made with the specific provision that if the amount borrowed is repaid, the assigned rights will revert (return) to the policyowner, and the assignment will no longer be effective. In that case, the policyowner will request that the assignee "release" the assignment—that is, complete and sign a statement that he no longer claims any rights under the policy. However, this is only a formality, to make it clear that the assignment is no longer in effect.

The American Bankers Assignment Form No. 10. Collateral assignments are difficult to define or discuss specifically because many lending institutions have their own forms, and no particular pattern is followed. However, the American Bankers Association has developed a standard form of collateral assignment called the American Bankers Assignment Form No. 10 (ABA Form No. 10), which is used by many banks and other lending institutions when life insurance contracts are assigned to them as security for loans. Under this ABA form, the following rights are expressly granted to the assignee:

1. The right to collect the net proceeds of the policy if it becomes a claim by death or maturity
2. The right to surrender the policy for cash
3. The right to obtain a loan either from the insurance company or from another lender, using the policy as security
4. The right to receive all dividends and to exercise all dividend options
5. The right to exercise all nonforfeiture options and receive all benefits.

These rights are subject to limitations. For instance, the assignee agrees not to surrender the policy for cash unless there has been a default in repayment of the loan or failure to pay a premium when due. Even then, he must give the policyowner a 20-day notice before he can exercise the right to surrender the policy.

The ABA form also limits the rights of the creditor with respect to the proceeds of the policy if the insured dies before the loan has been repaid. In that situation, the creditor may collect the total insurance proceeds, but any amount in excess of the loan must be paid to the person or persons who would have been entitled to it if the assignment had not been executed.

The following rights are not assigned under the ABA form and, therefore, remain with the policyowner:

1. The right to collect any disability income benefits that may become payable under the policy
2. The right to designate and change the beneficiary
3. The right to elect an optional mode of settlement.

Because the respective rights of both the borrower and the lender (the assignor and the assignee) are adequately and equitably protected under the ABA Form 10, the form is widely used for collateral assignments.

Conflicts Under Collateral Assignments

Since a collateral assignment usually gives the assignee some rights to the benefit payable at death, the rights of assignees and those of beneficiaries have frequently conflicted. It is generally held that a collateral assignee has a right to the proceeds of the policy, to the extent of the loan, that is superior to the right of the beneficiary. However, if there is any doubt, it may be necessary to obtain a court interpretation. A number of special procedures have been used in order to avoid such questions. For example, life insurance companies sometimes advise that the beneficiary designation be revoked and the proceeds made payable to the owner's estate before a policy is assigned collaterally. This clearly terminates the beneficiary's rights under the contract. The collateral assignment is then completed and the beneficiary is redesignated, in that order. The beneficiary's rights are then definitely subordinate to the rights of the collateral assignee, since the designation of the beneficiary has been made after the assignment was completed.

One of the simplest ways of avoiding any possible conflict between the rights of the beneficiary and the rights of an assignee after the insured's death is to include in the policy a provision clarifying the legal effect of an assignment, so far as the interest of a beneficiary is concerned. This is accomplished, with respect to revocable beneficiaries, in the second sentence of the policy provision quoted on page 154.

An irrevocable beneficiary is in a different position. The interest of an irrevocable beneficiary is said to be vested, which means that the policyowner cannot change or diminish the rights of such a beneficiary unless the beneficiary consents. Since an assignment could diminish the amount to which the beneficiary would be entitled, the policyowner cannot execute an effective assignment—either collateral or absolute—without the consent of an irrevocable beneficiary.

Life insurance contracts frequently specify that the optional modes of settlement may not be elected for or by assignees, trustees, executors, etc. This restriction is thought to be justified by the fact that the optional modes of settlement were developed primarily for the benefit of dependents of the insured, who may be quite unfamiliar with business practices and the handling of money. Since most assignments, and practically all collateral assignments, are made for business purposes, most assignees are businessmen or businesses. These people would not usually request an optional settlement for proceeds payable to them unless the interest rate or other guarantees of the insurer were considerably more favorable than other comparable investment opportunities. It is felt, therefore, that making the optional modes available to assignees, trustees, or executors could open the door to a special kind of antiselection, by a class of people who do not need these special services. To avoid any question as to whether settlement will be made to an assignee under a settlement option, the provision quoted on page 154 specifically states that such settlements will be made in one sum.

■ TRANSFER OF OWNERSHIP BY ENDORSEMENT

If a life insurance contract is to be used as collateral for a loan, an assignment is the only means of handling the transaction. If a complete and unconditional transfer of rights is intended, however, most life insurance contracts today provide a more convenient way to transfer ownership than by use of an absolute assignment. Under this contractual method, the policyowner merely requests the life insurance company to endorse the policy or otherwise take the necessary action to show that ownership is in a different person. Many policies provide for this type of ownership transfer in a policy provision similar to the following:

Change of Ownership. During the lifetime of the insured the ownership of this policy may be changed, subject to the rights of any assignee of record, by written request to the company accompanied by this policy for endorsement. No change of ownership will take effect until endorsed on this policy by the company, but when such endorsement is made the change will relate back to and be deemed effective as of the date the request was signed, whether or not the insured is living at the time such endorsement is made.

Any change of ownership will be subject to any payment made or other action taken by the company before the endorsement is made. A change of ownership, of itself, shall have no effect on the interest of any beneficiary. The rights of a deceased owner shall pass to the executors, administrators, or assigns of the deceased owner unless otherwise provided.

Under a policy provision of this kind, a transfer of ownership operates in much the same way as the endorsement method of making beneficiary changes. The transfer will not be effective under the provision quoted until it has been endorsed on the policy by the company, but when that is done, the transfer takes effect as of the date the request was signed. For instance, Joseph Kerr signs a request for a transfer of ownership of his policy on September 18 and sends it and his policy to the home office of the insurance company on that day. The transfer might not be endorsed upon the policy until September 24 or 25, depending upon the sequence of work days. When the endorsement is made, however, regardless of the date, the transfer will be effective as of September 18. After that date, the successor owner will be the new owner and may exercise all the rights and privileges formerly exercisable by Kerr.

Two aspects of this provision should be especially noted. The phrase "subject to any payment made or other action taken by the company before the endorsement is made" is included to protect the company in the event that a policy loan has been granted or the cash surrender value of the policy has been paid prior to the date the request was received. The next sentence makes it clear that nothing will be changed under a transfer of ownership except the ownership of the policy. If the new owner wishes to make a beneficiary change, he must do so in accordance with the applicable policy provision.

Endorsement Method versus Assignment

Whether the policyowner transfers his ownership rights by assignment or by the endorsement method, the legal effect should be the same. Neither method is necessarily superior to the other. However, there are significant and basic differences between the two methods that should be kept in mind.

First, the assignment method of transfer is not available as a contractual right. It is a right of ownership. The policyowner may assign his policy just as he may assign a certificate of stock and many other kinds of contracts. No special form of assignment is required, and whether the document he executes will have the legal effect he intends will depend upon many factors—the law of his state and the provisions of his policy, to list only two.

By contrast, the policyowner who transfers the ownership of his policy by following the procedure set forth in the transfer-of-ownership provision of the policy can be reasonably certain that the transfer will have the legal effect he intended, since he is exercising a right that is spelled out in the contract.

A second difference is found in the degree of responsibility assumed by the life insurance company with respect to the two methods of transferring ownership. The company clearly assumes no responsibility for the legal effect of any assignment. This is reasonable, since the company has no part in the transaction and thus no opportunity to protect itself against the added expense and problems that may result if the assignment proves to be inadequate in any way.

When ownership is transferred in accordance with a policy provision, however, the company's position is different. Here the request for transfer is sent to the company. If any technicalities are not complied with, the company has the opportunity to correct the situation before the transfer is completed. If it requires the policy to be submitted for endorsement, the company also has the opportunity to review the policy as well as the request document and to assure itself that they are in order. Under these circumstances, the company cannot claim not to be responsible for the validity and effect of the completed transfer, and it does not attempt to do so.

■ CHANGE OF PLAN

After a few years, the owner of a life insurance policy may find that his circumstances have changed sufficiently that a different kind of policy would be more suitable for him. Perhaps his income has decreased, or perhaps it has increased beyond his expectations. Perhaps his family or other responsibilities have changed. In such cases, if he is insurable, he can always apply for a policy more nearly suited to his circumstances, and either surrender his present policy for cash or permit it to lapse and continue as reduced paid-up or extended term insurance. However, it may be to his advantage financially to apply the accumulated values under his present policy toward a policy on a different plan but bearing the same policy date. Most insurers permit this kind of change as a contractual right, often in a simple policy provision such as the following:

Change of Plan. The plan or amount of insurance, or both, may be changed by mutual agreement with the company.

Policies that have been in force for many years may not include a provision of this kind. However, most insurers, by company practice, will permit a change of plan on the same conditions as if the policy specifically provided for it.

A change of plan may be made either to a higher-premium policy or to a policy with a lower premium, but the applicable requirements will usually differ according to the nature of the change. A change of plan to a higher-premium policy is generally granted on request and with no other condition than an adjustment in values. Thus the policyowner may be required to pay the difference in premiums from the issue date to the present, with interest, or the difference in the reserve or cash value. However, if the policyowner wishes to change to a lower-premium policy, satisfactory evidence of insurability will usually be required, and he will receive the difference between the cash surrender values of the policy to which he is changing and the one he has had.

These differences are understandable if the respective changes are considered carefully. If the policyowner is changing to a higher-premium policy, the values under his new policy will accumulate more rapidly, and the amount at risk will, therefore, be reduced more rapidly than would have been true under the old policy. This kind of change may be granted without evidence of insurability, because there is no danger of antiselection.

On the other hand, if the change is to a lower-premium plan, there is usually an immediate increase in the amount at risk; and the amount at risk will be subsequently reduced at a slower rate than under the former policy. Under these circumstances, antiselection is a very definite possibility, and evidence of insurability is required.

■ REINSTATEMENT

Life insurance companies are required by law to include a reinstatement provision in each policy. This is a provision permitting the policyowner to restore a lapsed policy to premium-paying status by meeting certain requirements. Generally, the policyowner must apply for reinstatement within a specific period of time (usually three or five years after lapse), furnish evidence of insurability, and pay all past due premiums, with interest. The following provision is illustrative:

Reinstatement. This policy may be reinstated at any time within five years from date of lapse, if a cash surrender value has not been paid. Such reinstatement shall be subject to:

(1) Evidence of insurability, including good health, of the insured satisfactory to the company

(2) Payment of all premiums in default, with interest at the rate of 5 percent per annum

(3) Payment or reinstatement of any loan secured by this policy on the date of premium default, with interest at the rate of 5 percent per annum from that date.

If the policy has been surrendered for cash, the policyowner customarily has no contractual right thereafter to reinstate it (as is true under the quoted reinstatement provision). Companies are legally permitted to deny reinstatement also if the policy has gone on extended term insurance and the term has expired, but most companies do not include this limitation.

Under most policies, therefore, reinstatement is permitted whether the policy has lapsed without values or has been continued under the extended term insurance or reduced paid-up insurance nonforfeiture option. All that is required is that the policyowner meet the requirements of the reinstatement provision. When this has been done, the policy is restored to full premium-paying status, on the same basis as if it had never lapsed.

■ NOTES ON CANADIAN PRACTICES

Assignments

In Canada, if there is no irrevocable or preferred beneficiary (or if there is such a beneficiary and he has attained the age of majority and gives his consent), the policyowner may exercise all rights under his contract, assign it, surrender it, and otherwise deal with it in any way agreed upon with the insurer.

The Uniform Life Insurance Act specifies that a policy provision prohibiting assignments is valid. This was included in the 1962 revision of the Uniform Life Insurance Act in order to permit contracts to be qualified as retirement saving plans under the Income Tax Act.

■ QUESTIONS FOR REVIEW

1. Briefly summarize an illustrative assignment provision of a life insurance contract.

2. Describe two kinds of assignments.
3. Alice Donahue purchased a life insurance contract on the life of her son, David, when he was five years old. When he was 21, she wanted to give the policy to him as a gift, but he insisted on paying her the cash value of the contract. What kind of assignment should be used?
4. What two basic rights are usually granted to the assignee when a life insurance contract is assigned as collateral security for a loan?
5. When a policyowner executes an ABA Assignment Form No. 10, what rights under the policy does he retain?
6. How do the rights of an irrevocable beneficiary differ from those of a revocable beneficiary in any conflict created by the collateral assignment of a life insurance contract?
7. Briefly describe a transfer-of-ownership by endorsement and a transfer by absolute assignment.
8. What is the general purpose of the "change of plan" provision in a life insurance contract?
9. Under what circumstances, if any, would a life insurance company require evidence of insurability in connection with a request for a change of plan? Under what circumstances would evidence of insurability probably not be required in connection with such a change? Explain.
10. What are the usual requirements for reinstatement of a lapsed life insurance policy?

9 THE PAYMENT OF BENEFITS

The basic promise under a life insurance contract is to pay a benefit on the death of the insured. Under any endowment contract, the company promises to pay the endowment proceeds if the insured survives until the maturity date of the policy or, alternatively, to pay a death benefit if the insured dies before that time. When the life insurance company has paid the benefits promised under one of its contracts, it has carried out its responsibilities and is discharged from any further liability so far as that contract is concerned. The purpose of this chapter is to discuss the payment of life insurance benefits.

■ LIVING BENEFITS

In 1970 death benefit payments made by life insurers in the United States and Canada totaled more than $7 billion.[1] During this same period, however, more than $9.4 billion was paid in the form of benefits during the lifetimes of insureds and annuitants by United States companies, while Canadian companies paid over $800 million in such benefits.

Benefits such as these, which are paid to the policyowner himself (or at his direction) during the lifetime of the insured, are often called living benefits. This distinguishes them from death benefits and emphasizes the numerous lifetime uses of life insurance. Policy dividends, surrender values, annuity payments, payments under

---

[1] *Life Insurance Fact Book*, 1971, pp. 44, 102.

matured endowments, and disability payments all furnish evidence of the value of the life insurance contract to the policyowner himself, not just to the beneficiary following the death of the insured.

Policy loans are not generally included in published figures of living benefits, but they constitute a sizable and important privilege and thus represent a definite benefit to the policyowner. In 1970 new policy loans were made in a total of $4.1 billion. (Policy loans outstanding at the end of the year exceeded $16 billion.)

Benefits Paid to Policyowners [2] (1970)

	United States Companies	Canadian Companies
Policy dividends	$3,577,400,000	$237,000,000
Cash surrender values	2,886,400,000	271,000,000
Annuity payments	1,757,100,000	250,000,000
Matured endowments	978,300,000	74,000,000
Disability payments	232,900,000	12,000,000
Total	$9,432,100,000	$844,000,000

In order to achieve a balanced view of modern life insurance, therefore, all the living benefits provided by the policies must be considered, as well as the death benefit payments. However, only matured endowments and cash surrenders will be discussed here.

Matured Endowments

Under an endowment insurance contract, if the insured dies before the maturity date, the death benefit is usually paid in the same way as it would be paid under any other life insurance policy —to the beneficiary. If the insured is living on the maturity date, however, the endowment benefit is payable to the policyowner himself or to someone else whom he has elected.

The payment of matured endowment claims does not usually involve many problems. The company knows when the endowment will become payable; and if there is any question, it can usually be settled with the policyowner himself. When an endowment policy matures, the contestable period has passed. If the insured is living on the maturity date, therefore, and if the contract has been kept in force, the benefit is payable.

Nevertheless, there are a few special matters that should be considered in connection with the payment of matured endowment

---

[2] *Ibid.*, pp. 43, 49, and 102.

proceeds. One of these concerns the right of the person entitled to payment (the payee) to elect a settlement option. Because of special provisions of the federal income tax law in the United States, it is often possible that by electing a settlement option for endowment proceeds, the payee can effect a considerable income tax saving compared to the tax he would have to pay if he received the proceeds in one sum. In the interest of good policyowner relations, therefore, the insurance company usually notifies the payee under a matured endowment of the approaching maturity of the contract and of his optional settlement privileges in sufficient time that these tax-saving possibilities can be considered.

Another situation which sometimes requires special attention in connection with the settlement of maturing endowments arises out of the fact that many endowments are purchased to provide funds for college education expenses. Often in such cases, the payee is a minor; and unless a guardian has been appointed, special settlement arrangements may be necessary, depending on the laws relating to minority in the jurisdictions concerned.

Cash Surrenders

Many life insurance contracts are surrendered for their cash value. In fact, as shown on page 165, cash surrender values totaling more than $3 billion were paid in 1970. Usually, the only requirement is a signed request from the policyowner and the surrender of the contract.

At one time, the surrender of a life insurance contract was thought of primarily as an emergency measure. Today, however, many surrenders are made when the policyowner retires, at which time he may elect to leave the proceeds under an optional settlement to provide additional income for himself.

Policies are often surrendered solely because there is no longer any need for them. For example, whole life insurance is sometimes purchased, instead of term life insurance, for needs that the buyer knows will be temporary. The policyowner knows that he will pay a higher premium for the whole life policy while it is in force, but that at the end of the period of need, he may surrender his policy for its cash value and achieve a lower net cash outlay for his protection than he would have had under a term life insurance contract.

Cash surrenders, therefore, do not necessarily mean that life insurance protection is being sacrificed. On the contrary, in many cases they mean that the insurance is being utilized wisely, in ways that best serve the needs of the insured and his beneficiaries.

■ DEATH BENEFITS

The processing of death claims is the final step in the story of the life insurance contract; and the insurance company makes every effort to carry out the terms of its contracts with as little delay as possible. This means paying the correct amount to the correct beneficiaries, in accordance with the expressed wishes of the policy-owner, and paying nothing if there is no liability on the company's part—for example, if the policy was not in force at the date of death.

The Policy Provisions

Most life insurance policies provide for the payment of the death benefit in a very simple statement on the face page of the policy. The following is illustrative:

The Ajax Life Insurance Company agrees to pay on receipt of due proof of the death of the insured the amount of insurance as a death benefit to the beneficiary.

Two other policy provisions are also of major importance in connection with the payment of death claims: the beneficiary designation and the settlement option election, if any. Before these provisions become significant, however, the liability of the company must be established.

The Liability of the Company

The most basic question to be answered when a death claim is received is to determine whether the policy was or was not in force on the date of death. If it was in force, the next question is whether the contingency insured against—that is, the death of the insured—has actually occurred. If the policy was in force and the insured is dead, then the next question is whether the cause of death was an excluded risk, such as suicide within the suicide exclusion period, usually the first two policy years.

Was the Policy in Force? In most instances, there will be no question but that a life insurance contract was in force on the date of death of the insured if premiums had been paid to and including the date of death or if the policy was "paid up." When a life insurance company is notified of an insured's death, the policy records are immediately searched to determine how many policies have been issued on the life of the deceased person and the status of each policy on the date of his death. Such policies will usually fall into one or more of the following groups: those that had lapsed without nonforfeiture values or on which the nonforfeiture benefits had expired prior to the date of death; those that had lapsed but were being continued under one of the nonforfeiture options; and those that were in force on a premium-paying or fully paid-up basis, at the date of death.

If the only policies the company has issued on this life have expired, a letter explaining this will be directed to the person who submitted the notice of death. However, if any policy was in force on any basis—under a nonforfeiture option, on a premium-paying basis, or on a fully paid-up basis—claim forms will be furnished.

Has the Contingency Happened? For the usual death claim, a certified copy of the death certificate or a physician's statement certifying to the death of the insured will be sufficient to constitute "due proof" of the death of the insured. If there is any question about the fact of death, the insurer will make a thorough investigation and take whatever steps are necessary or appropriate to ascertain the truth. One of the most difficult situations in this respect arises out of the unexplained disappearance of the insured.

Unexplained Absence. What to do about the property and personal affairs of someone who disappears and is never heard from again has presented a legal problem for many years. As a result, a basic rule of law has been developed, as a presumption, to help resolve it. A presumption is a legal device that is used in situations in which facts cannot definitely be established. The general presumption in the case of disappearance is that a person who has been continuously missing from his home for seven years will be presumed to be dead if: (1) there is no reasonable explanation for the disappearance, (2) the persons most likely to have heard from him have heard nothing, and (3) he cannot be located by reasonable methods.

Each of these three requirements is important. Thus, if there is some logical explanation for the absence—for example, if there have been domestic difficulties, or if the person was in trouble with the law—the presumption of death will not be effective. The fact that a man who was wanted by the police disappears is not in any sense an "unexplained absence." Also, persons with whom the missing individual would have been likely to communicate must have had no word from him during the seven-year period; and a serious attempt must have been made to locate him.

Applied to life insurance claims, this means that if the insured disappears under the circumstances necessary to satisfy the presumption, he will be considered to be dead at the end of seven years. However, there is no presumption of death prior to that time. The policy must be kept in force, therefore, by premium payments or under a nonforfeiture option, for the entire seven years if the death benefit is to be payable at the end of that time. After the expiration of that period, if no relatives or friends have heard from the insured, and if he cannot be located after diligent search, the presumption of death may be invoked and the claim settled on that basis.

Even after the expiration of seven years, the insurer cannot pay the proceeds to the beneficiary without some risk. If the insured should later reappear, there is usually nothing to prevent his reinstating the contract if the reinstatement period has not elapsed. In that case, the company might be required to pay the proceeds a second time, on his later death.

The company is legally entitled to recover the proceeds, if settlement has been made and the insured reappears; but if the beneficiary has spent the money, this right may be of little value. Companies usually will not pay a claim for any very large sum of money in situations of this kind, therefore, unless the evidence is clear and convincing or the question of death is decided in a court of law.

The Risks Not Assumed

Even if the policy is in force and there is no question as to the fact of death, there is a possibility that the claim may not be payable because of the nature of the death—that is, the cause of death may be a risk not assumed under the policy. This is much more likely to be true of the accidental death benefit (which will be discussed later) than of the life insurance coverage itself; but even under the basic life insurance policy, death as the result of war may be excluded, as may death resulting from certain aviation activities. (In such cases—that is, if death is the result of war or aviation—the sum payable is customarily defined as an amount equal to the reserve or to the premiums paid, whichever is the larger.) The most common risk not assumed under a life insurance policy is suicide within the suicide exclusion period.

The Suicide Clause

Most individual life insurance contracts include a provision limiting the liability of the company to the amount of premiums paid, in the event of the insured's death by suicide in the early policy years. A typical suicide clause reads as follows:

If, within two years from the date of issue, the insured shall die by suicide, whether sane or insane, the amount payable by the company shall be the premiums paid.

Not an Insurable Risk. One of the basic requirements of an insurable risk, it will be recalled, is that the event insured against must be "fortuitous"—that is, it must be unexpected and not deliberately brought about by the insured himself. If the event insured against is deliberately caused by the insured, there is no uncertainty; in fact, the result is about as certain as the insured can make it. In life insurance, this requirement is clearly violated if the company does not exclude the risk of suicide. Nevertheless, there are strong arguments against such an exclusion because of the special nature of the life insurance coverage.

Basically, life insurance is purchased to provide funds for the dependents of the insured after his death. Although suicide is not an insurable risk in the technical sense of the term, it nevertheless occasions the same loss to the family of the insured as if he had died from any other cause. For this reason, it presents a difficult problem so far as the life insurance contract is concerned. On the one hand, it would be inequitable to permit a man to benefit his family by procuring life insurance with the specific intention of paying a premium or two and then taking his own life. It would also be against public policy to lend any financial encouragement to persons with suicidal tendencies. On the other hand, the basic purpose of life insurance is defeated if the proceeds of a policy of life insurance are denied to beneficiaries who are innocent of wrongdoing and for whose benefit the insurance was purchased in the first place.

The suicide provision is intended to resolve this conflict. This provision is usually included in a life insurance policy, although it is not required by law. Briefly, it provides that, if the insured dies by suicide during a specified period following the effective date of the policy, a death benefit equal to the premiums paid is provided, and there is no further liability on the part of the insurer. The usual suicide exclusion period is two years, although some companies have a one-year period. After the expiration of this period, the exclusion is no longer effective. If the insured takes his own life later, the claim is treated no differently from any other death claim.

It is believed that establishing a period of this kind is sufficient to guard against the occasional situation in which a person might apply for life insurance with the deliberate intention of taking his own life. Any claim that arises after the expiration of the suicide period is paid on the same basis as if the insured had died of natural causes, and the basic purpose of the insurance is thus carried out.

Determining that the death of the insured resulted from suicide often presents a problem. Circumstances suggesting suicide frequently reveal a different situation on further investigation. For instance, murder is sometimes planned to appear as suicide, and accidents are frequently difficult to distinguish from deliberate acts of the insured. On the other hand, situations that do not seem suspicious at first may, on thorough investigation, be disclosed as suicides. When a life insurance company denies a death claim on grounds of suicide, however, it must have sufficient evidence to convince a jury, if necessary, that the insured took his own life and intended to do so. In legal terms, the life insurance company is said to "have the burden of proof," if suicide is used as the reason for denying the payment of a claim. This means that the life insurance company must prove that the insured intentionally took his own life. It is not the responsibility of the beneficiary to prove that he did not do so.

The Accidental Death Benefit

Many life insurance contracts are issued with a section providing an additional benefit in the event the insured's death is accidental or is caused by "accidental means." In such cases, additional proof may be required to establish that the death was accidental (or caused by accidental means). It is the responsibility of the beneficiary to furnish such proof. Here, too, some risks are excluded. Foremost among them, of course, is death by suicide—that is, intentional, self-inflicted injury—but in the accidental death section exclusion, there is no two-year limit. That is, the accidental death benefit is never payable if it can be proved that the insured took his own life intentionally.

Some of the other risks commonly not assumed under this accidental death benefit are death as the result of riot or insurrection;

death resulting from the inhalation of gas; death resulting from aviation, except as a fare-paying passenger on a regularly scheduled flight; and death resulting from the commission of a felony. Questions frequently arise as to whether a given set of circumstances falls within any of these exclusions, and legal advice is frequently required.

■ CONTESTABLE CLAIMS

The great majority of life insurance claims are paid promptly, as soon as claim proofs have been submitted. Nevertheless, if there is clear and convincing evidence that the claim is not valid, it will be denied.

Claims may be denied for any of several reasons—if the policy was not in force on the date of death, if the death of the insured resulted from suicide during the suicide period, if the death resulted from participation in aviation and the policy included an aviation exclusion, or if there was material misrepresentation or fraud in the application. An application is said to contain a material misrepresentation if misinformation is included and the insurance company would have taken different risk appraisal action if it had known the truth. Because of the incontestable clause, however, denials based on material misrepresentation or fraud cannot be made after the expiration of a period of one or two years after the issue date of the policy.

The Incontestable Clause

The incontestable clause, required by law to be included in a policy of life insurance, usually reads somewhat as follows:

This policy shall be incontestable after it has been in force during the lifetime of the insured, for a period of two years from the earlier of the policy date or the issue date, except for nonpayment of premiums.

The company may resist a claim because of material misrepresentation or fraud in the application, but the incontestable clause of the policy restricts this privilege to a short period following the issuance of the policy. In most instances, this "contestable" period is two years, although some insurers use a one-year period. After the policy has been in force for this specified period, it becomes incontestable. Thereafter, even fraud in the application usually cannot be used as a basis for denial of a claim (although by contrast, fraud may be used as a basis for claim denial in Canada at any time).

In this connection, a clear distinction should be made between denial of a claim because of fraud or material misrepresentation in the application and denial because the cause of death was a risk not assumed under the contract. When a claim is denied because of fraud or material misrepresentation, the contract is rescinded as a matter of law. When the cause of death is an excluded risk, denial of the claim carries out the terms of the contract; the validity of the contract is not questioned. Thus the only claim denials that are affected by the incontestable clause are those based on fraud or material misrepresentation. Claims cannot be denied on these bases after the end of the contestable period. By contrast, claims may be denied at any time if the cause of death is excluded by the terms of the contract.

Claims that arise during the contestable period are routinely reviewed for evidence of material misrepresentation or fraud. If such evidence is found, the claim and legal departments of the company will consider the advisability of contesting the claim. Occasionally, material misrepresentation seems to be indicated, but on additional investigation, it cannot be supported. Assume, for example, that a claim is based on the death of an insured age 28. The cause of death is leukemia, and the application, submitted only a few months before his death, represented him to be in sound health, with no significant medical history. On the surface, this might suggest material misrepresentation. Suppose, however, that investigation discloses that the questions on the application were answered correctly, that the insured had not consulted a physician except for minor problems during the preceding five years, as represented, and that the disease that caused his death had not been diagnosed until shortly before the insured's death, and after the policy was issued. In a situation of this kind, there is no evidence of misrepresentation. On the other hand, if treatment had been received prior to the date of the application and had not been noted on the application, the situation would be quite different. In that case, material misrepresentation could probably be proved.

Where evidence of material misrepresentation is clear, a claim will be denied and the denial defended in court, if the beneficiary sues the company for payment. If there is evidence of some misrepresentation but it is inconclusive, the final decision becomes a matter of judgment. Usually, however, a life insurance company does not deny a life insurance claim unless there is strong and convincing evidence to support its decision.

Reinstatement and Contestability. There is some question as to the legal effect of the incontestable clause if, after the original contestable period has expired, the policy has been permitted to lapse and has then been reinstated. Some courts have held that the contestable period starts again on the date of any reinstatement and that the insurer has a new period, equal in length to the original contestable period, during which it may contest the policy for material misrepresentation or fraud, but only with respect to the reinstatement application. Some states have statutes to this effect; and it is probably the law, either by statute or court decision, in the majority of states.

These and many other factors may need to be considered by a claim department in deciding whether a claim shall be denied on the basis of material misrepresentation or fraud. In general, however, the basic consideration is that a claim should be denied only if there is ample reason to justify a denial and not merely because there is a possibility of taking advantage of a technical legal point.

■ CLAIMANTS AND THEIR RIGHTS

The vast majority of claims presented to a life insurance company are valid, and there is no question of material misrepresentation or other basis for questioning the validity of the policy. The next question concerns the rights of the claimant or claimants. That is, the company must determine if claim has been made by the person or persons entitled to the proceeds. In most claim situations, the beneficiary designation is clear. Relatively few claims present a question as to the rights of an assignee, either because the policy was never assigned, or because any assignment that may have been executed, has been released. Usually, also, there is no question about the survival of the beneficiary or beneficiaries who have completed the claim papers. Nevertheless, each of these factors has an important bearing on the rights of the claimants, as the following discussion will show.

Problems Created by Assignment

The mere fact that a policy has been assigned does not create a problem. For instance, if the assignment was absolute, it will have transferred all rights, including the right to change the beneficiary.

Presumably, therefore, the new owner will have designated himself or someone else of his choice as beneficiary.

The collateral assignment, used when the policyowner assigns his policy as collateral security for a loan, is more likely to present a problem. In such instances, the lender usually has the right to recover any unpaid balance of the loan from the proceeds at the death of the insured. However, the remainder, if any, should be payable to the designated beneficiary.

Problems in connection with collateral assignments usually fall into two general groups. First, there is the situation where the debt has been repaid but the insurance company has not been notified of the release of the assignment. Second, there is the situation where the amount of the unpaid indebtedness is in dispute.

Many collateral assignments have been released and the insurance company has been so notified, long before the death of the insured. In any case, if the indebtedness has been satisfied, it is usually a simple matter for the beneficiary to obtain a release, and often it will be submitted along with the other claim papers.

Even when the loan has not been repaid, settlement does not necessarily create a problem. For instance, the American Bankers Association Assignment Form No. 10 is carefully drafted and is intended to be signed by the beneficiary as well as the policyowner, to signify that the beneficiary's rights are released to the extent of the assignment. If the insured dies before repaying the loan, the assignee has the right under this form to collect the proceeds in their entirety but is required to pay to the beneficiary any excess of the proceeds over the unpaid balance of the loan.

Nevertheless, there is always the possibility of a dispute in any assignment situation. Was the assignment legally effective? How much of the indebtedness remained unpaid at the death of the insured? These and other similar questions may be raised. It is highly important, therefore, that some method of resolving such questions be available.

Some general problems have been decided by the courts so many times that a relatively uniform approach has been developed. For example, when the proceeds of a policy are claimed by both the beneficiary and an assignee who has made a loan and accepted the policy as collateral security, the majority of courts have held in favor of the assignee to the extent of his loan. Thus he will be entitled to recover the unpaid balance of the loan out of the proceeds, and the remainder will be paid to the beneficiary.

It is also generally held that an absolute assignment, if given for the purpose of securing repayment of a loan, will be interpreted as if it were a collateral assignment. Thus, even though the document is an absolute assignment so far as its form is concerned, the court will look to the substance of the transaction and treat it as if it were a collateral assignment if it was given for that purpose.

Incomplete Beneficiary Changes

Most beneficiary designations are revocable. The only requirement for changing the designation, therefore, is that the procedure set forth in the policy shall have been followed. Unfortunately, this has not always been done by the time the claim arises.

Procedures for changing the beneficiary, as previously noted, fall into two principal groups: (1) those that require that the new beneficiary designation be endorsed on the policy itself; and (2) those that require only that the document effecting the change be recorded by the company. In either instance, if the required procedure has not been followed or completed at the time claim is made, there may be a question as to the effectiveness of the attempted change.

As a general rule, each case must be decided individually, but there are some helpful court decisions. For instance, when endorsement of the change is required, the beneficiary previously named may refuse to give up the policy, thus preventing the policyowner from submitting it for endorsement. In this type of situation, the majority of courts have held that if the policyowner has done everything he reasonably could do, the beneficiary designation has effectively been changed. This is sometimes referred to as the "substantial compliance rule." The reasoning is that the policyowner has the right to make a change of beneficiary and that he has done everything in his power to meet the requirements specified in the policy. Since nothing remains to be done except the ministerial act[3] of endorsing the policy, the courts hold that the policyowner has "substantially complied" with the policy requirements and that the beneficiary designation has, in legal effect, been changed.

Interpleader

In particularly difficult questions, where the rights of two or more claimants cannot otherwise be determined, a life insurance company

---

[3] A ministerial act is an act that does not require the exercise of judgment.

may pay the policy proceeds into a court and ask the court to decide among the claimants. This procedure is known as "interpleader" and the insurer is said to be "interpleading" the claimants.

Interpleader is frequently used to resolve questions between beneficiaries when the policyowner has attempted to make a beneficiary change and has not completed it in accordance with the procedures set out in the policy. The procedure may also be used in some instances where there is a conflict between the rights of a beneficiary and an assignee or where there is more than one assignment and thus a question as to the priority of the assignees' rights. Interpleader does not mean that the company is denying or in any way contesting the claim. On the contrary, it means that the insurer is ready and willing to pay and is only asking the court to decide which claimant is entitled to the proceeds. The procedure is used, however, only where there is no other reasonable way of establishing the rights of the various claimants.

Loss of Rights by Law

Divorce. Under the laws of a few states, divorce automatically terminates the rights of a beneficiary under a life insurance policy on the life of his or her spouse, even though the policyowner takes no action to terminate the beneficiary designation. In a few other states, the policyowner may terminate the rights of his spouse-beneficiary after divorce, even if the designation was made irrevocably. In situations such as these, the rights of the beneficiary may have been lost by operation of the law, in spite of the express provisions of the beneficiary designation of the policy.

The Murderer-Beneficiary. The beneficiary who murders the insured is almost never permitted to receive the proceeds. If the policy was applied for in good faith, the life insurance company is required to pay the proceeds, but payment will be made to someone other than the named beneficiary. Sometimes this is the estate of the insured; sometimes it is the contingent beneficiary. The laws of the various states differ as to how this question is answered.

Common Disasters and Short-Term Survivorship

Most present-day life insurance contracts provide that a beneficiary must survive the insured before becoming entitled to any share of the proceeds of the policy. Beneficiary designations include the phrase "if living" as a matter of course, and policies include specific provisions concerning the disposition of the proceeds in the event that no named beneficiary survives the insured. In most instances, therefore, if a beneficiary has died prior to the death of the insured, all that is necessary is to furnish evidence of the date of such beneficiary's death.

For instance, suppose that an unmarried woman, aged 24, loses her life in an accident, leaving a life insurance policy payable to her parents "equally or to survivor." Assume also that her father died a few months before she did but that her mother survived her. This claim would be quickly settled by payment to the mother, on presentation of a certified copy of the death certificate of the father, showing that he had predeceased the insured.

However, when the insured and the beneficiary die in the same accident, their deaths may occur at so nearly the same time that it is difficult to determine who died first. Such situations are termed "common disasters," because they are common to more than one person. Thus, if the young woman and her parents were traveling in a plane that crashed, killing all aboard, they would be said to have lost their lives in a common disaster.

The Uniform Simultaneous Death Act. Common disasters, though not frequent, may present a difficult problem when they occur. For that reason, they have been made the subject of legislation known as the Uniform Simultaneous Death Act. As it applies to life insurance, this law reads as follows:

> Where the insured and the beneficiary in a policy of life or accident insurance have died and there is no sufficient evidence that they have died otherwise than simultaneously, the proceeds of the policy shall be distributed as if the insured had survived the beneficiary.

This legislation is in effect in virtually all of the states, and a similar law is in effect in Canada. Under the Uniform Simultaneous Death Act, the young woman (the insured) in the above example, would be presumed to have survived her parents who were killed in the same plane crash, and settlement would be made to her estate. Thus, if there is no evidence to show that either the beneficiary or the insured survived the other, the Uniform Simultaneous Death Act provides a satisfactory and reasonable way to meet the common disaster problem.

A much more frequent and more serious problem may arise when the beneficiary survives the insured, but dies within a very short time afterwards. In that case, sometimes referred to as the "short-term survivorship" situation, the proceeds of the policy would be payable to the estate of the deceased beneficiary (since the beneficiary did survive the insured). Unfortunately, however, the insurance proceeds, as a part of that estate, may sometimes be distributed in ways far different from the wishes of the insured. The Uniform Simultaneous Death Act is of no value in situations of this kind, since there *is* evidence that the beneficiary survived the insured. In any situation where the heirs of the beneficiary may be different from those of the insured, therefore, special consideration should be given to the short-term survivorship problem in connection with beneficiary designations and settlement arrangements.

Short-Term Survivorship. The problems that may result when a beneficiary survives an insured for only a brief period may be illustrated by an example. For instance, Jack Perkins and his wife, Karen, who is the beneficiary of his insurance, die within a few hours of each other, although Jack dies first. Merely by surviving, Karen becomes entitled to the proceeds of Jack's insurance. Claim for the proceeds will be made by her executor or administrator, and those proceeds will be distributed in accordance with the terms of her will if she has one, or in accordance with the applicable state law if she died without a will.

If Jack and Karen have children, the proceeds not needed to pay Karen's debts will probably be distributed to the children, either under her will or in accordance with the applicable law. In either case, therefore, settlement would be made in accordance with the wishes of most insureds. If there are no children, however, and if Karen has no will, the law provides for distribution to her heirs, not Jack's heirs. In this situation, the proceeds of Jack's insurance would become the property of Karen's relatives, regardless of the members of Jack's own family whom he might have wanted to benefit. This result could be particularly unfortunate if this were a second marriage and Jack had children by the previous marriage. Even if such children were named contingent beneficiaries, they would not be entitled to the proceeds if Karen survived Jack by even a few moments. (It must be remembered that under a one-sum settlement, the contingent beneficiary has no rights to the policy proceeds unless the primary beneficiary dies prior to the death of the insured. Thus, the contingent beneficiary's rights are extinguished if the primary beneficiary survives the insured, even for a very brief time.)

There are other circumstances, also, in which this distribution might be contrary to the wishes of the insured. For instance, Karen's family might be comparatively well-to-do, in contrast with Jack's, or Jack's parents might be invalids requiring special care. In either case, the proceeds would probably not be distributed as Jack (or even as Karen) might have preferred.

The short-term survivorship problem, then, arises out of the fact that beneficiaries sometimes live just long enough to become entitled to the insurance proceeds and then die. In other words, they survive the insured but only for a short time. There are two commonly used methods of meeting the problem of how insurance proceeds are to be paid in situations of this kind. One is the use of a "common disaster" clause in the beneficiary designation. The other method is to elect an optional mode of settlement and designate a successor-payee or payees.

The common disaster clause is a clause included at the request of the policyowner which provides that payment of the proceeds shall be postponed for a stated period of time after the death of the insured. Typically, this is 30 or 60 days. A beneficiary designation of this kind might read as follows:

To Ruth Breton, wife of the insured, if living on the 30th day after the death of the insured; otherwise equally to the children of the insured, if any, who are living on the 30th day after the death of the insured.

This provision effects a satisfactory solution in many short-term survivorship situations. However, it does not provide for the possibility that the wife might live 31 days (or 61 days, if 60 is used) after the date of the insured's death and then die. In that case the insurance proceeds would still be payable to her estate (and thus, in most instances to her heirs). This provision, therefore, does not provide an entirely satisfactory solution to the problem, and it always delays payment of the proceeds until the stipulated period has expired.

The simplest and best way to assure that life insurance proceeds will be distributed in accordance with the policyowner's wishes even in a short-term survivorship situation is to elect an optional mode of settlement for the primary beneficiary and name successor payees for any proceeds not distributed to the primary beneficiary at that person's death. If Jack had done this, in the example given, he could have designated, as successor payees, his own children or any other relatives he wished to benefit, to receive any proceeds unpaid at Karen's death. Thus, any proceeds remaining unpaid at her death would have gone to persons of Jack's choice.

It should be noted that the problems of short-term survivorship of the primary beneficiary are not confined to the common disaster situation. The beneficiary may survive the insured by only a brief time, regardless of the causes of their respective deaths. However, the election of an optional mode of settlement, with successor payees, provides a simple way to avoid the short-term survivorship problem, regardless of the particular circumstances of the deaths.

■ SETTLEMENT OF THE PROCEEDS

The Amount Payable

The life insurance contract is not a contract of indemnity, and the beneficiary does not have to prove the amount of loss at the time claim is made. The amount of insurance payable is the amount provided by the policy. Nevertheless, some adjustments may be required in the sum payable even under the life insurance contract.

The most basic adjustment is made in the event that the correct age of the insured was not given in the application for the insurance. It will be recalled that age is a basic factor in establishing the premium for a life insurance contract. From an early date, therefore, life insurance companies have made adjustments when the age of the insured was misstated. One of the required policy provisions relates specifically to this right, and an illustrative misstatement-of-age policy provision reads as follows:

If the age of the insured has been misstated, the amount payable and every benefit accruing under this policy shall be such as the premiums paid would have purchased at the correct age according to the company's published rate at date of issue.

Under this provision, adjustments must be made in the amount of insurance rather than the premiums, if the age of the insured has been misstated and an incorrect premium has been paid. Thus, if the insured's age was understated, the policy will have been issued for a larger amount of insurance than should be payable; if the age was overstated, a smaller amount of insurance will have been provided by the policy. In either instance, the beneficiary will receive the amount of insurance that the premium actually paid would have purchased at the insured's correct age.

Subject to adjustments of this kind, the sum payable to the beneficiary will usually be computed as follows: Starting with the amount of insurance provided by the policy, add any paid-up or one-year term dividend additions payable; add any accumulated dividends and current dividends payable; add any premium refund due; subtract any outstanding policy loans, with accrued interest; and subtract any premium due and unpaid if death occurred within the grace period.

Depending upon company practices and policy forms involved, other factors may enter into this computation. Several annual premiums may have been paid in advance. If so, they may be refundable as a part of the sum payable. And in other situations, by company practice or policy provision, interest may be payable on the policy proceeds from the date of death to the date settlement is actually made.

One-Sum Settlement

Most policies provide that unless an optional method of settlement has been elected by the policyowner, the amount of insurance will be payable in one sum to the beneficiary or beneficiaries designated. Under these circumstances, if the beneficiary is living at the date of the insured's death, he or she will be entitled to the entire sum payable. If the beneficiary dies prior to the death of the insured, the sum payable will be divided among any contingent beneficiaries who survive; and if there are no contingent beneficiaries, the policy usually provides that the proceeds will be payable to the estate of the insured.

The Settlement Agreement

If the policyowner has elected a settlement agreement that is in effect at the death of the insured, the proceeds of the policy must be paid out in exact conformity with that agreement. If the beneficiary is entitled to a one-sum settlement, however, he or she may usually elect to receive the proceeds under an optional method (or optional methods) of settlement. Often, the terms and conditions of the optional settlements, whether elected by the policyowner before the death of the insured or by the beneficiary of a one-sum settlement, are summarized and incorporated in what is called a supplementary contract.

Supplementary Contracts

A supplementary contract is a separate contract issued when the company makes settlement of life insurance in any manner other than a one-sum payment. Thus, it differs from the settlement agreement, which is completed at the time the policyowner elects an optional mode or modes of settlement. The settlement agreement is a part of the contract with the policyowner. The supplementary contract is completed at the time the settlement is made and thus is a contract with the person or persons to whom the proceeds are to be paid.

Assume, for example, that Frank Horner has a $50,000 whole life policy on his own life, payable to his wife, Nancy, with his children named as contingent beneficiaries. If he elects an optional settlement for them, the details of this settlement will be incorporated in a settlement agreement and made a part of the policy. Usually a settlement agreement can be changed as often as the policyowner wishes to change it. At Frank's death, however, a supplementary contract will be drafted, incorporating the settlement arrangements that were in effect at the date of his death.

The supplementary contract will set forth the terms of the settlement provided, the name or names of the payee(s) entitled to payment and the manner of payment to each, as well as other significant rights or obligations of the parties. This contract will then be delivered to Nancy, since she is the person who will receive the initial payments.

Supplementary contracts are most typically issued in connection with the settlement of proceeds payable at the death of the insured. Thus, they generally reflect the settlement election of the policyowner, or of the beneficiary if the policyowner did not elect an optional method of settlement. However, the policyowner may surrender his policy if he wishes and have the cash surrender value applied under an optional method of settlement. Also, the owner of an endowment policy may elect to have the proceeds of the endowment applied under an optional method of settlement for his own benefit or the benefit of someone else. In any such situation, a supplementary contract will be issued at the time the insurance proceeds, cash value, or matured endowment become payable, and the contract will be delivered to the person entitled to the first payments it provides.

Finally, some kinds of life insurance contracts specifically provide for settlement in income installments instead of a lump sum. The most typical example is the family income policy (which will be described later in this text). In situations of this kind, a supplementary contract may be issued at the time the installments become payable, in order that the identity and rights of the persons to whom the payments are to be made, as well as the obligations of the company, may be clearly defined.

Payees. A person who is entitled to receive the payments under a supplementary contract is customarily called a "payee." This is distinguished from the term "beneficiary," which is used to designate the person who may become entitled to receive the proceeds under the life insurance contract itself. Often the payees under the supplementary contract are the same persons as the beneficiaries under the policy, but this is not always true. Moreover, even when they are the same persons, their rights may differ significantly, depending on the terms of the contracts. For instance, consider the following one-sum beneficiary designation:

To Pauline Emerson, wife of the insured, if living; otherwise to the surviving children of the insured by the said wife, if any.

If Pauline is living at the death of the insured, the rights of the children as beneficiaries under the policy are extinguished. If Pauline elects to take the proceeds of the policy under an optional settlement, she will receive a supplementary contract describing the terms of the settlement, her rights, and the obligations of the company. Usually, she will be permitted to name successor payees to receive any guaranteed installments remaining unpaid at her death, and she may name the children. However, their rights in this instance will be derived from the fact that she designated them, not the fact that they were contingent beneficiaries under the policy. Thus, she may designate another person or other persons as successor payees if she prefers.

Assume, however, that the policyowner elected an optional mode of settlement for Pauline and designated the children as contingent beneficiaries. Usually, in a situation of this kind, the contingent beneficiaries under the settlement agreement (which is a part of the policy) are expressly entitled to receive any installments remaining unpaid at the primary beneficiary's death. Under this kind of settlement agreement, therefore, the rights of the children to the policy proceeds are not terminated at the insured's death. A supplementary contract, therefore, would be prepared at the time of settlement, defining the terms of the settlement and naming the children as successor payees. Here, however, their rights would be derived from the fact that they were designated as contingent beneficiaries under the policy to receive any guaranteed installments remaining unpaid at the death of the primary beneficiary. In other words, this right was given them by the terms of the insurance policy.

Every company has its own practices with respect to the rights that may be granted under the supplementary contracts it issues. For instance, a payee who elects a mode of settlement for himself is usually free to exercise any rights provided under that mode. Thus, he can make withdrawals, change to a different mode and so on. However, if the option is elected by the policyowner, he may direct that such rights be restricted or denied altogether.

■ HOW LIFE INSURANCE BENEFITS ARE TAXED

It is customary to speak of the tax advantages of life insurance, as contrasted with the taxation of many other kinds of personal property. The person who receives life insurance proceeds enjoys a number of special tax exemptions, particularly in the area of state inheritance taxes. Nevertheless, life insurance proceeds are by no means completely tax-exempt. It is essential, therefore, to have some idea of the taxes that may be involved, if the problems of policyowners and beneficiaries in this area are to be understood.

Tax questions concerning life insurance are most likely to arise at the following times:

1. At the death of the insured, when the proceeds become payable.
2. Whenever installment payments become payable, either during the lifetime of the insured or after his death.

In the first instance, the questions usually relate to death taxes. In the second case, the questions concern income taxes.

Death Taxes

Both state and federal taxes are imposed on the property left by a person at his death. The most usual state tax is an inheritance tax, paid by the person receiving the property. However, many states have specifically exempted life insurance proceeds from the inheritance tax under certain conditions. For example, there may be no tax if the proceeds do not exceed a certain sum, or if they are payable to a named beneficiary. Nevertheless, a number of the states require that the tax department of the state be notified when a life insurance company settles a life insurance claim of more than a specified minimum amount. For amounts in excess of a stated minimum, such as $20,000, special permission may be required in the form of a tax waiver from the state before the insurer can make payment without itself incurring possible tax liability.

The federal estate tax is a different matter. This is a tax imposed by the federal government upon the property (estate) left by a person at his death, and there is no special exemption or deduction for life insurance. There is only a general exemption of $60,000, which applies to any property owned by the decedent, including life insurance. The federal estate tax, therefore, applies to any estate in excess of $60,000. The proceeds of life insurance are included in the insured's taxable estate in either of two instances:

1. If they are payable to the insured's estate.
2. If the insured possessed any of the ownership rights under the policy at the date of his death.

The tax law describes this second situation by saying that the taxable estate will include the proceeds of any life insurance payable to a named beneficiary if the insured owned the policy or possessed any of the "incidents of ownership" in it on the date of his death. "Incidents of ownership" is a technical phrase that refers to such rights as the right to change the beneficiary, to surrender the policy for its cash value, to make a policy loan, and to exercise any other ownership right. In other words, if a policy is owned by the insured, its proceeds will be included in his estate for federal estate tax purposes. A policy that is completely owned by someone else will not be included in the insured's estate unless the proceeds are payable to his estate. This is one of the reasons why life insurance is sometimes applied for and owned by someone other than the insured.

The Federal Income Tax

Life Insurance Proceeds. The basic rule in connection with the federal income tax is that the proceeds of a life insurance policy which are payable because of the death of the insured are not taxable income to the beneficiary.[4] For example, if James McBride has a policy of $50,000 payable to his wife, Lucy, she can take the $50,000 in a lump sum at the time of his death and no income tax will be payable on it. This will also be true of the actual proceeds even if she leaves the money under an optional mode of settlement. For instance, if she leaves the proceeds under the interest option,

---

[4] This rule is subject to an exception if a policy has been transferred for value, and this exception is in turn subject to certain exceptions. The basic rule, however, governs in the majority of federal income tax situations.

the interest will be income to her and, therefore, subject to income tax; but there will still be no income tax on the $50,000 of proceeds.

If Lucy elects to leave the $50,000 under an income option, each payment she receives will consist partly of principal and partly of interest. Only the interest part is income and subject to income tax. The amount that is considered income in each payment depends upon the settlement method she elects.

For example, assume that Lucy elects to leave the $50,000 under the fixed-period option and to take it in installments over a 20-year period. According to the fixed-years table given on page 122, she will receive $288.50 each month during the 20 years, or a total of $3,462 each year. Of this total, $2,500 ($50,000 divided by 20) will be a return of the proceeds and is not taxable. The remainder—$962—is income to her each year and, subject to the spouse's interest exclusion, discussed below, this amount is subject to income tax.

The Spouse's Interest Exclusion. The spouse of the insured is entitled to a special interest exclusion of $1,000 each year. This exclusion applies only to interest on life insurance proceeds; it is available to either husband or wife and applies to any option providing installment payments. Thus, it applies to any optional mode of settlement except the interest option.

In Lucy's case, this means that in addition to the $2,500 that she can exclude from her taxable income each year (because it represents the return of one-twentieth of the total insurance proceeds), she can also exclude up to $1,000 of interest. Since she receives only $962 as interest each year, she can, because of the spouse's interest exclusion, exclude this amount from her taxable income, as well as any additional interest payment she may receive from other life insurance proceeds (other than from the interest option), up to a maximum of $1,000 each year.

The Life Income Options. If insurance proceeds are applied under a life income option, the proceeds are divided by the beneficiary's life expectancy, determined in accordance with the mortality table used by the company in calculating the installments payable under the option. To illustrate, assume that Lucy McBride elected this option and assume further that her life expectancy according to the table, is ten years. In this case, she would be entitled to exclude $5,000 ($50,000 divided by 10) each year as a return of insurance proceeds; and she would pay income tax on whatever she receives above $5,000 each year, minus the spouse's annual interest exclusion of $1,000. It does not matter that she may outlive her expectancy. The exclusion is based on her life expectancy, but not limited to it. Thus, she is entitled to the same exclusion each year for the remainder of her life.

Matured Endowments. When the insured himself receives benefits from a life insurance company, the principle of taxation is the same, although the application of the principle is somewhat different. For example, assume that Fred Morrison has an endowment policy in the amount of $50,000. If he survives to the maturity date and receives the maturity proceeds, the gain over the net amount of premiums he paid will be taxable as ordinary income. (The net amount of premiums paid is equal to the premiums less dividends received, if any.)

If an optional settlement, other than the interest option, is elected for matured endowment proceeds, either before the maturity date or within 60 days after it, Morrison is entitled to spread his taxable gain under the contract over the entire period during which he will receive payments; and thus he will pay income tax on only a part of the gain in any one year.

If Morrison leaves the endowment proceeds with the company under the interest option, the interest will be taxed as income when he receives it. However, if he retains the right to withdraw the proceeds whenever he wishes, he will also be taxed (at ordinary income tax rates) on the entire gain under the contract in the year the contract matures.

At the present time, whether the owner of an endowment contract elects to take the proceeds under a fixed-period option or under a life income option, he is considered to have elected settlement under an annuity, and the annuity rules of taxation apply so far as the income taxation of the installments is concerned. Under these rules, a part of each installment is considered income and must be included in his taxable income. The remainder is considered a return of his "investment in the contract"—that is, a return of the premiums he paid to the insurance company. The rules for determining these two elements of the individual payments are established by the federal government.

■ NOTES ON CANADIAN PRACTICES

Taxation

Death Taxes. In 1971, the Canadian government announced its intention to discontinue levying estate taxes after January 1, 1972. Even before this, however, property passing to a spouse on the death of the owner was exempt from estate taxes. Thus, for practical purposes, much life insurance was already exempt from the federal estate tax.

Although all provinces except Alberta have levied a tax on property passing on death (succession duties), the levels of exemption have been such that smaller estates are generally exempt.

Federal Income Tax. The income tax treatment of life insurance proceeds in Canada is much the same as that in the United States, except that in Canada there is no spouse's interest exclusion.

■ QUESTIONS FOR REVIEW

1. List four benefits payable by life insurance companies that may be classified as living benefits to policyowners. How does the total of such benefits payable compare with the total death benefits paid in a given year?
2. Why does the settlement of matured endowments usually present fewer problems than the settlement of death claims?
3. List two basic questions that must be answered in connection with any death claim.
4. Briefly outline the presumption, based on the disappearance of the insured, that is sometimes relied upon in connection with the settlement of insurance claims.
5. For what reason is death from suicide not an insurable risk? What is the basic argument in favor of paying proceeds of life insurance even though the insured has taken his own life? How does the suicide clause resolve this conflict?
6. List four causes of death which are frequently excluded from the accidental death coverage as risks not assumed.
7. Briefly differentiate between denial of a claim because the cause of death was a risk not assumed and denial because of material misrepresentation in the application.
8. What is the "substantial compliance" rule with respect to incomplete changes of beneficiary?
9. Briefly summarize how a life insurance claim would be settled in accordance with the Uniform Simultaneous Death Act, assuming that it was impossible to determine whether the insured or the beneficiary died first.
10. What is the "short-term survivorship" problem? What two methods are commonly utilized in dealing with this problem? Which is the more generally effective? Explain.

10 SPECIAL WHOLE LIFE POLICIES AND ADDED BENEFITS

Most life insurers offer a broad variety of life insurance contracts. Term contracts for terms of different lengths, endowment contracts for different periods of time, and continuous-premium, whole life policies, as well as limited-payment plans, are basic. Many policies combine two or more of these basic plans. Other policies contain modified premium structures or special settlement arrangements. Almost all policies can be modified or expanded by additional policy sections called riders. This chapter will discuss some of the more common variations of the whole life plan, and benefits that may be added by rider.

■ VARIATIONS OF THE WHOLE LIFE PLAN

Policies with Varying Premium Rates

The fact that the premiums under most whole life policies are payable in a level amount from the very first policy year may present a special problem for the young person just getting a start in his life's work. Frequently, the premium for the amount of whole life insurance he really needs is considerably higher than he can comfortably afford for the first several years of his working career. He may have every reason to believe that his income will increase as he progresses in his work and that he will thus be able to pay the higher premiums at a later date. Nevertheless, the high premiums of the early policy years present a problem. Several modifications of the whole life plan have been developed to help meet this situation. One of the simplest is the whole life policy with graduated premiums.

Graduated-Premium Policies. The graduated- or graded-premium policy modifies the continuous-premium, whole life policy in this way: Under it, a specified amount of insurance is payable whenever the insured dies, but the premium is payable on a graduated or graded basis. Beginning at a rate appreciably lower than the premium rate for comparable level-premium coverage, the graduated premium increases each year through a period of several years until it reaches a rate that is slightly higher than that for a continuous-premium, whole life policy issued at the same age. The premium then remains at that level for the remainder of the lifetime of the insured.

FIGURE 10–1

Annual Premiums for a Graduated-Premium Policy, Issue Age 20 ($10,000 of insurance)

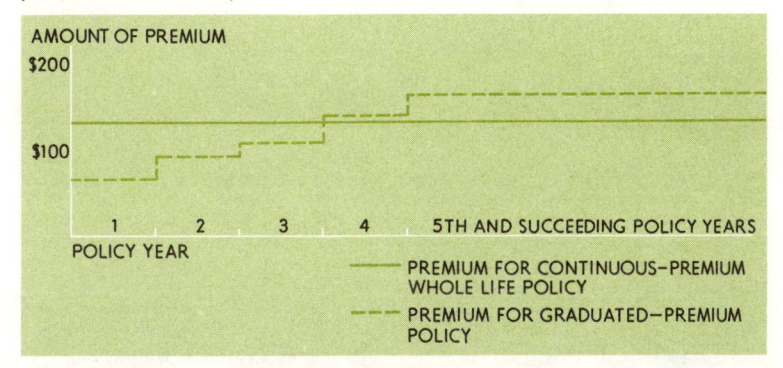

One company, for example, offers a policy under which the initial annual premium rate is 60 percent of the rate ultimately to be paid. Over the first 10 years this premium increases 4 percent a year to reach, in the 10th year, the premium that will be payable for the remainder of the lifetime of the insured. Cash values increase at a rate consistent with the lower premium payable and are, therefore, lower in the early years than they would be for a comparable level-premium, whole life policy.

192 ■ Principles of Life Insurance

Another company offers a policy at an initial premium rate that is slightly less than half the rate for a whole life policy issued at the same age. This premium rate then increases at the beginning of each of the second, third, fourth, and fifth policy years, remaining level thereafter in an amount slightly higher than for a continuous-premium whole life insurance policy issued at the same age. Figure 10–1 illustrates the premium structure for such a policy.

Modified Life Policies. Modified life policies are similar to the graduated- or graded-premium policies except that they usually provide for only two different premium rates. One rate applies to the first three or five years and the other, higher rate applies during the remainder of the premium-payment period. Thus, if the level premium were $150 for a $10,000 continuous-premium, whole life policy issued at age 20, the premium for a modified life policy of the same amount, issued at the same age, might be $110 for the first three or five years, increasing to $165 for the remainder of the premium-payment period. Regardless of the amount of the premium at any particular time, however, the amount of the death benefit would remain the same—$10,000. The premium structure for a modified life policy is illustrated in Figure 10–2.

FIGURE 10–2

Annual Premiums for a "Modified-5" Policy, Issue Age 20 ($10,000 of insurance)

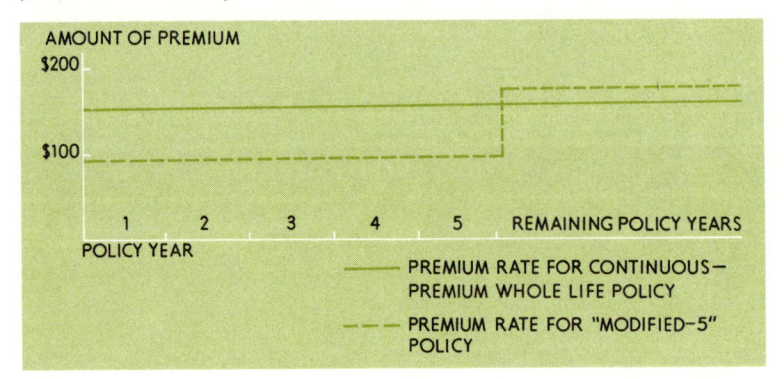

The modified life policies share with the graduated-premium plans the characteristic of having lower nonforfeiture values in the early policy years than are provided under continuous-premium, whole life plans. There is also a definite financial hurdle for the owner of a modified life policy in the year when his premium is increased. This problem is alleviated somewhat under participating policies, however, since policy dividends are usually being paid in increasing amounts by the third year. By using his dividends to help meet the increased premium payment, the policyowner has a kind of shock absorber at the time the premium is increased under the modified life plan.

Policies with Adjustments in Amount of Insurance

Graduated-premium and modified life insurance policies are based on the principle that a lower premium rate can always be charged in the early years of whole life insurance if the rate is increased sufficiently in the later years to make up the difference. A comparable adjustment is effected if the amount of insurance is reduced after a specified age, such as 60 or 65. By using this latter approach, the advantage of a lower premium is retained throughout the premium-payment period. At the same time, the full amount of insurance is maintained until the insured reaches an age at which his maximum family responsibilities (and his greatest need for life insurance) can reasonably be expected to have diminished. Usually the policyowner has the option of continuing his original amount of protection after the specified age, by paying an increased premium.

For example, one company offers a policy with level coverage until the insured's age 70. Thereafter, the policyowner may continue the same amount of insurance by paying twice the basic premium, or may continue to pay the same basic premium for a reduced amount of insurance. The amount of the reduction in the insurance depends upon the age of the insured at the time of policy issue. If the policy is applied for at age 25, the insurance reduces to $875 per $1,000 at age 70. If the policy is applied for at age 35, the insurance reduces to $831 per $1,000. (In either case, the original amount of insurance may be continued by paying a higher premium.) Plans of this kind permit the policyowner to carry, during a major part of his lifetime, a considerably larger amount of life insurance for a given premium outlay than he could have afforded under the continuous-premium, whole life plan. The disadvantages of term coverages are avoided, since cash values are accumulated and some permanent protection is maintained for the later years of life.

■ BENEFITS THAT MAY BE ADDED BY RIDERS

Coverages of a different nature, or for additional amounts, are frequently added to the life insurance contract by means of riders. Usually, though not always, a specified additional premium is payable for such coverages.

Riders may also be used to modify the coverage provided by the policy and to limit the liability of the company under specified conditions. For instance, many insurers use this method to limit their liability if the insured should die as the result of military aviation, or (less frequently) if he should die as the result of war.

Benefits frequently provided by means of riders are the waiver-of-premium for disability; the accidental death benefit; and the guaranteed insurability coverage, which permits the policyowner to purchase, without evidence of insurability, additional life insurance at intervals over a period of several years. Disability income riders are also available from some insurers. A recent development is the additional deposit privilege.

■ DISABILITY BENEFITS

The risk of income loss resulting when the insured is unable to work at his occupation because of accident or sickness is generally recognized as closely related to the life insurance risk. Often such disability results in death. Even when the insured recovers, his disability may have had such a serious financial effect that he is unable to continue premium payments under his life insurance policy. From an early date, this risk of economic loss as the result of total disability has been covered in connection with the life insurance contract in the form of a "waiver-of-premium-for-disability" benefit, usually available as a rider. Later a "disability income" benefit was introduced.

The Waiver-of-Premium Benefit

The waiver-of-premium-for disability benefit is usually available, either as a rider or as an integral part of the policy, in connection with any life insurance contract except a single-premium policy. The proposed insured must meet the insurability requirements of the company, and a specified additional premium may or may not be payable. (Under many policies, the benefit is said to be "folded in" and no identifiable extra premium is charged.)

The insured whose life insurance policy includes the waiver-of-premium coverage is protected against the possibility that prolonged disability might prevent him from continuing to make his premium payments. If he becomes totally disabled and if the total disability continues for a specified length of time, the company will forego (that is, it will *waive*) the payment of all premiums falling due under the policy for as long as the total disability continues. The effect is the same as if the policyowner had actually paid the premiums himself. That is, the cash value of the policy increases and dividends are paid (under participating contracts) just as if the premiums had been paid as they became due. This coverage is thus sometimes said to "insure the insurance," since it prevents the contract from lapsing for nonpayment of premiums if the insured is disabled.

Total Disability. It is customary to specify that premiums will be waived if the insured becomes "totally disabled" as that term is defined in the policy. However, insurers have not been very successful in developing satisfactory definitions of this term. The following definition has been widely used:

> Total disability is disability as the result of bodily injury or disease originating after the insurance under this policy took effect so that the insured is wholly prevented thereby from performing any work, following any occupation, or engaging in any business for remuneration or profit.

This definition, particularly the requirement that the disability must prevent the insured from "performing any work, following any occupation, or engaging in any business for remuneration or profit," has been extensively reviewed and interpreted by courts of law.

From the first, this requirement seemed harsh to many of the courts in which it was considered. Carried to its logical extreme, it would preclude anyone from qualifying for a disability benefit if he could perform the duties of any occupation whatsoever. Thus, the man who had performed highly technical work in nuclear physics would not qualify for the benefit, regardless of the severity of his disability, if he was able to perform any unskilled task. As a result, many courts took the position that, in using this definition, the life insurance company could not have intended to apply the requirement literally. The majority of the courts that have considered the question, therefore, have interpreted this definition as if it related to bodily injury or disease which "wholly prevents the insured from performing the duties of his *usual* occupation or any other for which his education and experience reasonably qualify him." Companies that have continued to use this traditional definition usually interpret it in accordance with these court decisions.

In the past several years, many life insurance companies have modified the traditional definition to reflect the usual court decisions. Such modified definitions read essentially as follows:

Total disability means disability resulting from bodily injury or disease which wholly and continuously prevents the insured from engaging in any occupation or employment for remuneration or profit for which he may be reasonably fitted by education, training, or experience.

Other life insurance companies have modified the traditional definition to clarify the meaning of "occupation" in a somewhat different way. The following definition is illustrative:

Total disability is incapacity as the result of bodily injury or disease originating after the insurance under this policy took effect, so that the insured is wholly prevented thereby from performing the duties of an occupation. During the first 24 months of disability, occupation means the occupation of the insured at the time such disability began; thereafter it means any occupation for which he is or becomes reasonably fitted by education, training, or experience.

A definition of this kind modifies the traditional requirement that the insured be unable to engage in *any* occupation, by requiring only that he be unable to follow his own occupation for the first two years of disability. This approach has a twofold advantage. First, it is more nearly in accord with the interpretation the insured would make as to the nature of the protection he has; and second, claim administration is considerably simplified if it is only necessary at the outset of disability for the company to determine whether the insured is or is not prevented by injury or disease from continuing the work he has been doing. (After two years, many disabled insureds will have recovered and returned to their regular occupation, while many of those who are unable to do this may have completed rehabilitation programs and found other employment "for which they have become reasonably fitted.")

The practical effect of these different definitions of total disability can be demonstrated most clearly by an example. Suppose a surgeon, as the result of an accident, has his hand so badly and permanently injured that he can no longer perform surgery. Under the traditional definition, if strictly interpreted, he would not be considered totally disabled if he could teach in a medical school, since this would, of course, be "an occupation." Nor would he, under these circumstances, be considered totally disabled under the generally-accepted court interpretation of that definition (and the first modified definition quoted above), since teaching in a medical school would presumably be work for which his education and experience would reasonably qualify him. Under the third quoted definition, however, since he could not perform the duties of his occupation as surgeon, he would be considered totally disabled for two years. After that, he would not be considered totally disabled if he could teach or engage in another area of medical practice, and the premiums under his policy would no longer be waived.

The Waiting Period. Originally, life insurers intended to provide the waiver-of-premium benefit only in situations where the disability of the insured might reasonably be expected to continue for a very long period of time. For this reason, the earlier definitions referred to "total and permanent" disability. It soon became evident, however, that the term "permanent" also needed clarification.

A truly permanent disability would, of course, continue until the insured's death. However, most policies provide that the benefit will cease upon the insured's recovery. Thus, a permanent disability in the literal sense of the word is not contemplated. In considering this question, therefore, the majority of courts have taken the position that a permanent disability is a disability that lasts for an indefinitely continuous period of time but not necessarily until death.

Today, there is a noticeable trend toward requiring only that total disability shall have continued for a specified length of time, such as six months, before disability benefits will be allowed. This avoids any question of whether the disability is or is not permanent and makes it clear that the only requirement in this respect is that the disability shall have continued for a period of six months during the insured's lifetime. In other words, the six-month period is simply a waiting period, which must be completed before the waiver-of-premium benefit is allowed. No matter how total (and permanent) the total disability is, this waiting period still applies before the benefit becomes available.

To keep the policy in force, the policyowner must continue to pay premiums as they fall due during this waiting period. However, most policies provide that if the insured's total disability has continued uninterruptedly for the required period, premiums will be waived retroactively, beginning with the first premium becoming due after the disability commenced. This means that premiums that became due and were paid after disability commenced but before the waiver-of-premium-for-disability claim was approved will be refunded. It is customary, however, to limit the period for which such refunds will be made. Usually, this period is limited to one year prior to the date the insurer received notice of the disability.

The policy usually provides that the mode of premium payment cannot be changed during a period of disability. Thus, if the insured is paying premiums on an annual basis and becomes disabled shortly after a premium has been paid, no premiums will be waived until the next annual premium becomes due and then only if he remains totally disabled on that date. In other words, the mode of premium payment cannot be changed to a more frequent mode in order to obtain the benefit of the waiver.

It frequently happens that by the end of the six-month waiting period the policy has already lapsed for nonpayment of premiums. It is customary to provide that the waiver-of-premium claim may nevertheless be allowed in such circumstances, if the insured became totally disabled prior to the end of the grace period following the due date of the first premium in default. For example, assume that an insured fails to pay a quarterly premium due on April 1. At the end of the grace period, the policy lapses, but sometime later he notifies the company that he is disabled as the result of an accident on April 17. Assuming that his disability qualifies as total and continues for the required waiting period, the waiver-of-premium claim will usually be allowed, although policy provisions differ as to whether the policyowner must pay the April 1 premium.

Limitations

Risks Not Assumed. The waiver-of-premium-for-disability section customarily specifies some "risks not assumed." This means that total disability resulting from some hazards will not qualify the insured for the waiver-of-premium benefit. The most typical risks not assumed are disabilities resulting from intentional self-inflicted injury and those resulting from war or any act of war while the insured is in military service for any country at war.

Age Limits. In most instances, the waiver-of-premium benefit is not provided for insureds who are less than 15 years of age, nor is the benefit extended to cover disability arising after ages 55 or 60. Since most insureds are not self-supporting prior to age 15, the disability coverage is not generally thought to be appropriate below that age. In some policies, however, such as endowments at age 18, it may be provided. In such cases, total disability is usually defined as inability to attend school.

The upper age limit is established because of the administrative problems involved in distinguishing between total disability resulting from accident or sickness and the general problems of aging. If the disability arises prior to the limiting age, however, premiums will continue to be waived as they fall due for the duration of the disability. Thus, if the disability coverage expires at the insured's age 55 under a whole life policy and if the insured becomes totally disabled before reaching that age, premiums will be waived as they fall due under his policy as long as his total disability continues, even though this may be many years after he attains age 55.

Provisions Relating to Claims. Written notice of claim for disability benefits is usually required to be presented during the lifetime of the insured and during the continuance of the disability. However, if notice is not given within these times, notice may be given as soon as is reasonably possible.

This modification is especially important in situations involving mental illness. The insured may be the only person who is aware that the waiver-of-premium benefit is provided in his policy. If he is mentally incapacitated, therefore, it may be impossible for notice to be given as required. In cases of this kind, courts have unanimously held that notice "as soon as reasonably possible" is sufficient, and most policies so provide.

Life insurers usually reserve the right to request proof of the continuance of the insured's disability after benefits have been allowed. Evidence of this kind is not usually requested more frequently than seems reasonable when the cause and probable duration of the disability are taken into consideration. For instance, proof of continuance of disability may be requested annually if the insured has osteomyelitis (an infection of the bone) whereas no followup would be necessary in connection with disability benefits allowed a factory worker for the loss of both hands. In fact, the latter situation is one of several types of loss that are customarily presumed to be total. Under the usual policy provisions, loss of both hands, loss of both feet, and loss of the sight of both eyes are all presumed to be totally disabling and will qualify the insured for the waiver-of-premium benefit even though he is able to work at an occupation for remuneration.

The Waiver-of-Premium Benefit in Term Policies

When premiums are waived under continuous-premium or limited payment policies, the benefit is continued until all premiums falling due under the policy have been waived or until the insured has either died or recovered from his disability and is able to resume payment of premiums. Under renewable term policies, if premiums are being waived at the end of the term or if the insured is entitled to have them waived at that time, it is customary for the policy to provide that it will be automatically renewed and premiums will continue to be waived. Convertible term policies, however, present a more complex problem.

A convertible term policy can be converted to a permanent plan of insurance without evidence of insurability. Therefore, the fact that the insured is disabled at the time will not preclude him from exercising his conversion privilege; but unless he furnishes satisfactory evidence of insurability, the new policy to which he converts will not usually be issued with the waiver-of-premium benefit.

However, a growing number of insurers are extending the waiver-of-premium benefit under these circumstances, by providing for automatic conversion if the conversion period terminates while the insured is totally disabled and premiums are being waived. In such situations, the term policy is automatically replaced with a specified permanent plan such as a whole life or a life paid-up at 85, to preclude antiselection to some extent. Premiums are then waived under the new policy for the duration of the insured's total disability.

The Disability Income Benefit

Some life insurance companies offer a disability income coverage in connection with the life insurance contract, as well as the waiver-of-premium for disability coverage. This disability income benefit provides an income of a specified amount—usually $5 or $10 per month for each $1,000 of face amount of insurance—if the insured becomes totally disabled as that term is defined in the policy, and if the total disability continues for a period of at least six months.

As a general rule, the definition of total disability in connection with this coverage is the same as for the waiver-of-premium for disability. Usually, also, the risks not assumed are similar, as are the provisions concerning notice of disability. Unlike the waiver-of-premium benefit, however, the disability income benefit is not usually paid retroactively. Instead, the income begins at the end of the first month after completion of the waiting period. Thus, if the policy provides a six-month waiting period, the first payment would be made at the end of the seventh month following commencement of the insured's total disability.

There are two basic classes of disability income coverages: short- and long-term plans. Short-term disability income is usually payable for a period of not longer than two years, or the duration of the total disability, if shorter. Under the long-term disability coverage, the income is payable for the duration of the disability or until age 60 or 65. At that time, the income will terminate or be continued at a reduced rate. Under some policies, if the insured remains totally disabled on reaching the limiting age, the policy in which the coverage is included will mature as an endowment, regardless of the kind of policy it may be.

The disability income benefit was widely sold at one time, particularly during the 1920's, and frequently at inadequate premium rates based on insufficient experience. As a result, a number of insurers suffered serious financial reverses in the late 1920's and early 1930's, when the widespread unemployment of the depression years resulted in many claims that were presented more because of lack of employment opportunities than because of the severity of the disability. Many of these claims might not have been presented in more prosperous times. Although this coverage was rather generally discontinued for some time after this experience, it is being issued by some insurers at the present time on a basis which is believed to be much sounder than that of the 1920's.

■ THE ACCIDENTAL DEATH BENEFIT

One popular benefit that can be added to a basic life insurance contract is the accidental death benefit or accidental means death benefit. Under this rider (or section of the policy) the insurer promises to pay an additional amount of insurance if the death of the insured is caused by an accident, or in some contracts, by "accidental means." Usually, the death must occur prior to the insured's age 65 or 70, and there are other requirements that must be met.

It is customary to provide an accidental death benefit in an amount equal to the face amount of the policy; hence the popular term, "double indemnity."[1] Thus, if the basic policy is in the amount of $10,000, the customary accidental death benefit would be an additional $10,000. If the death of the insured occurred accidentally, as defined in the policy, the total proceeds would be $20,000. Occasionally, the amount of the accidental death benefit is twice the amount of insurance provided by the policy, in which case it is called "triple indemnity." Payment, if the policy included a "triple indemnity" provision, would be made up as follows:

Face amount of the policy	$10,000
Accidental death benefit	20,000
Total proceeds	$30,000

Accidental Means

Traditionally, the accidental death benefit has been provided as an "accidental means" death benefit—that is, the insurer promises to pay the specified amount on receipt of due proof that the insured met his death as the result of accidental means. An illustrative policy provision might read much as follows:

The company will pay to the beneficiary, subject to the provisions of this policy, an additional sum equal to the amount shown as the "Face Amount of Insurance" on page 3 upon receipt of due proof that the death of the insured occurred, while this benefit is in effect, as the result, directly and independently of all other causes, of bodily injury caused solely by external, violent, and accidental means.

Many of the words in the quoted provision have been the subjects of court interpretation in disputes as to whether this benefit was or was not payable in a specific situation. However, the meaning of the term "accidental means" has probably been more frequently in controversy than any other aspect of this coverage. In general, death effected through accidental means is defined as death resulting from causes that are themselves accidental. Thus, the essential requirements are that both the cause (means) and the result must be accidental.

This definition, however, is deceptively simple. Identifying causes that are themselves accidental is not always easy. Generally,

---

[1] This term, though widely used, is not technically correct, because life insurance, as previously noted, is not a contract of indemnity.

death is not considered to have been caused by accidental means if it results from something the insured intended to do and did in the way he intended. Assume, for example, that a person takes a certain medication his physician has prescribed and that he takes it in the exact dosage prescribed. If, because of an unsuspected sensitivity on his part, he dies as the result of taking the drug, his death is not death by accidental means, since in this case the result (death) was accidental but the cause (taking the medication) was not. On the other hand, if he makes a mistake in dosage and accidentally takes a larger amount than prescribed, the cause is also accidental. In this latter situation, if he dies as the result of having taken the medication, his death will have resulted from accidental means.

Technical distinctions of this kind are frequently misunderstood by policyowners and beneficiaries. Most people feel that they know what constitutes an "accidental death," and the idea of "accidental means" as something different is not usually a part of their thinking. When claims have been denied on this basis, therefore, the beneficiary has frequently taken the question to court and in a great many instances has been successful in obtaining payment of the additional death benefit.

For a number of years, there has been a definite trend in court decisions away from the strict interpretation of the accidental means coverage, which was illustrated in the example given above. In fact, the courts of many states have specifically stated that the distinction between accidental means and accidental death has been abolished in their jurisdictions. This means that any question involving a claim for the accidental death benefit will be decided on a basis of whether the death was or was not accidental, regardless of the way the policy may read. Courts in other states have said that the accidental means requirement, if included in the policy, will be given effect, but that in any close question as to whether a given set of circumstances does or does not constitute accidental means, the decision will be in favor of the beneficiary—that death was the result of accidental means.

Even when court actions are not involved, however, such distinctions may result in misunderstanding and dissatisfaction among policyowners and beneficiaries. The trend, therefore, is away from technical interpretations when the accidental means terminology is still retained and away from the use of this language in many of the newer policies.

Many insurers today are reflecting this trend in their policy language and providing a true accidental death benefit, as in the following illustrative policy provision:

> The company agrees to pay an accidental death benefit on receipt at its home office of due proof that the death of the insured resulted, directly and independently of all other causes, from accidental bodily injury, provided that death occurred within 90 days after such injury and while this benefit is in effect.

This is a simple and more liberal provision so far as the insured is concerned. It eliminates any argument concerning accidental means and leaves as the only question to be answered—was the death accidental?

Risks Not Assumed under the Accidental Death Coverage

Life insurance companies usually exclude some risks from the accidental death section of their contracts. Different insurers exclude different risks, but there are a few exclusions that are relatively standard. The following are commonly used:

1. *Suicide.* Since suicide is the intentional taking of one's own life, such a death is not, of course, accidental. However, it is often difficult to establish intent. For this reason, the suicide exclusion is usually phrased very carefully. One insurer uses the following wording to exclude death resulting from:

> Suicide or any attempt thereat or intentional self-inflicted injury of any kind, whether the insured be sane or insane.

2. *Taking of Poisons or Inhalation of Gas.* Two risks that are frequently excluded from the accidental death coverage are death resulting from the taking of any poison or sedative, and death resulting from the inhalation of gas. Death from the inhalation of carbon monoxide gas presents an especially difficult claim problem. If intentional, the death is suicide, but proving that it was intentional is often difficult. For this reason, all such deaths are sometimes excluded from the accidental death coverage.

3. *Committing or Attempting to Commit a Felony.* A felony is any crime punishable by death or imprisonment in a penitentiary. Such crimes are inherently dangerous, and policy provisions excluding them from the accidental death coverage are frequently used for that reason and for reasons of public policy.

4. *War, Military Service, Riots, and Insurrection.* Some deaths that would otherwise qualify as accidental are excepted from the

accidental death coverage primarily because mortality statistics on which the premium rates are based do not generally include them. Among these exclusions are deaths resulting from war, military service, riots, and insurrection.

5. *Aviation.* It is also customary to exclude from the accidental death coverage death resulting from piloting a plane or flying in any aircraft "other than as a fare-paying passenger on a regularly scheduled airline."

6. *Bodily or Mental Infirmity.* Deaths resulting directly from bodily or mental infirmities are frequently excluded from the accidental death coverage. It is often difficult to establish that death was actually caused by a heart attack, for instance, if the insured is driving an automobile at the time the heart attack is suffered and is involved in an accident as the result. To minimize such problems, deaths resulting from bodily or mental infirmities may be specifically excluded.

Value of the Coverage

In this age of ever-mounting automobile fatalities, the possibility of accidental death seems more vividly real to many applicants for life insurance than almost any other risk to which they might be exposed. As a consequence, although accidental death benefits are payable only in connection with a relatively small proportion of death claims, the coverage is very popular.

Often, however, the policyowner does not have a very clear understanding of the coverage. For example, he may blend it, in his thinking, with his basic life insurance coverage and feel that he has twice (sometimes three times) as much life insurance protection as he actually has. In such cases, he may not have nearly as much "life insurance" as he thinks. However, if the accidental death coverage is considered as an accident policy, rather than as additional life insurance, it provides, for a small additional premium, a substantial additional benefit in the event of accidental death.

■ TERM LIFE INSURANCE BY RIDER

Most of the term life insurance coverages that are available as separate individual policies are also available as riders that may be attached to permanent life insurance contracts. (In some instances and with some insurers, term riders may be added to individual term policies.) These term life insurance riders are often convertible to permanent life insurance at the option of the policyowner; and the proceeds, if payable in one sum, may be applied under any of the optional modes of settlement provided by the policy to which they are attached. Often the rider itself provides for settlement in installments.

It is customary to offer five- and ten-year level term riders; decreasing term riders for periods much longer, such as 20, 25, and 30 years; and increasing term riders under some circumstances. This makes it possible to use term insurance riders to provide, for a relatively modest additional premium, a great deal of added coverage for periods when increased protection is especially needed. If these riders are attached to permanent life insurance contracts, the basic coverage may still be continued after the expiration of the term coverage, (assuming the insured is then living) and the insured will have had considerable added protection during the period covered by the rider.

The financial advantage of adding term insurance by rider to a whole life policy, as compared with purchasing whole life insurance in the full amount, is illustrated in Figure 10-3.

FIGURE 10-3

Comparison of Annual Premiums for $50,000 of Life Insurance, Issue Age 25

Provided entirely by whole life insurance	$846.00
Provided by a combination of whole life and term insurance:	
Whole life insurance of $25,000	$423.00
Level term insurance, for 20 years, of $25,000	$157.00
Total annual premium	$580.00

■ THE GUARANTEED INSURABILITY BENEFIT

The possibility of becoming unable to pay insurance premiums because of total disability and the risk of accidental death have traditionally been considered in connection with the basic life insurance risk. The risk of becoming uninsurable has also been recognized, particularly as a reason for purchasing insurance on the lives of children. Total disability and accidental death coverages had been available for a long time, however, before the risk of becoming uninsurable was recognized as one that could be made the subject of an insuring agreement. Protection against this risk was provided in the form of the guaranteed insurability rider, first offered in 1957.

Different variations of the guaranteed insurability coverage have been developed, but the general outline is as follows: For a small additional premium at the time a policy is issued, the policyowner is guaranteed the right to purchase additional policies, without evidence of insurability, at stipulated intervals over a specified period of time. The guaranteed insurability benefit is not insurance. It is only the right to purchase insurance in the future without evidence of insurability. As the new insurance is purchased, new policies are issued. An illustrative agreement reads, in part, as follows:

On each of the option dates the owner may purchase a new policy on the life of the insured without evidence of insurability, subject to the terms and conditions of this optional additional insurance section.

A typical set of option dates would fall on the policy anniversary dates immediately following the insured's attainment of ages 22, 25, 28, 31, 34, 37, and 40. Thus, if a policy including this coverage is issued to an insured age 20, he will have the privilege of purchasing seven additional policies during the next 20 years. If he is 32 years of age when the policy is issued, he can purchase three additional policies, and so on.

Just before each of the option dates, the insurer notifies the policyowner of his right to purchase additional insurance, subject to the terms and conditions of the coverage. The purpose of such conditions is to limit the company's possible liability and to reduce antiselection to some extent. The more typical of such terms and conditions are the following:

1. Both the base policy and the guaranteed insurability section must be in force on the option date.

2. The amount of insurance which each additional policy may provide is customarily limited to a maximum such as $10,000, $15,000, or $20,000, or the face amount of the policy to which the guaranteed insurability provision is attached, whichever is the smaller amount. Thus, if a $25,000 policy with this coverage ($15,000 limit) is purchased before the insured's age 22, the insured could, by the time he is 40, acquire seven more policies in the amount of $15,000 each, or a total of $105,000 additional life insurance. Each policy could be purchased at the standard premium rates in effect when the option was exercised and without submitting evidence of insurability.

3. The new policy is often limited to one of a few specified plans such as a whole life or endowment plan. However, retirement in-

come, term to age 65, and renewable and convertible short-term plans are sometimes permitted.

4. Added benefits such as waiver-of-premium-for-disability and the accidental death benefit may be available in connection with the new policy only with the consent of the company. A number of companies, however, will permit the waiver-of-premium coverage to be added if it is included in the base policy and if the insured is not disabled on the option date. Some companies also permit this disability coverage to be included in the new policy if it is on the whole life plan, even though the insured is totally disabled and premiums are being waived under the base policy at the time the new policy is issued. In that case, premiums are waived as they fall due under the new policy as well as the old, so long as the total disability continues. Requirements in this respect vary widely from company to company.

The policyowner is under no obligation to purchase additional insurance on any option date. He may purchase it, but he is not required to do so. If he fails to exercise the option on any one option date, that option will be lost to him, but this will have no effect on his right to exercise the option on the next option date.

Present-day guaranteed insurability coverages frequently include provisions making it possible to exercise an option in advance of the regular option date in the event of marriage or the birth of a child. For example, a young man may purchase, in 1972, a policy including this coverage, with options exercisable in 1975, 1978, 1981, etc. If he marries in 1973, he can exercise the 1975 option immediately, or within a period of 90 days following his marriage, instead of waiting until 1975.

Under such coverages, it is not unusual to provide, at no additional premium, automatic term insurance in the amount that would be available on the exercise of the option, for a period of 90 days following the insured's marriage or until the exercise of the option, if earlier. This means that if the insured dies within the 90-day period following his marriage, but before exercising the next option to purchase insurance, a death benefit will be payable in the same amount as if the option had been exercised and a new policy issued.

This same privilege is frequently provided on the birth of a child. Thus, if the same young man who marries in 1973 has a child in 1976, he can exercise the 1978 option immediately or within 90 days following the date of the child's birth. Here again term insurance may be provided automatically during the 90-day period in which the next option is exercisable, terminating with the end of the period or the effective date of the new policy if the option is exercised.

The guaranteed insurability coverage is ideally suited for the college student or for a young person just getting a start in business or a profession. Many people become uninsurable at an early age, but with this benefit they are assured of the right to purchase additional insurance as their insurance needs increase and their financial circumstances improve, regardless of their insurability at the time of actual purchase. The guaranteed insurability benefit, therefore, is particularly appropriate as an additional benefit for a policy on the life of a child or young adult and is especially attractive because of its modest cost. For example, one company makes the rider available on a $10,000 whole life policy at age 20 for an additional annual premium of $14.

■ THE ADDITIONAL DEPOSIT PRIVILEGE

The use of riders to provide privileges, rather than actual insurance coverages, is especially well illustrated by the additional deposit privilege. This rider permits a policyowner to deposit additional funds with the life insurance company when the cash value of a life insurance contract is placed under an option and to use the additional funds, together with the cash surrender value, to provide a life income for the insured. This privilege is offered by a number of insurers for use with life insurance that is sold in connection with formal corporate retirement plans, as well as with retirement plans for employees of unincorporated businesses.

Although the privilege has its most obvious use in connection with formal retirement plans, it is not confined to such plans. A policy including the additional deposit privilege may be purchased by any individual who plans to use it to provide for his own retirement, particularly if he has investments that he may wish to use in assuring himself a guaranteed life income at a future date.

Usually, there is a limit as to the amount of additional funds that may be deposited. Thus, if the cash value of the insurance policy would provide a retirement income of $10 per month for each $1,000 of face amount of insurance for the remaining lifetime of the insured, the additional deposit privilege might permit the deposit of an additional sum which, after deduction of an expense charge, would provide a retirement income of up to $20 per $1,000 of face amount of insurance.

■ QUESTIONS FOR REVIEW

1. Explain the principle underlying the graduated-premium or modified life plans. For what type of applicants are such plans particularly well suited?
2. Give one advantage and one disadvantage of the modified life and graduated-premium plans as compared with continuous-premium, whole life insurance.
3. Describe five benefits that may be added to a life insurance policy by rider.
4. Summarize the traditional definition of total disability used in disability coverages offered by life insurance companies. How has this definition been interpreted in the majority of court decisions? How has the traditional definition been modified?
5. Assume that Alex Dillon has a typical waiver-of-premium-for-disability coverage in his policy, and that premiums are payable quarterly on the 20th of March, June, September, and December. If he becomes disabled on March 21, and he is still totally disabled when the six-month waiting period is completed on September 21, which will be the earliest premium that will be waived under his policy? Explain.
6. Differentiate between the terms "accidental death" and "death by accidental means."
7. Describe three risks commonly excluded from the accidental death coverage.
8. What is the basic advantage in providing a specific amount of life insurance by a combination of whole life and term insurance, as compared with providing the total coverage by whole life insurance? The disadvantage?
9. Briefly explain the nature and purpose of the guaranteed insurability benefit. What modifications may be included in connection with the later marriage of the insured or the birth of a child?
10. What is the purpose of the additional deposit privilege?

11 SPECIAL POLICIES FOR FAMILY NEEDS

Although the basic plans of life insurance—term, whole life, and endowment—may be adapted to a wide variety of needs, some family situations are common to so many people that special combination plans have been developed for them. In one recent year, for instance, one out of every seven ordinary life insurance policies purchased was a family policy—under which all members of the family were covered. This chapter will discuss this and some of the other policies that have been developed especially to meet typical needs of families.

■ INSURANCE ON THE HUSBAND'S LIFE

Most families are primarily dependent on the continued life and earning ability of the husband and father. His death or total disability, therefore, constitutes a greater economic loss to the family than the death or disability of any other family member. For this reason, the largest share of family income allocated to life insurance premiums is usually devoted to insurance on his life. Even so, the amount of life insurance that can reasonably be purchased in most instances falls far short of the amount that would be needed to support the family in the event of the father's early death.

Because the need in such cases is so great, it is not very realistic for most families to attempt to meet this need in its entirety with whole life insurance. This would require a much larger premium than most families of modest incomes could afford. For example,

$25 per month in premium payments would provide about $20,000 of whole life insurance for a 25-year-old male; and $20,000 would not support an average family very long.

The amount of premium required for an adequate amount of whole life insurance becomes an even more serious problem when one considers the period in the life of the family during which the father's death would mean the greatest economic hardship. For most families this is the period when the children are very young. Since these are often the years in which a young father is also getting a start in his business or professional career, they frequently coincide with the period of his lowest earnings.

This coincidence of greatest insurance need with what is often a limited ability to pay premiums presents a difficult problem. However, it is usually confined to a fairly limited period of time. In most families, the children are grown and their formal education has been completed by the end of 20 or 30 years. Since this is the kind of situation for which term coverages are most appropriate, most life insurance plans developed especially for family protection utilize a considerable amount of term life insurance. Term coverages provide significantly more insurance protection for the same premium outlay than whole life plans for a period of several years in the life of a young adult, and the termination of some life insurance on the life of the father after the children are grown is not necessarily a disadvantage.

For these reasons, most life insurance companies offer combinations of term and whole life coverages especially for family protection. Typically, these policies utilize a large amount of term insurance to provide maximum protection during the period when children are growing up. Usually they combine the term coverage with permanent insurance, however, because some permanent life insurance is always advisable. At the end of the specified period, the term life portion of the policy expires, but the policyowner will still have his basic whole life coverage. One very popular combination of this kind provides whole life insurance plus decreasing term insurance payable in the form of a monthly income. This is generally referred to as a family income plan.

The Family Income Coverage

The earlier family income policies combined whole life insurance with decreasing term insurance in such amounts that the term insurance would provide a monthly income of a specified percentage, such as 1 percent, of the face amount of the policy for the remainder of the initial income period, typically 20 years, if the insured died during that 20-year period. Thus the policyowner who wanted to provide his family with an income of $300 per month in the event of his death during the specified period would purchase a $30,000 family income policy.

At the present time, the family income coverage is most frequently furnished by riders providing term life insurance for various periods—10, 15, or 20 years. These riders can be attached to any of several different policies providing whole life coverage. Some companies also make the coverage available in separate policies furnishing the term coverage only.

Regardless of how it is provided, however, the identifying characteristic of the family income coverage is that a death benefit is payable in monthly installments if the death of the insured occurs within a specified period. In that event, the income installments become payable when the insured dies and are paid until the end of the period. If the insured is still living at the end of the period, the family income coverage, like any other term coverage, expires.

Assume, for instance, that Peter Warren's whole life insurance policy in the amount of $50,000 includes a family income rider providing 15-year family income coverage of $250 per month. If the effective date of the policy and the rider is January 15, 1973, the family income rider will provide protection until January 15, 1988. If Peter is living on that date, the family income rider will expire, although his whole life coverage will remain in effect so long as he lives and continues to pay the premium.

If Peter dies at any time while the family income rider is in effect, the company will make a monthly payment of $250 to his beneficiary one month after his death; and it will continue making these payments each month until it makes the last payment in January, 1988 (the end of the 15-year period).

There are two periods to be considered in the family income coverage. One is the term of the coverage—that is, the number of years specified, such as 15, 20, or 25 years. This is determined at the time the policy is issued. The other period is the income payment period—that is, the period during which installments will be payable if the insured dies within the specified term of the coverage. The income payment period begins on the date of the insured's death if that occurs within the term of the coverage, and it continues to the end of the original term of coverage.

To illustrate, assume that Peter Warren, who has the 15-year family income coverage, dies on January 15, 1978. The family income benefits will become payable in this instance since he died during the term of coverage, and income payments will be made to the end of the term—that is, until January, 1988. These payments and the term of coverage can be charted thus:

15-Year Family Income Coverage

EFFECTIVE DATE OF COVERAGE	DATE OF DEATH	END OF COVERAGE
JANUARY 15, 1973	JANUARY 15, 1978	JANUARY 15, 1988

TERM OF COVERAGE
PERIOD DURING WHICH INSTALLMENTS ARE PAID

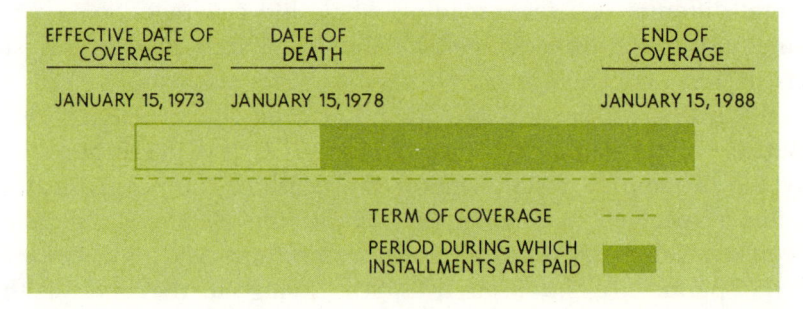

However, if Peter should die on January 15, 1983, the periods would be charted as follows:

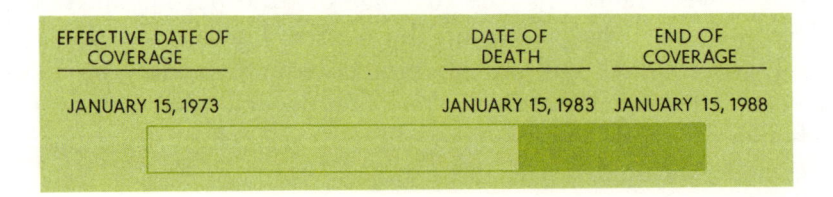

EFFECTIVE DATE OF COVERAGE	DATE OF DEATH	END OF COVERAGE
JANUARY 15, 1973	JANUARY 15, 1983	JANUARY 15, 1988

Note that the later date of death shortens the period over which income payments are made and thus reduces the number of installments that are payable. The family income coverage, therefore, is decreasing term insurance. It is term insurance because it is payable only if the death of the insured occurs during the term. Each month that the insured lives reduces the total number of income payments that can become payable at his death. Expressed in months, this decrease is readily apparent, as the graph on the next page shows.

If Peter dies after January 15, 1988, no payments will be made under the family income coverage. This illustration assumes, however, that the family income coverage was provided by rider. Under those circumstances, the base policy, to which the rider was attached, would be payable according to its provisions whenever the insured died, either during the installment-payment period or later. Similarly, if the family income coverage had been provided as a part of a family income policy, the whole life portion of the policy would remain in effect after the end of the installment-payment period, if the insured were still living at that time; and the whole life proceeds would be payable whenever the insured died.

15-Year Family Income Coverage

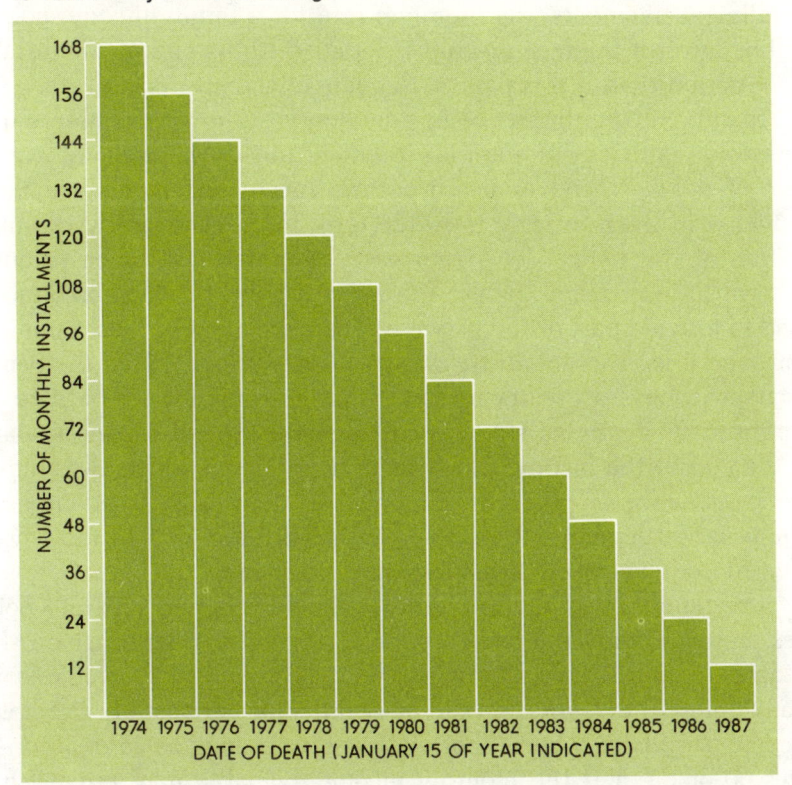

Under most of the earlier family income policies, however, the whole life proceeds were not usually payable immediately on the death of the insured if he died during the family income period. Instead, the face amount was retained by the company and the interest earned on it was used to make up part of the income payments. When the last income payment was made, the face amount became payable.

This arrangement permits a significant reduction in the amount of term insurance required to provide the installment payments. For example, if the face amount of the policy is $20,000 and the company is currently earning 5 percent on its investments, this face amount, when left at interest, will produce $1,000 each year. If income payments are provided in the amount of $200 per month, the interest earned on the face amount will provide all but approximately $1,400 of the funds required for the payments for one year. Since a significantly smaller amount of term insurance is required to provide the installment payments, the premium rate for a family income policy will be lower if the face amount is retained to the end of the installment period than if it is paid at the date of the insured's death.

In spite of the difference in premium cost, however, many family income policies provide for settlement of the face amount at the date of death whenever death occurs. Income payments are then provided in their entirety from the term insurance (family income) section of the policy. This requires a considerably larger amount of term life insurance than if the interest from the face amount is used to provide part of the necessary installments. For most families, however, it is a more realistic method of settlement. Often the beneficiary will have a greater need for the face amount at the date of the insured's death (to settle last illness and funeral expenses) than at the end of the income payment period. This is especially true if the family income policy is the only insurance the decedent had. The usual settlement options are available for any part of the whole life proceeds not needed for last illness expenses.

The family income coverage is available today in separate policies providing only the term coverage, as well as riders that can be attached to any whole life policy, and the coverage is available in many different amounts and for many different periods. For example, income periods may be as short as 10 years, as long as 25 or 30 or to ages 60 or 65, and the monthly income available may range from $10 to $25 or $30, occasionally as high as $50, for each $1,000 of basic coverage. Sometimes the amount of monthly income differs according to the length of the income period elected; sometimes it is larger in the first or early years of the payments and is reduced later. For example, one company offers a family income policy under which monthly income is payable in an amount that is 2 percent of the face amount of the policy during the first year and 1 percent in the succeeding years of the income payment period.

Some policies also guarantee that a minimum number of payments will be made, regardless of how late in the specified term the insured may die. Under these policies, payments may be made beyond the 15-, 20-, or 25-year term specified if the insured dies only a short time before the end of the period.

Although the family income coverage provides for settlement in income payments, many companies permit commutation of the payments so that a one-sum settlement may be elected in lieu of all income payments, either by the policyowner or by the beneficiary after the death of the insured.

The right to convert the family income coverage to a permanent plan of insurance may also be provided. In such instances, conversion is permitted on the same conditions as for any other term coverage. Thus the amount of insurance in force at the time of conversion (or a specified percentage of it, such as 75 or 80 percent) may be converted without evidence of insurability to any whole life or endowment plan offered by the company on the date of conversion.

The Family Maintenance Coverage

The family maintenance policy provides a combination of term and whole life insurance coverages similar to the coverages provided by the family income policy. However, the family maintenance policy has not proved as popular as the family income combination and it is not widely issued today.

The basic difference between the family maintenance and family income coverages concerns the period during which income payments will be made if the insured dies while the term coverage is in effect. As is true of the family income coverage, the family maintenance coverage provides monthly income payments, beginning at the death of the insured, if his death occurs within the specified period. In contrast with the family income payments, however, the family maintenance payments continue for a fixed number of years no matter when they start. If death occurs after the expiration of the income period, only the face amount is payable under either a family maintenance policy or a family income policy.

The difference between these coverages is more easily understood if an example is used. Suppose, for instance, that William Adams purchases a 20-year, $10,000 family income policy on July 1, 1973. His brother, Joseph, purchases a 20-year, $10,000 family maintenance policy on the same date. Both policies provide for monthly payments in the amount of $100, and monthly income will not be payable under either plan unless the insured dies within the initial 20-year period.

Assume, further, that both William and Joseph die on July 1, 1978. Under these circumstances, the family income plan will pay $100 per month to William's beneficiary, beginning at the date of death and continuing to the end of the original 20-year period—that is, until July 1993, or 15 years. The family maintenance payments (under Joseph's policy) also begin at the date of death; but they will continue for 20 years, that is, until July, 1998. The following diagram illustrates this difference.

Comparison of Payments under 20-Year Family Income and Family Maintenance Policies

ISSUE DATE JULY 1, 1973	DATE OF INSURED'S DEATH JULY 1, 1978	20 YEARS FROM ISSUE DATE JULY 1, 1993	20 YEARS FROM DATE OF DEATH JULY 1, 1998
	FAMILY INCOME PAYMENTS		
	FAMILY MAINTENANCE PAYMENTS		

As indicated in this diagram, the same number of installments will be payable under the family maintenance plan whether the insured dies early or late in the specified period. Thus, the same (that is, a *level*) amount of term life insurance will be required to provide the family maintenance payments, regardless of the date of the insured's death, so long as it is within the period of coverage.

Because the income benefits under the family maintenance policy are provided by level term insurance, this type of policy is more expensive than the family income policy, which provides the income installments by decreasing term insurance. Often there is no very great family need for an income that will continue for 20 years after the death of the insured. The period of greatest need—

when there are children to be cared for and educated—tends to decrease with each additional year. This is the pattern followed by the family income coverage; and, because it is also less expensive than the family maintenance coverage, the former has proven to be much the more popular of the two coverages.

Double Protection Policies

Family income and family maintenance coverages are only two of many different plans utilizing term insurance to increase, for temporary periods, the amount of insurance in force under permanent policies. Because this increase can be obtained for a relatively small additional premium when term coverages are added to permanent plans, most companies offer some policies, often called "double protection" or "double protection for a term of years," that are based on this principle. These policies usually provide term life insurance for a specified period of years in an amount equal to the face amount of the basic policy. Thus, double the face amount is payable if the insured dies during the specified term.

This type of policy is open to the criticism that one-half of the insurance is temporary. However, this criticism is applicable to any term insurance coverage. The advantage of such coverages is in the added protection afforded for the small increase in premium, during the years when family responsibilities are the heaviest and the economic loss by reason of the death of the insured would be the greatest.

The double protection policy consists of a basic whole life policy plus level term life insurance in the same amount as the face amount of the basic policy for a specified period of years or to the insured's age 60 or 65. In makeup, therefore, it bears a strong resemblance to the family maintenance policy. The principal difference between them is in the method of settlement of the term life insurance section. The term insurance section of the family maintenance policy is payable in installments (possibly with the right of commutation). The term insurance section of the double protection policy is usually settled in the same way as the whole life section. Thus, it may be settled in a lump sum or under any of the settlement options.

Double protection coverage may be provided in a special policy for which the premium is a level amount for the duration of the policy, or it may be provided by the addition of a level term rider to any policy providing permanent insurance. In the latter instance, the premium applicable to the term portion of the coverage will cease to be payable when the term insurance expires.

Since term insurance may be added in varying amounts to any basic whole life policy, within reasonable limits determined by the life insurance company, there are also "triple protection" policies and "multiple protection" policies, with added term coverages in varying amounts. All policies of this kind—double, triple, and multiple protection—have the advantage of furnishing a considerable amount of added protection for a relatively small additional premium, but they can be seriously misunderstood by policyowners and beneficiaries. If the limitations of these multiple protection policies are clearly understood, however—that part of the protection is temporary in nature—policies of this kind serve a very useful purpose.

■ INSURANCE ON THE LIVES OF CHILDREN (JUVENILE INSURANCE)

According to a survey made a few years ago by the Institute of Life Insurance, more than half of all American children under age 18 were then insured under some form of life insurance. This fact is especially significant because the financial loss resulting from the death of a child is, in most instances, limited to last-illness and funeral expenses. In fact, as a purely economic matter, the death of a child relieves the parents of the expenses of the child's education and support until he would have reached adulthood. Economically, the basic family need is for insurance on the life of the person on whom the child is dependent, not on the life of the child. Why, then, is insurance on the lives of children (juvenile insurance) so popular and so widespread?

The answer to this question reflects the constructive nature of life insurance and its lifetime benefits. Protection against the expenses that would result from the child's death is only one, and probably not the most important, reason why people apply for insurance on the lives of children. Most basic, probably, is the fact that it gives the child an early start in creating an insurance estate.

If life insurance is desirable for any young man or woman, and many people consider that it is, then there are significant advantages to an early start. First, as a matter of dollars and cents, the earlier a life insurance program is started, the lower the total dollar outlay will be. This statement sometimes seems surprising, but the following sample figures illustrate its truth:

Comparison of $10,000 Life Paid-Up-at-Age 65 Policies (Participating)
Issue Ages 1 and 20

	Issue Age 1	Issue Age 20
Gross annual premium	$ 114.60	$ 182.90
Cash value at age 65, assuming dividends are used to purchase paid-up additions	20,475.00	15,829.00
Total gross premiums paid to age 65	7,334.40	8,230.50
Difference between total premiums paid and cash value at age 65	13,140.60	7,598.50
Monthly income for life at age 65, male, 10 years certain, assuming paid-up additions	114.20	88.30

The explanation for these differences at the two issue ages lies in the remarkable effectiveness of compound interest. A much larger portion of the total cost of protection is provided by interest when the insurance is issued at the insured's age 1 than when it is issued at age 20.

A second advantage in establishing a life insurance program at an early age is that the child's insurability is protected. Accidents and illnesses may take their toll as the child grows older, but if the parents have provided some insurance on his life, his later loss of insurability will not leave him without protection. For many adults, a policy purchased for them in their childhood has proved to be the only individual life insurance for which they were able to qualify. Today, the guaranteed insurability [1] benefit is often available to increase the value of juvenile insurance in this respect.

Many parents also feel that, because of the cash values developed under whole life coverages, insurance on the life of a child constitutes a sound savings program for the benefit of the child. The necessity for making regular premium payments to keep the policy in force makes one reluctant to abandon a program once it has been started. There is no question about safety, and the cash value is readily available through a policy loan, if needed. Many people feel, therefore, that life insurance on the life of a child can encourage the development of good saving habits if, and when, the child later assumes the responsibility for making premium payments.

---

[1] See discussion of this benefit starting at page 206.

Statutory Limitations on Amount

At one time, there was considerable concern that insurance might sometimes be applied for on the lives of children by persons capable of taking the life of an insured child in order to collect the insurance. (This fear was no doubt based in part on the fact that the death of a child means a limited financial loss to his parents, as compared to their responsibilities for his continued care and education.) In any event, the laws of some of the states at one time limited the benefits that could be provided under insurance policies on the lives of children. Illustrative was a law requiring that a policy on the life of a child include a provision limiting the death benefit to $100, if the child died in the first year of its life. In the second year, a benefit of $200 could be paid; in the third year $400; in the fourth and fifth years, $600 and $800; and in the sixth year and thereafter to age 15, a benefit of $1,000 could be provided in the event of the child's death. Such laws are said to have required "graded benefits" in policies insuring the lives of children.

Today, these statutes have either been repealed or extensively amended. Reasonable amounts may be applied for and issued on the lives of children in any of the states. For instance, the New York Insurance Law establishes limitations for insurance on children under the age of 14 years and six months, but permits as much as $5,000 of insurance to be provided. Amounts in excess of $5,000 may be issued if the applicant (who is usually the father) is insured for at least twice the amount applied for on the life of the child (four times the amount applied for, if the child is under four years and six months of age).

Ownership Arrangements

The legal limitations involved in making contracts with a minor have previously been discussed. In the absence of a statute to the contrary, a minor has the same right to disaffirm a contract for the purchase of life insurance as for the purchase of a car or anything else that is not a "necessary." The Canadian provinces and many of the states have enacted statutes permitting minors of a specified age, typically 15 or 16, to make contracts of insurance on their own lives or the lives of others in whom they have an insurable interest, as if they were adults. In these jurisdictions, therefore, after a minor attains the age specified in the statute, he has the legal capacity to exercise ownership rights on the same basis as an adult.

Not every state has enacted this kind of statute, however, and, since an early start on a life insurance program has many advantages, both to the insured and to his parents, it has long been the practice to insure the lives of children under contracts owned by an adult, usually a parent of the child. One of the simplest ways of accomplishing this is for the parent to apply for and own the policy, without qualification as to the duration of his ownership. However, this is not consistent with the idea of "establishing a life insurance program for the child." Under such circumstances, the parent could continue to own and control the policy even after the insured was grown. The only alternative would be to assign the policy to the insured or transfer its ownership to him by endorsement. Most companies, therefore, offer ownership arrangements that are designed to follow the preferences of the applicant more closely.

Since parents generally wish to relinquish control of policies on the lives of their children (and the responsibility for premium payment) on or about the child's 21st birthday, it is customary for juvenile policies to provide that the applicant (the parent) will retain control of the policy only until the child attains age 21 or until the parent's death, if that is earlier. Such a provision would typically read somewhat as follows:

> Until the anniversary of the policy date on or next following the insured's 21st birthday, the owner of this policy shall be Philip Davis, father of the insured, while living; otherwise the insured. On or after the anniversary of the policy date on or next following the insured's 21st birthday, the owner of this policy shall be the insured.

A policy provision of this kind creates an ownership that shifts automatically. For instance, Philip Davis may purchase a $10,000 whole life insurance policy on the life of his daughter, Ellen, when Ellen is three years of age. The quoted policy provision would permit Philip to exercise all ownership rights under the policy while Ellen is growing up. He may obtain a policy loan if he wishes. He may assign the policy to a bank as collateral security for a bank loan. He may elect any dividend option provided by the policy, name and change the beneficiary as often as he wishes, or surrender the policy if he wishes. If the policy is still in force on the anniversary of the policy date on or following Ellen's 21st birthday, however, ownership will shift automatically to Ellen. After that date, Ellen will have all the rights and privileges of ownership previously exercisable by her father.

The Successor-Owner. The quoted ownership provision states that Philip Davis will own the policy for the specified period "while living." If he does not live until Ellen reaches age 21, therefore, Ellen may become the owner of the policy at a much earlier age. This can present several problems.

For example, Philip may die when Ellen is no more than 10 or 12 years of age. If so, Ellen will become the owner of her policy, but who will exercise the ownership rights or pay the premiums? The father's death might mean such a financial loss to the family that premium payments could not, under any circumstances, be continued (a possibility that will be considered later). Assume, however, that Ellen's mother does continue payment of the premiums. Unless she is named the legal guardian of her daughter's estate, she will have no right to effect a policy loan or exercise any other ownership rights under Ellen's policy.

Nor is Ellen in any better position. Although she is the owner, she has all the limitations of minority. Therefore, the company cannot safely recognize any action she might take in connection with the ownership rights under her policy, since any such action could be disaffirmed by her at a later date. In short, although the contract was not made with a minor, the company has, as the result of the adult's death, a minor policyowner with whom to deal.

The most logical and practical way to take care of these problems is to prevent their occurrence; and this can easily be done in the typical instance by the wording of the ownership provision. All that is needed is a successor-owner. Then if the parent-applicant should die before the insured reaches age 21, ownership will shift, not to the insured, but to the successor-owner (usually the surviving parent) for the intervening years. It will then vest in the insured at age 21, as originally provided. The previously quoted ownership provision would then be changed to read as follows:

> Until the anniversary of the policy date on or next following the insured's 21st birthday, the owner of this policy shall be Philip Davis, father of the insured, while living; otherwise Mary Davis, mother of the insured, while living; otherwise the insured. On and after the anniversary of the policy date on or next following the insured's 21st birthday, the owner of this policy shall be the insured.

Of course, if both the owner and the successor-owner die before the insured reaches age 21, the problems will still exist; but this is much less likely.

The Payor Benefit

The death of the parent-owner of a juvenile policy may have such severe financial consequences for the family that premium payments under the policy cannot be continued. If the owner suffers a long-term disability, the result could be the same. Most insurers, therefore, offer a waiver-of-premium-for-payor benefit designed to protect juvenile policies from lapsing under these circumstances. Usually, under this coverage premiums will be waived if the premium payor should die or become totally disabled prior to the insured child's attainment of a specified age. Different companies have their own name for this coverage, but probably the most widely used is "payor benefit."

The payor benefit may be in the form of an attached rider or, in the case of special policies, it may be an integral part of the policy itself. In either case, it provides a waiver-of-premium benefit applicable to the named adult (usually the parent) who is paying the premium for the policy on the child's life. Premiums are typically waived beginning with the first premium to fall due after the death of the payor and ending with the child's attainment of age 21 or 25. In the event of total disability of the payor which has continued for the required waiting period, premiums are waived retroactively, beginning with the first premium to fall due after the beginning of total disability. The waiver then continues as long as the payor remains disabled, or until the child's age 21 or 25, if disability continues beyond that date.

The premium for the payor benefit is small, because the amount of insurance needed to fund it is small. For instance, a $10,000 paid-up-at-65 policy on the life of a child age 5 is available from one life insurer for an annual premium of $110.90. If the payor benefit is effective until the child's age 25, the maximum period of coverage for the payor would be 20 years. The maximum payable under this benefit, therefore, would be 20 times the annual premium, or $2,218. Moreover, for each year the payor lives and does not suffer total disability, the amount of possible liability on the part of the insurer is reduced by one annual premium, or $110.90. The annual premium which this company charges for the payor benefit under this policy is $6.65, for a father age 28. It is somewhat higher for higher ages, of course, but even at the payor's age 40, it is only $12.20.

The payor benefit requires an application (though it is usually a part of the regular application for the juvenile coverage), some risk appraisal, and the additional premium. Usually, the payor's name, address, age, sex, occupation, height and weight, and a brief medical history are requested; and risk appraisal is made on the basis of that information. In most instances, insurability requirements are not very strict, and a medical examination is seldom required.

The payor benefit is of basic importance in connection with any juvenile coverage unless premium payment is assured in some other way.[2] For a small additional premium, a child's life insurance can be guaranteed until he reaches adulthood, regardless of the death or long-term disability of the premium payor. All the arguments in favor of establishing an insurance program on the life of a child in the first place also support establishing a coverage on the life of the payor that will continue the child's insurance program if the adult premium payor is no longer able to do so.

In a sense, the payor benefit "insures the insurance" under the juvenile policy just as the waiver-of-premium-for-disability coverage "insures the insurance" to which it applies. The payor benefit resembles the waiver-of-premium-for-disability coverage since it, too, provides the benefit in the form of a premium waiver. However, the payor benefit differs by providing the waiver in the event of death as well as total disability of the payor, and it concerns the death or disability of a person other than the person whose life is insured under the policy. By contrast, the usual waiver-of-premium-for-disability coverage operates only in the event of the disability of the insured.

The Guaranteed Insurability Coverage

The guaranteed insurability coverage is especially appropriate in connection with juvenile insurance programs. This coverage, it will be remembered (see chapter 10) guarantees the right to purchase additional amounts of insurance at specified intervals, over an extended period, without evidence of insurability. Thus, just as

---

[2] The payor coverage would not, of course, be needed in connection with a single-premium policy or a policy for which premiums have been paid in advance to the child's age 21 or 25.

the payor benefit can be said to "insure the child's insurance," the guaranteed insurability coverage "insures his insurability."

Typical Juvenile Plans

Most life insurance companies make a number of life insurance plans available as early as the first year of life (age 0, in insurance terminology). No special plans, therefore, are necessary for insuring the lives of children. In fact, limited-payment whole life policies and endowment plans are widely used for this purpose. Endowments maturing at a specified age, particularly 18 or 20, are especially popular, because of their convenience in providing funds for college. Sometimes these endowment policies have special settlement sections designed to provide funds over four years of college or some similar period of time. Nevertheless, most life insurance companies also offer some plans that have been expressly designed for juveniles.

One popular life insurance policy designed for juvenile insureds provides a nominal amount of insurance in the early years, which increases at a specified age, typically at or near age 21, to an amount five times the original face amount. Thus a $1,000 policy at age 5 would become a policy for $5,000 at age 21.

This policy is variously called "estate builder," "junior or juvenile estate builder," "junior guardian," and other similar names. (In fact, it is often unofficially called "jumping juvenile.") It is offered in a number of different variations. One plan, for instance, doubles the face amount at age 18, triples it at age 19, increases it to four times the original amount at age 20 and to five times the original amount at age 21. (This is perhaps the most "jumping" of the "jumping juvenile" policies.) Other policies may increase at two different ages. All, however, provide for an increase to a much larger amount of insurance at about age 21, although the premium remains the same—that is, the premium is level from the issue date.

A substantially higher premium is payable during the earlier years under a policy of this kind than would be required under a continuous-premium, whole life policy for the same original amount of insurance. As a result, cash values are built up much faster than under the whole life plans, and at the insured's age 21 the automatic increase in coverage is possible without any increase in premiums. Combined with the guaranteed insurability benefit, this kind of policy offers a limited amount of protection during the early years but permits a rapid expansion of insurance at a time when most insureds are beginning to assume the responsibilities of adulthood.

■ THE FAMILY POLICIES

There is some justification for life insurance on the life of every member of a family, and it is undoubtedly more convenient to pay only one premium (and have only one policy) instead of several. For these reasons, numerous attempts have been made to develop a policy under which all members of a family would be covered. The most successful policy of this kind is the family life policy, first introduced on a large scale in 1956.

Attempts had been made as early as the 1930's to provide coverage for all family members under one policy; and contracts insuring more than one person had been available to some extent for many years. However, the idea of insuring all members of a family under one contract had never before proved especially attractive.

For several reasons, the 1950's may have provided a more favorable climate for this idea of family coverage than did prior periods. First, improved infant mortality rates made it more feasible from the insurer's point of view to establish one premium to provide coverage for all children in a family, including those born after the issuance of the policy. Second, the "population explosion" of those years may have made such plans more attractive to the public; and, finally, a growing emphasis on "package policies" for other insurance needs may have played a part in the ready acceptance of "package" coverages for family life insurance needs. Whatever the reasons, the family life policies have proved to be very popular, and have accounted for about 20 percent of all ordinary life insurance sold in the United States for the past several years.

The Family Life Policy

In its most typical form, the family life policy provides coverage in units, each unit consisting of $5,000 of whole life insurance on the life of the husband; a lesser amount, typically about $1,000, of term insurance on the life of the wife; and $1,000 of term insurance on the life of each child in the family, regardless of the number of children there are or will be while the coverage remains in force. Different versions of this coverage have been developed by different companies, but this pattern remains reasonably typical of the family life coverages.

Insurance on the Life of the Husband. In most instances, the insurance provided on the life of the husband is whole life insurance; and usually additional benefits, such as family income or level term insurance riders, and similar coverages, are available on his life.

The premium for the policy is established on a basis of the husband's age and is usually level to his age 65. Typically, it reduces at that time and continues on a level, but lower, basis for the remainder of his life.

Insurance on the Life of the Wife. Under the most typical family life policy, the insurance on the life of the wife is term insurance and expires at the husband's age 65. This creates a problem if the wife dies before the husband. If a level premium is payable under the policy, the wife's death prior to that of the husband will, in the absence of a premium adjustment, mean that the premium for her death benefit will continue to be payable after her death. For this reason, some companies increase the amount of insurance on the life of the husband (after the death of the wife before his age 65) by the amount of the wife's death benefit on the same term-to-age 65 basis. Under this arrangement, if the husband dies later than his wife but prior to his age 65, the death benefit payable per unit will be his original insurance of $5,000, plus $1,000. (At his age 65, the $1,000 additional term insurance expires.) Other companies provide a premium reduction, rather than added insurance on the husband's life, after the wife's death benefit has been paid.

Since the premium for the family life policy is based on the age of the husband, variations in the age of the wife are usually reflected by adjustments in the amount of her insurance. Her death benefit, therefore, will be $1,000 for each $5,000 of insurance on the life of the husband only if she is the same age as the husband. If she is younger than he is, her insurance will be more than $1,000; if she is older, the benefit will be less. In order to establish a reasonable relationship between the amount of insurance on the wife and the amount of coverage on the husband, a maximum age difference is usually established. Thus the family policy may not be available if the wife is more than 12 years younger or more than 7 years older, than her husband. Different companies establish different limits, but the principle remains the same.

Insurance on the Life of Each Child. For each unit of $5,000 on the life of the father, a benefit of $1,000 is usually provided on the life of each child, at a premium that is established on an average basis, regardless of the number of children in the particular family. The premium rate is established by assuming a specified number of children per family, such as two or three, and the premium is not increased regardless of the number of children born after the policy is issued (after-born children). Any child of the insured is eligible if he is named in the application and is 15 days but not yet 18 years of age. As a general rule, also, any child born to or adopted by the insured after the policy has been issued will be covered automatically on and after the age of 15 days. Insurance on the lives of the children is term insurance, and it typically expires at the child's age 21 or 25, or at the father's age 65, whichever is earlier.

Conversion Privileges. Since the insurance on the lives of the wife and children under the typical family life policy is term insurance, there is a conversion privilege, very similar to the conversion privilege under individual term insurance policies. However, the value of this privilege is somewhat limited with respect to the insurance on the life of the wife, because it is available only at the time her insurance would otherwise expire—that is, at the husband's age 65. Usually, any permanent plan to which her coverage might be converted at that time would require a relatively high premium.

The child's conversion privilege is more attractive. In the first place, it is available at a much more favorable age—21 or 25, depending on the policy wording. And in the second place, it usually includes the privilege of increasing the amount of permanent insurance to as much as the amount of insurance on the life of the father, if desired. Thus, if Thomas Briggs has a $5,000 family life policy, each of his children will have the option of converting his or her $1,000 of term coverage to $1,000 of permanent insurance, or to a larger amount if preferred, subject to a maximum of $5,000, without evidence of insurability.

Conversion is usually permitted on written request within a conversion period, typically 31 days following expiration of the term insurance coverage. The usual conversion requirements are imposed. The new policy must be a whole life or endowment plan then issued by the company; it will be dated as of the day following the day the term coverage expired; and additional benefits—such as accidental death and waiver-of-premium-for-disability coverages—are available only if evidence of insurability for those benefits is submitted. A death benefit may be provided during the 31-day conversion period in the event the person entitled to exercise the privilege dies during the conversion period and before conversion has been requested or completed.

Other Benefits and Privileges. The family life policy frequently provides an additional accidental death coverage on the lives of the husband and wife, but not generally on the lives of the children. This benefit is payable in the event of the accidental death of either husband or wife, or both of them, and is subject to the customary terms and provisions of the usual accidental death coverage. The only difference is that two people have the coverage under the family life policy instead of one.

Waiver-of-premium-for-total-disability is usually provided for the husband only and follows the usual pattern of this coverage in individual plans.

Most family life policies provide a valuable additional benefit in the form of paid-up term insurance benefits in the event of the death of the husband prior to age 65. If he dies prior to this age, the insurance on the life of his wife, if she survives him, and on any surviving children, is continued on a paid-up basis for the remainder of their respective terms. This, it will be remembered, is to age 21 or 25 for each child of the insured. For the wife, the insurance is continued to the date the husband would have attained age 65.

Risk Appraisal. The application for the family life coverage requires risk appraisal information on all members of the family who will be covered under the policy when issued, and all must be insurable in accordance with the risk appraisal rules of the company. Later-born children will be covered automatically and without evidence of insurability, when they reach the specified age (typically 15 days). However, children living at the time the policy is issued must satisfy the risk appraisal requirements of the company.

Ownership and Control. The family life policy in its typical form is issued on the application of the husband. From the outset, therefore, he is the owner of the policy and has the sole right to change the beneficiary, elect any options available, and exercise any other rights under the policy, for as long as he lives. It is quite possible, however, that he may be the first to die. If so, the insurance benefit will be paid to the beneficiary; but contrary to the situation under an individual policy, the contract will not terminate. Instead, it will continue as paid-up term insurance on the life of the wife and the lives of each of the children for the remainder of their respective terms. These paid-up benefits may have cash values, and the insurance is convertible. Someone, therefore, must have the right to change beneficiaries, surrender the contract, if necessary, and otherwise exercise the ownership rights under the contract.

There may be other deaths also, prior to the date when the last of the term insurance coverages expires or is converted. Thus, there may be more than one change in the ownership situation. Without a relatively well-defined succession-of-ownership provision, therefore, problems could be numerous. For this reason, it is customary to outline in the contract the succession of ownership of the policy. A typical provision of this kind might specify that the insured shall be the owner, while living; otherwise the insured's wife, while living; otherwise the children of the insured who are insured under the policy at the time the ownership right in question is to be exercised.

Beneficiary and Settlement Provisions. The owner has the right to designate and change the beneficiary for each death benefit provided by the policy. However, the policy is designed to cover a typical family situation; and, for this reason, a relatively standard beneficiary provision is frequently included in the policy. An illustrative beneficiary provision might read as follows:

The beneficiary for any benefit payable on the death of the insured shall be the wife of the insured, if living; otherwise the executor or administrator of the insured.

The beneficiary for any benefit payable on the death of the wife of the insured shall be the insured, if living; otherwise the executor or administrator of the wife of the insured.

The beneficiary for any benefit payable on the death of any child of the insured shall be the insured, if living; otherwise the wife of the insured, if living; otherwise the executor or administrator of such child.

Other Policy Provisions

The family life policy contains all of the provisions found in the typical whole life policy since it provides whole life insurance on the life of the husband. However, the additional benefits payable on the death of the wife and each of the children of the insured require revisions in some of the whole life provisions. Differences in the ownership provision and the standard beneficiary designation have been discussed previously. Another typical difference is found in the reinstatement provision.

Under the family life policy, the reinstatement provision requires evidence of insurability, including good health, with respect to everyone who will be insured under the reinstated policy, not just the principal insured. Therefore, children born to or adopted by the insured after the policy was issued will be subject to risk appraisal for the first time if the policy lapses and reinstatement is requested.

The incontestable and suicide provisions also reflect the fact that more than one person is insured. Thus, the policy is declared to be:

... incontestable with respect to the insurance provided on the life of any person insured under this policy after such insurance has been in force during the lifetime of such person for a period of two years from the policy date or the issue date, whichever is the earlier.

The suicide provision reads:

Neither the suicide of the insured nor of the wife of the insured, within two years of the policy date or the issue date, whichever is the earlier, is a risk assumed under this policy.

Identification of Wife and Children. One of the special problems in connection with issuing and administering the family life coverage concerns the identification of the wife and children who are insured. The policy usually identifies the wife as "the wife named in the application." Thus, if Herbert Ritter is married to "Elizabeth" at the time the policy is issued but they are later divorced, Elizabeth will still remain insured under the family life policy unless Herbert (the owner) requests termination of her coverage.

Identification of the children presents a somewhat more complex question. All children named in the application who are between the ages of 15 days and 18 years are eligible for insurance. Later born children, however, are also covered and they, as well as children who are adopted after the issuance of the policy, will not be named in the policy. In order to identify the persons insured as "children" under this policy, therefore, a special definition of the phrase "child of the insured" is usually included in the policy. The following is illustrative:

Child of the insured means any child, stepchild, or legally adopted child of the insured named in the application for this policy who, as of the policy date or issue date, whichever is the earlier, has not attained his or her 18th birthday, and any child, stepchild, or legally adopted child acquired by the insured (1) after such date and (2) prior to the child's 18th birthday.

Usually the benefit provision makes it clear that the death benefit is not payable on the death of any child of the insured who has not attained the age of 15 days.

Variations of the Family Life Policy

The policy form discussed thus far is relatively typical. However, as previously mentioned, many variations of the family life coverage have been developed. One such variation provides endowment insurance on the life of the husband; another provides permanent insurance on the life of the wife. This latter variation is especially attractive because the wife's insurance under the typical policy is on a term basis and expires at the husband's age 65. If this is converted to permanent insurance at the husband's age 65, the new policy will usually require a relatively high premium. It is more than probable, therefore, that the wife's term coverage under the typical family life policy will be permitted to expire at a time when she may still need some protection. This possible disadvantage is especially easy to overlook when it is included in a "package" policy which provides many benefits with respect to other members of the family. Nevertheless, it remains a disadvantage when the total insurance needs of the family are considered, and plans that provide permanent insurance on the life of the wife have been developed to meet this particular need.

Other Family Plan Coverages

Today, the family plan coverages are being offered in the form of riders with increasing frequency. Thus, a rider may be offered under which one parent is insured on a term-to-age-65 basis and the children (including those born or adopted after the issue date of the rider) are insured on a term-to-age-21 or -25 basis, in much the same way as the wife and children are insured under the family life policy. This rider can be attached to any whole life coverage on the life of the father, and the basic result is much the same as that achieved by the family life policy. Alternatively, one rider can be used to insure the wife and a separate rider to insure the children of the insured. This approach permits a great deal of flexibility as to amounts of coverage for the various lives.

Using riders also permits family coverages for families in which one parent is uninsurable or for family units that include only one parent. For situations of this kind, the typical family life policy is not suitable. One-parent "family" policies have been developed to insure the one parent and children, but when riders are used, it is possible to assemble in one policy exactly the coverage needed for any particular family unit.

■ THE JOINT WHOLE LIFE POLICY

Except for the family life coverages, no ordinary life insurance policies providing insurance on the lives of more than one person have proved especially popular. One such coverage, however, has recently received attention and with some added benefits may prove to be a very appropriate coverage for husband and wife. It also has some advantages in business situations, such as partnerships. This is the joint whole life policy.

In the form in which it was generally offered in the past, the joint life policy insured the lives of two people, but the amount of insurance was paid only on the death of the first of the insureds to die. When this payment had been made, the contract terminated. Plans of this kind had the advantage of a lower premium than would have been payable for individual policies providing the same amount of insurance on each life, but had the disadvantage that the insurance on the life of the survivor was terminated at the death of the first insured to die. Often this occurred at a time when continued insurance was needed but unavailable because of age or uninsurability. Often, also, this possibility was not fully understood by either insured when the insurance was purchased.

Today, a number of life insurers offer a joint life insurance policy with two significant added benefits. First, the survivor is covered by term insurance for a specified period (90 days, for example) after the death of the first insured to die. Second, during this 90-day period, the survivor has the option of purchasing, without evidence of insurability, a new whole life or endowment policy on his own life for as much insurance as was provided on the death of the first insured to die.

The premium for a joint whole life policy is established on the basis of a joint "equivalent" age, which means that the ages of the two insureds are adjusted and an equivalent single age is established. Typically, term insurance on the life of the survivor is provided for 60 or 90 days, and there are age limitations. For example, the 90-day term insurance may be provided only if the first insured to die is not more than 65 or 70 years of age when he dies. However, the joint life policy is available at a significantly lower premium rate than would be necessary for whole life insurance on one insured plus level term insurance on the other, and in many ways the effect is the same.

Assume that Richard and Lois Noyes apply for a $10,000 joint whole life policy of this kind, at ages 24 and 26. Assume further that Richard dies at age 30 and that Lois is the beneficiary, to receive the benefit payable on his death. Lois will receive $10,000, but the insurance on her life will also continue in the amount of $10,000 for a 90-day period. During that period, she may apply for a $10,000 individual policy (whole life or endowment) without evidence of insurability; and if she dies during the 90-day period, her beneficiary will receive $10,000. These added benefits remove the basic objection to the traditional joint whole life policy—that the survivor of the joint insureds was left without coverage after the death of the first insured to die.

■ QUESTIONS FOR REVIEW

1. What is the basic advantage in using some term insurance to meet the life insurance needs of the head of a family?
2. Describe the family income coverage. How does this differ from the family maintenance coverage?
3. What is the usual makeup of a "double protection" policy? What is the principal advantage of such policies? A disadvantage?
4. Discuss briefly three reasons justifying purchase of insurance on the life of a child.
5. Why is it customary to provide for adult ownership and control of insurance on the life of a child?
6. Briefly discuss the payor benefit and guaranteed insurability coverages as they are used in connection with juvenile insurance.
7. List the principal death benefits usually payable under a family life policy. What plans of insurance are used for each of these?
8. Why is the conversion privilege under the family life policy more valuable with respect to the term insurance on the lives of the children than to that on the life of the wife?
9. Under what circumstances may it be advantageous to provide the family life insurance coverages by rider rather than in an integrated policy?
10. Briefly describe a joint life insurance policy. What two special benefits are sometimes included in this policy as it is offered today?

12 INDUSTRIAL LIFE INSURANCE AND THE DEBIT SYSTEM

Industrial (or debit) life insurance is generally defined as life insurance provided under individual policies issued in small face amounts—typically less than $1,000—and marketed by agents who call at the policyowner's home to collect premiums, usually on a weekly or monthly basis.

Today the survivors' benefits under the Social Security programs, as well as group life insurance plans, have alleviated to a very marked extent the life insurance needs of the low-income workers that industrial life insurance was designed to meet. In 1970, however, some 77 million industrial life insurance policies were in force in the United States, for a total of $38.6 billion. Industrial life insurance seems, therefore, to continue to meet the need for some life insurance protection for many low-income persons.

The purpose of this chapter is to discuss the general characteristics of industrial life insurance, with particular attention to policy forms, premium rates, and marketing methods.

■ HISTORICAL BACKGROUND

Industrial life insurance originated in England in 1854, as a means of making actuarially sound life insurance available in amounts and at premiums that the industrial workers of that time could afford. In those days, people who worked in industry received very low wages;

and ordinary life insurance was generally beyond their means. Premiums for ordinary life insurance plans could not be paid more frequently than quarterly; and even quarterly premiums were too large for most wage earners to pay.

In earlier days, many of the working people had belonged to local burial clubs and friendly societies and, through such associations, had been able to make some provision for a burial fund or for benefits if they became ill. As England became more highly industrialized, however, these local societies began to disappear. Larger friendly societies took their place, drawing their membership from wider geographical areas. Though larger in size, these societies still operated on some variation of the assessment plan and were subject to the basic weaknesses of such plans. By the middle 1800's, these weaknesses had become so apparent, and administrative abuses within the societies so widespread, that an investigation into their activities was made by the British Parliament.

About this time, a newly formed life insurance company—later known as The Prudential Assurance Company—made a study of the possibilities of making life insurance available to industrial workers. The company, already writing insurance on ordinary life plans, concluded that life insurance on an actuarially sound basis could be provided at premiums lower-income people could afford, if some of the practices associated with ordinary life insurance were modified.

The company proposed, therefore, to offer insurance in smaller face amounts, with premiums payable weekly and, in some instances, in amounts as small as three or five cents. To encourage the payment of these premiums, the insurance agent would collect them at the home of the insured. One other departure from ordinary life insurance practices was also introduced—the amount of insurance purchased was determined by the amount of premium the policyowner could pay, instead of determining the premium on the basis of the amount of insurance purchased. In other words, the applicant would decide how large a premium he could pay, and the amount of insurance he purchased would be the amount which that premium would buy.

Industrial life insurance was introduced in the United States about 20 years after it had its beginnings in England. The first policy in the United States was issued in 1875, by the Prudential Insurance Company of America. Later, Metropolitan Life Insurance Company and John Hancock Mutual Life Insurance Company entered the industrial business; and these companies became and remained for many years the largest writers of industrial life insurance in the United States. All three have now discontinued the issuance of new industrial life insurance policies, although many other companies have continued to sell industrial life insurance.

■ DISTINCTIVE CHARACTERISTICS

The insurance law of one representative state defines industrial life insurance as ". . . that form of life insurance, either (1) under which the premiums are payable weekly, or (2) under which the premiums are payable monthly or oftener, but less often than weekly, if the face amount of insurance provided in any such policy is less than one thousand dollars and if the words 'industrial policy' are printed upon the policy as a part of the descriptive matter."

This definition emphasizes two important characteristics of industrial life insurance. The first is the frequency of premium payments. At first industrial insurance premiums were always payable weekly, but this is not necessarily true today, and that fact is reflected in the quoted definition. The second characteristic is the small face amounts of the individual policies. Historically, industrial life insurance policies have been issued in very small amounts, often less than $100. Thus, in addition to weekly-premium policies, the definition includes insurance under which the premiums are payable monthly or "oftener, but less often than weekly," if the amount of insurance is less than $1,000 and the policy is described as "industrial insurance."

Although this definition emphasizes two significant characteristics of industrial life insurance, there are other important characteristics also. The first of these is the marketing (sales) approach. Industrial life insurance is sold in a way that is distinctly different from the marketing of ordinary life insurance. Second, industrial life insurance plans are usually more limited in number than those offered in ordinary life insurance; and, finally, industrial life insurance premium rates are generally higher per $1,000 of insurance than are premium rates for ordinary life insurance plans.

Marketing

From the beginning, industrial life insurance was sold differently from ordinary life insurance. Because these plans were designed for persons of extremely limited means, it was recognized that there would be strong competing (noninsurance) demands for even the small amounts of money which the premiums involved. For this reason, a special agency system—the "debit" system—was developed to bring the insurance to the policyowner and keep it in force.

The word "debit" has several different meanings, as it is used in industrial life insurance. Originally, it meant the total weekly premiums which the agent was to collect on policies in force in the territory assigned to him. In bookkeeping terms, these premiums were "debited" to him on the company's records and thus referred to as his "debit." Today the word "debit" is frequently used instead of the word "industrial," to describe the line of insurance—that is, "debit" insurance. It may also be used to refer to the geographical area served by the debit agent (his debit being the area he is assigned to serve), or to the marketing system itself (the debit system).

Fundamentally, the debit system is a door-to-door method of selling and servicing life insurance. Originally, the debit agent called on his policyowners once a week, and he still does so for weekly premium policies, unless the policyowner elects to pay the premium less frequently. Today the policyowner may pay his premium at the home office or an agency office if he prefers, and most companies grant a premium refund if industrial premiums are paid at such an office over as long a period as a year.

When the debit agent sells a policy or policies to a new family, he delivers a premium receipt book, usually one book for all the policies in the family. As premiums are paid, the agent enters the amount paid in the receipt book and does not give a separate premium receipt. In his report to his office, he reports only the total amount collected on all of the policies in force on his debit. Thus, the company does not maintain detailed records for individual policies either at its home office or at the agency office. It does not even have a record of the names and addresses of the insureds. (Such records, of policies and insureds, are kept by the agent.)

A marketing system of this kind involves considerably more expense to the company than the system used for marketing ordinary life insurance, but the practice of collecting premiums at the policyowner's home has been considered an important factor in keeping industrial policies in force. The company, the agent, and the policyowner all benefit by this practice.

Because the agent becomes so well acquainted with the families on whom he calls, he is in a particularly favorable position to understand and help them meet their new insurance needs as those needs become apparent. He makes every effort to prevent the policies for which he is responsible from lapsing; he informs the policyowners of dividends when they are declared, helps to insure additional members of a family, assists with beneficiary changes and the completion of claim papers, and generally does everything in his power to see that the policyowners and beneficiaries obtain the full benefits provided by their insurance. All these are services other life insurance agents also perform, but because of his close and continuing contacts with his policyowners and their families, the debit agent often occupies an almost unique position as an insurance advisor.

Fewer Plans

Most companies do not offer many different plans of industrial life insurance. Typically, a life paid-up-at-65 or -70 policy may be offered, as well as a 20-payment life policy and endowments at 65 or 70. Term plans are rare. In most instances, whole life policies paid up at 65 or 70 are offered, rather than the continuous-premium, whole life plan. This avoids the need for paying premiums in the insured's later years but continues his protection throughout his lifetime.

Higher Premium Rates

Premium rates for industrial life insurance are characteristically higher per $1,000 of insurance than premium rates for similar plans of ordinary life insurance. There are several reasons for this. One is the premium collection service of the debit agent, previously mentioned. Collecting premiums at the policyowner's home as often as weekly clearly involves more expense than is incurred in connection with premium collection under ordinary life insurance.

The owner of an industrial life insurance policy also has the benefit of two coverages, at no specified extra cost, that are provided under the ordinary life insurance policy only for specific extra premiums, if they are available at all. Disability benefits in the form of a lump-sum payment in case of dismemberment or blindness, as well as an accidental death benefit, are included as a part of the typical industrial life insurance policy, without additional premium. These coverages are somewhat different from benefits of the same general description offered in connection with ordinary life insurance contracts. As a result, there is no accurate basis for comparing the costs of these added benefits, but they help to account for the higher premium rates for industrial policies.

A third reason for the higher premium rates for industrial life insurance is found in the applicable mortality rates, which are generally higher for these insureds than for persons of the same age insured under ordinary life insurance policies. Much industrial life insurance is sold to low-income persons, whose circumstances, both at work and at home, are not as favorable to good health or freedom from accidents as those enjoyed by persons in higher-income groups. Greater exposure to industrial hazards, less adequate health care, and less comfortable living conditions, all contribute to a higher mortality rate among lower-income groups. Nevertheless, better health care, more effective accident prevention, and general improvement in living standards for all income levels are steadily reducing this difference between the mortality rates for industrial insureds and those for persons insured under ordinary life insurance policies.

A fourth major reason for the generally higher premium rates for industrial life insurance is found in the risk appraisal practices used in this line of insurance. Risk appraisal procedures used in this line of life insurance are significantly less refined than those used in considering applications for ordinary life insurance. Medical examinations and inspection reports are rarely required, and many persons who would be accepted only at substandard rates for ordinary life plans are accepted at standard rates for industrial life insurance. As a result, standard premium rates generally are higher for industrial life insurance than for similar ordinary life insurance policies.

For these reasons, mortality tables based on industrial experience rather than experience under ordinary life insurance plans are used for calculating reserves and premium rates for industrial life insurance. The following figures show the death rates at different selected ages according to the 1958 Commissioners' Standard Ordinary (1958 CSO) Mortality Table and those at the same ages under the 1961 Commissioners' Standard Industrial (1961 CSI) Mortality Table.

Comparison of Mortality Rates—Ordinary and Industrial (deaths per 1,000)

Ages	1958 CSO (Ordinary)	1961 CSI (Industrial)
5	1.35	1.44
10	1.21	1.23
15	1.46	1.53
20	1.79	1.97
25	1.93	2.19
30	2.13	2.55
35	2.51	3.34
40	3.53	4.84
45	5.35	7.28
50	8.32	10.77

Administrative costs are also a significant factor in considering the higher premium rates for industrial life insurance. Industrial life insurance policies are issued in very small amounts. (The average size of such policies in force for United States companies in 1970 was $500.) Yet some expenses in connection with the issuance of a policy are the same whether the amount of insurance is $500 or $5,000. Consequently, it is definitely more expensive per $1,000 of coverage to issue and administer small policies than policies for larger amounts. In addition, the lapse rate for industrial business has always been higher than that for ordinary life insurance. Often the company's cost of issuing a policy is never met out of premium income from that policy simply because the policy is not kept in force long enough. All these factors must be taken into account in explaining the higher premium rates for industrial life insurance.

■ THE INDUSTRIAL LIFE INSURANCE POLICY

In most respects, the provisions of industrial life insurance policies are similar to those of ordinary life insurance contracts. However, some provisions typically found in ordinary life insurance contracts are modified as they appear in industrial life insurance plans, and other provisions are included that are unique in industrial plans.

Option to Surrender

One of the distinctive provisions in an industrial life insurance policy permits the policyowner to hold the policy for a short while—usually two or three weeks—and then return it, if he wishes, and have his entire premium refunded. In effect, this gives him free insurance coverage for the period which has elapsed. An illustrative provision of this kind reads as follows:

Option to Surrender within Three Weeks. If this policy is not satisfactory it may be surrendered for cancellation, within three weeks from its date of issue, at the district office through which it was delivered, and the premium or premiums paid will be returned.

Premium Payment

An industrial life insurance contract expresses the usual promise to pay the stated amount of insurance on receipt of due proof of the death of the insured and contains the usual consideration provision relating to payment of premiums. Nowhere, however, does it specifically provide that the premiums will be payable at the home of the insured or that the agent will call at the home to collect the premium. This service is implied by the inclusion of a provision unique to the industrial life insurance policy—a provision for a refund of part of the premium if the policyowner pays the premium at an office of the company for a specified period, usually a year. One company captions such a provision, "Refund on Direct Payment of Premiums." The gist of this provision is that the company will grant a refund of 10 percent of the total year's premiums if they are paid directly to an office of the company that maintains facilities for receiving such direct payments.

Nothing in the industrial life insurance policy relieves the policyowner of the obligation to pay the premium and to take the initiative, if necessary, in doing so. Thus, if the agent does not call and if the premium is not paid, the policy will lapse.

The Grace Period

The grace period provision differs somewhat from that of the ordinary life insurance policy. Generally, the insurance laws require a grace period of four weeks for industrial policies, although a 31-day period is required if premiums are payable monthly. (It will be recalled that a 31-day grace period is required for ordinary life insurance contracts.)

Dividend Provisions

Dividends are apportioned annually under participating industrial life insurance policies (as is true of ordinary participating policies). However, because of the small amounts involved, the methods used for allocating industrial policy dividends are not generally as refined as those used in ordinary life insurance. Dividends are customarily apportioned on a calendar-year basis rather than a policy-year basis, and generally by year of issue. Thus dividends for policies issued in 1973 would not be applied on the anniversaries of the various policy dates but at the end of the calendar year for all such policies. (Occasionally, the methods differ by plan of insurance.)

Because the amounts involved are usually small, industrial policies customarily provide only one method in which dividends may be applied (that is, there are no dividend "options"). For example, the policy may provide that dividends will be applied to purchase paid-up additions or that they will be used as premium credits, but the policyowner usually does not have a choice, as he does under an ordinary life insurance contract. If the policy specifies the paid-up additions method, the amount of the paid-up insurance will be established as a percentage of the face amount, rather than a specific dollar amount as would be true under the paid-up additions dividend option of ordinary life insurance plans.

Assignment

The assignment provision found in most industrial life insurance policies differs in a fundamental way from the assignment provision customarily found in the ordinary life insurance contract. The early industrial life insurance policies specifically stated that they were not assignable, and the policies of many companies still declare any assignment void. This approach was felt to be justified because of the very small amounts for which such policies were issued, as well as the fact that industrial policies frequently provided the only funds available for burial expenses. It was considered undesirable, therefore, to encourage or permit assignment, since a valid assignment existing at the date of the insured's death could virtually wipe out the already limited amount of insurance payable to the beneficiary. Prohibition of assignments also reduced the company's administrative expense.

Today, however, companies operating in the state of New York are required to permit an industrial life insurance contract to be assigned to a bank as security for a loan. Often this permission is specifically granted in the policy and any other kind of assignment is declared to be void. The following policy provision is illustrative:

Assignability. This policy may be assigned to any national bank, state bank, or trust company, but any assignment or pledge of this policy or any of its benefits to an assignee other than one of the foregoing shall be void. No assignment of this policy shall be binding upon the company unless and until it has been filed with the company at its home office or one of its head offices. The company assumes no obligation as to the validity or sufficiency of any assignment.

Settlement Provisions

Beneficiary Designations. The early industrial life insurance policies made no provision for naming a specific person as beneficiary. Under what was called a "facility of payment" provision, the policy provided for payment to anyone who appeared "equitably entitled to the proceeds." Generally, this meant someone who had paid or incurred the expenses of the insured's last illness or burial. However, present-day industrial policies usually permit policyowners to name and change beneficiaries on much the same basis as ordinary life insurance policies.

Facility-of-Payment Provision. Even though a beneficiary is named, many situations may exist at the time a claim arises which could result in a delay in settlement. The policy may have been lost or the beneficiary may have died. Ordinary life insurance policies usually provide that if the named beneficiary and any contingent beneficiaries have died prior to the death of the insured, payment will be made to the insured's estate. This requires the court appointment of an administrator or executor, and entails some legal expense. However, such expenses are not usually a significant factor in the settlement of ordinary life insurance claims, since the proceeds often amount to many thousands of dollars.

Under an industrial life insurance policy, however, such legal expenses could easily amount to half the proceeds or more. Obviously, this would defeat the basic purpose of the insurance, create delay, and in many cases make settlement difficult. For this reason, a "facility-of-payment" provision is still frequently included in industrial life insurance policies. The following provision is illustrative.

Facility of Payment. If the beneficiary does not surrender this policy with due proof of death within 60 days after the death of the insured, or if the beneficiary is the estate of the insured, or is a minor or incompetent, or dies before the insured, the death benefit will, upon surrender of this policy with due proof of death, be paid to the executor or administrator of the insured; but in any such case the company may, in lieu of payment to the executor or administrator, pay the death benefit to any person named as beneficiary, or to any relative by blood or connection by marriage of the insured appearing to the company to be equitably entitled to such payment. The company may, if the insured is incompetent, make any other payment or grant any right or benefit provided in the policy to any of the persons described in this paragraph.

This provision specifies three situations in which the insurer has the right not to make payment to the named beneficiary, even if the beneficiary is living. They are (1) if the beneficiary does not make claim for the proceeds within 60 days after the death of the insured,

(2) if the beneficiary is a minor, and (3) if the beneficiary is mentally incompetent. In any of these situations, the company may pay the death benefit to the executor or the administrator of the insured. Under this provision, however, it also has the option of paying either "to any person named as beneficiary, or to any relative by blood or connection by marriage of the insured appearing to the company to be equitably entitled to such payment."

The basic objective of this kind of clause is to permit payment of the policy proceeds with as little delay or expense as possible. In most instances, the insurance money is badly needed, and settlement without delay is in the best interests of the payee as well as of the company.

Benefit for Loss of Eyesight or Limbs

Industrial life insurance policies typically include, at no specified additional premium, a provision for a benefit in the event the insured loses his sight or limbs. This benefit differs in several ways from the disability benefits provided under ordinary life insurance policies. One company's industrial policy, for example, provides a lump-sum benefit in the same amount as the death benefit, which is payable in case of the loss of both hands or both feet, or one hand and one foot, or the total and irrecoverable loss of sight. One-half this amount is payable if the insured loses only one hand or one foot. In any of these situations, in addition to the payment of the specified amount, the policy will be endorsed as fully paid, and no further premiums will be payable.

The Accidental Death Benefit

The accidental death benefit (sometimes called "accidental means death benefit" and sometimes referred to as "double indemnity") follows the same general lines as the comparable benefit that is offered in connection with the ordinary life insurance contract. Usually, death must result "directly and independently of all other causes, from bodily injuries caused solely by external, violent, and accidental means." The benefit is not payable if death occurs by suicide, as a result of excluded aviation activities or war, or when the insured is attempting to commit a felony. Excluded also are deaths in which disease or bodily or mental infirmity are contributory factors. Under some policies, the accidental death benefit is reduced by any amount payable under the loss-of-eyesight-or-limbs provision if the loss of eyesight or limbs resulted from the same accident.

■ INDUSTRIAL INSURANCE FOR CHILDREN

Since industrial life insurance policies were issued in small amounts and for small weekly premiums, it was not unusual, from a very early date, for a family to purchase several policies so that every member of the family would be insured. Children were thus insured under industrial policies at a time when other forms of juvenile insurance were very rare. Since the death of a child can easily mean financial hardship to a family of limited means, insurance to protect against that possibility is not only appropriate but clearly within the primary objective of industrial life insurance—that of providing a burial fund.

■ INDUSTRIAL LIFE INSURANCE—AN EVALUATION

Industrial life insurance has been criticized from time to time, particularly on the basis of its cost to the policyowner. In its defense, however, it should be pointed out that the industrial, or debit, system has made life insurance available to many people who could not or would not have purchased insurance under ordinary plans. Policies were issued in very small amounts, but those amounts were enough to meet, or help to meet, the costs of burial. Premiums were payable literally in pennies, but the agent was at the door regularly each week; and often the cash value of a policy on which such small premiums had been paid represented the only funds of any kind available to the family in an emergency.

Since the mid-1950's, there has been a slight decrease in the total amount of industrial life insurance in force. This continues a trend that began shortly after World War II, when the amount of industrial life insurance in force in the United States began to show a much slower rate of increase from year to year than did either ordinary life or group life insurance. There are several reasons for this apparent trend.

First, many people who once would have purchased industrial life insurance policies are now able to afford ordinary life insurance. This has been made easier by the development of "monthly debit ordinary" life insurance, under which premiums for ordinary life insurance policies are payable on a monthly basis but collected at the policyowners' homes by a debit agent.

Second, more and more industrial workers are being covered by group life insurance plans; and third, the survivors' benefits and the lump-sum death benefit under Social Security have further reduced the need for industrial life insurance coverage. Finally, insurance on the lives of children is readily available now under ordinary life insurance policies—family plans as well as individual policies—whereas many years ago, an industrial policy was often the only life insurance available for young children. All of these factors have been influential in the decline in total amount of industrial life insurance in force. However, the purchase of nearly 8 million industrial policies for a total of more than $6 billion of insurance in one recent year suggests that this line of life insurance continues to meet an important part of the public's total life insurance needs.

■ QUESTIONS FOR REVIEW

1. Explain why industrial life insurance was originally developed.
2. Outline an illustrative definition of industrial life insurance.
3. List four possible meanings of the word "debit" as it is used in industrial life insurance.
4. Summarize the role of the agent in industrial life insurance.
5. Describe the differences between industrial and ordinary life insurance with respect to:
   a) plans of insurance
   b) amount of premium
   c) mortality rates.
6. Explain how the following provisions differ in industrial contracts from comparable provisions in ordinary life insurance policies:
   a) the premium payment provision
   b) the grace period provision
   c) the assignment provision.
7. Briefly describe the facility-of-payment clause. What is its purpose?
8. Discuss briefly the disability benefits typically provided under industrial life insurance policies.
9. In the past several years the amount of industrial life insurance in force has diminished. Give three major reasons for this trend.

13 HEALTH INSURANCE

Loss of income because of illness or accident, as well as the expenses of hospital, medical, and surgical care, are all economic losses in the true insurance sense of the term; and they are measured in billions of dollars every year. It is hardly surprising, therefore, that health insurance, which reimburses the insured for such losses, is one of the fastest-growing and most dynamic coverages in the present-day insurance world.

Some of the reasons for this growth, some of the problems involved, and some of the principal forms of health insurance offered today will be discussed in this chapter. As has been true of the life insurance coverages, this discussion will be concerned mainly with individual coverages offered by life insurance companies in the health insurance field.

■ HEALTH AND INSURANCE

There is no question about the average individual's need for health insurance. In fact, most people are more keenly aware of their need for health insurance than of their need for life insurance. Accidents are constantly occurring—on the job, on the highways, in the home, and elsewhere. And illnesses, both major and minor, are continuing reminders that economic loss must be measured in terms of days away from work, as well as the expenses of hospital, medical, and surgical care.

The possible loss of income because of extended periods of disability is a vital consideration to almost anyone who is employed. However, medical and hospital expenses are significant possible losses for everyone. Medical expenses, routine for children, are especially serious for older people, whose extended periods of illness and hospitalization often threaten—and sometimes result in—the complete exhaustion of their financial resources. At one time or another, therefore, the vast majority of people will be seriously concerned with the problem of how to meet medical and hospital expenses, often at a time when they are also faced with a serious loss of income because they are unable to work.

The Development of Health Insurance

The economic consequences of accidents and illnesses have long been recognized, and many different arrangements have been made to alleviate them. Individual insurance contracts for this purpose, however, have been available in the United States only since the mid-1800's.

The earliest health insurance contracts were written by casualty insurers, companies that wrote liability insurance of various kinds as well as burglary and robbery insurance and accident insurance. Later, companies were formed to write health insurance only and called, for that reason, monoline (or one-line) insurance companies. Still later the life insurance companies entered the field. During the past several decades, they have written a larger and larger share of this business, with the result that the health insurance which life insurance companies now write accounts for more than 87 percent of the total premium income received from health insurance written by commercial insurers.

The earliest health insurance contracts covered disability if it resulted from an accident, and the first such disability policy in the United States was issued in 1850. Sickness insurance was introduced in that same decade; but it did not prove successful, and it was not offered again until shortly before the end of the century. About that time, policies were introduced covering disability resulting from specified diseases and, somewhat later, these coverages were expanded to include benefits for hospital and medical care.

The period between 1910 and the late 1920's was characterized by further extension of the benefits offered under policies such as these, particularly disability income (loss-of-income) coverages. During this period, noncancellable and guaranteed renewable policies were introduced. (Both of these terms will be explained later.) The great depression of the 1930's, however, brought unfavorable experience to the insurers, particularly in connection with sickness benefits; and a number of companies discontinued loss-of-income coverages for sickness.

The most striking development since the 1930's has been the tremendous emphasis upon medical care and medical expense benefits. Prior to that time, health benefits were primarily confined to loss-of-income payments and were available, therefore, only to employed persons. Other benefits, in most instances, were incidental to these loss-of-income coverages; and family members were not covered. Since about 1930, hospital and medical expense benefits have been increasingly offered under contracts designed solely to provide such coverages; and husband, wife, and dependent children are often insured under the same policy.

In the mid-1940's, special policies were introduced to reimburse the insured for expenses incurred for treatment of poliomyelitis. These policies were followed by others providing benefits payable for treatment of cancer and other "dread diseases." In the late 1940's and early 1950's, the "major medical" coverages were introduced, which reimbursed the insured for medical expenses up to maximums ranging from $5,000 to $25,000.

Several factors have contributed to this increasing emphasis on medical care benefits. For one thing, the migration from farm to city, which began in this country nearly a century ago, has accelerated even more rapidly during the last 40 years. This movement has undoubtedly been a factor in the increased use of hospital services. In the rural areas, disabled people were cared for to a much greater extent in their homes. In the cities, all adult members of the family often work outside the home, leaving no one to care for those who are ill. The sick and disabled of the city, therefore, often have been hospitalized by necessity.

Advances in medical science and surgery have also been important factors in the increasing emphasis on medical care benefits. The dramatic reduction in the number of deaths from pneumonia, scarlet fever, rheumatic heart disease, and many other similar diseases is eloquent evidence of the almost miraculous effects of sulfa, penicillin, and other "wonder drugs." Many of these "miracles," however, have meant added medical expense; and awareness of such expenses has prompted the purchase of an ever-increasing amount of medical-expense health insurance.

The changing pattern of health insurance needs is also significant. Because of better medical care and improved living conditions, people generally are living to more advanced ages. As a consequence, more people are suffering from chronic and long-term illnesses than was formerly the case. In addition, medical discoveries have increased the possibility of effective treatment, and sometimes cures, in areas that once were considered hopeless. Mental illness and treatment of the mentally retarded are examples. It is only reasonable, therefore, that medical expense and medical care insurance, as ways to meet these rapidly increasing and expanding medical costs, have had their greatest growth in the period since the early 1930's.

Other factors also have had an important influence on the expansion of this form of insurance. One was the difficulty experienced by many hospitals in making collections from their patients during the depression years. Problems of this kind gave rise to plans for prepayment of hospital bills, the effectiveness and popularity of which demonstrated the need for insurance as a means to help meet such expenses. Another factor has been the interest of employers in such plans, as a means of strengthening employer-employee relations, and the emphasis upon such benefits in the collective bargaining of unions.

■ HEALTH INSURANCE BENEFITS

Health insurance has been developed by many different kinds of organizations and for many different situations. It is provided under individual policies insuring individuals and their dependent family members; it is provided under master contracts insuring groups of employees, borrowers, members of associations, and so on; and it is provided under area-wide plans to provide hospital accommodations (Blue Cross Plans), and surgical benefits (Blue Shield), as well as under government-required disability payment plans. In fact, there sometimes seem to be as many different kinds of health insurance plans as there are diseases and disabling conditions that may result in medical expenses or loss of income.

Some policies list specific accidents, for which specified benefits will be paid; and policies insuring against only one or a few related diseases have not been uncommon. Viewed generally, however, the benefits payable under commercial health insurance policies fall into one or more of the following groups:

1. Disability income benefits (loss-of-time)
2. Accidental death and dismemberment benefits

3. Expense reimbursement benefits
    a) Hospital expense benefits
    b) Surgical expense benefits
    c) Regular medical expense benefits
    d) Major medical expense benefits.

■ DISABILITY INCOME BENEFITS

The majority of employed persons have little income except their salaries or wages. For them, and for persons financially dependent on them, any disability that might interrupt their continued ability to work means a genuine possibility of economic loss. In the case of long-term disabilities, salaries or wages, if continued at all, will eventually be terminated. This is a risk of economic loss in the true insurance sense of the term; and insurance against it—that is, loss-of-income or disability income insurance—was the first of the health insurance coverages to be widely developed and sold.

Disability income contracts are outnumbered today by other kinds of health insurance policies. However, the disability income coverage must still be considered the basic coverage in the health insurance field. Hospital and medical expense coverages have definite economic value, but they would fall far short of meeting the true needs of an insured in the event of prolonged disability. In such situations, the basic need is for income; and this is what the disability income coverage provides.

In general terms, a disability income policy provides that the insurance company will make payments of specified amounts at regular intervals to the insured, if he becomes unable to work because of disability resulting from injury or sickness. The most important features of this coverage concern the following:

1. The amount of income
2. When the income becomes payable
3. How long the income will be paid
4. Related benefits
5. Excluded risks

The Amount of Income

The disability income benefit is usually expressed as so many dollars per week or month and, for reasons that will be discussed later, insurers customarily limit this amount to substantially less than the amount of the applicant's usual earnings. It is customary also to set an overall (issue) limit beyond which the insurer will not go, regardless of the applicant's earned income. A company's risk appraisal rules, for example, might permit applications to be approved for amounts up to two-thirds of the applicant's usual earnings but not to exceed a maximum of $1,500 per month. Some companies have much higher issue limits, however, and maximums of $2,000 or $2,500 are not uncommon.

When the Income Becomes Payable

Definition of Disability. Disability income is customarily payable if the insured becomes totally disabled as the result either of an accident occurring, or of sickness "first manifesting itself," while the policy is in force. As pointed out in the discussion of disability benefits offered in connection with the life insurance contract, total disability as an insurable risk is difficult to define. In general, however, definitions used in health insurance policies have been similar to those used in disability coverages issued in connection with life insurance.

The early health insurance policies defined total disability as the total inability of the insured to engage in "any gainful occupation." When this definition was interpreted by the courts, however, it was generally held to mean the inability of the insured to perform the duties of his own occupation or do other work compatible with his experience and training. Today, a growing number of insurers define "occupation" in their policies in such a way as to provide for the payment of benefits for a specified period, such as two years, if the insured is unable to engage in his own occupation. This is followed by a second, usually longer, period of benefits, perhaps for life, if the insured is unable to engage in any occupation for which he is reasonably fitted by education, training, or experience.

Confining or Nonconfining Disability. At one time, it was customary to distinguish between confining and nonconfining disabilities due to sickness. So long as the insured's disability was sufficiently severe to confine him to his home or a hospital, benefits were paid at the maximum rate. Later, when his disability was not so severe —that is, when he was not confined by it—a smaller benefit would be paid, if he remained unable to work. Benefits in each instance were limited to a specified maximum period of time. Usually, a disability was considered to be "confining" only so long as the patient was treated by a doctor in a hospital or his home. As soon as he was able to call at the doctor's office for treatment, his disability was considered to be nonconfining.

The confining or nonconfining distinction is not widely used in policies that are currently being issued; but for policies where the language still appears, the trend is toward a liberal interpretation. Because many doctors no longer make house calls, the fact that an insured is able to see his doctor in the latter's office is no longer considered sufficient to establish that a disability is "nonconfining."

The Elimination Period. Even though the insured has become totally disabled, as this term is defined in the policy, income payments may not begin immediately. Many policies provide for a specified period of time between the onset of disability and the date the company will begin the income payments. This is the "elimination period," sometimes referred to more simply as the "waiting period." In some disability income plans, the elimination period may be as brief as seven days; in other plans, it may be 30, 60, 90, 180, or even 365 days.

At one time, it was customary to have an elimination period for disability resulting from sickness but to have none if the disability resulted from accident. This was intended to provide some protection to the insurer against antiselection, because of the highly subjective nature of disability resulting from sickness. As disability income coverages began to be issued in larger amounts, however, insurers sought ways by which they could reduce the premium rates. One way was to eliminate any benefit payments during an initial period of a week or longer.

Most insurers writing disability income coverages today offer a wide choice of elimination periods, thus permitting the applicant to select the period most appropriate to his needs. For example, consider the office manager whose employer, as a matter of personnel policy, continues the salary of any disabled employee for 60 days. When this office manager applies for disability income coverage, he may very logically apply for a policy providing a 60-day elimination period for any disability, regardless of whether the cause is sickness or accident. This will give him the benefit of a lower premium and tailor the policy more closely to his particular situation.

How Long the Income Will Be Paid

Disability income policies are often classified as either short- or long-term policies, depending upon the maximum length of time the benefit will be paid, assuming that the insured's total disability continues. Individual contracts under which the income is payable for up to two years are generally referred to as short-term contracts.

Long-term disability income contracts provide for the payment of an income for longer than two years, perhaps to age 65 or longer. Benefits are frequently payable for life in the event of total disability resulting from accident, but lifetime benefits are not common for total disability resulting from sickness.

Related Benefits

Disability income policies often include other benefits in addition to the income payments for total disability. For example, a smaller benefit may be payable for partial disability, and some policies may also include a waiver-of-premium benefit.

Partial Disability. When a disability income policy includes a benefit for partial disability, this term is typically defined as inability to engage in one or more, but not all, of the important duties of the insured's occupation. The partial disability benefit is almost always in a significantly smaller amount than that for total disability, typically 50 percent of the latter; and it is usually payable for a shorter period, such as three or six months. Quite often the partial disability benefit is payable only if the partial disability follows a period for which the total disability income benefit was paid.

Waiver of Premium. Most disability income contracts, if they are guaranteed renewable, include a provision for waiver of premium. Under this provision, premiums are usually waived after total disability has continued for a specified period, such as three or six months. The waiver usually begins with the first premium becoming due after the end of the specified period, and it continues for as long as the disability income is paid. However, the waiver benefit is sometimes continued for as long as total disability continues, even though the maximum income period for that disability may be shorter. Thus, if the policy provides a maximum of two years of income payments for disability resulting from any one accident or sickness, the waiver-of-premium disability benefit might continue for as long as the total disability continues even though the income payments for that particular disability would terminate at the end of two years. The policy would thus be kept in force and provide coverage in the event of a different and later disability.

Excluded Risks

It is customary to exclude some risks from coverage under a disability income policy. These exclusions vary, but as a general rule, disability resulting from war or any act of war is excluded, and coverage may be suspended while the insured is in military service. Other common exclusions in disability income coverages are disabilities resulting from attempted suicide or self-inflicted injuries, pregnancy, and extensive residence or travel abroad.

Business Overhead Expense Benefits

The Business Overhead Expense Coverage, or Business Expense Disability Benefit, is a special form of disability income coverage. The intent, however, is not to replace lost income but rather to provide the funds necessary to keep a business or professional office going during a period when the owner is totally disabled. Basically, this benefit covers such business expenses as rent, mortgage interest, utilities, and office payroll, up to a stated maximum. Usually, there is a waiting period of 14 or 30 days and a maximum benefit period of from one to two years.

The business overhead expense coverage is sold mainly to self-employed professional people, such as architects, doctors, and attorneys, whose personal skills are essential to their business. Benefits are payable only if the business expenses continue and are payable in the amounts actually required for the covered expenses, up to a maximum stated in the policy.

■ ACCIDENTAL DEATH AND DISMEMBERMENT BENEFITS

Disability income policies often provide lump-sum benefits in the event of accidental loss of life, sight, or limbs; and these benefits are also frequently provided in separate policies, often referred to as "A.D. and Dis." policies. Traditionally, the basic benefit for such losses has been expressed as the "principal sum," but more recently other terminology, such as "accident amount," has begun to be used. Usually, the principal sum is payable in the event of accidental death of the insured, loss of both hands, both feet, or the sight of both eyes. Lesser amounts, customarily expressed as fractions of the principal sum, are payable for loss of one hand, one foot, or the sight of one eye.

If a policy of this kind is issued with a principal sum of $10,000, that amount would be paid if the insured lost his life, or if he lost both hands, or both feet, or the sight of both eyes, or one hand and one foot. If he lost one hand, or one foot, or the sight of one eye, the benefit would be $5,000. It is customary to provide that if more than one of these losses is suffered as the result of any one accident, payment will be made for the loss entitling the insured to the largest settlement.

■ EXPENSE REIMBURSEMENT BENEFITS

Expense reimbursement coverages repay the insured for the expenses of medical care necessitated by accident or illness. In one form or another, coverages of this kind have been available for many years. As previously pointed out, however, they have had their greatest growth since 1930. Standards of health care have improved markedly during this period, and the expenses of hospital care and medical treatment have increased many times. As a result, expense reimbursement coverages have had a very rapid growth.

Expense reimbursement coverages are written in many different forms. Some policies cover hospitalization expenses only; others cover medical and surgical expenses also, if the insured is hospitalized. Still others provide medical expense benefits if such expenses are incurred without hospitalization but as a result of accident or sickness. The earliest of the health insurance expense coverages to be developed on anything like a major scale provided reimbursement for hospital expenses. Coverage for surgical expenses followed, and the last in point of time was coverage for medical expenses.

Hospital Expense Benefits

Hospital expense insurance is an extremely popular and valuable coverage. It accounts for a very large part of the health insurance premium income, as well as for the largest number of insureds. In general terms, the purpose of this coverage is to reimburse the insured, at least in part, for expenses of hospitalization necessitated by accident or sickness.

Most hospital expense reimbursement policies provide two general classes of benefits. One, the daily room benefit, is designed to help meet the expenses of room and board and the general nursing care furnished by the hospital. The other, the miscellaneous expense benefit, provides coverage for the special services incident to hospital care, such as the use of the operating room, X-rays, and special medications.

The Daily Room Benefit. Reimbursement for room and board

expenses may be provided in any of several ways. The customary approach among commercial insurance companies is to reimburse the insured in the amount of the actual charge, up to a specified daily maximum. Usually, there is a maximum number of days for which the benefit will be payable for any one period of hospitalization. For example, one company offers a daily benefit in maximums from $10 to $50, for a maximum period of 365 days for any one period of hospital confinement. The applicant indicates the maximum benefit amount he wishes; and, in the event of hospitalization, benefits will be paid in the actual amount of daily expenses incurred, up to the maximum amount selected.

A second way of providing room-and-board benefits in hospital policies is to provide a stated kind of accommodation for a maximum number of days, without specific reference to cost. Thus, the insured may be entitled to a semi-private room—that is, a room shared with at least one other patient—for a maximum of 45 to 120 days. This is the "service" type of benefit. It is most closely identified with the Blue Cross plans for hospital service, although it is not limited to such plans.

Some hospital policies—often called hospital indemnity policies—pay a flat sum per day while the insured is hospitalized, regardless of the actual hospital charges. Such policies state the maximum only in terms of the number of days for which this specified benefit will be paid for any one hospital confinement. Such a policy might, for instance, pay a $20 per day benefit, with a maximum of 365 days, for hospital care necessitated by any one cause or related causes. This coverage is easy to understand and easily administered; and a number of insurers have introduced some variation of it in the past few years.

Miscellaneous Hospital Expenses. Benefits for other hospital expenses are sometimes listed in a schedule of maximum amounts which apply to each of the different types of services. Thus, laboratory services will be reimbursed up to one maximum, X-rays will be paid for within another maximum, and drugs and special treatments will have still another maximum.

Alternatively, reimbursement for these hospital expenses may be provided without regard for individual items—that is, on a blanket basis—up to a stated maximum amount for each hospitalization. This maximum amount may be expressed as a multiple of the daily room-and-board benefit instead of a specified dollar figure. Frequently, this is 20 times the daily room-and-board maximum.

Maternity Benefits. The problem of providing maternity benefits without inviting antiselection is resolved by different insurers in different ways. Pregnancy and childbirth are not insurable risks in the generally accepted meaning of the term except for complications of pregnancy, which are frequently defined and covered. Nevertheless, there is a very strong feeling on the part of many insureds that maternity benefits should be included in hospital expense reimbursement policies. Accordingly, maternity benefits are usually available as an optional benefit that may be included at an added premium. Often the maternity benefit is a flat amount, frequently expressed as a multiple of the daily room benefit maximum. Ten times the daily room benefit is often used.

Generally, the maternity benefit is payable only if the pregnancy had its inception after the effective date of the policy; and frequently the benefit is payable only if both husband and wife are insured under the policy.

Surgical Expense Benefits

The surgical expense benefit reimburses the insured for professional charges incurred for surgical operations. Maximum benefits are customarily established for different kinds of operations, which are listed in a surgical schedule. The insurer will pay the amount of surgical expenses actually incurred by the insured, up to the stated maximum for the particular operation performed. Shown on the next page is a portion of an illustrative schedule providing a maximum benefit of $600 for any one operation.

Schedules of this kind are not intended to cover every possible operation. Benefits for operations not listed, therefore, are paid on a comparable scale, based on the degree of seriousness of the surgery actually performed.

Regular Medical Expense Benefits

Medical expense benefits relate to the expenses of treatment by physicians other than surgeons. In most instances, benefits are payable in specified amounts if the insured incurs medical expense for nonsurgical treatment while he is a patient in a hospital; and coverage is also available to meet the expense of visits to the doctor's office and for house calls.

Surgical Schedule Excerpt

Cardiovascular System	
Aortic valvuloplasty, open repair of	$600
Myocardial aneurysm, repair of	600
Atrial septal defect, open repair of	600
Chest	
Bronchoscopy	60
Lobectomy, total or subtotal	400
wedge resection, single or multiple	320
Lung, removal of	400
Dislocation, Simple, Closed Reduction of	
Ankle	40
Elbow, jaw, shoulder or wrist	20
Finger	12
Hip	80
Ear, Nose and Throat	
Mastoidectomy, simple	200
radical, without skin graft	280
with skin graft	320
Sinusotomy, frontal, external, simple	80
Submucous resection of nasal septum	120
Laryngectomy, without neck dissection	400
Eye	
Cataract, operation for intracapsular or extracapsular, unilateral	$320
Detached retina, operation for	400
Eyeball, removal of	160
Fracture, Treatment of	
Ankle, simple, closed reduction	100
Elbow, distal end of humerus or proximal end of radius or ulna, one or more bones, simple, closed reduction	80
Femur, shaft, including supracondylar simple, closed reduction	160
simple or compound, open reduction	320
Nose, simple, uncomplicated, closed reduction	20
complicated, closed reduction	40
Tibia, shaft, simple, closed reduction	100
simple or compound, open reduction	200
Tibia and fibula, shafts, simple, closed reduction	120
simple or compound, open reduction	240

Major Medical Expense Benefits

Major medical insurance was a new and fresh approach to health insurance when it was introduced around the early 1950's. Instead of benefits payable for specified kinds of expenses and subject to various kinds of limits, the original major medical benefits were payable in broad categories up to $5,000, $7,500, or $10,000. (These limits have since been expanded to $20,000, $25,000, and often much higher.) The purpose was to afford protection against extremely large medical expenses.

The exact coverages provided by major medical plans vary from company to company. In general, benefits are available to meet expenses in all of the following categories:

1. Hospital daily room charges
2. Miscellaneous hospital services, such as use of the operating room, X-rays, laboratory
3. Drugs and medicines (whether insured is hospitalized or not)
4. Physicians' and surgeons' services (whether insured is hospitalized or not)
5. Nursing services (whether insured is hospitalized or not)
6. Artificial limbs and rehabilitation treatment and devices.

The earliest major medical plans covered eligible expenses up to the overall limits of the policy, regardless of the amounts of the various kinds of expenses. However, this resulted in some unfavorable experience in a period of rapidly increasing hospital and medical costs; and, as a result, many insurers began to include some limits on different categories of expense. A daily hospital room maximum, for example, was established under many plans; and surgical schedules were introduced. Usually, such maximums are similar to the upper limits established in regular hospital and surgical expense policies.

■ FAMILY COVERAGES

Hospital and medical expense benefit coverages are customarily available for the dependents of the insured under a policy issued to the insured. Dependent, unmarried children are usually covered until they reach a specified age, such as 18 or 19 years. However, it is becoming increasingly common to extend this coverage to ages 22 or 23, if the child is unmarried and a student at an accredited institution of learning. In either instance, when the child reaches the limiting age, a conversion privilege is available. This means that the insurer will, on request, issue an individual policy of hospital and surgical expense insurance to him, without evidence of insurability, at the premium rate for his attained age.

Many states have special laws that require the insurer to permit continuation of the coverage of a dependent child under a parent's policy, if at the time the child reaches the limiting age, he is so mentally or physically handicapped as to be incapable of self-support.

■ LIMITED POLICIES

One of the major difficulties in understanding health insurance coverages results from the wide variations in terminology. As new coverages or new combinations of coverages have been introduced, new names have been given them. Thus, there are accident policies, loss-of-income policies, dread-disease policies, noncancellable policies, guaranteed renewable policies, and industrial policies, to name only a few. Often the same benefits are provided under different names; often the name gives only a hint of the nature of the coverage or the benefits actually provided. However, when benefits are small or restricted in duration—or when broad coverage is provided, but in connection with one or a few specific hazards only—the policy is customarily referred to as a limited policy.

Such accident policies as the automobile accident policy and the aviation accident policy are examples of limited policies. The automobile accident policy typically provides an accidental death benefit, medical expense benefits, and a monthly income for total disability, but they are payable only for injuries resulting from automobile accidents.

Aviation accident policies were originally sold by airline ticket agents over the counter. The early policies provided insurance in the amount of $5,000 for accidental death or dismemberment. In recent years, amounts as high as $100,000 have been made available, with medical expense reimbursement up to stated limits for injuries sustained as a result of aviation accidents. Since 1946, this type of policy has been sold extensively through vending machines.

Limited sickness insurance policies were first issued in the mid-1940's, providing benefits to meet medical and hospital expenses incurred in connection with treatment of poliomyelitis. Later, the coverage was broadened to include treatment for such specific diseases as diphtheria, scarlet fever, leukemia, spinal meningitis, and other similar diseases. In this form, it was often known as "polio and dread diseases" insurance. Cancer expense policies are also examples of this type of coverage. Such policies may provide payments up to $5,000 or $10,000 for medical and hospitalization expenses incurred for treatment of the specified diseases. However, these coverages are being prohibited in some of the more populous states because of their limited coverages and the possibility that the insured will be misled into believing that he has more extensive coverage than he actually has.

■ RISK APPRAISAL IN HEALTH INSURANCE

General Objectives

Risk appraisal is necessary in health insurance for essentially the same reasons that it is necessary in life insurance. Premium rates are based on statistics of past losses, and they will not be adequate if an unreasonably large proportion of persons in poor health or in especially hazardous occupations are included in the insured group. Risk selection, therefore, is necessary to assure that persons accepted for health insurance will fall within the general underwriting limits the company has established, and that appropriate premiums may be charged. By far the majority of health insurance applications are accepted.

Sources of Risk Appraisal Information

Health insurance underwriters use much the same sources of underwriting information as their life insurance counterparts. Health insurance applications include questions designed to cover most of the significant factors of insurability: age of the proposed insured, sex, medical history, height and weight, habits, and occupation. In addition, medical examinations are sometimes required, though not usually as often as for life insurance; and specific information may be requested from physicians who have treated the proposed insureds. The latter is generally furnished on what are called "Attending Physicians Statements." Investigations from commercial inspection agencies are also sometimes used, especially in connection with disability income coverages.

Antiselection

Health insurance risk appraisal differs from life insurance risk appraisal in some respects, but these differences are primarily differences of degree. This is especially true of the problem of antiselection, which is a more serious and continuing consideration in health insurance than in life insurance. One reason, no doubt, is the fact that health insurance benefits are customarily payable to the insured himself rather than to a beneficiary who receives them after the insured is dead.

People sometimes apply for health insurance knowing that they will shortly need to be hospitalized or otherwise treated for health conditions of which they are aware at the time of application. If a policy would not have been issued if the truth had been disclosed, an early claim may be denied and the policy rescinded on the basis of material misrepresentation, just as is true of the life insurance contract under similar conditions. However, adequate evidence of the facts misrepresented is not always available. Even when it is, denial of claims, whatever the reason, often results in serious misunderstandings and bad public relations. Such problems are much better avoided, if at all possible. The risk appraiser, therefore, must be especially alert for any evidence that the information given in the application is not complete.

Factors of Insurability

Although the same factors of insurability are considered in health insurance underwriting as in life insurance, they are not always considered in the same way. Here, too, the differences are primarily differences of degree. Usually, if a proposed insured's medical history is favorable for life insurance, it will be favorable for health insurance also. However, this is not always true. Such conditions as back disorders and allergies, for example, may be relatively unimportant as far as the life insurance risk is concerned. They may be very unfavorable for health insurance coverages, however, for they indicate the possibilities of hospitalization and medical costs, to say nothing of prolonged periods of disability.

The occupation of the proposed insured is especially significant in health insurance risk appraisal for disability income coverages; and it is customary to group the different occupations into several classes, depending on the degree of hazard they present. Higher premium rates are charged as the occupational hazard increases; and persons in especially hazardous occupations may not be accepted at any premium.

Some health insurers use as few as three or four different occupational rating classes; others as many as nine or ten. Usually they consider persons with such occupations as attorney, accountant, insurance agent, librarian, and pharmacist (to name only a very few) insurable at the most favorable rates. A more hazardous class, insurable at an increased premium, would include persons who work as occupational or physical therapists, supervising plant managers, shipping clerks, and building contractors who supervise construction (again only a few examples are listed). A higher degree of hazard, and thus a higher premium, would apply for blue collar workers, persons who drive passenger or light delivery vehicles, and foremen who directly supervise manual workers. Persons who handle explosives and those who do stunt work, or test or race vehicles, would present the highest degree of hazard and may be considered uninsurable.

Some occupations may not present particularly serious hazards in themselves but could require extensive periods of recuperation from relatively minor accidents or illnesses before the insured would be able to return to his work. (Professional athletics is an example.) This characteristic is reflected in the classifications to which such occupations are assigned. Seasonal work is unfavorable, but for a different reason—the fact that the insured may have no work to return to after his recovery. Therefore, the date of recovery—and thus the date his disability benefits are terminable—would be more difficult to establish than if he had regular employment. All these considerations are significant in evaluating the insurability of a person who wishes to purchase health insurance coverage.

Amount of Benefit

The amount of the benefits applied for, as compared with the amount of the insured's probable loss, is also an important consideration, especially in relation to applications for disability income coverages. Consider, for example, a person who earns $12,000 per year and applies for a disability income policy that will pay him $1,000 per month if he suffers a disabling illness or accident and is unable to work. If a policy providing benefits of that amount is issued to him, his disability income benefits would be considerably in excess of the take-home pay he would have had while working, since disability income benefits are not subject to income tax if the insured has paid the premiums on the policy.

In such situations, even a relatively minor injury may result in a longer-than-average loss-of-income claim, for there is very little incentive for this insured to return to work. In borderline situations, therefore, where the work is sporadic or unusually taxing, it is sometimes extremely difficult to distinguish between a valid claim, where the insured is truly disabled over a longer than usual period, and a form of semiretirement, financed by the health insurance coverage.

Health insurance is especially vulnerable to situations of this kind because of the subjective nature of disability. In other words, two people with essentially the same kind of disability may be affected quite differently by it. People have worked in extreme discomfort when they felt it necessary or when they were motivated by strongly compelling reasons. Other persons have prolonged their periods of illness far beyond any reasonable convalescent period, if they have had no especially strong financial incentive to return to work.

There are few stronger reasons for working than the need for income; and insurance companies have had some vivid lessons in what happens when this motivating factor is removed by a too-generous schedule of benefits in disability income contracts. Most companies, therefore, establish "issue limits" which specify maximum monthly income amounts that will be issued to any one person. Usually this is a dollar amount which varies according to the occupation of the proposed insured. Typically, it is limited to a percentage, such as one-half or two-thirds or perhaps as much as three-fourths, of the proposed insured's earned income, up to a specified maximum amount. This maximum may be as much as $2,000 or $2,500 per month. Often a second limitation, called a "participation" limit, is established. This is the maximum amount of income benefits from all such sources as Social Security and other insurers that the applicant's insurance company will "participate" in. If the applicant's present coverage would provide him with that amount of income, an application for additional amounts of disability income insurance will not be accepted.

■ CONTRACTUAL SAFEGUARDS

The health insurance risk does not meet all the requirements of an insurable risk as adequately as does the risk in life insurance. This is especially true of the requirements that the loss must be definite and that it not be trivial. The subjective nature of disability makes it difficult in some instances to establish that the insured is in fact disabled; and health insurance claims have long been characterized by a multiplicity of relatively small losses. Because of differences such as these between the health insurance risk and the risk of loss because of early death, insurance companies use a number of contractual provisions in health insurance that have no counterpart in life insurance. Among these are provisions for deductible amounts and percentage participation [1] (or coinsurance), as well as waiting periods, specific exclusions, and some provisions relating to pre-existing conditions. These concepts will be discussed in the order given above.

The Deductible Amount

Most major medical policies specify that the insured must incur eligible medical expenses up to a specified amount, such as $200 or

---

[1] This term has been recommended by the Commission on Insurance Terminology of the American Risk and Insurance Association, because of the many different and entirely unrelated meanings the word "coinsurance" may have.

$500 (sometimes more), before any benefits will become payable under the policy. These amounts are termed "deductibles" or "deductible amounts." The purposes of such provisions are to limit the benefits payable under the policy to significant or "major" medical expenses and to keep the premium lower than would otherwise be necessary. Often there is a time limit, such as 90 days, within which these expenses up to the deductible amount must be incurred.

From the beginning, the major medical coverages were intended to supplement any basic hospital and surgical coverages the insured already had. In other words, they were designed to provide benefits payable after the basic coverages were exhausted and thus to insure against genuinely *major* medical expenses. For this reason, the deductible amount was established to reflect the maximum payable under most such basic coverages. Today, major medical policies which are intended to supplement basic hospital plans sometimes define the deductible amount as the amount actually paid under the basic coverage, plus a flat amount—typically $100. This flat amount is sometimes called a "corridor" deductible.

In the past few years, several leading insurers have offered major medical policies under which the deductible amount is defined in a way that combines the above approaches. Called a "floating" deductible, the deductible amount is expressed as the larger of (1) a flat amount, such as $500; or (2) the amount actually received by the insured under any basic medical, hospital, or surgical coverage he may have. For every dollar by which the amount paid under the basic coverage exceeds the flat amount, three dollars are added to the maximum that will be payable under the major medical coverage. For example, if the flat amount is $500 and benefits are paid in a total of $550 under the insured's basic coverage, the deductible amount will be $550 and the maximum payable under his major medical coverage will be increased by $150.

Illustrative major medical limits used by two leading insurers

Illustrative Major Medical Limits

	Maximum Benefit	Deductible Amount
Insurer A:		
Plan I	$15,000	$ 750
Plan II	$25,000	$1,000
Insurer B:		
Plan I	$10,000	$ 500
Plan II	$15,000	$ 750
Plan III	$25,000	$1,000

are shown on page 269, to illustrate how the deductible amounts typically vary with the maximum benefit payable.

Some major medical plans are available with lower deductible amounts, from $50 to $250, for instance. These plans, intended primarily for persons who have no other coverages, are frequently called "comprehensive major medical" plans. Since a very large number of persons have some basic hospital and surgical coverage, this type of plan is not nearly so widely sold as the major medical plans with higher deductibles.

Percentage Participation

After the insured has incurred expenses equal to the amount of the deductible, a major medical policy will pay a specified percentage—75 or 80 percent—of all additional covered medical expenses, up to the overall maximum limit of the policy. For example, if the deductible amount is $500, the insured must have $500 of eligible medical expenses before anything becomes payable under his major medical coverage. Then, if he incurs additional expenses, the insurance company will pay, under the percentage participation clause of the contract, the greater part, but not all, of the expenses he incurs over the amount of the deductible. The insured thus "participates" in the additional expenses, paying 25 or 20 percent as provided in the contract. (The percentage participation clause is sometimes referred to as the "coinsurance" clause.)

Waiting Periods

Hospital expense policies frequently provide what may be referred to as "waiting periods," although the term "probationary period" is frequently used to mean the same thing. Waiting period will be used here because it seems to indicate the meaning more clearly.

A waiting period is a specified number of days following the effective date of the coverage, during which time benefits are not payable. Thus, hospital expense policies may provide a waiting period such as 14 or 30 days for hospital confinement caused by sickness, with benefits payable from the first day for hospitalization resulting from an accident. Under such a policy issued with an effective date of June 1, with a waiting period of 14 days for sickness, no benefits would be payable until June 15 for hospitalization due to sickness.

Hospital expense policies sometimes provide a longer waiting period of 90 days or six months following the issue date, during which period no benefits will be payable if the hospital confinement is the result of specifically named conditions such as hernia, tonsillitis, appendicitis, and so on. Conditions of this kind are sometimes acute, requiring immediate hospitalization and treatment. However, they are also often chronic. In the latter circumstances, antiselection is especially possible on the part of an applicant who may postpone needed surgery for a hernia or for appendicitis, for instance, until after he has had the "foresight" to obtain insurance coverage. Excluding treatment for such conditions for a specified period after the policy becomes effective is considered a more satisfactory way of minimizing such antiselection than trying to establish that the condition was known to the insured but not mentioned on the application when the insurance was applied for.

Exclusions

Policies providing reimbursement for medical expenses usually exclude some kinds of expenses, such as those resulting from:

1. Injury or sickness resulting from war or any act of war, declared or undeclared
2. Injury or sickness covered under workmen's compensation, or Occupational Diseases Laws
3. Care or treatment given in any government facility, unless the insured is legally required to pay for it
4. Cosmetic surgery, unless required because of injury (or because of congenital defect in the case of newborn children covered by the contract)
5. Pregnancy, except as specifically provided in the contract
6. Mental, nervous, or emotional diseases or disorders.

Pre-existing Conditions

Most medical expense or disability income contracts insure against losses resulting from injuries "occurring" or sickness "first manifesting itself" while the policy is in force. The intent of this provision is to exclude health conditions that existed prior to the issuance of the policy but which occasion medical expenses after the effective date of the policy. If insurance is provided for medical expenses incurred in connection with health problems that existed prior to the effective date of the insurance, the situation is somewhat analogous to insuring a building against fire after the fire is already smouldering. The situation in health insurance, however, is not quite so easily summarized.

Insurers frequently intend to provide coverage for a pre-existing condition when it has been disclosed on the application. Usually the conditions covered are chronic or recurrent in nature, such as elevated blood pressure; and in such situations a higher premium is charged to cover the added risk.

In other situations, the applicant may disclose a pre-existing condition in his application and the company will accept the application but issue a policy with a specific exclusion, excluding any benefits for treatment of that particular condition.

If the applicant discloses a physical impairment on his application and the company issues a policy of health insurance but does not specifically exclude treatment of the impairment, a question arises if a claim is later presented for expenses occasioned by a recurrence of that condition. For instance, the application states that the insured had an automobile accident three years before. He states that he suffered a back sprain but that recovery was complete. Now, after the policy has been in effect eight or nine months, a claim is presented for hospitalization because of a recurrence of this back injury.

If the provisions of the policy are followed literally, this claim will not be paid, since the hospitalization was caused by an accident that occurred prior to the effective date of the policy. Under generally accepted claim practices, however, the insurer is considered to have waived any right to deny a claim in situations of this kind, even though the condition existed prior to the effective date of the contract if, having been informed of the condition, it issued a policy without a specified exclusion. The theory is that the company had the opportunity to exclude the condition if it had wished, when the policy was issued. Since it did not do so, the insured is justified in believing that the company intended to assume the risk of future treatment for that condition.

One of the legally required policy provisions specifically provides that after the policy has been in effect for three years, no claim will be denied or benefits reduced because of a pre-existing condition.

The Policyowner's Right to Renew

Health insurance contracts may be divided into two broad general groups with respect to the policyowner's right to renew his coverage. One group consists of policies under which the insurance company reserves the right either to cancel the policy or refuse to renew it; the other group is made up of policies under which the insurer does not reserve either of these rights. As a result, the policyowner has the right to renew a policy in the latter group, although the insurance company may reserve the right to increase the premium rates for certain classes of insureds under some policies in this group.

Cancellation and Refusal to Renew. An insurer's right to cancel a health insurance policy should be clearly differentiated from the right to refuse to renew it. If a cancellation provision is included in a policy, the insurer may terminate the coverage at any time, including any time during a period for which the premium has been paid. Appropriate notice must be given, and the premium applicable to the unexpired period of time (the *unearned* premium) must be returned. By contrast with this situation, if the company reserves the right only to refuse to renew a policy, coverage may be terminated only at the end of a period for which premiums have been paid. In this situation, the policy is said to be *optionally renewable*, that is, it is renewable at the option of the company. When a company refuses to renew a policy, however, it is a different situation from a cancellation.

These differences are more easily understood if an example is used. Assume that a policy includes the cancellation provision and a quarterly premium has been paid to provide coverage to June 15. This policy could be cancelled effective as of May 1 (or any other time prior to June 15), if the necessary advance notice is given and the unearned premium refunded. By contrast, the same policy, if optionally renewable, would have to be continued to June 15 and then, with appropriate prior notice, the company could refuse to renew it.

Many insurers today issue policies with only a limited right on their part to refuse renewal. Such policies frequently state that the insurer will not refuse to renew the policy solely because the health of the insured has deteriorated; and the insurance laws of some of the states require that the insurer's right to refuse renewal shall be so limited.

Policies with the Right to Renew. Policies guaranteeing the policyowner the right to renew, by payment of renewal premiums, to a specified age, such as 60 or 65 or later, are of two kinds. Under some of these policies, the insurer reserves the right to change the premium for any class of insureds [2] on any renewal date. These are called "guaranteed renewable" policies. Policies under which the company does not reserve the right to increase premium rates, and which the policyowner can renew just by paying the renewal premium on time are called "noncancellable."

The differences between guaranteed renewable policies and those that are noncancellable may be summarized as follows: The owner of a guaranteed renewable policy has the right to renew it by paying the appropriate premium until the limiting date of the coverage. The insurer cannot refuse to renew the policy so long as the premium is paid on time, but it can, if it wishes, raise the premium rate on a class basis for such policies. The owner of a noncancellable policy also has the right to renew his policy until the limiting age, by paying the premium by the due date or within the grace period, but the insurer cannot raise the premium rates on any basis for these policies. Thus it is not necessary to describe noncancellable policies as "noncancellable and guaranteed renewable" as is sometimes done. If the policy is noncancellable, it is guaranteed renewable and the latter term is not necessary in describing it.

■ THE INDIVIDUAL HEALTH INSURANCE CONTRACT

Individuals purchase health insurance in exactly the same way they purchase life insurance, by applying for the coverage they wish and paying the required premium. The same principles of contract law that apply to the formation of the life insurance contract also apply to the formation of the contract of health insurance and, as is true of life insurance, many laws have been enacted that concern the health insurance contract specifically.

Approval of Policy Forms

Most states require that health insurance policy forms, like life insurance policy forms, be submitted to each state insurance department for approval before they may be used in that state. A uniform policy provisions law for health insurance, or similar legislation, has

---

[2] Usually this phrase refers to a broad category of insureds such as all insureds whose policies are issued on a specified form.

been enacted by the legislatures of all the states; and most states also have additional special laws that apply to health insurance and health insurance contracts. The health insurance laws of the various states, therefore, are generally similar in content, although a great many specific variations exist.

Policy forms for health insurance plans are customarily prepared in much the same way as those for life insurance plans. They are printed in large numbers after having been approved by the various state departments. Appropriate forms are then prepared for issuance to individual applicants by preparing a special insert schedule on which are typed (or printed by computer) the identifying data for the individual contracts.

Suppose Maurice Watson applies for a hospital surgical policy. If his application is accepted, the proper policy form will be selected and prepared for issuance to him. A special section of the front page (or an inner page that is visible through a window) will be completed specifying Watson's name, the policy number, the policy date, the amount of the premium and the premium payment mode, as well as any other details of the coverage that may have been elected. It will thus specify the coverages, limits as to amounts and the periods for which the different benefits are payable; deductible amounts and elimination periods if appropriate; the effective dates of the various coverages; and any other specific information relative to that particular contract. Figure 13–1 shows an illustrative schedule.

The health insurance contract, when issued, will typically consist of the following sections:

1. A face page
2. A policy schedule
3. Benefit provisions
4. A section titled "Exceptions and Exclusions"
5. A general section.

The Face Page

The face page of a health insurance policy includes the name of the insurer and an insuring statement such as the following:

The Ajax Life Insurance Company hereby promises to pay the benefits herein specified for injury or sickness of any covered person, subject to the provisions, limitations, and exceptions of this policy.

276 ▪ Principles of Life Insurance

FIGURE 13–1

POLICY SCHEDULE

INSURED	WATSON, MAURICE	$78.80	INITIAL PREMIUM
POLICY NUMBER	X0040139	$78.80	RENEWAL PREMIUM
POLICY DATE	OCTOBER 15, 1972	QUARTERLY	PREMIUM MODE

FIRST RENEWAL DATE JANUARY 15, 1973

THE BENEFITS AND PREMIUMS SHOWN ON THIS SCHEDULE ARE EFFECTIVE OCTOBER 15, 1972

COVERAGE SUMMARY

FORM	COVERAGE INFORMATION	MAXIMUM	QUARTERLY PREMIUM
77004	BASIC POLICY--HOSPITAL-SURGICAL		$78.80
	HOSPITAL DAILY BENEFIT	$30 PER DAY	
	MAXIMUM BENEFIT PERIOD	365 DAYS PER CONFINEMENT	
	SURGICAL EXPENSE	$600 SCHEDULE	
	MISC. IN-HOSPITAL EXPENSE	$450	
	EMERGENCY ACCIDENT EXPENSE	$25	
	PHYSICIANS IN-HOSPITAL EXP.	$5 PER DAY	
	MAXIMUM BENEFIT AMOUNT	$150	

OTHER COVERED PERSONS

WATSON, JANE   SPOUSE   WATSON, COLLEEN CHILD
WATSON, WILLIAM   CHILD

Most health insurance contracts also include on the face page a special notice giving the policyowner 10 days in which to review the policy and decide whether or not he wishes to keep it. If he does not wish to keep the policy, he may return it within the 10-day period and receive a full refund of his premiums. This notice is required by many of the states and typically appears on the face page of the policy, as follows:

NOTICE OF 10-DAY RIGHT TO EXAMINE POLICY

Please read this policy and the attached copy of the application carefully. If you are not satisfied with the policy for any reason, you may return it within 10 days after receipt and any premium paid will be refunded.

Included also on the face page of the policy are the provisions defining the policyowner's right to renew. For example, a guaranteed renewable policy would give the policyowner the right to continue the policy in force to a specified date by payment of premiums when due or within the grace period, but reserve to the company the right to change "at any time and from time to time" the table of applicable premium rates.

The Policy Schedule

An illustrative policy schedule was shown on page 276. The amount of information included in such a schedule will vary from only a relatively few items to a great many, depending upon the number of benefits provided and the number of variable items involved.

The Benefit Provisions

The benefit provisions describe the benefits payable under that particular policy and may occupy several pages of the policy. This is especially true if a surgical expense benefit and a surgical schedule are included. On the other hand, the benefit provisions of a disability income policy are usually relatively brief.

Exceptions and Exclusions

Many health insurance contracts include a section titled "Exceptions and Exclusions," in which only provisions limiting or reducing the coverages will be listed. These may be grouped together or included with the special benefit provisions to which they apply.

The General Section

A major section of the policy, which may be referred to as the general section, contains provisions required by law to be included in all individual health insurance contracts. The section usually also contains any provisions the insurer wishes to use (optional provisions) that are permitted but not required by law. The law which defines and prescribes these provisions is called the Uniform Individual Accident and Sickness Policy Provisions Law. A general acquaintance with this law is essential to an understanding of individual health insurance contracts.

■ THE UNIFORM POLICY PROVISIONS LAW

In 1950, the National Association of Insurance Commissioners recommended a model law for health insurance contracts called the Uniform Individual Accident and Sickness Policy Provisions Law. This law, or similar legislation, has been enacted in all the states. The model law is detailed, and only a few of its provisions will be summarized. In general, however, it concerns provisions that must be included in health insurance policies as well as some that may be included. These provisions are set forth in recommended language and classified as "required" provisions or "optional" provisions.

Required Policy Provisions

Required policy provisions are provisions that must be included in every health insurance contract that is issued or delivered in the state concerned. The exact language of the law does not have to be used in the policy, but if different wording is used, it must be equally favorable to the insured or more so, and it must be approved by the insurance department of the state concerned. Among the most significant of the policy provisions required to be included in the health insurance policy are those relating to (1) the grace period, (2) reinstatement of the policy, (3) change of beneficiary if the policy provides a death benefit, (4) time limit on certain defenses, and (5) claims.

The Grace Period. If the premium is payable other than weekly or monthly, the health insurance contract must provide a 31-day grace period. For monthly-premium policies, a 10-day period is permitted, and for weekly-premium policies, a 7-day period may be used.

If the policy is cancellable, that fact may be reflected in the grace period provision. Thus, a policy that includes a cancellation provision may include the following words at the end of the grace period provision:

. . . subject to the right of the company to cancel in accordance with the cancellation provision hereof.

If the policy is not cancellable but the company has reserved the right not to permit renewal, the provision must be introduced with the following:

Unless not less than 30 days prior to the premium due date the company has delivered to the insured or has mailed to his last address, as shown by the records of the company, written notice of its intention not to renew this policy beyond the period for which the premium has been accepted, . . .

Reinstatement. The reinstatement provision required for health insurance contracts differs from the reinstatement provision of the life insurance contract in several respects. One basic difference is that reinstatement is specifically granted as a right under the life insurance contract, subject to stated conditions. Under the health insurance contract, the right of the policyowner to reinstate his contract is assumed. The reinstatement provision merely clarifies the circumstances under which a reinstatement becomes effective, limits the amount of past-due premium that may be collected by the insurer, and specifies the losses that will be covered by the reinstated policy.

The provision makes it clear that the reinstated policy will cover only losses resulting from accidental injury that occurs after the reinstatement, or sickness that begins more than 10 days after the date of reinstatement. For example, an insured may permit his policy to lapse and then have an accident or become ill before he reinstates it. In that case, reinstatement may be permitted, but no benefits will be payable for the accident or illness he has suffered during the period the policy was lapsed. (The prior accident or illness will not be covered, just as a house cannot be insured against a fire that has already occurred or is in progress.) Except for injuries and sickness that have occurred while the policy was lapsed and prior to the date of reinstatement, however, the rights and responsibilities of the insurance company and the insured under the reinstated policy will be the same as they were prior to the date the policy lapsed, subject to any provisions endorsed on or attached to the policy in connection with its reinstatement.

Change of Beneficiary. If the health insurance policy includes an accidental death benefit, it must contain a change-of-beneficiary provision. This gives the insured the right to change the beneficiary without the consent of any prior beneficiary or beneficiaries unless he has designated the prior beneficiary irrevocably.

Time Limit on Certain Defenses. All health insurance policies must also include a provision that is similar to the incontestable clause of the life insurance contract. This provision consists of two paragraphs and is titled "Time Limit on Certain Defenses." A "defense," in the sense in which the word is used here, means a legal defense—that is, a legal reason—which the company might use in a court of law, if necessary, to support (or defend) its denial of a claim or rescission of a policy.

For optionally renewable policies, the first paragraph of this provision must state that, after three years, "no misstatements except fraudulent misstatements may be used to avoid the policy or to deny a claim as to loss incurred or disability commencing after the three-year period."

For guaranteed renewable or noncancellable policies, this provision may be titled "Incontestable" and this first paragraph may state that, after the policy has been in force for a period of three years, it will be incontestable as to the statements in the application.

The second paragraph of this provision, for either kind of policy, must provide that after the policy has been in effect for three years, no claim will be denied or benefits reduced because a disease or physical condition "not excluded from coverage by name or specific description effective on the date of loss" had existed prior to the effective date of coverage.

Claim Provisions. The Uniform Individual Accident and Sickness Policy Provisions Law includes several provisions specifically relating to claims and proof of loss. This is important in health insurance, since numerous claims may be payable under the same contract over a period of years. It is essential, therefore, that requirements relating to such matters as giving the company notice of a claim, filing of claim and proofs of loss, payment of benefits, and other similar matters be detailed and clear.

Written notice of claim must be given to the insurance company within 20 days after the occurrence of any loss covered by the policy "or as soon thereafter as is reasonably possible." The company must furnish claim forms within 15 days after receiving notice of claim; and proof of loss must be submitted in writing, usually within 90 days after the end of the period for which payments are due, or within 90 days after the date of death or dismemberment.

The law specifically says that failure to furnish the required proof within these times "will not invalidate nor reduce" a claim if it can be shown that it was not reasonably possible to furnish it as required and that proof was furnished as soon as was reasonably possible. Except in situations involving lack of legal capacity, however, proof must be given within one year.

There are two required provisions concerning the payment of claims. The first of these provisions specifies how frequently and when claim payments must be made. Periodic benefits—disability income payments, for example—must be paid not less frequently than monthly. Other benefits must be paid "immediately upon receipt of due written proof of such loss."

A second required policy provision concerning the payment of claims states that any payment for loss of life will be payable in accordance with the beneficiary designation. If no beneficiary designation is in effect at the date of death, payment will be made to the estate of the insured. All other indemnities will be paid to the insured.

Optional Policy Provisions

Provisions Relating to Occupation. Occupation is one of the basic factors involved in appraising the insurability of an applicant for disability income insurance. Often, however, an insured may be accepted for such insurance while he is working at one occupation and later change to an occupation more hazardous than the one he had on the date of his application. In that event, the premium he should be paying after the change may be significantly higher than the one he is actually paying. On the other hand, if his current occupation is less hazardous than the one he had at the time he applied for his insurance, he may be paying a higher premium than would be necessary.

Health insurance policies may, at the option of the insurance company, include a provision that permits the company to make adjustments in cases of this kind. Under this optional provision, if the insured's occupation at the time of his claim is more hazardous than the work he was doing at the time of application, the benefits payable will be adjusted to the amount or amounts that the premium he has been paying would have purchased at his present, more hazardous occupation. There is no change in premium; the entire adjustment is in the amount of the benefit.

On the other hand, if the insured's current occupation is less hazardous than his occupation at the time the premium rate was determined, the company will reduce the premium on receipt of proof of the less hazardous occupation. The excess premium paid for any period after the date of the occupation change will be refunded.

Provisions Relating to Other Insurance and Earnings. Whenever an insured has a reasonable expectation of receiving, while he is not able to work, disability income benefits from his insurance policies in amounts equal to or in excess of the amounts he would receive as salary or wages if he were working, he is said to be overinsured. Overinsurance has a very unfavorable effect on the incidence of claims under any health insurance coverage. Consider, for instance, a person who earns $9,000 a year performing work that requires a certain amount of lifting. He suffers a back injury and is totally disabled. He undergoes surgery and has a reasonable period of convalescence. He is now able to return to work but not to his former job. He is, therefore, assigned to a different job at a lower salary. Now, if he has a disability income policy providing payments of $500 per month, and his new salary is only $450, a relatively minor injury may be claimed as a recurrence of his former back problem, and another claim may be presented.

In other words, under circumstances of this kind, there is a tendency to exaggerate somewhat minor illnesses and to prolong major disabilities beyond the normal recovery period. To reduce this possibility, the insurance company may include provisions limiting the benefits payable if the insured has other insurance covering the same losses, or if the insured's total disability income benefits exceed his monthly earnings at the time his disability began.

These provisions spell out in some detail the methods of settlement if the insured has additional insurance in force, either with the same insurer or with other companies. For example, the policy may provide that if all the insured's policies of a specified kind of accident and sickness insurance with this insurer exceed a specified maximum dollar amount, all of his insurance of this kind in excess of that maximum will be void. In that event, the premiums paid for the excess insurance will be returned to the insured or to his estate. An alternative provision permits the insured to elect which of the policies he wishes to retain. The insurer will then return the premiums paid for the others.

The "Relation of Earnings to Insurance" provision outlines the method of settlement that will apply if the insured's benefits under all disability income policies he may have with any insurer are in excess of his monthly earnings at the time his disability began, or the average of his monthly earnings for the two years immediately preceding his disability, whichever is greater. If the total of his disability income benefits exceeds his monthly earnings, the insurer will pay only a proportionate part of the benefits provided by the policy.

Assume that Joyce Lee has policy A, which includes this provision and provides a benefit in the amount of $400 per month during her total disability. Assume further that she has policies B and C which provide $200 each (and do not include this Relation of Earnings to Insurance provision), that her monthly earnings at the time she became disabled were $600, and that the average of her monthly earnings over the preceding two years was $500. Here, Joyce's total disability income from the three policies would be $800 and thus in excess of her monthly income of $600. In that case, the insurer's liability under policy A would be limited to the same proportion of the benefit promised as her monthly earnings bear to the total benefits under all policies providing this type of coverage. This is 600/800, or three-fourths, of $400—a liability of $300. Note, however, that Joyce is still overinsured, since policies B and C will pay the full amounts promised, for a total of $700 under all policies. Thus, unless the Relation of Earnings to Insurance provision has been included in all policies concerned, overinsurance cannot be prevented.

Because the Relation of Earnings to Insurance provision includes a basic minimum, it will not operate to reduce the total benefits payable to a policyowner under all his disability income policies to the lesser of either $200 per month or the total amount of all benefits provided under all disability income coverages he may have. The lower of these two minimums will be payable even if the insured's income was less at the time his disability began.

■ THE NAIC ADVERTISING CODE

In 1955, the National Association of Insurance Commissioners (NAIC) recommended the adoption of a uniform code of health insurance advertising, designed to reduce misleading advertising of health insurance policies. This relatively extensive code has been incorporated into the insurance rules and regulations of nearly half the states. It defines advertising to include all printed and published material used in newspapers, magazines, radio and TV scripts, as well as billboards and similar displays, sales aids of all kinds, prepared sales talks, presentations, and other similar materials used by agents.

Any such advertising material must disclose exceptions, reductions, and limitations included in the health insurance policy if the advertisement includes any mention of specific policy benefits. If renewability is mentioned, all the requirements of the policy relating to renewability must be set forth; and misleading words and phrases are specifically prohibited.

■ NOTES ON CANADIAN PRACTICES

Canadian insurers and other insurance companies operating in Canada generally offer the same classes of benefits under health insurance contracts as are offered in the United States, except for benefits to cover hospital expenses. Since all provinces have government-sponsored plans for prepayment of hospital expenses, insurers in Canada have generally ceased offering this coverage.

Government-sponsored plans for prepayment of hospital expenses date back to 1947, when Saskatchewan initiated a hospital plan. British Columbia followed in 1949. In 1958, the federal government enacted legislation making it possible for the federal and provincial governments to share the costs of prepaying hospital expenses for their residents. In the next three years the other provinces also enacted the necessary legislation to put such plans into operation.

These plans provide for universal coverage, and a person becomes eligible for the coverage in his province after three months of residence. (The government plans are optional in Ontario and Prince Edward Island, but private insurance of ward-level hospital expenses is not permitted. Consequently, persons in these provinces who wish insurance for these expenses must obtain it through the government.)

In five of the provinces—Alberta, British Columbia, Manitoba, Ontario, and Prince Edward Island—premiums for the government plans are paid directly, and in the other provinces, the premiums are paid by means of a tax.

No distinction is made between the benefits for room and board and benefits for other hospital expenses, such as the use of the operating room or the cost of medications. The government plans incorporate an average charge for these services into their general premium rate.

A Uniform Accident and Sickness Act, very similar to the Uniform Accident and Sickness Policy Provisions Law in the United States, is in force in all provinces of Canada except Quebec.

The Canadian law does not require policies to include provisions concerning incontestability or the barring of defenses based on pre-existing conditions. Instead, general provisions which apply to all policies are included in the law itself. However, companies generally include such provisions, as well as a grace period provision, in their policies, even though they are not required to do so.

Quebec has no laws relating specifically to health insurance policies, but companies generally operate in that province in the same manner as in the other provinces and use the same policy forms.

■ QUESTIONS FOR REVIEW

1. Briefly review the development of health insurance in the United States.
2. List three probable reasons for the strong emphasis upon hospital and medical expense coverages during the period since the 1930's.
3. Describe briefly three basic kinds of health insurance benefits.
4. Outline two ways in which total disability may be defined in health insurance contracts.
5. Distinguish between total and partial disability, as these terms are used in disability income contracts.
6. Briefly explain the meaning of the following terms as they are used in major medical coverages:
   a) the deductible amount
   b) percentage participation.
7. List four risks of loss that are commonly excluded from health insurance coverages.
8. Describe the policyowner's right to renew under each of the following:
   a) a cancellable policy
   b) an optionally renewable policy
   c) a guaranteed renewable policy
   d) a noncancellable policy.
9. Describe at least three provisions which are required to be included in health insurance policies issued in the United States.

14 ANNUITIES

In addition to the risks of economic loss due to death and loss of health, life insurance companies are concerned also with the risk of loss of income resulting from old age. Life and health insurance offer protection against the first two risks of loss; the annuity offers protection against the loss of income resulting from old age.

The purpose of this chapter is to discuss some of the more common annuity plans available from life insurance companies and the basic principles that make annuities possible.

■ WHAT AN ANNUITY IS

A Series of Payments

The dictionary defines an annuity as a payment of a fixed sum of money at intervals of time, especially yearly. The word itself is derived from the Latin word for year. Today most annuities are paid at more frequent intervals, usually monthly; and under one form, the variable annuity, the payments may differ in amount. In every instance, however, an annuity is a series of payments.

The annuity is sometimes defined as a contract providing a series of payments made at regular intervals. This is what people usually mean when they mention that a certain person "has an annuity" or when a company explains that annuities are purchased for its retiring employees. The contract, however, is the agreement under which one person or organization promises to pay the annuity to another.

Commercially, annuities are available from life insurance companies. However, annuity contracts are frequently entered into between individuals or between an individual and a not-for-profit organization. Annuities that are payable under contracts with a person or an organization other than a life insurance company are referred to as *private* annuities. This discussion will be concerned with annuities provided by life insurance companies.

If an annuity is thought of as a series of payments, it is easier to understand the various kinds of annuity contracts offered by a life insurance company. Often, several different optional annuity plans are included in the same annuity contract. The owner then elects which plan he wishes in his particular case. The same contract may also include some life insurance as well as the annuity provisions; and other benefits are sometimes included, as will later be explained.

The basic operation of an annuity contract can be more clearly illustrated than explained. Assume that Mrs. Hallam, a widow with no close relatives, finds herself, at age 75, having to make frequent financial decisions concerning the investment of the property her husband has left her. She is concerned that the income from her investments may not be enough to support her if interest rates decline; and she hesitates to spend more than the income earnings, knowing that this would further reduce her investments and thus reduce the income they produce. In other words, she is faced with the possibility of outliving her income.

Mrs. Hallam's investment adviser, recognizing that these are legitimate reasons for concern, suggests that she use $50,000 of her available funds to purchase an annuity from a life insurance company. By doing this, he explains, she can assure herself of an income for life, and she will not need to worry about interest rates or other returns on her investments. The insurance company will pay her a fixed amount each month, and the payments will be guaranteed for as long as she lives.

In accordance with his suggestion, Mrs. Hallam discusses annuities with a life insurance agent, Mr. Lucas. After referring to his rate manual, he tells her that his company will guarantee payment of a lifetime income to her, beginning at her age (75), in the amount of $9.41 per month for every $1,000 she deposits with the company. If she deposits $50,000, the company will send her a monthly check for

$470.50 ($9.41 x 50), as long as she lives, no matter how long that may be.

Mr. Lucas assures Mrs. Hallam that these payments are guaranteed, but he adds that the payments would stop at her death, regardless of how much (or how little) she had then received. Under a somewhat different plan, he continues, the company would pay her a slightly smaller income each month, but it would guarantee that payments would be made for not less than a specified number of years, for example, for 10 years. These payments would be made to her during her lifetime and, if she died before the end of the 10-year period, they would be continued until the end of the period, to whomever she designated. On that basis, the company could guarantee that payments would be made for not less than 10 years (and for as long as she lived if she lived longer than 10 years) and provide $8.06 per month for every $1,000 deposited with it, or $403 per month, in return for her $50,000 premium.

After some consideration, Mrs. Hallam decides that she would prefer the smaller monthly payments and would like to have her niece receive any guaranteed payments remaining unpaid if she (Mrs. Hallam) died before the end of the 10-year guaranteed period. Mr. Lucas then completes an application for Mrs. Hallam's signature. She pays a single premium of $50,000 to the company; and the company issues a policy under which it promises to make payments in the amount of $403 per month to her for as long as she lives. If she dies before payments have been made for 10 years, the payments will be continued to her niece until the end of that period.

The Applicant Has Many Choices

Because Mrs. Hallam's needs and financial situation were fairly well defined, Mr. Lucas did not outline all the choices she might have had in connection with the purchase of an annuity. If he had thought it appropriate, however, he could have mentioned several choices that are available to the applicant for an annuity. For ease of discussion, these choices may be grouped as follows:

1. Choices as to the way the applicant will pay for the annuity
2. Choices as to minimum guarantees the company will make
3. Choices as to when the annuity payments are to begin
4. Choices as to the number of lives to be covered.

■ HOW THE APPLICANT WILL PAY

Single-Premium Annuities

One of the basic choices that must be made by the applicant for an annuity concerns the way he will pay for it. Since Mrs. Hallam had a sizable sum of money available, she paid for her annuity in a single sum and thus purchased what is called a "single-premium annuity." (It is also an immediate annuity, which will be described later.)

Annual-Premium Annuities

Younger people (than Mrs. Hallam) often purchase what are called annual-premium annuities. Under this kind of annuity contract, the owner pays premiums to the company over a period of several years (often 25 or 30), in order to accumulate the fund necessary to provide the income payments he wishes eventually to receive. During this premium-payment period, the owner of such an annuity contract pays premiums in just the same way he would pay them under a life insurance contract.

■ CHOICES AS TO MINIMUM GUARANTEES

A second basic choice that the applicant for an annuity must make concerns the question of guarantees. The monthly payment amount Mr. Lucas first mentioned to Mrs. Hallam could have been paid by his company to Mrs. Hallam as long as she lived, but no longer. This type of annuity is called a straight life annuity.

Under a straight life annuity, the insurance company has no further obligations after the annuitant's death. Because of this, the company is able to make payments in a larger amount than if it guaranteed to make payments for a specified number of years, but the annuitant who dies shortly after having purchased a straight life annuity may have paid a much larger amount to the insurer than he will have received in payments at the time of his death. (On the other hand, if he lives a long time, he has the same advantage under this type of annuity that he has under all life annuities—he may receive a great deal more in annuity payments than the amount he paid for the annuity.)

It is this uncertainty as to how long an annuitant may live (as was true in Mrs. Hallam's case) that prompts him or her to purchase an annuity. Nevertheless, the fact that one may not live to receive payments totaling the amount he paid for the annuity raises a problem in the minds of many prospective purchasers of annuities. There are, therefore, other more popular forms of the annuity, which guarantee that the insurance company will make a specified minimum number of payments, or that it will pay not less than a specified amount, to someone, even though the annuitant himself may die soon after payments begin. Among these more popular forms are annuities with periods certain and refund annuities.

The Annuity with Period Certain

Under the annuity plan that Mrs. Hallam chose, the company promised to pay an income to her for as long as she lived but also guaranteed to make payments to someone—either Mrs. Hallam or her niece, if living—for at least 10 years. A life annuity with a guarantee of this kind is called an annuity with a period certain. Life insurance companies customarily offer annuities of this type with guaranteed periods (periods certain) of 5 years, 10 years, 15 years, or 20 years.

The person to whom the payments are continued, if the annuitant dies before the end of the specified period, is sometimes called a successor-payee. If the successor is not living at the death of the annuitant, or if no successor-payee has been designated, the annuity contract usually provides that the present value (commuted value) of all guaranteed payments remaining unpaid at the annuitant's death will be paid to the annuitant's estate. Usually, the successor-payee, if living, may elect to receive in a lump sum the commuted value of any payments he or she may become entitled to receive.

It may be interesting to note what would happen if the successor-payee survived the annuitant but then died before receiving all of the guaranteed payments. In that case, the commuted value of the guaranteed installments remaining unpaid at the successor-payee's death would be paid to his estate.

Refund Annuities

Two very popular types of annuities provide guarantees in the form of a refund rather than a minimum number of payments. Under either type of refund annuity, the insurer promises to make payments in a certain amount, at regular intervals, to the annuitant for as long as he lives, just as it does under both the straight life annuity and the life annuity with period certain. However, under a refund annuity, the insurer guarantees that if the total of the payments actually made to the annuitant at the time of his death does not equal or exceed the purchase price he paid for the contract, the difference will be paid to a successor-payee, if living, otherwise to the annuitant's estate.

Assume that Mrs. Hallam had purchased an annuity of this kind. If the total of all payments made to her before her death had not equalled the $50,000 single premium she paid, the difference would have been payable to her niece, if living; otherwise to Mrs. Hallam's estate. Refund annuities are classified, according to the way in which this difference will be paid, as either installment refund annuities or cash refund annuities.

The Installment Refund Annuity. Mrs. Hallam might have purchased a refund annuity under which any difference between what she had received from the company in payments prior to her death and what she paid for the contract ($50,000) would be made up by *continuing the installments* to her niece for the necessary length of time. Annuities of this kind are called installment refund annuities. It is customary to permit the remaining guaranteed installments under a contract of this kind to be commuted and the commuted value (present value) to be paid in one sum to the successor-payee, if any, or to the annuitant's estate.

The Cash Refund Annuity. If Mrs. Hallam had purchased a cash refund annuity, the situation would be somewhat different. Under this type of refund annuity, if the payments made to the annuitant at the time of her death do not equal or exceed the amount she paid for the contract, the difference will be payable to the successor-payee in a lump sum, not in installments. If the successor-payee (the niece, in Mrs. Hallam's situation) is not living, then the payment will be made to the annuitant's estate.

The premium for a cash refund annuity will be somewhat higher than that for an installment refund annuity providing income payments of the same amount. This is because, under the cash refund annuity, the difference between the annuitant's purchase price and the total payments received is paid immediately in a lump sum at his death. Under the installment refund annuity, by contrast, the company has the benefit of interest earnings on the declining balance during the period in which installments are being paid. The premium for the installment refund annuity, therefore, can be somewhat lower.

■ WHEN INCOME PAYMENTS BEGIN

The annuitant who pays for his annuity in a single sum may elect to have his income payments begin immediately, or he may have them deferred, to begin at a later date. Thus a single-premium annuity may be either *immediate* or *deferred*.

Even under an immediate annuity, however, the annuitant does not pay the single premium and receive his first income payment "immediately," as this term is ordinarily understood. Instead, he will receive his first income payment at the end of the first income period, and succeeding payments will be made at regular intervals thereafter. Thus, if payments are to be made monthly and the policy date is January 15, the annuitant will receive his first income payment at the end of the first month following the policy date, or February 15. If payments are on a quarterly basis, he will receive the first payment at the end of the first quarter, or April 15; and, if annual payments are elected, he will not receive the first income payment until the end of a year from the policy date.

Deferred annuities provide for income payments to begin at a specified date in the future, usually several years from the issue date of the contract. Often the contract permits the owner to select any date between specified ages (50 to 70, for example) on which he wishes his income payments to begin.

Most deferred annuity contracts are annual-premium deferred annuity contracts. In fact, one of the principal reasons individuals purchase annuities is to assure themselves of a retirement income by making regular premium payments during the years in which they are employed.

The Annuity Due

An annuity under which the first payment is due at the beginning of the first payment period, instead of at the end of the period, is called an "annuity due." Since this concept is used in the computation of life insurance and annual-premium deferred annuity premium rates, it is an important concept, although it is not found among the individual annuities offered for sale to the public. The individual who purchases an annuity may purchase either an immediate or a deferred annuity, but not an annuity due.

■ ANNUITIES ON MORE THAN ONE LIFE

Most life insurance companies offer what is called a "joint and last survivor" annuity. This is a contract under which the insurance company pays an annuity to two or more annuitants jointly, for as long as both or all are living, and continues to make payments thereafter to the survivor or survivors for as long as they live. This type of annuity is especially attractive to husbands and wives, for it assures an income as long as either of them lives.

Usually the joint and last survivor annuity provides for smaller payments after the death of the first annuitant. For instance, payments may be made in the amount of $300 each month while both annuitants are living but be reduced to $150 after the first death. Annuities of this kind are popularly called "joint and one-half" annuities. Sometimes the reduction is smaller—as from $300 to $200—in which case the annuity may be referred to as a "joint and two-thirds" annuity.

■ THE SURVIVORSHIP ANNUITY

A somewhat different annuity plan from any of the plans discussed thus far provides a lifetime annuity for a designated person, the annuitant, if another person named in the contract dies before the annuitant dies—that is, if the annuitant survives the designated person. If the annuitant dies before the designated person, the contract terminates without values.

Assume that a young woman is the sole support of her elderly father. So long as she lives she will see that he is cared for, but in the event of her death while he is still living, there will be no one to assume the financial responsibility for his support. She can name him beneficiary of her life insurance and elect the life income option. However, she can provide a larger life income for him by purchasing a survivorship annuity that will pay him an annuity if he survives her, but will terminate without values if she outlives him. This type of annuity is especially appropriate in situations such as the one described—where a young person wishes to be sure that a much older person will have a lifetime income if the younger dies first. However, few insurers offer it at the present time.

■ ANNUITIES AND THE SETTLEMENT OPTIONS

In one sense, an annuity is available under almost every ordinary life insurance contract sold today—as an optional mode of settlement. The life income option, or some variation of it, is almost always offered. When it is elected, either by the policyowner for the beneficiary or by a beneficiary after the death of the insured, the proceeds of the insurance policy will be used as a net single premium to provide a life income—that is, an annuity on the life of the beneficiary. If the option is elected without a period certain, it provides a straight life annuity. If it is elected with a period certain, it provides an annuity with minimum guarantees. The life income option with cash refund is also sometimes offered.

The optional modes of settlement are also usually available to the policyowner himself, if he wishes to surrender his life insurance policy for cash. When a cash value life insurance contract is surrendered and the cash value applied under the life income option for the benefit of the insured, the result is very much the same as if a retirement income contract (which will be discussed later) had been purchased in the first place. The applicant for a whole life policy does not usually purchase it for retirement purposes, but the fact that the cash value may be used in this way is only another in a fairly impressive list of valuable uses of the whole life contract.

Another of the settlement options, the fixed-period option, illustrates a different kind of annuity from any discussed thus far—the annuity certain. An annuity certain is a series of payments guaranteed to be made for a specified period, but no longer, regardless of how long the payee may live. Thus, the beneficiary who elects to receive the proceeds of a life insurance policy under the fixed-period option for a period of 20 years is electing an annuity certain for that period. At the end of 20 years the entire annuity will have been paid and no further payments will be due. (By contrast, under the *life* annuity with period certain, payments will be made to someone for the period selected; and then, if the original payee is still living, the payments will be continued for the remainder of his or her life.)

Annuities certain are classified as "annuities without life contingencies," by contrast with the other annuities discussed in this chapter, which are "annuities *with* life contingencies." The number and the amount of the individual payments under the fixed-period option are not affected by the age, sex, or date of death of the payee, as are the payments under any of the life annuity options.

■ HOW ANNUITY PAYMENTS ARE CALCULATED

Annuities are possible because the law of large numbers can be applied to the risk of living a very long time, just as it can be applied to the risk of premature death. The individual annuitant does not know whether or not he will be living at the end of any given year, and neither does the insurer. When annuitants are considered in groups, however, the insurer can use statistics to predict, with a reasonable degree of accuracy, how many annuitants per thousand at various ages will survive each year. This is accomplished in much the same way as the insurer predicts the number of insureds who will die in any given year—using statistics of past experience. Using these statistics, and assuming that deaths will occur in the future at approximately the same rate as in the past, the insurance company can estimate the number of payments it must reasonably be prepared to make for each 1,000 annuitants to whom it issues contracts. Then, knowing the number of such payments it must make, the company can calculate the amounts of the payments it can safely make for each $1,000 deposited with it by annuitants of various ages.

This principle can be illustrated by an oversimplified (and therefore somewhat unrealistic) example. Suppose five men, 90 years of age, wish to purchase annuities that will provide monthly income payments for each of them for the remainder of their respective lives—that is, straight life annuities. Each man pays a single premium of $10,000, making a total of $50,000 paid to the insurance company. Assume that statistics show that one of these men can be expected to live to receive income payments for one year only, another for two years, a third for three years, and so on. On this basis, assuming one death each year (at the end of the year in each instance), the company must be prepared to make monthly income payments as follows:

Payments to:	Assumed Date of Death	Number of Monthly Payments
Annuitant No. 1	End of 1st Year	12
Annuitant No. 2	End of 2nd Year	24
Annuitant No. 3	End of 3rd Year	36
Annuitant No. 4	End of 4th Year	48
Annuitant No. 5	End of 5th Year	60
Total estimated number of payments to be made to the group		180

Since the insurer will have the $50,000 at the beginning of the first year (and will invest it), the interest to be earned on the fund while these payments are being made must be taken into consideration. This interest will increase the amount of the individual payments the insurer will be able to make. The amount of each individual monthly income payment in this example, therefore, will be $50,000 divided by 180, or $277, plus interest earnings and less an allowance for expenses of administration.

Each payment the individual annuitant receives is made up of three elements. One element is a share of the *principal* amount (premium) he contributed. A second element is made up of interest earned on the declining balance of that principal. The third element is sometimes called a "survivorship benefit." This refers to the annuitant's share of all amounts contributed by other annuitants who have died before the payments made to them or their successors have equalled the amounts they originally contributed.

Note, for example, that the annuitant to whom payments are made for just one year, receives only 12 × $277, or $3,324 plus. The remainder of his $10,000, plus interest, is thus released for use in making payments to the survivors; hence a "survivorship benefit" to them. The annuitant who lives for two years receives $6,648 and releases the remainder of his $10,000 contribution, and so on. Thus each annuitant who dies prior to receiving in payments the equivalent of his total contribution plus interest releases the remainder for use in making payments to the surviving members of the group.

Annuity Tables

For several reasons, life insurers do not use the same mortality tables in calculating annuity payments that they use in calculating life insurance premiums. Probably the most important reason is the fact that annuitants, as a group, tend to live longer than similar groups of insureds. Several explanations have been suggested for this. For one thing, annuitants have traditionally lived in reasonably comfortable financial circumstances. (The very poor, for obvious reasons, do not purchase annuities.) This fact alone gives annuitants certain advantages in the areas of medical care, living conditions, and retirement, if and when they wish, to favorable climates. The annuity then makes it possible for them to retain these advantages, thus continuing environmental factors that are favorable to a lengthened life span.

Annuitants are also a select group at the outset so far as health is concerned. The person in poor health is not usually concerned about outliving his income. It is the person whose health is good who wishes to assure himself that he will have an income for the rest of his life. It is not surprising, therefore, that death rates at the various ages are generally lower for annuitants than for insured lives and that different mortality tables are used in computing annuity rates and payments than are used for life insurance purposes.

Nevertheless, there is another basic reason why life insurance companies use different tables for annuity calculations. This is the fact that changes in the timing of annuitants' deaths have a very different (and opposite) effect on the financial position of the company from changes in the rates of death of insured lives at the various ages.

Consider, first, the effect of the death of an insured at any time, on the obligations of the company under a life insurance contract. The insured's death brings about an immediate financial obligation on the part of the company—payment of a death claim. By contrast, the death of an annuitant means that the company has to make no further payments (or, under some annuity contracts, only a limited number of further payments).

Under life insurance contracts, therefore, if insureds as a group tend to live longer than the mortality tables would indicate, the life insurance company will be receiving premium payments over a longer period of time than was assumed in establishing the premium rates. Therefore, it will have more money than it anticipated, out of which to pay claims as they arise. By contrast, if annuitants as a group tend to live longer than available statistics would indicate, the company will be in exactly the opposite financial position. It will be obligated to continue annuity payments for longer periods than were assumed in calculating the payments, and the result may be a serious financial drain on the assets of the company. To guard against this possible adverse result, different safety factors are necessary in annuity tables from those used in mortality tables for life insurance premium rates.

Mortality rates used in calculating life insurance premium rates contain safety factors in the form of an upward adjustment, so that they somewhat overestimate the rates of death actually expected at the different ages. This establishes a higher premium rate and thus operates as a safeguard to the company against upward fluctuations in the death rates actually experienced. However, an upward adjustment in death rates on which annuity calculations are based would have the opposite effect and would result in premium rates that would be inadequate.

To illustrate, suppose the death rates of the annuitants in the example given on page 295 were increased by one death in each of the first two years, with the fifth annuitant dying in the third year. In that case, the table of payments would read as follows:

Payments to:	Assumed Date of Death	Number of Monthly Payments
Annuitant No. 1	End of 1st Year	12
Annuitant No. 2	End of 1st Year	12
Annuitant No. 3	End of 2nd Year	24
Annuitant No. 4	End of 2nd Year	24
Annuitant No. 5	End of 3rd Year	36
Total number of payments to be made to the group		108
Total contributions for annuities		$50,000
Approximate monthly payments (* $50,000 divided by 108)		$463*

In other words, if annuity tables were adjusted in the same way as mortality tables are adjusted for life insurance purposes—that is, by assuming a higher death rate at each age than the actual statistics show—fewer total payments would be required, and each payment could therefore be larger.

Now, consider what it would mean if the insurance company established its annuity rates on the assumption that deaths would occur among this group of annuitants at the accelerated rate shown in the table above. In that case, annuities would be issued providing for monthly payments of approximately $463, in return for a single premium of $10,000. However, if the annuitants died in accordance with the statistics used in the illustration on page 295, a total of 180 payments of $463 each would have to be made, although the insurer would have exhausted the funds derived from premium payments under these contracts by the time 108 payments had been made.

As a matter of fact, any downward trend in the death rates of annuitants means that the insurer will have to make annuity payments for longer periods. If this has not been anticipated, the insurer may have a larger total financial liability than it has prepared for. And the trend in death rates during most of the present century has been downward. Until fairly recently, mortality rates had shown an almost steady decrease, and any new breakthrough in the medical treatment of degenerative diseases could renew the trend.

For all these reasons, life insurers use tables for annuity calculations that are different from the mortality tables used for life insurance purposes. Annuity tables are based on the experience of annuitants rather than insured lives, and the actual death rates among annuitants are reduced slightly at the various ages to provide a safety factor for annuity purposes (as contrasted with the upward adjustment used for life insurance purposes).

Annuity Rates for Women. In considering the longevity of annuitants generally, one other factor should be mentioned—the significant difference in life expectancy among women as compared to the life expectancy of men of the same age. This difference has been demonstrated statistically for a number of years, although it was not generally given effect in life insurance premium rates until relatively recently. In the computation of annuity rates and payments, however, the fact that women tend to outlive men by a significant number of years has been recognized and taken into account for a long time. This is because the difference, significant in itself, is accentuated by the high percentage of annuitants who are women.

The most common method of adjusting for this difference is to make annuity payments to women on the same basis as to men four or five years younger. Thus, a woman age 65 might receive income payments on the same basis as a man age 60 or 61. Some companies, however, establish separate and higher premium rates for women annuitants or lower income amounts per $1,000, instead of using an age adjustment.

■ RETIREMENT ANNUITIES

The annuity is an especially appropriate way for an individual to provide an income for himself to begin after he retires from active employment. The single-premium immediate annuity, though suitable for this purpose, requires a fairly substantial single premium at the time of retirement and, therefore, is not very practical for most people who are concerned about retirement income. The annual-premium deferred annuity is a much more realistic plan, since it permits the individual to accumulate the necessary fund through premium payments during his working years. When the annuitant retires, the insurance company begins making income payments to him. There are several different variations of this basically simple plan.

The Annual-Premium Deferred Annuity

The typical retirement annuity contract is designed to accumulate a sufficient fund by the time the annuitant reaches retirement age to permit the insurance company to make income payments to him in a specified amount per $1,000 of cash value, for the remainder of the annuitant's lifetime. If the annuitant dies before the date income payments are to begin, the cash value of the contract as of the date of death, or the total premiums he has paid, if larger, will be paid to his beneficiary.

Often a waiver-of-premium-for-disability benefit will be included in a policy of this kind, since the policyowner is undertaking a financial program involving the payment of premiums over a long period of time. If he becomes totally disabled before he completes this program, the waiver-of-premium-for-disability coverage will continue his premium payments for him and thus "insure his annuity plan," just as the waiver-of-premium-for-disability coverage insures the insurance under a life insurance contract.

During the period before income payments begin, an annual-premium deferred annuity contract operates in very much the same way as the cash value portion of an individual life insurance contract. Premiums paid to the company are invested by the company and accumulated until the date when the income payments are to begin. After that date, the contract operates as an annuity.

Assume that a contract of this kind is purchased when the applicant is age 25. He pays premiums for 40 years and then elects to begin receiving income payments. The coverage under an illustrative contract having a $100 annual premium is charted in Figure 14–1.

Although a "death benefit" is paid under this contract if the annuitant dies before the income payments begin, it is not true life insurance, since there is never any amount at risk. The company never pays out more than the amounts received plus earned interest, adjusted for expenses of administration.

There is no reason, however, why life insurance cannot be provided under an annual-premium deferred annuity contract, to increase the benefit payable during the period in which premiums are being paid. Contracts which combine the annual-premium deferred annuity and life insurance may be called retirement income contracts, income endowment contracts, endowment income contracts, or any of several other similar names. Probably the most popular plan of this general type is the "retirement income contract."

FIGURE 14–1

Annual-Premium Deferred Life Annuity (issue age 25, retirement age 65; premium $100 annually; income payments $85 per month, $1020 per year)

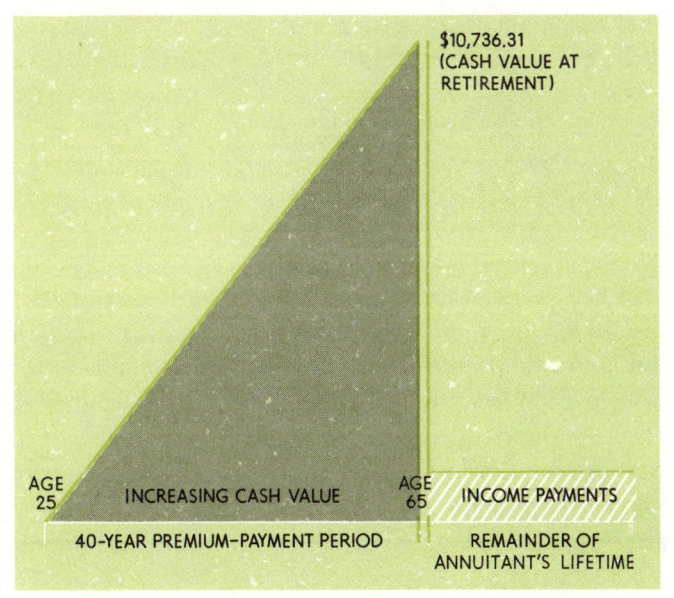

[Figure showing a triangle labeled INCREASING CASH VALUE from AGE 25 rising to $10,736.31 (CASH VALUE AT RETIREMENT) at AGE 65, with INCOME PAYMENTS continuing for REMAINDER OF ANNUITANT'S LIFETIME after the 40-YEAR PREMIUM-PAYMENT PERIOD.]

The Retirement Income Contract

The retirement income contract is basically an annual-premium deferred annuity policy, with the addition of some term life insurance. If the annuitant pays the required premiums each year until he reaches an age specified in the contract, the company will begin making income payments to him and will continue these payments for as long as he lives. In other words, the retirement income contract is no different from the annual-premium deferred annuity contract after income payments begin. However, during much of the period before the payments begin, the retirement income contract provides a true insurance benefit. If the annuitant does not survive to the specified age, the company will pay a life insurance benefit of not less than a specified amount (not just the amount of premiums paid) to the beneficiary.

The typical retirement income contract is designed to provide decreasing term insurance, so that a death benefit of at least $1,000 can be provided for each $10 of monthly income ultimately to become payable. However, $1,000 of cash value at age 65 is not enough to provide a life annuity of $10 per month, as indicated in the following excerpt from a settlement options table:

Guaranteed Monthly Income $1,000 of Cash Value Will Purchase

Age M	Age F	Life Income	Life Income with 10 Years Certain
61	65	$6.04	$5.74
62	66	6.22	5.88
63	67	6.41	6.03
64	68	6.62	6.18
65	69	6.84	6.34

As shown in this table, $1,000 of cash value will provide a life income of only $6.84 per month for a male at age 65. More than $1,000, therefore, will be required if $10 of monthly income is to be provided for life, as promised; and this amount must be accumulated by the time the annuitant attains age 65. The cash value of this contract, therefore, will exceed $1,000 per $10 of monthly income provided, for a period of some time prior to his age 65. That is, for that period of time, the cash value will exceed the face amount of the contract.

The relationship of the increasing cash value, amount at risk, and face amount, for each $1,000 of a retirement income contract may be charted as shown in Figure 14–2.

The cash value of this particular contract exceeds the $1,000 face amount of the policy during every year after the annuitant's age 56. By the time he reaches age 65, the cash value is $1,578. The policy, therefore, pays a death benefit that is defined as the "face amount of the policy or the cash value, if larger," if the annuitant dies prior to the date income payments begin. The insurance is decreasing term life insurance, expiring at the annuitant's age 56. After that, the death benefit is the cash value of the contract (as would be true also under an annual-premium deferred annuity contract).

If the annuitant is living at retirement age, the company will begin making the income payments whenever the annuitant elects to have them begin. After that election, the contract operates as an annuity and not an insurance contract.

Most companies give the annuitant as many choices as possible under such contracts. Usually, the annuitant may elect to have his income payments begin at any time between ages 50 and 70, or later. Usually, also, he may receive the payments as a straight life annuity

FIGURE 14–2

Retirement Income Contract (issue age 25; retirement age 65; income payments $10 per month, $120 per year)

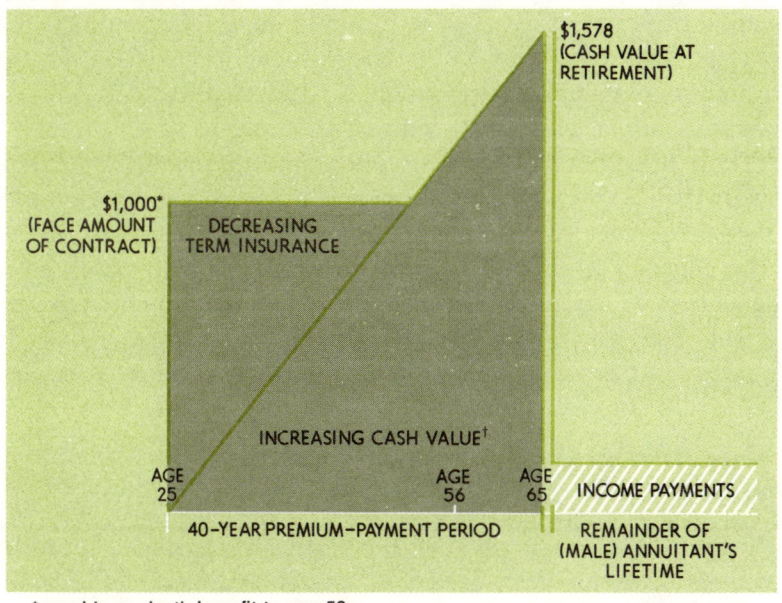

[Figure: Diagram showing $1,000* (FACE AMOUNT OF CONTRACT) with DECREASING TERM INSURANCE and INCREASING CASH VALUE† reaching $1,578 (CASH VALUE AT RETIREMENT) at age 65. 40-YEAR PREMIUM-PAYMENT PERIOD from AGE 25 to AGE 65, with AGE 56 marked. INCOME PAYMENTS during REMAINDER OF (MALE) ANNUITANT'S LIFETIME.]

*payable as death benefit to age 56
**payable as death benefit, ages 56 to 65

or with any of several periods certain—10, 15, or 20 years, for instance. Alternatively, he may elect a joint and last survivor annuity, if he prefers. The amount of each payment will be determined in accordance with the annuitant's choices in each of these respects, as well as by the sex of the annuitant and his or her age when the payments begin.

The Flexible-Premium Annuity

Under either the annual-premium deferred annuity or the retirement income contract, the policyowner pays premiums in a predetermined level amount throughout the premium-payment period. Sometime during the late 1950's and early 1960's, however, a new concept was introduced—the idea of permitting different amounts to be paid as premiums through the premium-payment period, depending upon the funds the annuitant had available or wanted to invest for his retirement. Policies based on this principle are called flexible-premium annuities.

A flexible-premium annuity contract operates in essentially the same way as an annual-premium deferred annuity except that the policyowner has the right to make premium payments in different amounts from year to year. For example, he might pay $1,000 the first year, $800 the second, $1,600 the third, and so on. Usually, there is a minimum annual amount, such as $100, that must be paid; and there is usually a maximum such as $2,500 per year.

These premium payments are accounted for and accumulated at not less than a specified rate of interest until the policyowner elects to begin receiving his retirement income. At that time, the cash value of the contract is applied to provide whatever amount of income payments it will purchase at rates that have been guaranteed from the issue date of the contract; and the company begins to pay him his retirement income. This type of contract is charted in Figure 14–3.

■ THE VARIABLE ANNUITY

Until recently, annuity contracts always provided for income payments to be made in fixed and guaranteed amounts of money. Traditionally, this arrangement—a guaranteed income of a specified (and adequate) amount, for life—has implied financial security. It was recognized, of course, that there would be periods when the purchasing power of a fixed income would be higher, and other periods when it would fall. The choice, however, was always thought to be between the security of guaranteed payments, such as were available under annuities (backed by fixed-dollar investments), and the risk of greater financial loss if one's investments were in equities.

The terms "equities" or "equity investments," refer to investments in property such as land and buildings or certificates of stock. Such ownership involves values that tend to rise with rising economic trends and to fall with a declining economy. Investments of this kind, therefore, involve a special kind of risk not present in investments which guarantee a specified return or a fixed future value. At times, and for some people, equity investments have been the source of extraordinary gains; and at other times, notably in the great depression of the 1930's, they have meant extensive financial losses.

During most years since the early 40's, however, this country has been experiencing some degree of inflation. As a result, the gen-

FIGURE 14-3

Flexible Premium Annuity (issue age 25, retirement age 65; income payments in whatever amount the cash value at age 65 will provide, according to tables included in the contract)

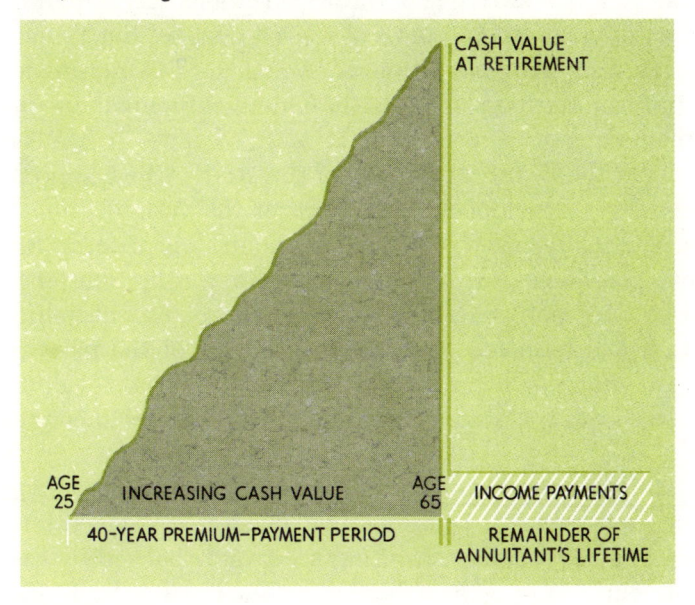

- CASH VALUE AT RETIREMENT
- AGE 25 — INCREASING CASH VALUE — AGE 65 — INCOME PAYMENTS
- 40-YEAR PREMIUM-PAYMENT PERIOD — REMAINDER OF ANNUITANT'S LIFETIME

eral level of prices is now much higher than it was a few decades ago; and equity investments have generally been advantageous. Persons who invested their money in traditional, fixed-dollar annuities, however, have had the unfortunate experience of finding that the dollars they are receiving as annuity incomes today have much less purchasing power than the dollars they paid to the insurance company as premiums some 30 or more years ago.

This is a plight they share with all persons whose investments provide an income in guaranteed numbers of dollars. Insurance policies, the traditional annuity contracts (such as those discussed thus far), bonds, and mortgages all may be classified as fixed-dollar contracts or investments; and all are payable in a specified number of dollars. These fixed-dollar investments and the guaranteed incomes they provide represent stable purchasing power in times of economic stability and increasing purchasing power when price levels tend to decline. When price levels are rising, however, such investments may mean substantial losses in purchasing power.

The disadvantages of fixed-dollar investments in periods of rising prices have long been recognized, and the hardships to retired persons attempting to live on fixed-dollar incomes during such periods have been acknowledged. For many years, however, it was generally assumed that nothing could be done about it.

Following World War II, one of the organizations best acquainted with the effect of inflation on groups of retired persons, the Teachers Insurance and Annuity Association of America (TIAA), made a thorough study of the possibility of providing retirement incomes which might reflect, to some extent at least, changes in the purchasing power of the dollar. As a result of this study, a new approach to the annuity was developed in the form of the variable annuity.

A variable annuity may be defined, in nontechnical terms, as a contract that guarantees to pay an income for the lifetime of the annuitant but does not guarantee the amounts of the installment payments that will be made. Instead, the amount of the payments varies upward and downward according to the market value of funds that have been invested largely in equities, usually in common stocks.

The variable annuity required some basic changes in the investment practices of insurers. Annuities that guarantee payments in a specified amount (fixed-dollar annuities) are largely backed by fixed-dollar investments. In other words, the insurer invests the funds it holds in such securities as federal government, municipal, and industrial bonds and well-secured mortgages. For variable annuities, the insurer invests its funds mainly in equities, primarily common stocks.

The variable annuity plan developed by the Teachers Insurance and Annuity Association had its beginning in 1952, when the New York Legislature enacted a law creating the College Retirement Equities Fund (CREF). This organization worked hand in hand with TIAA to provide a combination of annuities—a fixed-dollar annuity through TIAA and a variable annuity through CREF.

These annuities were made available to college and other teachers only; and because it was felt that some guaranteed dollar amounts were basic to a retirement plan, the variable annuity could not be purchased unless at least 50 percent of each premium was invested in a fixed-dollar annuity. Later, as inflation continued and increased, this limit was relaxed, and today the total annuity premium submitted may be applied toward the purchase of the variable annuity or the fixed-dollar annuity in any proportions desired, up to 100 percent for either.

Because the variable annuity was essentially a new concept, several legal questions were presented by it. One of these was the question of how such annuities were to be regulated. At the present time, this question has been resolved, with the Securities and Exchange Commission regulating the issuance and marketing of variable annuities on the basis that they are essentially securities rather than insurance contracts. Special legislation has also been enacted by many of the states permitting life insurance companies to hold funds in separate accounts, thus permitting variable annuity funds to be invested separately from the general assets of the company. More than 40 life insurance companies today offer variable annuities or similar retirement plans.

Operation of the Variable Annuity

Variable annuities, like fixed-dollar annuities, may be purchased by paying a single sum or by paying premiums over a period of years. If the purchase price is paid in a single sum, the annuity may be either immediate or deferred. A contract under which premiums are paid over a period of years is a deferred variable annuity contract, under which income payments will begin on the date the annuitant chooses. In its general outlines, this kind of variable annuity will provide for a premium-payment, or accumulation period and an income, or pay-out period.

The Accumulation Period. During the accumulation period, each premium payment made by the annuitant is used by the insurer to purchase "accumulation units" for the annuitant's account. Accumulation units are shares in an equity fund administered by the insurer. The value of these units fluctuates in accordance with the value of the equity investments. (It is found by dividing the total value of the investments of the fund by the number of accumulation units.) The number of units that will be purchased by a given premium, therefore, will depend upon the value of the units on the day the premium is paid.

Assume, for example, that the market value of all fund investments is such as to produce a value of $20 for each accumulation unit on September 15 when Gregory Harrison's premium of $100 is received. In that case, five accumulation units will be purchased for him. If the value of each accumulation unit is $12.50 at the time he pays the next premium of $100, his premium will purchase eight units. These eight units will be added to the five units he has already purchased, and this process will be continued until he reaches retirement age.

The Income or Pay-Out Period. At retirement age, the total accumulation units of the annuitant are valued (at whatever value these units have on that date), and the total value is used to purchase annuity (or pay-out) units. Annuity units are valued separately from the accumulation units and less frequently. The valuation method is different also, in order to give effect to mortality guarantees and expenses, as well as the value of the equity fund.

Annuity units fluctuate in value just as the accumulation units do. Thus, the number of annuity units that can be purchased for an annuitant when he reaches retirement age will depend upon two things: the value of the accumulation units, to establish the amount of the fund to be applied; and the value of the annuity units, to establish the number of annuity units to which the annuitant will be entitled. Once annuity units have been purchased for the annuitant, the number of units to which he is entitled will not change.

The value of annuity units is customarily recalculated once each year, and this value determines the amount of the monthly payments that will be made to the annuitant for the coming year. For example, if 100 annuity units were purchased for the annuitant and each would provide $3 per month, he would receive $300 per month until the annuity units were revalued. At the end of the year, the value of the annuity units is again recalculated to determine the amount that can be paid out for each annuity unit for the next year, and so on.

The variable annuity has been one of the most discussed subjects in life insurance circles since it was first introduced. Those who have been its strongest advocates believe that it represents a workable solution to the problems of assuring adequate retirement incomes in periods of constantly rising prices. Those who take a less enthusiastic view agree that the variable approach has much to recommend it in periods of rising prices but point out that there is no guarantee that equity investments will automatically increase in value even in times of inflation, and severe declines in value could have a very serious effect on the income payments so provided. At this time, however, there seems little justification for prolonged debate, for the variable annuity principle is already widely used and seems likely to increase in popularity in the coming years.

■ TAX-SHELTERED ANNUITIES

Eligible Organizations

One of the significant developments in the field of annuities during the past several years has concerned what are popularly called "tax-sheltered" annuities. These are annuities purchased for their employees by certain types of tax-exempt organizations and, more recently, by public school systems, under a provision of the federal Internal Revenue Code that grants special tax privileges in such instances. The term "tax-sheltered annuity" does not refer to any special kind of annuity. Any annuity will qualify, provided that it is purchased under conditions set out in the federal income tax law.

501(c)(3) Organizations. Prior to 1961, the only organizations eligible to purchase tax-sheltered annuities for their employees were those described in section 501(c)(3) of the Internal Revenue Code, as follows:

Corporations, and any community chest, fund, or foundation, organized and operated exclusively for religious, charitable, scientific, testing for public safety, literary, or educational purposes, or for the prevention of cruelty to children or animals. . . .

This description includes so many different kinds of not-for-profit organizations that they are frequently referred to as "501(c)(3)" organizations.

Public Educational Institutions. In 1961, Congress extended this tax-sheltered annuity privilege to employees of public educational institutions, although such organizations were not always free to take full advantage of it because of limitations of local laws. These limitations are rapidly being removed, however, and the number of tax-sheltered annuities purchased for employees of public school systems has been increasing accordingly.

Requirements

A tax-sheltered annuity is an annuity contract purchased by an eligible organization for an employee of that organization. One or several employees may be so benefited. There are no requirements that all—or even a minimum number—of the employees must be selected; and retirement income contracts as well as fixed-dollar or variable annuities will qualify.

Although the employee must be the owner of the annuity, the employer-organization must apply for the contract and pay the premium. It may pay the premium as an addition to the employee's salary, or the employee may make a salary reduction agreement with the employer. Under a salary reduction agreement, the employee gives up a salary increase to which he would otherwise be entitled, or he accepts a reduction from his current salary, in the amount necessary to pay the premiums for his annuity.

The "Tax Shelter"

When an eligible organization applies for and pays premiums on a contract of this kind for one of its employees, the employee is entitled to exclude from his current taxable income the amount the organization pays in premiums even though this is, in effect, current income to him. So long as these amounts do not exceed an "exclusion allowance" specified in the law, he pays no federal income tax on them until he begins receiving income benefits under the contract, or until he withdraws the cash value by surrendering the contract or making a policy loan.

The formula for the exclusion allowance is 20 percent of the employee's current salary—16⅔ percent, if he has agreed to a reduction in salary—multiplied by the employee's total number of years of service, and reduced by the total of all amounts contributed on his behalf in prior years which were excluded from his gross salary.

The essence of the tax shelter lies in this privilege, on the part of the employee, of excluding premium payments from his current taxable income. Although he will be taxed on the entire income as he receives it after retirement, his tax will ordinarily be less at that time, since he will have the "over-65" additional personal exemption and will usually be in a lower income tax bracket.

An illustration may help to show the advantages of the tax-sheltered annuity. Assume that Keith Martin is considering the purchase of an annual-premium deferred annuity and that he can devote approximately $1,000 per year of his salary to that purpose. If he must purchase the annuity himself and is in a 20 percent tax bracket, he will pay an income tax of $200 on this $1,000 and will then have only $800 with which to pay his annuity premium. On the other hand, if he is employed by an organization that is eligible to purchase a tax-sheltered annuity for him, he can request his employer to reduce his salary by $1,000, and the employer can pay this total amount as an annual premium on a tax-sheltered annuity for him.

When these two situations are compared, the advantages of the tax-sheltered annuity become apparent. It makes no difference to Keith's employer whether the $1,000 is paid as salary to Keith or as a premium for an annuity for him. It is the same outlay to the employer in either case. To Keith, however, the difference is striking, for a 25 percent greater premium can be paid under an annuity purchased for him by his employer, and a 25 percent larger annuity can be purchased than if he applied for it and paid the premiums himself.

■ HOW ANNUITY INCOME IS TAXED

Although the payments an annuitant receives under his annuity contract are often referred to as "income" payments, they are not income in the same sense as interest payments on bonds or dividends on stock, and they are not taxed in the same way. Under most annuities, as previously explained, each payment is made up partly of money the annuitant paid to the insurance company in the first place, partly of interest earned on the accumulated funds, and partly of a "survivorship benefit." Accordingly, the income tax law recognizes that under the typical annuity contract a part of each payment the annuitant receives is really a return to him of money he originally paid for the contract. Thus, a part of each payment is considered a partial return of the annuitant's "investment in the contract" and is excluded from his taxable income. The remainder is considered income and is subject to federal income tax. (The tax-sheltered annuity is an exception to the usual situation. Since it is purchased by the employer, the employee has paid nothing toward its purchase and thus has no investment in this contract. Consequently, income payments received by the annuitant from a tax-sheltered annuity are subject to income tax on the same basis as any other income.)

The annuitant's "investment in the contract" is the amount he actually paid to the insurance company—either in a lump sum or in premium payments—less any dividends he has received. Under the tax rules for annuities, this amount is divided by the annuitant's "total expected return" under the contract; and the resulting percentage is the percentage of each payment that he can exclude from his taxable income. This percentage is known as the "exclusion ratio."

Computing the exclusion ratio is not as complicated as it seems. Under a life annuity, the "expected return" is based on the payee's life expectancy, calculated in accordance with special Internal Revenue Service mortality tables. Assume an annuitant has a straight life annuity contract for which he has paid a total of $10,000 in premiums. Assume also that he retires at an age when his life expectancy, as shown in the table, is 20 years, and his monthly income payments are $65. In this case, his investment in the contract is $10,000, and his total expected return will be his annual income ($65 x 12), or $780, multiplied by 20 (years), or $15,600. When his investment in the contract ($10,000) is divided by his total expected return ($15,600), the result is 64 percent, which is the exclusion ratio. This means that he can exclude 64 percent of each $65 payment he receives ($41.60) from his taxable income. The remainder of each payment—$23.40—is taxable at ordinary income tax rates.

The annuitant may live beyond the 20 years, for as previously noted, the life expectancy concept has no relationship to the length of time any particular individual will actually live. However, he can continue to exclude 64 percent of each payment from his taxable income for the rest of his life.

For cash or installment refund annuities, the exclusion ratio is computed in the same way, after adjusting the annuitant's "investment in the contract" in accordance with Internal Revenue Service rules.

The annuity rules of the Internal Revenue Code also apply to all benefits payable in periodic installments under life insurance contracts if they are paid during the lifetime of the insured. Thus these rules apply to cash surrender values that are left under the optional modes of settlement, as well as to the proceeds of endowment policies.

■ NOTES ON CANADIAN PRACTICES

Individuals in Canada may make contributions towards retirement income on a tax-sheltered basis, within government-defined limits, either to a Registered Group Retirement plan to which the employer also contributes or to an individual Registered Retirement Savings Plan. Any life insurance policy which includes a savings element may be registered, but only the savings portion is eligible for tax exemption. Premium payments are excluded from current taxable income (so long as the total amount of the payments does not exceed the limits set by the government). However, the full amount of annuity payments must be considered as income for tax purposes when the payments are received.

■ QUESTIONS FOR REVIEW

1. Briefly define an annuity.
2. Outline the two principal ways in which a person may pay for an annuity.
3. Distinguish among the following:
   a) Straight life annuity
   b) Annuity with period certain
   c) Annuity with installment refund
   d) Annuity with cash refund
4. Distinguish between an immediate and a deferred annuity. How does an annuity due differ from an immediate annuity?
5. Briefly describe the three basic elements which make up the periodic income payments under an annuity.
6. Contrast the effect of the death of an annuitant on the financial situation of a life insurance company with the effect of the death of an insured.
7. Why are life insurance mortality tables not suitable for use with annuities?
8. In what two major ways do variable annuities differ from the traditional fixed-dollar annuities?
9. Explain the advantages to the annuitant of the tax-sheltered annuity.

15 GROUP LIFE INSURANCE

The history of life insurance includes many innovations, but few have been more readily accepted or more widely utilized than the idea of group insurance. Introduced in 1911-1912, the group approach has had such general acceptance that group plans account for more than one-third of the total life insurance in force in the United States today. Some of the reasons for this growth and some of its implications, as well as the general principles on which group life insurance plans are based, will be examined in this chapter.

■ ORIGIN AND DEVELOPMENT

Life insurance could be offered to any large segment of the general population with no risk appraisal whatever, if adverse selection could be avoided. In fact, it is sometimes said that a life insurance company could insure every person who passed by its front door if all such persons would accept the insurance and keep it in force. In that case, losses could be predicted and rates could be calculated for the group just as effectively as if the insureds had been individually selected. In addition, many of the expenses incident to applications, risk selection, policy issue, and recordkeeping for individual insureds could be eliminated. Group life insurance is a practical application of this approach.

The Earliest Group Plans

Group life insurance in the form in which we know it today began with the establishment of two employer-employee group plans, in 1911 and 1912 respectively. In 1910, the Montgomery Ward Company contacted several life insurance companies about the possibility of providing low-cost life insurance to all Montgomery Ward employees. Since all employees were to be insured, individual risk appraisal was precluded.

The plan selected by Wards was developed by the Equitable Life Assurance Society and established in 1912. It provided life insurance for all the employees under one general contract, without individual medical examinations and at no cost to the employees. That is, the employer paid the entire cost of the insurance. Under this plan, life insurance was provided for 2,912 employees, in amounts roughly approximating one year's salary for each, subject to a maximum of $3,000 on any one life.

A similar plan had been established in 1911 by the same insurer (the Equitable Society) for the employees of Pantasote Leather Company of Passaic, New Jersey. Together, the Montgomery Ward and the Pantasote plans set a pattern for group life insurance for employer-employee groups which is still followed in its general outlines.

The NAIC Model Group Insurance Bill

For a few years after these first group life insurance plans were introduced, there was a considerable difference of opinion as to the acceptability of group plans. Many life insurance leaders felt that life insurance coverage without individual underwriting was completely unsound. In 1917, however, the National Association of Insurance Commissioners (NAIC) officially recognized the soundness of group life insurance by recommending a model group life insurance bill for enactment by the legislatures of the various states. This bill included standard provisions for group life insurance contracts and a definition of group life insurance as a form of life insurance covering employer-employee groups which met certain requirements.

In 1946, after reconsidering the group life insurance laws, the NAIC recommended broadening the definition of group life insurance to include, in addition to employer-employee groups, debtors of the same creditor (creditor group insurance); members of a labor union, under a policy issued to the union; and employees of two or more employers in the same industry or members of one or more labor unions, under a master policy issued to a common trustee for the benefit of the employees of the employers or the members of the labor union or unions.

The groups listed in the 1946 Model Bill still remain the most typical groups acceptable for group life insurance plans, and they account for the major part of the group life insurance in force. Other groups, however, such as national guard units, state police organizations, and associations of public employees, also constitute acceptable groups under the laws of many of the states.

■ INSURANCE FOR EMPLOYER-EMPLOYEE GROUPS

Employer-employee groups account for approximately 65 percent of the total group life insurance in force today. There are several reasons for this. Employee groups were the first to be insured on a group basis, and they remain among the most suitable for group insurance purposes so far as underwriting requirements are concerned.

Most employees have a very definite need for life insurance. It has been estimated that as late as 1960, one worker in every four covered by group life insurance had no individual life insurance, and an additional 7 percent had less than $1,000 of individual coverage.[1] This situation has undoubtedly improved, but the fact remains that many employees have little, if any, life insurance on an individual basis. Employers have been interested in group life insurance plans for their employees as a way of meeting this need. For similar reasons, unions have made group life insurance plans covering their members a matter of collective bargaining. As a result, group life insurance plans have made substantial amounts of life insurance available to millions of persons who otherwise would have had little or no life insurance protection.

The federal tax law has also been a significant factor in the development of group life insurance plans. Employer contributions to employee group term life insurance plans are deductible from the employer's taxable income, as a business expense; and these con-

---

[1] Gregg, Davis W., *Group Life Insurance,* 3d ed. (Homewood, Ill.: Richard D. Irwin, Inc., 1962), p. 21.

tributions are not considered taxable income to the employees, so long as the insurance does not exceed a specified limit. These tax advantages have proved to be strong incentives for employers to work with unions and life insurance companies in developing group life insurance plans for their employees.

Legal Requirements

The legal requirements for an acceptable employer-employee group were included in the original (1917) NAIC Model Group Life Insurance Bill as a part of the definition of group life insurance, which read as follows:

Group life insurance is that form of life insurance covering not less than 50 employees with or without medical examination, written under a policy issued to the employer, the premium on which is to be paid by the employer or by the employer and employees jointly, and insuring only all of his employees, or all of any class or classes thereof determined by conditions pertaining to the employment, for amounts of insurance based upon some plan which will preclude individual selection, for the benefit of persons other than the employer; provided, however, that when the premium is to be paid by the employer and employee jointly and the benefits of the policy are offered to all eligible employees, not less than 75 percent of such employees may be so insured.

The original requirement that not less than 50 employees be covered has been relaxed considerably. All states now permit group coverage for groups of ten or more employees, and many states permit it for even smaller groups. The other requirements, however, have been changed very little, if at all. Thus, individual medical examinations are permitted but not required. The group insurance policy must be issued to the employer, but the insurance cannot be for his benefit. (That is, the employer cannot be the beneficiary, and he cannot name the beneficiary.) Premiums may be paid by the employer alone, or they may be shared by the employer and the employees. (If premiums are paid by the employer, without contributions by the employees, the plan is said to be "noncontributory." If premiums are paid in part by the employees, the plan is said to be a "contributory" plan.) Under state laws patterned after the NAIC Model Group Life Insurance Bill, some part of the premium must always be paid by the employer; it cannot be paid entirely by the covered employees. In fact, several of the states have established legal limits beyond which employee contributions will not be permitted under contributory group term life insurance plans. Sixty cents per month per $1,000 of insurance has been a typical maximum rate for such contributions.

A plan under which the employer pays all the premiums must insure all the employees or all employees in specified classes. These classes are determined by the nature of the employment. If the plan is contributory, at least 75 percent of the eligible employees must be insured. Finally, the definition specifies that the amount of insurance provided for each covered employee must be established on a basis that does not permit the employee himself to choose the amount of coverage he will have.

The Selection Process

The selection process in group life insurance differs markedly from the risk selection process for individual plans. The basic purpose, however, is the same in both instances—to select risks of such a nature that predictable mortality experience will be developed. To accomplish this, certain general underwriting principles have been developed in group insurance. Among the most important of these general principles are the following:

1. *The group should have been formed for some purpose other than to obtain insurance.* This requirement is clearly met in the usual employer-employee situation, but that may not be true of some associations. In such instances, the law itself may include a requirement pertaining to associations. For example, one state permits group life insurance covering the "full privileged, voting and contributing members of any association which has been in existence for at least a year, not formed for the exclusive purpose of procuring insurance . . ." In other words, insurance must be an incidental consideration, not the primary reason for the existence of the group.

2. *There should be a relatively steady flow of new members into the group.* This requirement, too, is met to a reasonably satisfactory extent by the usual employer-employee situations. New employees are continually being taken into the group; and employees are continually resigning, retiring, or otherwise being terminated. As a result, the group continues with much the same general spread of ages through many years, instead of repeating the unhappy experience of the assessment groups previously described.

Generally speaking, underwriting requirements need not be as strict for employee group life insurance as for individual life insurance. There are at least three reasons for this. First, the fact that the persons whose lives will be insured are employed operates to some extent as an underwriting safeguard. Some individuals may be insured under employee group plans who would not be insurable on an individual basis, but it is not likely that many very seriously impaired individuals will be working on a full-time basis at any time. Usually an employee must be at work on a full-time basis when a group life insurance plan goes into effect or he will not be covered until he has returned to work.

A second reason is that many of the possibilities for antiselection are automatically precluded if the applicable legal requirements are met. Thus, as a matter of law, eligibility for coverage must be determined by conditions of the employment and not the wishes of the employee; and the amount of coverage for each employee must be established on a basis "precluding individual selection."

A third reason why underwriting requirements for group plans need not be so strict as those for individual coverages is the fact that the premium rates for group plans, unlike the rates for individual coverages, can usually be adjusted in later years if the experience of the group is such that adjustment is indicated.

General Characteristics of Employee Group Plans

Eligibility of Employees. Under the usual legal requirements for employee group plans, all employees of the employer must be eligible for insurance, or all employees in a class or classes determined by conditions of the employment. Thus, the eligible group may be defined in the plan as "all employees paid on an hourly basis," or "all clerical workers," or "all nonsales personnel." As mentioned earlier, employees are usually required to be at work on a full-time basis in order to be eligible; and "full-time" is generally defined in terms of number of hours per week or year.

Most employee group plans require the employee to have worked for the employer for not less than a specified period of time before becoming eligible for insurance under the plan. This period is called a "probationary" or "waiting" period. Waiting periods vary in length from one to twelve months, with one or two months being typical.

The purpose of the waiting period is to reduce the administrative costs of a group life insurance plan by eliminating from coverage those employees who either do not meet the employer's standards of performance or who, for other reasons, are terminated or resign after having been employed by the firm for only a few weeks or months. Recordkeeping and administrative expenses are thus reduced, since it is not necessary to establish insurance and then terminate it for those employees who stay with the company for only a brief time.

If the group plan is noncontributory, all eligible members of the group must be insured when the plan is installed and all new members must be insured when they become eligible. (This is a legal requirement.) If the plan is contributory, the individual members will not become insured until they have signed a participation form and agreed to make the necessary premium payments (usually by authorizing a payroll deduction). Thus, the fact that an employee has become eligible for insurance under a contributory group plan does not mean that he will automatically become insured. A contributory plan must, however, insure at least 75 percent of the eligible employees.

Under contributory plans there is usually an additional period of time, following the probationary period, during which the eligible employee may apply for insurance without submitting evidence of insurability. This is called the "eligibility" period. It is usually limited to 31 days.

The purpose and effect of the eligibility period become clear when one considers the effect of permitting an employee to enter the insuring plan whenever he wishes, without evidence of insurability. In that case, some employees might prefer to wait until there was some apparent need, such as ill health, to become interested in life insurance. Restricting the period in which the employees can obtain insurance without evidence of insurability tends to guard against this kind of antiselection.

For the same reason, evidence of insurability may be required of an employee who once was a member of the insured group but who has withdrawn, whether by resignation, transfer to an ineligible position, or otherwise. If he later wishes to reenter the insured group, he may be required to furnish evidence of insurability satisfactory to the insurance company.

From time to time, contributory group insurance plans are reopened for limited periods, during which all uninsured employees who wish to do so may enroll without evidence of insurability. These "enrollment campaigns" represent an effort to obtain a greater participation, often when membership has dropped to near the minimum 75 percent level. This, obviously, opens the way for some adverse selection by nonparticipating employees who are no longer insurable or who are no longer "standard" risks. Thus, it is a calculated risk which the insurer is willing to take rather than have the entire group become ineligible for the insurance.

The Amount of Insurance

The amount of insurance provided for each individual insured under an employee group life insurance plan may be established in any of several ways, so long as it is based on some plan that makes it impossible for an individual member of the group to decide for himself how much insurance he will have. In the absence of a requirement of this kind, the opportunity for antiselection would be almost unlimited. Persons with unimpaired health would tend to elect minimum amounts of insurance, if any; and uninsurable persons or those of border-line insurability probably would tend to apply for the largest amounts of insurance available. Thus, some objective method of establishing the amount of insurance to be provided for each member of the group would be necessary as an underwriting requirement, if it were not required by law.

Under most group life insurance plans, the amounts of insurance to be provided for the various members of the group are determined in accordance with the participants' salaries, in accordance with their positions, or (rarely) in accordance with their lengths of service. Occasionally, a flat amount is provided for everyone, regardless of salary or position.

In Accordance with Salary. Probably the most generally satisfactory way of establishing the amount of insurance to be provided is to relate it to the employees' salaries. The life insurance needs of the various employees are important but not controlling, since group life insurance is seldom intended to provide all the insurance the employees may need. Originally, the objective was merely to furnish some basic life insurance to persons who would otherwise have had very little or none. However, the insurance needs of the employees are significant; and in contributory plans, the employees' ability to pay their share of the premium must be considered. The amount of insurance to be provided under a group life insurance plan should, therefore, be large enough to meet some of the basic life insurance needs of the employees, and yet, under contributory plans, it should not be so large as to be inconsistent with the employee's probable ability to pay his share of the premiums. Both of these considerations are given weight if the amount of insurance is related to salary.

One of the traditional objectives under employee group life plans was to provide insurance in amounts roughly approximating the compensation of the individual employees for one year. More recently, this approach has been expanded; and a modern salary schedule might read, in part, as follows:

Annual Compensation Rate	Amount of Insurance
Less than $4,000	$ 4,000
$ 4,000– 4,999.99	10,000
5,000– 6,999.99	14,000
7,000– 8,999.99	18,000
9,000–10,999.99	22,000
11,000–12,999.99	26,000
13,000–14,999.99	30,000
15,000–16,999.99	34,000
17,000–18,999.99	38,000
19,000–20,999.99	42,000
21,000–22,999.99	46,000
23,000 and over	50,000

In Accordance with Position. Theoretically, establishing the amount of the insurance on a basis of the position of the employee should accomplish essentially the same objective as determining it by salary. A well-administered salary plan relates the salary scale to the positions of the employees, and usually some weighting is given to seniority. A typical position schedule might read as follows:

Class	Position	Amount of Insurance
I	Officers	$20,000
II	Department Managers	15,000
III	Salesmen and Foremen	10,000
IV	All Other Employees	5,000

With a schedule of this kind, where all employees in Class I are insured for $20,000, those in Class II are insured for $15,000, and so on, the effect should be much the same as if benefits had been related to salary in the first place. However, one of the major disadvantages of position schedules is the difficulty of defining employee classes in such a way that antiselection is precluded.

In Accordance with Length of Service. At one time, the amount of insurance provided under many group life insurance plans was established in accordance with the employee's length of service. This approach reflected the belief that employees who had been with the company longest were entitled to the largest benefits. This method is not so common as it once was, for a very basic reason. The amount of insurance provided under this plan is seldom related in any way to the needs of the employee. That is, many young married persons who have been employed for only a short while may need much more life insurance than persons who have been with the firm for 35 or 40 years. However, this problem also exists to some extent when the amount of insurance is based on salary.

Level Amount Plans. Some group plans do not determine the amount of insurance on any of the above bases. Instead, they provide for payment of a flat amount of insurance on the death of any member of the insured group. This is the simplest approach and, in some instances, it may be adopted because of the ease of administration. For example, if a plan covers the employees of several employers or the members of different labor unions, the insurance may be part of a collective bargaining agreement. In such situations, the administrative advantages of providing a flat amount of benefit for each member of the group may be sufficiently persuasive that other considerations seem relatively minor. Under most employee-benefit plans, however, a schedule of insurance that gives some recognition to the factors of need and ability to pay is more appropriate.

Maximum Limits. Most life insurance companies have maximum limits for the amount of life insurance they are willing to provide on any one life under a group life insurance plan. The objective is to achieve a reasonable balance between the amounts of insurance provided on individual lives and the total amount of insurance on the group. For example, for a group representing total insurance in force of $1 to $1.5 million, the maximum amount of insurance on one life might be established at $20,000; for a group of $1.5 to $2 million, $25,000, and so on.

Maximum limits are established for two reasons. First, they protect against adverse selection in small groups, where one or a few persons might be able to obtain large amounts of insurance on their own lives. Second, they reduce the fluctuations in claim costs over the years. For instance, if there is no possibility of any one claim exceeding $20,000, a considerably more uniform claim cost will be achieved from year to year than if one or two $50,000 or $60,000 claims could be presented in any one year.

Maximum limits for group life insurance coverage on any one life have been established by law in some states, although the advisability of such absolute limits has been debated extensively. One representative law limits the amount of insurance that may be provided for any one person under a group life insurance plan to $20,000 or 150 percent of the person's annual compensation, whichever is greater, subject to a maximum of $40,000. The following table may help to make this clear.

Annual Compensation	150 Percent of Annual Compensation	Maximum Amount of Insurance	
$12,000	$18,000	$20,000	(Because anyone may have this amount)
25,000	37,500	37,500	(Because $37,500 is greater than $20,000)
39,000	58,500	40,000	(Because $40,000 is the maximum permitted)

Thus, if one's salary is $12,000, he could have as much as $20,000 of insurance, since 150 percent of $12,000 does not exceed $20,000. If a person's salary is $25,000, the maximum group life insurance he could have would be $37,500 (150 percent of $25,000); and the maximum permitted for a person with a salary of $39,000 would be $40,000, since 150 percent of $39,000 exceeds the alternate maximum limit of $40,000. However, many states have been abolishing maximums they had previously established.

■ GROUP LIFE INSURANCE PREMIUMS

Minimum Premium Rates

Minimum premium rates for group life insurance plans have been established by law in some states, including New York. Usually such laws specify minimum rates that may be charged during the first policy year, although the company is free to charge higher rates if that seems advisable. Rate reductions may be made after the first year, depending on the experience of the group.

Most such laws have applied only to group contracts issued in the state having the law, but the New York law applies to all contracts issued by insurance companies licensed to operate in New York. As a result, New York licensed companies have experienced some competitive problems in states where other insurers (not licensed in New York) were not subject to similar regulatory laws.

General Principles

Unlike most individual life insurance coverages, group life insurance plans are customarily funded on a pay-as-you-go, yearly-renewable term basis. Nevertheless, premium rates for group life insurance are governed by the same general principles as those for individual life insurance. Premiums must produce funds sufficient to meet all expected claim costs, plus administrative expenses—that is, they must be adequate. Premiums must be established on a basis reflecting the degree of risk presented by each group—that is, they must be equitable. And, finally, premium rates must be low enough to be competitive.

The three basic factors of mortality, assumed rate of interest, and expenses enter into the computation of group life insurance premiums just as they do in the calculation of premium rates for individual plans, although they do not have the same relative significance.

Mortality. The mortality experience under group plans is comparable to that under individual plans, even though no medical examination is required and other means of individual selection are not generally used. This is because the group definition and the risk appraisal process generally result in the selection of groups for group coverage which do not differ a great deal from individually selected lives, especially after the expiration of four or five years.

Interest and Expenses. Since most group plans are on the yearly-renewable term basis, no large policy reserves are built up. Consequently, the interest factor is less significant than for ordinary life insurance plans. Expenses also represent a smaller item for each $1,000 of coverage. There are several reasons for this. Since there is no medical examination, there are no medical examiners' fees. Policy issue expense is lower because only one *policy* is issued, no matter how many persons are included in the insured group, and simpler *certificates* are issued to the individual insureds. Commission rates are lower; and, under the great majority of group plans, many of the administrative activities—enrolling, recordkeeping, beneficiary changes, claim handling, and so on—are assumed by the employer. For these reasons, the interest and expense factors account for a much smaller percentage of the group life insurance premium than is true of the ordinary life insurance premium.

Premium Computation. A detailed and technical discussion of the computation of group life insurance premiums is beyond the scope of this book. In a general sense, however, the procedure may be summarized as follows. First, an initial monthly premium is computed by using gross premium rates by age and calculating the premiums payable for each member of the group at his or her attained age, for the amount of insurance to be provided. These premiums for the individual members of the group are then totaled and adjusted by the application of a loading or discount formula. The result is the total amount of monthly premium payable when the policy is issued.

Second, the average monthly premium rate per $1,000 is calculated by dividing the initial monthly premium by the total amount of insurance in force on the group. This average monthly premium rate per $1,000 is used for any premium adjustments for lives added or terminated during the policy year, regardless of the respective ages of those persons who enter or leave the group during the year. For example, assume that a new employee becomes eligible for insurance on September 1. Regardless of this employee's age, the premium for his insurance for the remainder of the policy year will be based on the average monthly premium rate for that year.

This same process is repeated at the beginning of each new policy year. The premium is computed for each member of the group at that person's attained age and for the amount of insurance for which he or she is eligible. Also, a new average monthly premium rate is calculated at the beginning of each new policy year, and it is used to calculate the premium adjustment, whenever anyone enters or leaves the group during the year.

Group premiums are customarily paid on a monthly basis. This arrangement is usually more convenient for the employer as a matter of accounting, and it permits immediate adjustments for changes in personnel. The premium may be paid at less frequent intervals, however, if the employer prefers.

It is customary for group life insurers to guarantee premium rates for a specified period after a group plan goes into effect. One year is a typical period for such a guarantee, and the policy usually provides that annual rate adjustments may be made by the insurer after that period. A guarantee of this kind does not, of course, mean that the monthly premium remitted to the insurer by the employer will remain the same, even for each month of the first year. The premium payable will depend upon the number of insured employees, their respective ages, and the amounts of insurance provided for them. The actual *premium* payable, therefore, may vary a great deal throughout the guaranteed period even though the *rate* remains the same. Under the typical plan, however, the premium rates applicable to the various ages may be changed by the insurer at the end of any policy year after the expiration of the original period for which rates have been guaranteed.

Dividends and Experience Rating

Premium refunds are customarily provided under group life insurance policies, even by companies whose ordinary life insurance contracts are issued on a nonparticipating basis. However, premium refunds may or may not be referred to as "dividends." A company that issues nonparticipating group plans usually refers to premium adjustments as "experience rating refunds," whereas a company issuing participating group plans usually refers to premium adjustments as "dividends."

Experience Rating. As with dividends on ordinary life insurance, interest, expenses, and mortality are all taken into consideration. So far as the interest and expense factors are concerned, premium refunds in group life insurance are allocated in very much the same way as dividends are in ordinary life insurance. With respect to the mortality factor, however, it is customary for all companies to use a procedure known as "experience rating."

Experience rating procedures are not normally applied to smaller groups, since the mortality experience of such groups can fluctuate widely and little credibility can be given to it. The minimum group size at which companies begin to use experience rating is determined by company formula. In addition to the number of employees who are insured, the formula may also take into consideration the amount of premiums, the volume of insurance, and the amount of insurance on individual lives.

The basic idea of experience rating is that the mortality experience of a particular group is considered in relation to the average mortality experience for similar groups insured by the same insurance company. If the experience of the particular group indicates a significant variation from the average experience of similar groups, favorable or unfavorable, this difference will be reflected in the experience refund for that group. If the experience is sufficiently adverse, there will be no refund.

Under noncontributory plans, dividends or experience rating refunds are paid to the employer, since he has paid the premiums.

They are usually paid to the employer under contributory plans also, but for a different reason. Although the employees have shared in paying the premium under these plans, it would be impracticable, and in many cases impossible, to return dividends to each employee in accordance with his contribution toward the premium. Even under contributory plans, therefore, the employer is entitled to all dividends until they exceed his share of the total cost. Any dividends in excess of that amount are required by law to be "applied by the employer for the sole benefit of the employees." Usually, they would be used to reduce future contributions of employees or to provide additional benefits for them.

Reserves

Since group life insurance is generally written on a yearly-renewable term insurance basis, there is no need for policy reserves on anything like the scale of the policy reserve liability required for most ordinary life insurance plans.

The policy reserve for group life insurance is essentially an "unearned premium" reserve. The "unearned premium" reserve is computed by assuming that the premiums collected are earned on a continuing basis throughout the period for which they were paid. At any time prior to the end of that period, therefore, some part of the premium will be "unearned." Thus, if the reserve is computed as of December 31, two-thirds of a quarterly premium paid on December 1 will be unearned. If premiums are payable monthly on the first of the month, no part of the December premium would be unearned on December 31. By contrast, if the monthly premium had been paid on December 15, approximately one-half of the December premium would be unearned on December 31. In other words, the premium reserve is the amount that would be required to continue the coverage to the end of the period for which premiums have been received or are due.

A second kind of reserve is established for claim purposes. Group life insurance written on the yearly-renewable term basis contemplates the payment of claims arising in any one year out of premiums paid for that year. Actually, of course, claims are not always presented in the year in which death occurs. A claim reserve, therefore, is necessary to compensate for the fact that some claims may have been incurred but not reported at the end of the year.

A third class of reserve is established for the extension of benefits under the disability provision of a group life policy. Today most group policies include a waiver-of-premium disability benefit which is effective after nine months of continuous total disability. Once this waiting period requirement has been satisfied and satisfactory proof of total disability has been submitted to the insurance company, the insurance of the disabled person will be continued, with premiums being waived so long as he submits proof of the continuance of his disability. Regardless of when he dies, therefore—in one year, five years, or ten years—the insurance company will pay the amount of the insurance provided for him. For this reason, a death claim is considered as having been incurred at the time of disablement, and a reserve is established at that time, usually in an amount equal to approximately 75 percent of the death benefit provided.

A fourth class of reserve is established in the sense that assets are set aside for the purpose of paying unusually large claims, or claims in unusual numbers. Called "contingency reserves," these reserves help to guard against the adverse effects of severe fluctuations in mortality experience.

■ THE GROUP LIFE INSURANCE POLICY

Group life insurance is provided under an insuring agreement called a "master policy." For employer-employee groups, this agreement is established between the life insurance company and the employer (or a trustee representing one or several employers). The master policy specifies the designated classes of employees who are eligible for the insurance and sets forth the details of the insurance plan. It thus sets out the eligibility requirements, the schedule of amounts of insurance, the premium rates, and other elements of a group insurance plan that have been discussed thus far.

The basic principles of contract law apply to the group life insurance contract, just as they apply to any other insuring agreement. The insurance laws of many states also specify certain provisions that must be included in a master policy of group life insurance. Among these required provisions are a grace period provision, an incontestability provision, a beneficiary provision, and provisions guaranteeing certain conversion rights.

The Grace Period

Group life insurance policies, like individual life insurance contracts, must grant a grace period of 31 days for the payment of any premium after the first. The insurance under the group policy continues in force to the end of the grace period unless the policyowner terminates it earlier. In either instance, a pro rata premium will be payable for the insurance provided during the grace period or during that part of the grace period in which the insurance remained in force. By contrast, the individual life insurance policy makes no provision for termination by the policyowner during the grace period and provides only that the insurance will remain in effect until the end of the period. If a claim arises during the grace period under an individual policy, the unpaid premium may be deducted from the death benefit, but the individual policyowner is not liable for a pro rata premium for the coverage he has had during the grace period if he merely permits the policy to lapse.

The Incontestable Clause

The incontestable clause must provide that a policy cannot be contested except for nonpayment of premiums after it has been in force for two years from the issue date. In group insurance, however, people are continuously entering and leaving the group. For this reason, the incontestability provision of a group life insurance policy must also provide that no statement made by a participant concerning his insurability may be used to contest the validity of that person's insurance after the insurance has been in effect for two years "nor unless it is contained in a written instrument signed by the participant." The effect of this provision is to establish, throughout the lifetime of the contract, a two-year contestable period for those incoming participants who are required to furnish evidence of insurability.

The Beneficiary

The master policy must state that at the death of a participant, his insurance under the policy will be paid to the beneficiary designated by that participant. Usually, the designation is required to be "on a form satisfactory to the insurance company." As in individual life insurance, most beneficiary designations are revocable, and the beneficiary may usually be changed by filing written notice of the change.

Complex beneficiary designations—such as class designations—that could present problems when a claim is presented are commonly discouraged, both to reduce delay and to minimize expenses. However, benefits may usually be made payable to two or more individuals as primary beneficiaries; and contingent or successor beneficiaries are usually permitted.

Group life insurance contracts frequently provide that if there is no named beneficiary living at the time of the insured's death, the company may pay the proceeds, at its option, to one of his relatives, such as the spouse, parent or parents, or children of the insured. This is sometimes referred to as a "preference beneficiary" provision. The purpose of including such a provision is to avoid having to pay the death benefit to the estate of the deceased employee.

Sometimes group policies also include a provision that if no beneficiary is designated for all or a part of the insurance payable, the insurance company may pay as much as $500 of the proceeds to anyone who seems to be entitled to the payment by reason of having paid the funeral or last illness expenses of the insured. The remainder, if any, would be paid to the estate of the insured.

Optional Modes of Settlement. In most instances, the earliest group life insurance plans did not provide optional methods of settlement. Often the amount of insurance payable was very small, and optional modes of settlement were neither justified nor appropriate. For some time, however, as the amounts of insurance have become progressively larger, there has been a trend toward the use of settlement options. Both the fixed-amount and the fixed-period options are often provided; and other settlement arrangements, such as the life income option, if not specifically provided, may be available by special agreement. Usually, the beneficiary may elect an optional settlement method after the death of the employee, for insurance proceeds that would otherwise be paid in one sum.

Conversion Provisions

An employee's insurance under a group life insurance plan may be terminated in any of three different situations:

1. If the master policy is terminated, or if it is amended to terminate the insurance for his class of employees
2. If his employment is terminated—that is, if he ceases to work for the same employer
3. If he ceases to work in a class of eligible employees

In the first instance—if the master policy is terminated or is amended to terminate the insurance of any class of insured persons—each person who has been insured for at least five years before the termination is entitled to the privilege of converting his insurance. That is, each such person has the right to exchange his coverage under the group policy for a policy of individual life insurance without evidence of insurability. In the second and third instances—if the employee's employment is terminated, or if he ceases to work in a class of eligible employees—he is entitled to a conversion privilege regardless of how briefly he has been insured.

As is true of the conversion privilege under individual term life insurance contracts, the conversion privilege in group contracts is subject to certain conditions that are set forth in the conversion section of the master contract and in the certificate which the employee receives. The employee who wishes to convert to individual coverage must submit his application for an individual life insurance policy within 31 days from the date the master policy is terminated or the date he leaves his employment or ceases to work in an eligible class of employees. The insurer is not required to include disability benefits or any other supplementary coverage in the new individual policy it issues; and the insured may apply for and be issued any type of policy, other than term insurance, then being issued by the insurance company. However, under the New York Insurance Law (which applies to every insurer licensed to operate in New York), a terminating employee must be given the right to convert to a policy of individual life insurance "preceded by single-premium term insurance for a period of one year." This permits him to continue his coverage on a term basis for a full year while he looks for employment elsewhere or makes other arrangements for continuing his life insurance protection.

The premium for the individual policy to which conversion is made must be based on the company's standard premium rate for that kind of policy, the amount of insurance provided, and the current age of the insured. If the group policy is terminated (either by the employer or by the insurer) or if it is amended to terminate the insurance of any class of persons, the amount of insurance to which the covered employees are entitled may be limited to the smaller of (1) $2,000, or (2) the amount of insurance they had under their former group plan less any amount provided under a new group policy replacing the terminated plan. Thus, if a group life insurance policy is terminated and is replaced by another group policy providing benefits in the same amount, there is no right of conversion.

If the employee's insurance terminates either because his employment with the company is terminated or because he is no longer working in a class of eligible employees, the amount of insurance for which he may apply on an individual basis is limited to not more than the amount of insurance he had under the group plan.

The insurance of a terminating employee must be continued under a group policy until the end of the conversion period, whether or not the participant applies for an individual policy. The effect of this requirement is to continue the insurance for 31 days beyond the termination of the insured's eligibility for the group coverage.

Assignment of Group Life Insurance

Group life insurance contracts have customarily included a provision prohibiting assignment, for essentially the same reasons that this right is limited or denied under industrial life insurance plans. Originally, group life insurance provided only a relatively modest death benefit, and assignment to a creditor could have defeated even this limited objective. Today, however, many group life insurance plans provide relatively large amounts of insurance. The proceeds may, therefore, constitute a significant portion of the insured's taxable estate at his death; and assignment of the insurance—especially the absolute assignment of it, so that someone other than the insured employee would own it—may be a desirable objective.

The Internal Revenue Service has issued several rulings concerning the legal effect of an assignment of group life insurance proceeds, and many of the states have enacted laws to clarify the insured's right of assignment under a group life insurance policy. Group life insurance contracts, therefore, have frequently been amended specifically to permit the assignment of the individual insured's interest under the contract.

Individual Certificates

The Model Group Life Insurance Law requires the issuance of individual certificates to employees who are insured under a group policy issued to an employer. This certificate is not a contract and merely "certifies" that the employee to whom it is issued is insured under a master policy issued to the employer. The certificate must state (1) the amount of insurance to which the employee is entitled; (2) the person or persons to whom his insurance benefits will be paid; (3) the conversion privilege available on termination of the group coverage; and (4) the fact that a death benefit will be paid if the certificateholder should die during the conversion period but before conversion of the insurance.

Booklets. At the time a group life insurance plan is established, booklets are usually printed by the insurance company and furnished to the employer, to be distributed to all insured employees and new employees who become eligible for coverage. These booklets describe and explain the group life insurance plan and are written in simple language that is more easily understood than the provisions of the certificate or master policy. In recent years, some insurers have issued combined certificate-booklets, which incorporate simplified language into the certificate.

Administration of the Plan

Group life insurance plans may be self-administered or insurer-administered. Under self-administered plans, the employer has the major responsibility for keeping all necessary records—adding, removing, or reinstating employees; preparing the individual certificates; taking care of beneficiary designations and changes of beneficiary, changes of address, and so on. The employer makes reports to the insurer monthly, listing the changes that have taken place during the month, showing the number of lives insured and the amount of insurance in force at the end of the month, and including a calculation of the premium then due. If the plan is insurer-administered, the insurance company takes care of these administrative details, relying for that purpose on periodic reports from the employer.

Since insurer-administered plans require fairly detailed reporting on the part of the employer, plus additional recordkeeping on the part of the insurance company, the cost of an insurer-administered plan tends to be higher than when the employer takes care of more of the administrative details. Many plans, therefore, are self-administered.

■ PERMANENT LIFE INSURANCE FOR EMPLOYEE GROUPS

Many larger employers have initiated the practice of continuing group life insurance, in reduced amounts, for employees after their retirement. However, a large number of plans remain that provide insurance for participants only until they retire. The retiring employee has a conversion privilege, but conversion is not a very realistic possibility for most retirees. The insured must pay the entire premium for the converted policy (by contrast with paying only a part or none of the premium for his group coverage); and the premium will be based on his age at the date of conversion. This presents a definite problem for many insureds at retirement.

Consider a man retiring at age 65. If he purchases individual life insurance at that time, a typical annual premium rate for whole life insurance (which would usually be the least expensive insurance available to him at that age) is around $75 per $1,000. When this is compared with nothing or, at the most, the annual rate of $7.20 per $1,000 that he would have been paying under a typical contributory plan, the difference is significant.

If the employer wishes to continue the insurance for his retiring employees under a group plan, the greatly increasing costs of the yearly-renewable term plan in the later years of life become evident. There are three principal ways of avoiding this problem:

1. The employer may provide permanent insurance under a group life insurance plan
2. He may provide group paid-up insurance
3. He may provide a plan of group/ordinary life insurance.

Level-Premium Group Permanent Life Insurance

Group permanent life insurance may be provided for employee groups under much the same administrative arrangements as group term insurance plans. Group underwriting and administration reduce costs and simplify handling. Certificates are issued to the individual insureds instead of policies. A level premium is paid, and nonforfeiture values are provided, just as they are under individual life insurance contracts.

In 1950, however, a federal tax ruling made it clear that premiums paid by employers for permanent life insurance for employees would be taxable as current income to the insured employees. This ruling discouraged the growth of group permanent insurance plans. Consequently, alternative approaches—group paid-up and group/ordinary plans—have proved to be more popular as ways of providing permanent life insurance for employees in recent years.

Group Paid-Up Insurance

Under a group paid-up insurance plan, the employees are insured in accordance with a schedule showing the total amount of insurance provided for each. By its nature, a group paid-up plan must be on a contributory basis, but the amount contributed by each employee is not applied toward term life insurance. Instead, it is used to purchase a unit of paid-up whole life insurance in whatever amount it will buy at the employee's age that year. The employer's premium is then established in the amount necessary to pay for enough group term life insurance to bring the total coverage for the employee (the paid-up whole life plus the group term) to the amount provided in the schedule.

The amount of paid-up insurance for each employee increases from year to year as additional units are purchased, and this reduces the amount of term life insurance necessary to bring the total up to the scheduled amount of insurance to which the employee is entitled. The paid-up insurance has cash or paid-up values, although the employee cannot withdraw them prior to termination of his employment.

The group paid-up plan has the advantage of providing the participant with some paid-up insurance after his retirement and, since the employer's payment is applied only toward the purchase of group term insurance, the premium paid each year by the employer is not considered income to the employee. Thus, it is not subject to income tax.

Group/Ordinary Life Insurance

In the late 1960's, many insurance companies began offering plans of group life insurance that were commonly referred to as "group/ordinary" plans. Under these plans, the individual participant may elect to have some or all of his group life insurance coverage in the form of permanent life insurance, with cash values. The total amount of insurance to which he is entitled will be established in the same way it would be under a group term plan; and such permanent plans as whole life, life paid-up at 65, or life paid-up in 10 years are usually available. If the participant does not elect to have all of his insurance on a permanent plan (or if underwriting requirements do not permit him to do so), the remainder of his coverage will be made up of term insurance—for which the employer pays the total premium.

The premium for the whole life portion of the group/ordinary coverage is shared by the employer and employee, on a basis that is most easily understood by reference to the diagramed analysis of a continuous-premium whole life policy shown on page 32. There, it will be recalled, the cash value of a whole life policy was shown to increase from year to year throughout the remaining lifetime of the insured, while the amount at risk decreased.

This characteristic of increasing cash value and decreasing amount at risk is shared by all whole life plans of insurance, including the whole life portion elected by the participant in a group/ordinary plan. The premium for the whole life coverage, therefore, is divided by the insurer into the portion applicable to the increasing cash value, which amount is paid by the insured, and the portion applicable to the decreasing amount at risk, which is paid by the employer. Premiums for both employer and employee are level and are established on the basis of the age of the insured when the insurance was purchased, the sex of the insured, and the plan of insurance elected.

The basic advantage of a group/ordinary plan is that it is easier for the participant to continue the permanent insurance he has under such a plan than to convert the term insurance under a group term plan when he retires, or if he terminates his employment with that employer before reaching retirement age. Typically, at such retirement or termination, he may continue his permanent coverage on a paid-up basis, surrender it for cash, or exchange it for an individual policy at rates based on his age when the permanent insurance was first purchased.

A recent tax ruling has made it clear that group/ordinary plans will not receive the favorable tax treatment given group term life insurance for employer contributions if the employer pays any part of the cost of the permanent insurance. That is, although the employer's contributions toward a plan of group term insurance for his employees is not taxable as income to the insured employee, this is not true of a group/ordinary plan where the premium for the permanent insurance is shared by employer and employee. This situation does not meet the requirements set out in the Internal Revenue Code and, as a result, all employer payments under the plan are considered current income to the employees and therefore subject to income tax.

■ ACCIDENTAL DEATH AND DISMEMBERMENT INSURANCE

Accidental death and dismemberment insurance is generally considered to be a form of health insurance. However, the coverage is very commonly issued as a supplement to group life insurance. When this is done, the result is to provide an additional benefit in the event the insured person dies as the result of an accident, and lump sum benefits in the event of loss of a limb or limbs by severance, or the total and irrecoverable loss of sight as the result of accidental bodily injury. Usually, these benefits are established in amounts that are equal to the amount for which the participant's life is insured under the base policy. Thus, the beneficiary of a participant whose group term life insurance is $20,000 would be entitled to an additional $20,000 under the accidental death and dismemberment coverage, if the participant were killed in an accident. If the participant survived the accident but lost a limb or the sight of both eyes, he would be entitled to a lump sum benefit of $20,000 under this supplementary coverage.

■ CREDITOR GROUP LIFE INSURANCE

Creditor group life insurance is life insurance purchased by a creditor to protect himself against loss in the event of the death of a person to whom he has loaned money or extended credit. If the debtor dies before repaying the loan or completing installment payments he has agreed to make, the insurance will be payable to the creditor in the amount of the loan or the installments remaining unpaid. Creditor group life insurance is provided for this purpose under a master contract issued to the creditor, insuring the lives of his debtors, for the creditor's benefit.

The advantages of creditor group life insurance to lenders and companies doing an extensive installment credit business are obvious. It provides a simple and inexpensive way to protect them against loss in the event of the death of a debtor. They avoid the delay and expense of trying to collect the debt after the death of the borrower, as well as the ill will which often results from efforts to collect remaining payments or to repossess articles that have been purchased on installment payment plans.

The advantages to the borrower are also clear. A loan that is covered by credit life insurance will be paid in full at the death of the borrower; and, if an installment purchase agreement is so protected, the death of the purchaser will leave his family with the car, television set, refrigerator, or other major appliance, free of debt, instead of the obligation of continuing the unpaid installments.

Makeup of the Group

Legally, if a creditor has a creditor group insurance plan, it must be offered to all of his debtors whose indebtedness is repayable either (1) in installments or (2) in one sum at the end of a relatively short period—typically 18 months from the date the debt is incurred; or to all of any class or classes of his debtors, "determined by conditions pertaining to the indebtedness or to the purchase giving rise to the indebtedness."

A group of this kind is well suited to meet the underwriting requirements for group life insurance. Clearly the group is formed for a purpose other than that of obtaining life insurance. Usually also, there is a constant flow of new people into the group. In fact, the model group legislation for creditor group plans requires at least 100 new entrants into the group each year, or a reasonable expectation that there will be at least that many new entrants. The duration of any one person's membership in the group is relatively short; and the same characteristics that make a borrower a good credit risk usually are considered to indicate insurability.

Premium Payment

Premiums for creditor group insurance may be paid by the creditor (policyowner) entirely out of his own funds or out of funds contributed partly by the insured debtors and partly by the creditor. They may also be paid entirely out of funds collected from the persons insured. (By contrast, the model legislation for group life insurance requires that for employer-employee groups, the employer contribute at least part of the premium.)

Creditor group life insurance has been subjected to considerable misuse, primarily because the individual borrowers, in most instances, have had very little choice as to the terms or even the fact of their insurance coverage. That is, they have had little bargaining power. Dividends or experience rating refunds are usually paid to the creditor, since he is the policyowner; and he often receives the commissions also, since he is frequently the agent for credit insurance purposes. The result is a kind of "reverse competition." Instead of seeking lower premium rates, some creditors are said to have sought plans with higher premium rates because in this way they could obtain larger commissions and higher dividends or experience rating refunds.

Other abuses also were associated with the lack of bargaining power on the part of many insured debtors. More insurance was sometimes purchased than was necessary to cover the indebtedness; debtors were sometimes not informed of their coverage or its cost; and the unearned portion of the premium the debtor had paid was not always refunded when the indebtedness was repaid sooner than the loan agreement provided and the insurance was, therefore, terminated.

In an attempt to correct these problems, a model bill for the regulation of credit life insurance, and credit life and accident insurance, has been prepared by the NAIC for consideration by the various states. This law requires unearned premiums to be refunded if a debt is repaid in a shorter time than agreed upon and requires the issuance of a certificate to the person insured. Policy forms and premium rates must be filed with the state insurance department prior to being used, and the rates can be disapproved by the insurance commissioner if the premium rates are excessive in relation to the benefits provided. The model law also provides that when credit life or health insurance is required of a debtor, he must be given the option of furnishing the coverage through existing policies or of obtaining the coverage from a different company if he wishes.

■ NOTES ON CANADIAN PRACTICES

Group Life Insurance

In Canada, group life insurance is regulated under the Uniform Life Insurance Act in all provinces except Quebec. In *all* provinces, group life insurance is also governed under a set of 10 Rules established by the provincial superintendents. Three of these Rules apply to creditor's group life insurance. The Uniform Act defines group life insurance as insurance, other than creditor's group insurance, "whereby the lives of a number of persons are insured severally under a single contract between an insurer and an employer or other person." By contrast with the United States definition, there is no mention of minimum number of lives, premium payors, participation requirements, and other similar details. Nor are standard contract provisions required. However, the master contract must specify:

1. The method of determining which lives are insured
2. The amount, or method of determining the amount, of coverage
3. The grace period, if any
4. A statement as to whether the contract is a participating one.

As in the United States, an individual certificate must be issued to each individual insured under a master contract. This certificate must state the amount of coverage (or the method by which the amount is determined), the circumstances of termination, and the insured's rights on termination.

The Uniform Life Insurance Act provides that misrepresentation involving one insured life does not affect the group contract as a whole, but the insurance on the individual is voidable within two years (or at any time for fraud) if evidence of insurability was required.

The Superintendents' Rules supplement the Uniform Act. For example, these Rules state that:

1. Death benefits do not discriminate among group members (or members of the same class within the group)
2. Every group life insurance contract must include a provision permitting a member to convert his insurance, without evidence of insurability, within 31 days after termination of his employment or group membership, provided he is less than 65 years of age at the time of conversion.

Creditor's Group Life Insurance

Creditor's group life insurance is regulated under the Uniform Life Insurance Act and is defined as insurance effected by a creditor on the lives of his debtors under a single contract. There are no requirements concerning premium payors, minimum number of new entrants, issuance of certificates, or inclusion of standard provisions; and the law does not specify maximum amounts of coverage. However, the Superintendents' Rules state that the amount of insurance may not be greater than the amount of the unpaid debt. In addition, under certain circumstances, the applicant for insurance must be given a copy of his application at the time he signs it.

QUESTIONS FOR REVIEW

1. Outline briefly three reasons why employer-employee groups are especially suitable for coverage under group life insurance plans.
2. Discuss the requirements of the NAIC model definition of group life insurance as they concern
   a) payment of premiums
   b) employees to be insured
   c) determination of the amount of insurance to be provided.
3. Briefly define a contributory group life insurance plan. A noncontributory plan.
4. Briefly discuss two general underwriting principles specifically applicable to group life insurance.
5. Define the following terms as they relate to group life insurance:
   a) waiting period
   b) eligibility period
   c) experience rating.
6. List four methods by which the amount of insurance benefits may be determined under a group life insurance plan.
7. Discuss briefly the functions of the master policy, the individual certificates, and announcement booklets in the operation of a group life insurance plan.
8. Briefly summarize the conversion rights provided participants under an employer-employee group life insurance plan.
9. List three ways in which some permanent life insurance may be provided under group life insurance plans.
10. Briefly outline the nature and purpose of creditor group life insurance.

16 GROUP HEALTH INSURANCE AND RETIREMENT PLANS

Group plans have been used with marked success to provide life insurance for many groups other than employer-employee and creditor groups. Many other kinds of insurance coverages are provided through group plans also. Coverage under group health insurance far outdistances individual health insurance, especially in the areas of hospital and medical expense coverages; and group insurance is used to provide retirement benefits under many different kinds of retirement plans. This chapter will discuss group health insurance and retirement plans.

■ GROUP HEALTH INSURANCE

The same factors that gave impetus to the growth of individual health insurance in the 1930's also favored the development of group health insurance plans. There were especially strong incentives for their expansion during World War II, when the wage freeze emphasized the importance of fringe benefits for employees; and in 1947, the National Labor Relations Board declared group medical care programs one of the subjects with respect to which employers must bargain if so requested by the union.

Group health insurance is generally available for the same groups as those eligible for group life insurance plans. Employee groups constitute the largest single category covered by group health insurance. Members of labor unions, as well as associations of employers and members of other associations, also constitute qualified groups for health insurance under the laws of most states. Group disability benefits are widely available for creditor groups also.

Group health benefits for employee groups are usually provided in conjunction with other group insurance benefits. Thus, the same administrative facilities for enrollment, recordkeeping, and claim handling are utilized. Group health insurance plans for employee groups may be contributory or noncontributory, and benefits are often extended to include dependents of employees.

FIGURE 16-1

Persons Having Health Insurance Coverages under Group and Individual Plans, End of 1970

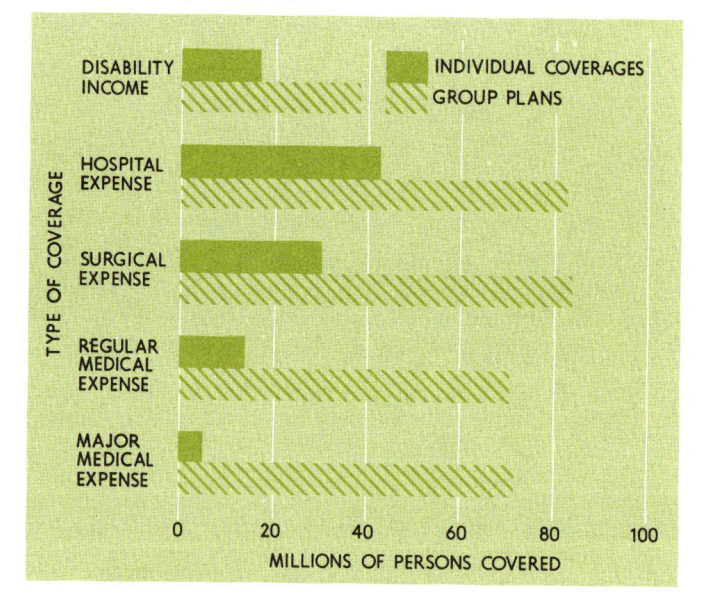

Benefits under group health insurance plans are provided in the same general areas of coverage as benefits under individual health insurance plans. Thus, they include disability income coverages; hospital, surgical, and regular medical expense benefits; and major medical plans. All are widely provided, especially for employer-employee groups. Figure 16-1 shows the numbers of persons insured for each type of benefit under group plans, as compared with the numbers insured for similar coverages under individual plans in an illustrative year.

Disability Income Benefits

Group disability income plans are generally classified as either short- or long-term disability plans, as suggested in Figure 16–2. Either type of plan customarily provides disability income benefits in accordance with a schedule, or as a percentage of the insured's salary, during a period of disability resulting from accident or illness, subject to specified maximum time limits. Plans that provide benefits payable for up to two years are considered short-term plans.

FIGURE 16–2

Persons Having Group Disability Income Coverages (in millions)

Year	Short-Term	Long-Term
1966	26.3	2.4
1967	27.6	3.8
1968	30.8	4.7
1969	30.9	5.7
1970	31.5	7.2

Short-Term Disability Plans. Short-term disability income plans typically provide benefit amounts of 50 to 70 percent of the insured's wages, subject to an overall maximum limit, such as $150 per week. In some instances, a flat amount is provided, regardless of salary. Usually there is a waiting period for disability resulting from sickness, but this may or may not be true of benefits payable in case of accident. Waiting periods of three or seven days are most commonly used. Short-term benefits are usually provided for 13, 26, 52, or 104 weeks. Typical maximum benefits would be $150 per week, for 26 weeks, but many insureds would receive far less.

Benefits are not generally provided for disabilities resulting from accidents or illnesses if the insured is entitled to workmen's compensation benefits. However, pre-existing conditions are usually covered immediately under group policies (by contrast with most individual contracts), and the disability income coverage is characterized by fewer exclusions than are customarily found in other health insurance coverages. Thus, there may be only two or three exclusions (other than the workmen's compensation exclusion), such as disability resulting from pregnancy, self-inflicted wounds, or war.

Long-Term Disability Plans. Long-term disability income plans typically provide benefit amounts of 50 percent, 60 percent, or 66⅔ percent of wages. Maximum benefits under such plans are usually higher than under short-term disability plans, with $1,500 per month being quite common. Typical waiting periods for disability resulting from both sickness and accident are 30, 60, 90, and 180 days. Common benefit periods are two, five, and ten years, or to age 65.

Long-term disability benefits payable under a group policy are usually reduced by income and benefits received by the insured from other sources, such as Social Security, workmen's compensation, or the employer's pension plan.

Medical Expense Benefits

Hospital, surgical, and medical expense benefits are often grouped together as basic medical expense coverages. The great majority of persons having group health insurance have one or more of these coverages, as indicated in Figure 16–1; and the numbers have been growing steadily, as shown in Figure 16–3.

FIGURE 16–3

Persons Having Group Medical Expense Coverages (in millions)

End of Year	Hospital Expense	Surgical Expense	Regular Medical	Major Medical
1966	158.0	144.7	116.5	56.7
1967	169.5	155.7	129.1	66.9
1968	162.9	150.4	122.6	62.2
1969	175.2	162.1	134.9	72.3
1970	181.5	169.0	145.3	78.2

Hospital Expense Benefits. Group health insurance plans provide hospital expense coverages on many different levels and in different ways. In some instances, room and board benefits are payable in a specified number of dollars per day of hospitalization. Alternatively, the actual expense incurred may be reimbursed, up to a specified maximum. Expenses for other hospital services are similarly covered. Maternity benefits are customarily provided, but usually only for pregnancies which have their inception after the claimant becomes insured under the plan.

Surgical Benefits. Surgical expenses are reimbursed under group plans on much the same basis as under individual coverages. In most instances, a schedule of maximum benefits is included in the contract, and operations not listed are provided for on a comparable basis.

Regular Medical Expense Benefits. Regular medical expense insurance generally provides benefits to help pay physicians' fees for care received while the insured is hospitalized (in-hospital physician's visits) as well as for care given in the patient's home or the doctor's office. Other benefits frequently included are diagnostic X-ray and laboratory benefits, supplemental or emergency accident benefits, and X-ray and radioactive treatment expense benefits.

The Major Medical Plans

Major medical plans were first offered nationally about 1950, although there had been prior scattered experiments with this approach under both group and individual plans. Major medical plans are intended to cover all kinds of medical expenses (subject to only a few exclusions). Thus, the coverage includes expenses of hospitalization, physicians' and surgeons' fees, nursing care, laboratory charges, drugs, medicines, oxygen, wheelchairs, braces, and so on. Maximums are generous and range from $7,500 or $10,000, through $20,000, $25,000, or $30,000 and even higher under some plans.

Group major medical plans are typically provided as supplements to basic hospital-surgical or regular medical insurance programs, and resemble the individual major medical plans in most respects. Usually, there is a deductible amount, though it may be defined in any of several ways. All medical expenses of the insured above that amount are shared by him and the insurance company on a percentage participation (coinsurance) basis, with the insurance company paying 75, 80, or as high as 90 percent, and the insured paying the remainder.

Major medical coverages are generally considered to be attempts to apply true insurance principles to the problem of medical expenses. The hazard insured against—major medical expense—is sufficiently large to constitute a definite hardship. It was originally believed also that expenses of such magnitude were not likely to occur to any large number of insureds, so that the cost would be reasonable in relation to the possible benefits. This has not been borne out by experience, however, and internal limits (such as maximums for the daily hospital expense benefits) are frequently used today in an attempt to hold down the claim costs under such coverages.

Among the more common exclusions in group major medical contracts are dental expenses, alcoholism, injuries or sickness covered by workmen's compensation or occupational diseases laws, self-inflicted injuries, and sickness or injuries resulting from war and military service.

Comprehensive Major Medical Plans. Comprehensive major medical plans provide essentially the same benefits as the major medical coverages, but they are designed to meet minor as well as major medical expenses of the insured. In other words, they are intended for use by groups having no other medical coverage. Thus, they usually provide a lower deductible amount, often as low as $25 per year; and they cover all eligible expenses above that on a percentage participation basis, up to specified maximums.

Deductible Amounts and Percentage Participation. Insurance companies use deductible amount requirements in group major medical and comprehensive major medical plans in much the same ways that they use them in individual plans. In plans designed to provide the only medical coverage for the group (comprehensive major medical), a small deductible amount is used. In plans designed to supplement basic hospital plans (sometimes referred to as supplementary major medical plans), the deductible amount may be a dollar amount, such as $500, or it may be defined as the total of all benefits collected under the basic plan.

Many plans use what is called a "corridor" deductible, defining the deductible amount as an amount equal to the total of all benefits provided by the basic coverage, plus a "corridor" deductible of a flat amount, such as $100. A modification of the "corridor" deductible—referred to as an "integrated" deductible—defines the deductible amount as the greater of a specified dollar amount *or* the amount of benefits payable under the basic plan. The deductible amount for representative group health insurance plans is shown in Figure 16–4.

Percentage participation requirements are also utilized in group major medical coverages on very much the same basis as in individual major medical coverages, and for essentially the same reasons. Such requirements are generally believed to encourage the insured to cooperate in limiting costs by not incurring unnecessary expenses, since he will have to meet a part of the expenses out of his own pocket. Figure 16–4 illustrates typical percentage participation requirements under group health insurance coverages.

Other Health Coverages

In recent years, group health insurance plans have been expanded to cover expenses for health care in additional areas. Group policies providing coverage for dental care as well as for medications and vision care have been developed. The popularity of such plans is increasing, as employees and unions look to employers to provide additional fringe benefits.

FIGURE 16-4

Typical Deductible Amount and Percentage Participation Requirements under Group Health Insurance Coverages

Plan	Deductible Amount	Percentage Participation by Insurer	Percentage Participation by Insured
Basic hospital-surgical plan	—0—	100 percent [1]	—0—
Supplementary major medical plan	$500 or corridor deductible [2]	80 percent	20 percent
Comprehensive medical plan	$25, $50, or $100 [3]	80 percent	20 percent

[1] Under a basic hospital-surgical plan, the insurer usually pays 100 percent of the incurred expenses, up to limits specified in the policy, beginning with the first dollar of expenses. That is, there is no deductible amount.

[2] Under a supplementary major medical plan, the insured is assumed to have a basic hospital-surgical plan. The deductible amount under the supplementary major medical coverage, therefore, is usually either an initial deductible (with benefits received under the basic plan applied toward meeting it) or a corridor deductible.

[3] Under a comprehensive medical plan, the deductible amount is low, because it is assumed that the insured does not have a basic medical plan. The comprehensive medical plan, therefore, is designed to provide benefits that will take the place of benefits payable under basic plans as well as those provided under supplementary major medical plans.

■ BLUE CROSS AND BLUE SHIELD PLANS

Health insurance is written by life insurance companies, by companies organized to write casualty insurance, and by many insurers—known as "monoline" insurance companies—organized specifically to write health insurance. Many cooperative associations, such as group practice prepayment plans and trade union organizations, also furnish health services to their members on a basis similar to insurance, although the associations may not be insurers in the technical sense of the word.

The term Health Maintenance Organization (HMO) is now used to indicate any of a number of different prepaid health care systems, whether provided by one organization or a group of cooperating organizations, which furnish a wide range of health care services—such as physicians' services, hospital services, diagnostic services, emergency care—to enrollees on a prepayment basis. Examples are the Health Insurance Plan of Greater New York, which has about 750,000 members and furnishes hospital services for them under contracts with Blue Cross; the Kaiser Foundation Health Plan, which has 2,100,000 members, and owns and operates a number of hospitals in the areas it serves; and Group Health Cooperative of Puget Sound, which has about 150,000 subscribers. The most widely known cooperative plans for hospital and medical care, however, are the Blue Cross and Blue Shield plans.

Blue Cross Plans

Blue Cross plans are generally considered to have originated at Baylor University, where a plan was established in 1920, to enable teachers to pay hospitalization costs in advance. This prepayment principle was later adopted elsewhere; and the American Hospital Association developed standard requirements for any association organized to provide group hospitalization benefits on a prepayment basis. These standards provided that members must be guaranteed a free choice of physicians and hospitals, and the organization was required to operate on a nonprofit basis.

Characteristics of Blue Cross Plans. As they were originally developed, Blue Cross plans offered coverages that differed in certain characteristic ways from commercial insurance plans for hospital expense benefits. These differences have become less distinct over the years, however, and today there are few features of either type of plan that may not be found to some extent in the other. Nevertheless, Blue Cross coverages are generally considered to differ from commercial insurance plans in the following ways:

1. *Blue Cross benefits are usually furnished on a service basis.* This means that the benefit the Blue Cross member is entitled to is described as a certain number of days in a member hospital, with the type of accommodation specified. Commercial insurance contracts, by contrast, typically pay the insured the cost of hospital accommodations up to a specified dollar maximum, or a fixed number of dollars for each day of hospitalization.

2. *Blue Cross plans customarily pay the benefits to the hospital which provides the service, while commercial contracts provide for payment to the insured.* If the hospital is not one with which the Blue Cross plan has a contract, however, the plan will usually make a cash settlement with the subscriber in much the same way as the commercial insurer does. Conversely, if the benefits under a commercial insurance policy have been assigned to the hospital, the insurer will usually pay the hospital, just as Blue Cross does.

3. Benefit limitations in Blue Cross agreements are typically expressed in terms of a maximum number of days' service. In commercial policies, maximums are usually expressed in dollar amounts, but many commercial policies provide also for maximums in terms of days of hospitalization.

Most Blue Cross agreements furnish semiprivate room accommodations; a few, ward facilities. Most agreements provide that if the member has a private room, Blue Cross will pay the hospital the cost of semiprivate room accommodations, and the member will be responsible for the difference in cost.

In addition to the hospital accommodations, the Blue Cross coverage includes the expenses of general nursing care and the use of the operating room and equipment. Maternity benefits are usually provided. Excluded are diseases or conditions covered by workmen's compensation or by hospital coverages provided by municipal, state, or federal agencies.

Benefits are furnished by Blue Cross plans under both group and individual contracts, with about 75 percent of the membership being group. A third classification, sometimes referred to as nongroup, is made up of persons who were formerly group members but who have left the group and converted to individual membership. Blue Cross plans typically cover employee groups, making contracts on a regional basis to provide hospital expense protection for the employees so covered and the Blue Cross contracts with member hospitals to make the services available. Many other types of groups are covered, however, including residents of certain specified areas.

Members are accepted for group membership regardless of health, although many of the Blue Cross associations require a health statement for individual membership. A conversion privilege is available to group subscribers on termination of their group membership and to dependents who become ineligible for group coverage because of marriage or reaching the limiting age of dependency. Contributions (premiums) are generally the same for nongroup and individual members, but they are considerably less for group members.

Operation of Blue Cross Plans. Blue Cross plans are separate, nonprofit organizations, organized and operating, for the most part, under laws that specifically relate to prepayment plans for health care. In many, though not all, of the states, they are regulated by the state insurance department, and they are exempt from most state and local taxes, including premium taxes. This gives them a significant competitive advantage over commercial insurers.

Blue Cross plans are organized on a territorial basis, often statewide, but a few states have more than one Blue Cross plan operating within their borders, and a few Blue Cross plans operate in more than one state. In 1972, there were 74 Blue Cross plans in the United States.

Each Blue Cross plan is autonomous and has its own board of directors, which elects the officers and determines overall policies. Each Blue Cross organization also issues its own contracts, which typically may differ in some respects from those issued by other Blue Cross plans. Thus, there is no such thing as a standard Blue Cross policy. The person who has Blue Cross coverage must examine his policy or certificate to determine the nature of the benefits to which he is entitled. However, the local Blue Cross organizations are affiliated on a national basis in a coordinating association called the Blue Cross Association, Inc.

Blue Shield Plans

Blue Shield plans were organized as a means of prepaying medical and surgical expenses, just as the Blue Cross plans provide for hospitalization expenses. Blue Shield plans had their beginnings in the California Physician's Service in 1930 and were associated with the American Medical Association until 1949. Since 1950, they have been known as Blue Shield Medical Care plans.

In 1972, there were 71 Blue Shield plans in the United States, all members of a national coordinating association, the National Association of Blue Shield plans. Legally, Blue Shield plans are completely separate from the Blue Cross plans, and each one issues its own separate policies to its own members. Nevertheless, the operations of the Blue Shield and Blue Cross plans are closely coordinated, and often there is a single executive director for both Blue Shield and Blue Cross plans.

■ GROUP COVERAGES AND RETIREMENT PLANS

The tremendous increase in the number of persons living into their seventies and eighties has given many more people a longer period of retirement today than has ever been true before. At the same time, higher tax rates and higher costs and standards of living have made it increasingly more difficult for the average person to save enough during his working years to assure an adequate retirement income for himself.

The need for retirement incomes for older people has become increasingly apparent during the past few decades. Some part of this need has been met by Social Security benefits, and many people have individual annuities or other sources of income for their retirement years. Nevertheless, the vast majority of employees have little, if any, savings; and Social Security benefits provide, at best, a minimum retirement income.

Retirement plans have become an integral part of the employee benefits offered by many businesses today and for several reasons. The basic reason is the fact that a well-planned and adequately funded retirement plan makes it relatively simple to retire employees who have reached an age where their health and initiative are beginning to decline. Such a plan will help an employer compete for and retain competent employees, since most job applicants consider the prospective employer's retirement plan, as well as other employee benefits, significant factors so far as desirable jobs are concerned. Such plans are also important in establishing and maintaining good employee morale.

A "Qualified" Retirement Plan

In a general sense, any plan, no matter how informal, under which an employer provides benefits for retiring employees is a retirement plan. Most forward-looking employers, however, are interested in establishing and maintaining what is called a "qualified" retirement plan. This means a retirement plan that meets requirements set forth in the Internal Revenue Code and Regulations of the federal government and that has been approved by the Internal Revenue Service.

Tax Advantages. A retirement plan that is "qualified" in this sense provides the following tax advantages:

1. The contributions of the employer are deductible as a business expense from the employer's gross income
2. The earnings on all funds held under the plan are exempt from income tax
3. The employees are not subject to income tax on the employer's contributions or on the earnings of the fund until they begin receiving their income after retirement.

At retirement, the employees will usually have two "after-65" income tax exemptions, and they will usually be in a lower income tax bracket than during the time they are working. The financial advantages of a qualified retirement plan, therefore, are substantial, for both the employer and his employees.

Tax-Sheltered Annuities Compared. A qualified retirement plan differs from a tax-sheltered annuity plan in at least two major respects. First, any corporation may establish a qualified retirement plan by meeting the IRS requirements outlined briefly below; but only certain organizations, described in chapter 14, may purchase tax-sheltered annuities for their employees. Second, any discrimination in favor of certain employees is prohibited under a qualified retirement plan, but there are no regulations to prevent such discrimination under a tax-sheltered annuity plan.

Requirements and Specifications. A complete discussion of all of the requirements that must be met before a retirement plan can be considered "qualified" is beyond the scope of this book. In general, however, the most essential requirements may be summarized as follows: The plan must be (1) a written plan, intended to be permanent, and established by an employer, (2) to provide definitely determinable retirement benefits on a nondiscriminatory basis, (3) for the benefit of his employees or their beneficiaries, and (4) it must be impossible for the employer himself to benefit from the plan until and unless all his obligations to the employees and beneficiaries under the plan have been fulfilled.

A qualified plan may exclude part-time and seasonal employees; a minimum age requirement may be included, such as 25 or 30; and a waiting period, such as three years, may be imposed. An employer who establishes a retirement plan has a certain amount of freedom in connection with specifications such as these. However, they must be applied on a nondiscriminatory basis. That is, requirements that apply to any participants must apply to all.

Normal retirement age is customarily fixed at age 65, but earlier retirement is generally permitted, usually with some reduction in benefits. Generally, also, a participant may be permitted to work beyond normal retirement age on a year-by-year basis, but with no increase in retirement benefits by reason of the extended period of employment.

Usually there is some provision for the vesting of employer contributions after the participant has been included in the plan for a specified minimum number of years. Benefits are said to be "vested" when a participant cannot be deprived of his right to receive the contributions (or benefits purchased by the contributions) made on his behalf by the employer, even though he leaves the employment of the employer prior to retirement. If his employment is terminated by death, his beneficiary will receive any such vested benefits. (Contributions made by the participant himself are vested from the date that they are made.)

Prototype and Master Retirement Plans. Since a qualified retirement plan must be a written plan, it has been customary for the employer who wishes to establish a plan to have its attorney incorporate the required provisions and specifications in a specially prepared legal document. The attorney submits this individually prepared plan to the Internal Revenue Service for approval, and the corporation then adopts it by an appropriate resolution of the board of directors. Today, many life insurance companies have prepared standardized retirement plans, called "prototype" or "master" plans, that simplify this procedure considerably.

Both prototype and master plans are "model" retirement plans that have been prepared by a sponsoring organization, such as a life insurance company or a bank, and submitted to the Internal Revenue Service for approval as to form. After this approval has been obtained, individual corporations have only to insert a few provisions relating to their own situations—benefit formulae, funding methods, and so on—and submit the completed plan to the Internal Revenue Service for approval. This procedure eliminates the expense and time required to develop an individually prepared plan in every case, and greatly simplifies the matter of obtaining IRS approval.

Definitely Determinable Benefits

The amount of the retirement benefit to be provided for a retiring employee under a qualified plan must be "definitely determinable," but within that requirement, the employer has several choices. If retirement plans are classified in terms of the type of retirement benefits provided, there are three principal classes:

1. Defined benefit plans
2. Money-purchase (defined contribution) plans
3. Assumed benefit plans.

A defined benefit plan establishes the retirement benefit as a fixed percentage of compensation or as a flat dollar amount, sometimes also taking into account years of service. Thus a plan providing a pension of $100 per month would be a defined benefit plan, as would one providing a pension equal to "one percent of annual compensation for each year of service." Contributions under a defined benefit plan are made in whatever amounts are required to provide the specified benefit at the time the retiring employee becomes entitled to it.

A money-purchase (or defined contribution) plan defines the amount to be contributed each year for each employee, such as a specified percentage of the employee's salary for that year. The amount of the retirement income for that employee, then, will be whatever can be provided with the total contributions that have been made on his behalf.

An assumed benefit plan establishes the benefits to be provided according to a benefit formula, just as is true of a defined benefit plan. Contributions are made to a trust fund on each employee's behalf, in accordance with that formula. The trust fund is invested, and the retirement benefits actually payable will depend upon the investment experience of the fund. If the experience is more favorable than expected, the retirement benefits will be larger. If the experience is less favorable, the benefits will be less than anticipated. An assumed benefit plan, then, is a defined benefit plan so far as contributions are concerned, but it becomes a money-purchase plan when the employee is ready to retire, since the retirement income is whatever the available funds will purchase at that time.

For employees who have been with the firm for several years when a pension plan is first established, past-service benefits—that is, benefits attributable to services performed before the pension plan became effective—are usually provided. Various methods are used to spread the expense of providing these benefits over the years remaining until such employees are ready for retirement.

How Retirement Plans Are Funded

So far as the life insurance company is concerned, the most important aspect of a qualified pension plan is its funding. Funding is the process of accumulating the assets that are necessary to provide the benefits contemplated by the plan. A qualified retirement plan may be funded either by contributions by the employer alone (a noncontributory plan), or by contributions from employees as well as the employer (a contributory plan). Funding may be allocated, unallocated, or combination. Contributions to a qualified retirement plan may be made to a trustee or they may take the form of payments to a life insurance company.

Contributory and Noncontributory Plans. Although benefits may be provided on a more generous basis if employees as well as employer make contributions to the plan, there is a tax disadvantage to the employee under contributory plans that is avoided if contributions are made solely by the employer. This is because the employer's contribution is deductible as a business expense from its taxable income, and there is no comparable privilege available to the employee. Even at the lowest income tax rate, therefore, an employee must earn considerably more than one dollar in order to make a one-dollar contribution toward his own retirement. By contrast, any corporation that has a taxable income in excess of $25,000 can make a one-dollar contribution to a retirement plan for its employees at a net cost of slightly more than 50 cents.

An illustration may help to show the importance of this tax situation. Assume that an employee who is in the 20 percent income tax bracket makes a $200 contribution each year to a retirement plan, and his employer contributes an equal amount. This employee must earn $250 in salary, out of which he would pay $50 in income tax, in order to have $200 to contribute. The employer, however, can deduct its entire $200 contribution from its taxable income and thus pay no income tax on the $200. If the employer had no retirement plan, its income tax on this $200 would be a little less than 50 percent, and the employer would be left with slightly more than $100. By making the $200 contribution to a pension plan, therefore, the corporate employer is, in effect, spending only about $100 more than it would have paid in income taxes. Thus it is making the $200 contribution at a net cost of only slightly more than $100.

Allocated and Unallocated Funding. If the contributions to a retirement plan are apportioned among the various participants as they are made and used to purchase insurance or annuity contracts for each of the participants, the plan is said to have "allocated" funding. If the contributions are accumulated in a general fund and not apportioned to the various participants until benefits are paid, the plan is said to use "unallocated" funding. A plan under which a portion of the funds is invested on an unallocated basis and the remainder is used to purchase insurance contracts for the various participants is said to be a "combination" plan and to use "combination" funding.

Trusteed Retirement Plans

Many qualified retirement plans are funded by contributions made to a trustee, usually a corporate trustee. A trust is a legal arrangement under which a person transfers money or other property to another person or corporation, called a trustee, to be used for the benefit of a designated person or persons. The trustee may be an individual or a financial organization, such as a bank. A trusteed retirement plan (pension trust) is a retirement plan under which contributions are made to a trustee for the purpose of providing pensions for designated employees after their retirement.

Some trusteed pension plans are said to be "insured"; others are "noninsured." Under an insured pension trust, the employer deposits funds with the trustee at regular intervals, and the trustee uses those funds to purchase annuity contracts for the employees for whom retirement benefits are to be provided. When an employee retires, the insurance company begins paying him his retirement income in accordance with the contract or contracts that have been purchased for him by the trustee.

Under a noninsured trusteed retirement plan, the employer also deposits funds with a trustee at regular intervals, but the trustee invests the funds in securities instead of using them as premiums for annuity contracts. When an employee retires, his retirement benefits are paid to him out of the trust fund.

The employer who establishes a noninsured trusteed retirement plan for his employees assumes full responsibility for the adequacy of the fund and usually bases his contributions on the estimates of a consulting actuary. If those estimates are not sufficient, or if the investment experience of the fund is less favorable than anticipated, the trust fund may not be adequate to provide the retirement benefits that are contemplated. In such situations, the participants will receive only those retirement benefits that can be purchased by the funds that are available. Under an insured pension plan, by contrast, retirement incomes are guaranteed by the life insurance company and payable as provided by the policies that have been purchased for the various participants.

Group Deferred Annuities

On the group basis, insured retirement benefits are most frequently provided through group deferred annuities or under a deposit administration plan. The group deferred annuity plan of funding retirement benefits was introduced in the 1920's. Its plan of operation is simple. The life insurance company issues a master annuity contract to the employer; individual certificates are issued to the employees. Each year the employer purchases a unit of single-premium deferred annuity for each employee in an amount that is usually determined by the employees' earnings during the year.

An illustrative plan might provide that each year the employer would purchase a deferred annuity for each participating employee which would provide monthly income payments for the employee at retirement, equal to one percent of the employee's earnings in the year the annuity was purchased. This would be a defined benefit plan. If a money-purchase plan were used, the employer would contribute a stipulated amount as a premium on a deferred annuity that would provide an income in whatever amount the premium would purchase. The premium would be established as a specified percentage of the earnings of the employee for that particular year—for example, 5 percent.

Each single-premium deferred annuity that is purchased will pay a life income of a stated amount, beginning at the employee's normal retirement date. With each additional year of employment, an additional annuity is purchased. The employee's retirement income is the total income provided by the accumulated annuities that have been purchased for him.

The principal advantage of group deferred annuity plans is the advantage of all insured plans: they relieve the employer of all technical responsibilities. Actuarial, investment, and many administrative responsibilities are assumed by the insurance company, and the benefit payments are guaranteed. In addition, when group deferred annuities are used, if the retirement plan is discontinued, the annuities already purchased for the employees will remain fully paid-for and effective in amounts that are clearly stated.

Deposit Administration Plans

A deposit administration plan is a plan under which contributions are made to a life insurance company to provide retirement benefits for employees, but these contributions are handled on an unallocated basis—that is, they are not treated as premiums for agreed-upon benefits for the individual employees.

Under a deposit administration plan, a contract setting forth the mechanics of the plan is issued to the employer, and the employer makes regular contributions to the insurance company in amounts that may be determined either by the insurance company or by an actuarial firm hired by the employer. Generally, the amounts of the contributions are not rigidly established and need only fall between specified minimums and maximums.

These contributions are invested by the life insurance company and held on an unallocated basis until they are needed to provide retirement benefits for retiring employees. When each employee retires, the company calculates the amount that will be required, as a single premium, to provide the retirement income to which he is entitled. This amount is then transferred (in an internal transaction) from the deposit fund to the appropriate department of the insurance company, and a single-premium immediate annuity is purchased for the retiring employee. Thereafter, the insurer pays him his retirement income on the same guaranteed basis that it makes annuity payments to all other annuitants.

Since no annuities are purchased until the employees are ready to retire, the amount of benefit to be provided under a deposit administration plan can be established on any of several bases. The usual practice is to base benefits on the average earnings of the retiring employee for the last five or ten years immediately prior to retirement. With a group deferred annuity plan, it is difficult to do this, since the deferred annuities are purchased each year in amounts based on the employees' earnings for that year.

The insurance company guarantees a minimum interest rate on the funds deposited with it, and it guarantees the fund itself against loss. In addition, the employer's deposits are based on actuarially determined assumptions. However, it is the responsibility of the employer, not the insurance company, to see that the fund is adequate to provide the benefits contemplated. Of course, once an annuity has been purchased for a retiring employee, he has all the usual guarantees of an individual annuity contract.

Combination Plans

A pension plan that involves both insurance policies and an auxiliary or "side" fund is commonly referred to as a "combination," or "split-funded," plan. Usually a pension plan of this kind is trusteed, and a portion of each year's contribution is used to purchase individual life insurance contracts for participating employees, while the remainder is held in a separate, invested fund. When a participant retires, the life insurance contract is surrendered for its cash value and the separate fund is drawn upon for sufficient additional funds to purchase an immediate annuity that will provide the retirement income to which he is entitled. Then, as is true with the deposit administration plans, the retiring employee has the same guarantees as any other annuitant of the company.

■ RETIREMENT PLANS FOR SELF-EMPLOYED

For many years, self-employed persons could set aside funds for their retirement only out of after-tax dollars, although the employees of a corporation, including officers, enjoyed retirement plans funded by contributions that were deductible as business expenses by the employer and not considered income to the employees. In 1962, the United States Congress remedied this inequity by enacting the Self-Employed Individuals' Tax Retirement Act, otherwise known as H.R. 10, or the Keogh Act.

Briefly, the Keogh Act broadened the Internal Revenue Act by revisions and amendments to permit the self-employed person (who is termed an "owner-employee" under the act) to make contributions on his own behalf and for any employees he may have, and to deduct these contributions from his taxable income. The deductible contributions he makes for himself are limited to 10 percent of his earned income or $2,500, whichever is the smaller, and he must make contributions for each of his employees at the same rate as for himself. An owner-employee cannot receive benefits from his Keogh plan before he reaches age $59\frac{1}{2}$ unless he is totally disabled. If he dies prior to that time, the benefits will be paid to his beneficiary.

In general, a qualified retirement plan for self-employed persons and their employees is treated much the same as a qualified corporate pension plan, and many of the same requirements apply. Thus, a Keogh plan must be a written plan, just as is true of a qualified corporate retirement plan. However, even before prototype and master plans were acceptable for corporate retirement plans, they were widely developed and used for Keogh plans. In addition, a Keogh plan may be established as a trusteed plan, as a custodial account with a bank, or by direct investment in a special series of Government bonds.

Contributions toward a Keogh plan may be invested in mutual funds under the trusteed or custodial account plans, in life insurance so long as not more than a specified percentage of the total contributions are so invested, and in annuity and retirement income contracts, as well as in the special Government bonds. The flexible-premium annuity described in chapter 14 is especially well suited to Keogh plans because the premiums may be varied from year to year to correspond to the fluctuations of the self-employed person's income and to permit him to take advantage each year of the maximum amount of contributions deductible under the law.

Contributions made to a qualified Keogh plan give the self-employed person many, though not all, of the tax advantages enjoyed by participants in a qualified corporate retirement plan, including the following:

1. The owner-employee may deduct from his taxable income his contributions, up to 10 percent (or $2,500, if less) of his earned income each year, and the contributions he makes for any employees he may have.

2. Neither the owner-employee nor his employees will be taxed on any earnings on the retirement funds as they accumulate.

3. Both owner-employee and his employees will be taxed only as they receive the retirement benefits after they retire.

■ NOTES ON CANADIAN PRACTICES

Health Insurance Plans

Blue Cross and group health insurance plans in Canada differ in one significant respect from similar plans sold in the United States. As previously noted, all provinces in Canada have government-sponsored plans for prepayment of certain hospital expenses. Hospital benefits under group insurance plans, therefore, as under individual plans, are customarily limited to the difference between the costs of private or semi-private accommodation and the general ward costs (which are provided under the province plans).

Group Coverages and Retirement Plans

In general, group coverages for retirement plans in Canada are similar to those in the United States. Contributory plans are more attractive in Canada, however, because of a difference in the tax law as it applies to employee contributions. Employee contributions for retirement benefits (as distinguished from insurance benefits), when made under approved pension trust and group retirement plans, are deductible from taxable income, up to substantial limits. As in the United States, employer contributions for retirement benefits are considered an expense and are therefore deductible for income tax purposes and are not considered income to the employee in the year they are made. Income at retirement under such plans is generally fully taxable.

■ QUESTIONS FOR REVIEW

1. Briefly summarize the typical ways in which disability income benefits are provided under group disability income plans.
2. List four exclusions commonly found in group major medical contracts.
3. In what way or ways do comprehensive medical plans differ from major medical plans?
4. List three ways in which Blue Cross plans for hospital care may differ from hospital insurance plans of commercial insurance companies. In what respects, if any, have these differences been modified?
5. What is meant by a Health Maintenance Organization?
6. What is a qualified pension plan? What important income tax advantages are enjoyed by employees covered by such plans?
7. Distinguish between contributory and noncontributory retirement plans; allocated and unallocated funding.
8. What is a Keogh plan?
9. What important tax advantage is provided in Canada with respect to the employee's contributions to a retirement plan?

GLOSSARY OF COMMON LIFE INSURANCE TERMS

Absolute Assignment. An irrevocable transfer, from one person to another, of all ownership rights under an insurance policy. *See also* Collateral Assignment.

Accidental Death Benefit. A benefit in addition to the face amount of a life insurance policy, payable if the insured dies as the result of an accident or, depending upon the policy definition of the term, as a result of accidental means. Sometimes referred to as "double indemnity."

Actuary. A technical expert in life insurance, particularly in mathematics. The actuary applies the theory of probability to the business of insurance and is responsible for the calculation of premiums, policy reserves, and other values.

Administrator. The person who is appointed by a court of law to settle the estate of a person who has died without a valid will.

Adverse Selection. (Also referred to as "antiselection" or "selection against the company.") The tendency of persons with greater likelihood of loss to apply for or continue insurance to a greater extent than others. These persons are also more inclined to take advantage of favorable privileges such as renewal and conversion of term life insurance policies.

Glossary of Common Life Insurance Terms ▪ 365

Agent. A person who represents a life insurance company for the purpose of soliciting applications, collecting initial premiums, and servicing insurance contracts. Also known as a "life underwriter" or "field underwriter."

Amount at Risk. The amount by which the face amount of a life insurance contract exceeds the reserve.

Annuitant. The person during whose life an annuity is payable, usually the one who receives the annuity payments.

Annuity. A specified sum payable at regular intervals during the lifetime of one or more persons (Straight Life Annuity). Also payments at regular intervals for a stipulated period (Annuity Certain). *See also* Annuity with Period Certain, Deferred Annuity, Immediate Annuity, Joint and Last Survivor Annuity, Refund Annuity.

Annuity Certain. A contract providing payments at regular intervals for a specified period of time, without reference to the life or death of the individual(s) concerned.

Annuity with Period Certain. An annuity that is payable for the lifetime of the annuitant but with payments certain to be made (guaranteed) for a specified length of time, such as 10 or 15 years, whether or not the annuitant lives to the end of the period.

Antiselection. *See* Adverse Selection.

Assignee. The person to whom certain rights under an insurance policy are transferred under an absolute or collateral assignment. *See* Assignment.

Assignment. The legal transfer of ownership rights under a life insurance policy from one person to another; also the document effecting the transfer.

Assignor. The person who executes an assignment.

Automatic Premium Loan. A policy loan authorized in advance by the policyowner and established by a life insurance company to pay a premium which remains unpaid at the end of the grace period.

Beneficiary. The person to whom the proceeds of a life insurance policy are payable at the death of the insured.

Binding Receipt. A form of premium receipt which provides that life insurance will be payable, subject to the terms of the receipt, if the proposed insured should die before a policy is issued or the application is denied. *See also* Conditional Receipt.

Broker. An insurance representative who places business with more than one insurance company but not as an agent.

Business Life Insurance. Life insurance purchased for business uses, rather than for personal uses. Examples are life insurance owned by a business organization on the life of a key man, insurance owned by one business partner on the life of another partner, or by one stockholder-officer in a close corporation on the life of another stockholder-officer.

Cancellable Policy. A health insurance policy which the insurance company may cancel at any time, if advance notice is given as provided in the policy and any unearned premium is refunded. Cancellation has no effect on claims incurred prior to the effective date of the cancellation.

Cash Surrender Value. The amount payable to the owner of a whole life or endowment insurance policy on surrender of the policy to the company prior to the maturity of the policy as a death claim or matured endowment. Some term life insurance policies also have cash values during some periods.

Certificate. A statement issued to the individuals insured under a group insurance policy, setting forth the essential provisions relating to their insurance coverage.

Claim. A demand presented, usually by the beneficiary, for payment of the proceeds of a life insurance contract.

Coinsurance. *See* Percentage Participation.

Collateral Assignment. The legal transfer of all or a part of the ownership rights under an insurance policy as security for an indebtedness, on condition that if the indebtedness is repaid, the rights so transferred will revert (return) to the person who made the assignment.

Commuted Value. The present value of a series of payments to be made in the future. Also referred to as "discounted value."

Comprehensive Major Medical Insurance. A form of major medical insurance designed to combine the protection afforded by a basic health insurance policy (usually hospital insurance) with that afforded by a major medical policy. Typically, a comprehensive major medical policy has a low deductible amount and high maximum benefits.

Conditional Receipt. A premium receipt which is given to the applicant who pays all, or a specified portion, of the initial premium at the time he applies for life insurance. Such receipts generally provide that if the proposed insured is found to have been insurable as of a specified date (usually either the date of the application or of the medical examination, if later), a death claim arising prior to the issuance of a policy will be payable. Some conditional receipts provide for payment of a claim only if the application is approved prior to the death of the proposed insured.

Contingent Beneficiary. The person designated under a life insurance contract to receive the proceeds payable on the death of the insured if there is no primary beneficiary living at the insured's death. Sometimes referred to as "secondary beneficiary."

Conversion. The exchange of an insurance policy of one kind for a policy of a different kind. Specifically, the exchange of a term life insurance contract for a whole life or endowment contract in accordance with the terms of a policy provision granting that right. Also the right of a certificateholder under a group insurance contract to purchase individual insurance on a permanent plan, without evidence of insurability, at termination of his group coverage.

Convertible Term Insurance Policy. A term life insurance policy which, by its provisions, may be exchanged for a whole life or endowment plan of insurance without evidence of insurability.

Credit Life Insurance. Life insurance, usually group, purchased as protection to one who has loaned money or extended credit to the insured. The amount of the insurance at any point in time is the amount of the unpaid balance of the loan.

Deductible Amount. A specified amount of medical expenses that an insured person must incur before benefits will be payable under a health insurance policy.

Deferred Annuity. An annuity contract under which the income payments are not to begin until the end of a specified period or the annuitant's attainment of a stipulated age.

Disability Income Benefit. A disability benefit provided under a health insurance contract or a rider attached to a life insurance policy, which provides an income of a specified amount at regular intervals, during any period in which the insured is disabled as defined in the policy.

Disability Income Insurance. Health insurance under which benefits are payable in regular installments designed to replace some of the insured's income when he is unable to work because of accident or illness.

Disability Waiver-of-Premium Benefit. A disability benefit which provides that a policy of life or health insurance will be continued in force without payment of premiums during any period in which the insured is totally disabled as defined in the policy. During such periods, the premiums are said to be *waived* by the company—that is, premiums are not required to be paid.

Dividend. An amount which is refunded to the owner of a participating life insurance policy, if the company has operated with sufficiently favorable mortality, interest, and expense experience.

Double Indemnity. *See* Accidental Death Benefit.

Endowment Insurance. An insurance contract that pays an amount of insurance if the insured should die during a specified term of years, or the same amount as an endowment if the insured survives to the end of the specified term.

Executor. The person who is appointed by a court of law to carry out the provisions of the will left by a deceased person. The court will appoint a person who is designated in the will to be the executor, if that person is living, consents, and qualifies. *See* Administrator.

Extended Term Insurance. Term life insurance granted under the nonforfeiture section of a life insurance contract, if a policyowner ceases to pay premiums at any time after the contract has acquired a cash value. The cash value will be applied to purchase term insurance in the face amount of the policy, less indebtedness, for as long a period as the cash value will provide, or for the original term of the policy, if shorter. Under endowment contracts, any excess of the cash value not used to purchase term insurance for the remaining term of the policy will be used to purchase a pure endowment payable on the date the contract matures.

Face Amount. The amount stated in the policy that is payable at the death of the insured or at the maturity of the contract, subject to adjustments for indebtedness, dividend additions, additional benefits, etc. Also called "amount of insurance."

Facility-of-Payment Clause. A provision commonly included in industrial life insurance contracts, under which the insurer reserves the right to pay the policy proceeds, under specified conditions, to any person who appears equitably entitled because of having paid funeral or other expenses incident to the last illness of the insured.

Family Income Policy. A policy under which a specified amount of permanent insurance is payable at the death of the insured, and, if such death occurs within a designated period, an income will be paid from the date of such death to the end of the period. The permanent insurance may be payable either at the date of death or, if death occurs within the specified period, at the end of all income payments.

Family Life Policy. A policy that provides insurance on the lives of all members of a family. A typical form provides permanent insurance on the life of the husband and a lesser amount of term insurance on the lives of the wife and children. Children born or legally adopted after the policy is issued are automatically insured under the policy with no increase in premium.

Fraternal Life Insurance. Life insurance provided in connection with membership in a lodge or fraternal order. At one time such insurance was funded primarily by the assessment system, but most fraternals today operate on a legal reserve basis.

Grace Period. The period of 30 or 31 days, granted under the terms of a life insurance contract, following the day a premium becomes due and during which the payment may be made without loss of any rights. The policy remains in force during this period but lapses if the premium is not paid at the end of the grace period. If the insured dies during the grace period, the death benefit is payable but the premium is deducted from the proceeds.

Gross Premium. The total premium for a life insurance policy, composed of the net premium plus a loading for expenses.

Group Life Insurance. Insurance on the lives of several persons as a group, written under one policy called a master policy, and evidenced by individual certificates issued to the persons whose lives are insured.

Guaranteed Renewable Contract. A health insurance policy which the policyowner has the right to continue by paying premiums when due or within the grace period, until he reaches a specified age or for the remainder of his lifetime, subject to the insurer's right to increase premium rates for policyowners as a class.

Health Insurance. A form of insurance providing benefits in the event of economic loss resulting from sickness or injury. It thus includes loss-of-time and all medical expense reimbursement coverages. Sometimes referred to, especially in legislative language, as "accident and health insurance."

Immediate Annuity. An annuity under which income payments are not deferred but which begin instead at the end of the first payment interval after purchase. Thus, if payments are to be made on a monthly basis, the first payment under an immediate annuity will be made at the end of the first month following purchase of the contract.

Industrial Life Insurance. Life insurance under which premiums are payable more frequently than under ordinary life insurance, typically weekly, and characterized by collection of premiums and servicing of the policy at the home of the insured by agents called "debit agents."

Insurable Interest. A beneficiary has an insurable interest in the life of the person insured if he has a reasonable expectation of benefit from the continuance of the insured's life or of suffering a loss if the insured should die.

Insurability. Those qualifications of age, health, occupation, etc., which enable the proposed insured to meet the requirements of a life insurance company for the issuance of insurance.

Insured. The person whose death is the contingency on which life insurance is payable. (Under the Uniform Life Insurance Act of Canada, the insured is defined as the person who applies for the insurance and may therefore be someone other than the person whose life is insured.)

Irrevocable Beneficiary. A beneficiary whose interest cannot be cancelled without his or her consent.

Joint Life Annuity. An annuity payable during the joint lives of two or more persons and terminating at the death of the first such person to die.

Joint and Last Survivor Annuity. An annuity payable during the joint lives of two or more persons and continuing, sometimes in a reduced amount, for as long as the survivor or survivors live.

Joint Life Policy. A contract insuring the lives of two or more persons, providing for payment of the proceeds on the death of the first insured to die, with insurance provided on a limited basis, if any, to the survivor. Under present-day joint life policies, the survivor may have a right to purchase an equal amount of insurance, without evidence of insurability, during a limited period of time following the death of the first insured to die.

Juvenile Insurance. Life insurance written on the lives of children under a specified age. This insurance is usually owned by a parent or parents.

Lapse. Termination of a life insurance contract because of nonpayment of premiums. If there are nonforfeiture values, the policy lapses but may remain effective as extended term or reduced paid-up insurance.

Legal Reserve. Policy reserve established as a liability and maintained by a life insurance company in accordance with standards established by state laws.

Level Premium. A premium established in such an amount that it will be sufficient to meet the increasing number of death claims expected under a group of life insurance policies without the need for increasing it at any time during the duration of the policies.

Life Annuity. A contract providing for specified payments at regular intervals for the lifetime of the annuitant, with payments ceasing at the annuitant's death. *See* Annuity.

Life Expectancy. The average number of years a group of persons of a stated age may be expected to live, according to a given mortality table.

Limited-Payment Life Policy. A policy of whole life insurance for which the premium payments will terminate at the end of a specified term of years or at the death of the insured, if it occurs before that date.

Major Medical Insurance. Health insurance designed to cover catastrophic medical expenses. Usually there is a deductible amount, percentage participation, and high maximum limits.

Master Policy. The policy that is issued to an employer or trustee, establishing a group insurance plan for designated members of an eligible group. The various insured members of the group receive individual certificates which describe the insurance benefits to which they are entitled.

Maturity Value. The amount payable under an endowment insurance contract if the insured person is living at the end of the specified endowment period. Also, the amount payable under a whole life insurance policy if the insured lives to the last age of the mortality table on which the values of the contract were based.

Monthly Debit Ordinary. Ordinary life insurance sold on a monthly premium basis with premiums collected by a debit agent.

Mortality Table. A statistical table showing, for each age from 0 to some agreed-upon upper age such as 100 or 110, the number of persons living, the number dying, and the rate of mortality per thousand, for a specified number of persons, such as 1,000,000. The fixed number selected is the *radix*.

Mutual Life Insurance Company. A life insurance company owned by its policyowners, who have the right to elect directors.

Net Premium. The premium calculated using a specified mortality table and a given rate of interest, but without allowance for expenses.

Noncancellable Policy. A health insurance policy which the policyowner has the right to continue in force to a specified age, such as 60 or 65, by paying premiums as they fall due or within the grace period, and with respect to which the insurer has not reserved the right to increase premium rates.

Nonforfeiture Provisions. Provisions required to be included (in the United States but not in Canada) in any long-term, whole life, or endowment life insurance contract, guaranteeing at least minimum values to the policyowner who has paid premiums long enough to establish an equity in the policy.

Nonparticipating Policy. A life insurance policy which does not grant the policyowner a right to policyowner dividends.

Option. A choice. Most life insurance policies provide options with respect to settlement arrangements, dividends, and nonforfeiture values.

Optionally Renewable Policy. A health insurance policy which may be renewed by the policyowner, only with the consent of the insurance company.

Ordinary Life Insurance. One of the broad classes of life insurance (the others are group and industrial). The term "ordinary" is also used to refer to continuous-premium, whole life contracts.

Paid-up Policy. A life insurance policy under which no further premiums are payable but under which the insurance coverage continues in effect.

Participating Policy. A policy under which policyowner dividends are payable—that is, a policy that entitles its owner to participate in any allocations of surplus.

Payee. The person to whom benefits are payable under a supplementary contract.

Payor Benefits. Coverages available in connection with juvenile insurance policies, that provide waiver of premiums under such policies in the event the premium payor, usually a parent of the insured, becomes totally and permanently disabled or dies within the term specified (usually the minority of the insured child).

Percentage Participation. A practice followed in major medical insurance, in which both insurer and insured share the hospital and medical expenses incurred by the insured, in accordance with a specified ratio, such as 80 percent to be paid by the insurer and 20 percent by the insured.

Policy. The written instrument issued to the applicant, which expresses the insurance contract between the company and the applicant.

Policy Loan. An advance made by a life insurance company to a policyowner, on the latter's request, secured by the cash value of the policy.

Premium. The payment, or one of several payments, required to establish and keep a life insurance policy in full effect.

Present Value. The single sum which, together with interest at a specified rate, will equal a stated sum at a given future date or a series of sums at specified future dates.

Proceeds. The amount of money payable under a policy at the death of an insured or at the maturity of a policy.

Pure Endowment. A sum of money payable at the end of a stated period, provided a designated person is living at the time. If the person specified dies before the end of the period, nothing is payable.

Rated Policy. A policy that is issued at higher than the standard premium rate because the insured does not meet the company's insurability requirements for standard rates.

Reduced Paid-up Insurance. One of the nonforfeiture benefits, under which the cash value of the policy is used as a single premium to purchase paid-up insurance of the same kind as the policy itself (whole life under a whole life policy, endowment under an endowment policy, term insurance under a long-term contract for the term of the policy) in such an amount as the cash value will provide.

Refund Annuity. An annuity that is payable for the lifetime of the annuitant, but with a provision that if the annuitant should die before receiving a total amount in income payments at least equal to the total premiums paid for the annuity, the company will pay the difference between the total of the payments made under the annuity and the purchase price to someone designated for that purpose or to the estate of the annuitant. Under an installment refund annuity, this difference is payable by continuing the installments for the necessary length of time. Under a cash refund annuity, the difference is payable in one sum.

Reinstatement. Restoration of a lapsed policy to premium-paying status on compliance with the conditions set forth in the policy.

Renewable Term Insurance. Term insurance that may be renewed for another term of the same length, usually subject to an upper age limit beyond which renewal will not be permitted.

Reserve. The amount required to be carried as a liability in the financial statement of a life insurer, to provide for future commitments under policies outstanding.

Revocable Beneficiary. A beneficiary whose rights are subject to the rights of the policyowner to revoke or change the beneficiary designation and to exercise any ownership rights under the policy without the beneficiary's consent.

Rider. A special policy provision or group of provisions which may be added to a policy to expand or limit the benefits otherwise payable. Examples of benefits often added to a basic policy by rider are the accidental death benefit, waiver of premiums for disability, and family income.

Risk Appraisal. The process of selecting those persons proposed for life or health insurance who meet the insurability requirements of the company, and of classifying them according to degrees of insurability so that appropriate premiums may be charged. Also known as "underwriting."

Secondary Beneficiary. *See* Contingent Beneficiary.

Selection against the Company. *See* Adverse Selection.

Settlement Option. A choice given the policyowner (or, in some cases, the beneficiary) with respect to the sum payable under a life insurance contract. Usually any substantial sum, whether payable as an endowment, death benefit, or cash surrender benefit, may be settled under any of several alternative methods.

Stock Life Insurance Company. A company owned by its stockholders, who elect the directors and who may or may not be policyowners of the same company.

Straight Life Insurance. *See* Whole Life Insurance.

Supplementary Contract. A contract issued by a life insurance company when policy benefits are applied under one of the optional modes of settlement. The supplementary contract specifies the amounts to be paid, the dates of such payments, the payee or payees, and all other pertinent details of the settlement method elected.

Survivorship Annuity. A contract that provides for payment of a life annuity to a specified person, at the death of the insured. No benefits are payable if the specified person dies prior to the death of the insured.

Term Insurance. Life insurance under which the benefit is payable only if the insured dies during a specified period of time or term, nothing being payable if he survives to the end of the term.

Underwriting. See Risk Appraisal.

Variable Annuity. An annuity under which the amount of payments that will be made to the annuitant may vary in accordance with the value of an account invested primarily in common stocks.

Waiver of Premium. A provision under which payment of premiums is waived (that is, not required) on and after the occurrence of a contingency, such as the insured's becoming totally and permanently disabled.

Whole Life Insurance. Insurance that may be kept in force by the owner for the remainder of the lifetime of the insured.

INDEX

A

ABA Assignment Form No. 10, 156, 175
Absolute assignment, 154
  for collateral purposes, 176
Accident policies, 264
Accidental death and dismemberment, 258, 338
Accidental death benefit, 171, 201, 247
  amount of, 202
  industrial life insurance, 247
  policy provision, 204, 245
  risks not assumed under, 171, 204
  suicide and the, 204
Accidental means, 202
Additional deposit privilege, 209
Adhesion, contract of, 82, 84
Adverse selection; *see* Antiselection
Advertising Code (NAIC), 283
Administrator, 111
Age, misstatement of, 181
Agency, law of, 85
  principles, 86
Agency system, 85
Agent's statement, 97
Agents, authority of, 86, 95
Aleatory contract, 81
Amicable Society for a Perpetual Assurance Office, 65
Amount at risk; *see* Net amount at risk
Annual-premium deferred annuity, 289, 300
Annual statement, 69
Annuitants, life expectancy of, 296
Annuities
  annual premium deferred, 289, 300, 301
  calculation of payments under, 295
  cash refund, 291
  definition of, 3, 286
  deferred, 292

Annuities—*Cont.*
  flexible premium, 303, 305
  group deferred, 358
  immediate, 292
  installment refund, 291
  with and without life contingencies, 294
  minimum guarantees, with, 289
  on more than one life, 293
  operation of, 287
  with period certain, 290
  private, 287
  for retirement, 299
  settlement options and, 294
  single premium, 289
  straight life, 289
  survivorship, 293
  survivorship benefit, 296
  tax sheltered, 309
  used by Romans, 6
  variable, 304, 306, 307, 308
Annuity due, 292
Annuity rates for women, 299
Annuity tables, 296, 297
Antiselection
  definition, 24
  health insurance, 265
  life insurance, 99
  term insurance renewals, 24
Application, 90
  agent's statement in, 97
  contractual information, 91
  for nonmedical insurance, 95
  signatures to, 97
Approval-type premium receipts, 103
Assessment plans
  for fire losses, 53
  inadequacies of, 55
  for life insurance, 54
  post- and pre-assessment plans, 57

377

Assignee and assignor, 153
Assignments, 153
  ABA Form No. 10, 156, 175
  absolute, 154, 176
  collateral, 155, 157, 175
  group life, 333
  industrial policies, 245
  problems of, 174
  versus transfer of ownership by endorsement, 159
Authority of agent, 86, 95
Automatic premium loan, 132, 136
Automobile accident policies, 264
Average-age problem, 55
Aviation accident policies, 264

B

Backdating, 107
Baltimore Life Insurance Company, The, 66
Beneficiaries
  brothers and sisters as, 110
  children as, 110
  contingent, 111
  divorce and, 177
  final, 111
  minors as, 113
  primary, 110
  revocable and irrevocable, 111, 112
Beneficiary changes, 109, 115
  endorsement method of, 115
  by guardian, 110
  group life, 330
  health insurance, 279
  incomplete, 176
  power-to-appoint, 110
  procedures for, 115
  recording method of, 116
  "substantial compliance" rule, 176
Beneficiary designation
  by applicant, 109
  class designations, 114
  group life, 330
Bilateral contracts, 78
Benefits
  added by rider, 194
  cash surrender, 144
  death, 167
  living, 164
  nonforfeiture, 33, 68, 71, 144
  reduced paid-up, 33, 146
Binding receipts, 103
Blue Cross Plans, 253, 349
  characteristics of, 350
  operation of, 351
Blue Shield Plans, 253, 349, 352
Booklets, group life insurance, 334
"Burden of proof," 171
Business overhead expense insurance, 258

C

Cancellation of health insurance, 273
Cash refund annuity, 291
Cash surrender
  continued privilege of, 149
  reasons for, 166
Cash surrender benefit, 144
Cash surrender value, 31, 144
Cash value; see Cash surrender value and Nonforfeiture benefits
Certificates, group life insurance, 333
Change of beneficiary
  endorsement method, 115
  group life, 330
  health insurance, 279
  ordinary life insurance, 109, 115
  recording method, 116
Change of plan, 160
  requirements for, 161
Children, life insurance for, 220
  advantages of, 220
  juvenile plans, 227
  ownership of, 222
  payor benefit, 225
  statutory limits on, 222
Claimant's rights, 174
Claims
  contestable, 172
  during contestable period, 172
  denial of, 172, 173
  health insurance
    notice, 280
    payment of, 281
    proof of loss, 280
  waiver-of-premium disability, 199
Class designation of beneficiary, 114
"Clean-up" funds, 122
Coinsurance; see Percentage participation
Collateral assignments, 155
  claim problems and, 175
  conflicts under, 157
  irrevocable beneficiary's rights and, 157
  release of, 175
Common disaster, 177
Common disaster clause, 180
Commutative contract, 81
Compound interest, effect of, 58
Comprehensive major medical
  deductible amounts, 269
  group plans, 348
  individual plans, 269
Computer preparation of policy forms, 104
Connecticut Mutual Life Insurance Company, 67
Consideration, 78
  adequacy of, 78
  bilateral contract, 78

Consideration—*Cont.*
  definition of, 78
  in life insurance, 79, 130
  for a promise, 78
Construction, rule of, 85
Constructive delivery, 106
Contestable claim, 172
Contestable period, 172
Contingent beneficiary, 111
Continuous-premium, whole life policy, 29
Contract, life insurance
  adhesion, a contract of, 82, 84
  aleatory, 81
  contract of good faith, 83
  nature of, 82
  not a contract of indemnity, 82
  unilateral, 78, 82
Contract(s)
  adhesion, 82, 84
  aleatory, 81
  bilateral, 78
  of business organizations, 77
  commutative, 81
  competent parties, 74
  definition, 74
  formal, 74
  formation of, 73
  good faith, 83
  indemnity, 82
  informal, 74
  of insane persons, 77
  insurance as a, 73
  of minors, 75
  "necessaries," 76
  requirements as to form, 79
  unilateral, 78, 82
  void or voidable, 75
Contributory and noncontributory plans
  group life insurance, 317
  retirement, 356
Conversion
  automatic, 26
  current date, 26
  family life policy, 230
  group life insurance, 331
  original date, 26
Corridor deductible, 269, 348
Cost-of-living riders, 29
Counteroffer, 78
Creditor group life insurance, 338
  premium payment under, 339

D

Death
  and economic loss, 2
  increasing probability of, 18
  as an insurable risk, 17

Death—*Cont.*
  rates of, 47, 49, 242
  totality of, 18
  uncertainty of, 18
Death benefits, 167
Death claims
  basic question, 167
  "due proof" in, 168
Debit, definition, 240
Debit life insurance; *see* Industrial life insurance
Decreasing term life insurance, 29
Deductible amounts
  comprehensive major medical, 269
  "corridor" deductible, 269, 348
  floating deductible, 269
  integrated deductible, 348
Defense, time limit on, 280
Deferred annuity, 292
Delivery of policy
  constructive, 106
  for inspection, 107
  manual, 106
Deposit administration, 359
Disability
  confining and nonconfining, 255
  definitions, 255
  partial, 257
  subjective nature of, 267
Disability income benefits, 200, 254
  group plans, 344, 345
Disability income insurance, 254
  amount of income, 254
  business overhead expense, 258
  definition of disability, 255
  elimination period, 256
  excluded risks, 257
  features of, 254
  income payment period, 256
  waiver-of-premium under, 257
Disability waiver-of-premium in life insurance, contracts, 132, 194, 199
Dividend options, 93, 138
  cash payment, 138, 139
  dividend additions, 138, 140
  interest option, 138, 139
  one-year term, 140
  premium reduction, 138, 139
Dividends
  in general, 142
  group life insurance, 327
  industrial life insurance, 244
  options, 93, 138
  policyowner, 93
Divorce, of beneficiary, 177
Dodson, James, 13
Double protection policies, 219
Dread disease policies, 252
"Due proof," 168

E

Economic loss
  death and, 2
  definition, 1
  how met, 3
  life insurance and, 2
  may be assumed, 4
  may be shared, 5
  may be transferred, 4
  problems of, 1
Effective date, 106
Eligibility period, group life insurance, 320
Endorsement
  method of beneficiary change, 115
  method of transferring ownership, 159
Endowment life insurance, 36, 42
  analysis of, 38
  compared with term life insurance, 38
  compared with whole life, 36
  education plans, 42
  make up of, 37
  retirement needs, 43
  uses of, 37, 42
Endowment privilege, 143
Entire contract provision, 105
Equities, 304
Estate tax, 186
Exclusions, health insurance, 271
Executor, 111
Expense reimbursement benefits, 259
Experience rating, 327
Extended term insurance, 33, 147

F

Face amount, 30
Facility of payment, industrial life insurance, 246
Family health policies, 263
Family income coverage, 212
  conversion rights, 217
  income payment period, 213
  settlement arrangements, 215
  term of coverage, 213
Family life policy, 228
  beneficiary and settlement provisions, 232
  conversion privilege, 230
  identification of wife and children, 233
  incontestability provision, 233
  ownership and control, 231
  reinstatement of, 232
  risk appraisal of, 231
  suicide provision, 233
  variations of, 234
Family maintenance coverage, 217
Family needs
  special policies for, 211
  term insurance for, 212

Final beneficiary, 111
Fixed-amount option, 123
Fixed-period option, 122
Flexible-premium annuity, 303, 305
Floating deductible, 269
Fraternal benefit associations, 56
Funding of pension plans, 356

G

Good faith, contract of, 83
Grace period provision
  group life insurance, 329
  health insurance, 278
  industrial life insurance, 244
  ordinary life insurance, 132
Graduated-premium policies, 191
Graunt, John, 13
Gross annual premium, 64
Group deferred annuities, 358
Group health insurance, 343
  benefits, 344
  comprehensive major medical, 348
  disability income, 344, 345
  hospital expense, 344, 346
  major medical, 344, 347
  medical expense benefits, 346
  regular medical expense, 344, 347
  surgical expense, 344, 346
Group life insurance
  creditor groups, 338, 339
  definition, 20
  for employer-employee groups, 316
    administration of, 334
    amount of insurance, 321
    booklets, 334
    certificates, 333
    claim reserve, 328
    contingency reserve, 329
    contributory and noncontributory, 317
    dividends and experience rating, 327
    eligibility, 319
    eligibility period, 320
    enrollment campaigns, 320
    general characteristics, 319
    group/ordinary, 336
    group paid-up, 336
    legal requirement, 317
    length of service plans, 322
    level amount plans, 323
    level-premium group permanent, 335
    maximum limits, 323
    permanent life insurance plans, 334
    position schedules, 322
    premium computation, 325
    premiums, 324
    probationary period, 319
    reserves, 328
    salary schedule, 321, 322
    selection process, 318

Group life insurance, for employer-employee groups—*Cont.*
  unearned premium reserves, 328
  waiting period, 319
  legal requirements for, 317
  origins and development, 314
Group life insurance policy, 329
  assignment provision, 333
  beneficiary, 330
  booklets, 334
  certificates, 333
  conversion, 331
  grace period provision, 329
  incontestable clause, 330
  optional modes of settlement, 331
Group/ordinary life insurance, 336
Group paid-up life insurance, 336
Guaranteed insurability benefit, 206, 226
Guaranteed renewable policy, 251, 274
Guardian, of minor, 113

H

Halley, Sir Edmund, 13
Hand-in-Hand Insurance Company, The, 65
Health insurance, 3
  antiselection in, 265
  development of, 251
  economic losses and, 250
  limited policies, 263, 264
  need for, 250
  risk appraisal, 264
Health insurance contract
  benefit provision, 277
  cancellation, 273
  earliest, 251
  exceptions and exclusions, 271, 277
  face page of, 275
  general section of, 277
  individual, 274
  policy schedules, 276, 277
Health Maintenance Organizations, 349
Hospital expense insurance, 259
  daily room benefit, 259
  group, 344, 346
  maternity benefits, 261
  miscellaneous hospital expenses, 260
  surgical expense benefits, 261
  surgical schedule in, 262
Human life value, 3

I

Immediate annuity, 292
Incidents of ownership, 186
Income tax, federal, 186
  life insurance proceeds, 186

Incomplete change of beneficiary, 176
Incontestable clause, 172
  group life insurance, 330
Indemnity contract, 82
Individual Accident and Sickness Policy Provisions Law, 278
Industrial life insurance, 237
  for children, 248
  definition of, 20, 237
  distinctive characteristics, 239
  an evaluation, 248
  historical background, 237
  mortality rates, 242
  premium rates, 241
  trends in, 248
Industrial life insurance policy, 243
  accidental death benefit, 247
  assignment provision, 245
  benefits for loss of eyesight or limbs, 247
  dividend provisions, 244
  facility of payment provision, 246
  grace period, 244
  option to surrender, 243
  premium payments, 243
  settlement provisions, 245
Inspection, delivery for, 107
Inspection receipt, 107
Inspection reports, 100
Installment refund annuities, 291
Insurability type premium receipt, 102
Insurable interest, 13, 80
Insurable risk, requirement of, 14
Insurance
  beginning of, 5
  definition, 5
  fire, 7
  loss sharing, 7
  marine, 5
  risk reduction, 10
Insurance Company of North America, 66
Insuring Agreements
  Babylonian, 5
  concerning lives, 7
  Egyptians and Greeks, 6
  forerunners of, 2
  Romans, 5, 6
  wagering, 7
Intangible personal property, 152
Integrated deductible, 348
Interest, 60
  estimation of, 61
  on policy loans, 133, 134
  rate of, 61
Interest exclusion, spouse's, 187
Interest option, 120
Interim insurance, 103
Interpleader, 176
Investment element, whole life policy, 31

382 ▪ Index

Irrevocable beneficiary, 111
  and collateral assignments, 157
  vested interest of, 112

J

Joint whole life policy, 235
"Junior estate builder," 227
Juvenile plans, 227

K

Keogh Act, the, 361
Keogh plans, 361
  advantages of, 362

L

Lapsation of policy, 144
Large numbers, law of, 12
Legal reserve, the, 68, 69
Legal reserve laws, first, 68
Level premium, 19, 50
  basis of, 57
  investment and the, 58
Level premium group life insurance, 335
Level premium system, 47
Level term policies, 28
Life expectancy of annuitants, 296
Life income settlement options, 124
  with period certain, 125
  straight life income, 125
  taxation and, 187
Life insurance companies, early, 65
Life Insurance Company of North America, 66
Life insurance contract, as property, 152
Life insurance plans, 20
Limited payment whole life plans, 29, 33
  advantages and disadvantages, 33
  cash values, 33
  premium, 33
  savings element, 35
Limited policies, health, 263
Limited sickness insurance policies, 264
Living benefits of life insurance, 164
Lloyds of London, 6
Loading, 64
Loan, policy
  automatic premium, 132, 133, 136
  request, 133
Loss of eyesight or limbs benefit, 247
Loss of health, 3
Loss of income coverages, 251, 253
Loss sharing, 7
Losses
  economic, 1
  prediction of, 10

M

Major medical plans
  comprehensive type, 269, 348

Major medical plans—*Cont.*
  individual, 252
  group, 344, 347
Marketing system, industrial life insurance, 239
Material misrepresentation, 84, 87, 172
Maternity benefits, 261
Massachusetts Hospital Life Insurance Company, The, 66
Matured endowments, 165
  for college education, 166
  optional settlements and, 166
  settlement under, 165
  taxation of proceeds, 188
Medical care benefits, 252
Medical examinations, 94
Medical examiner, 94
Medical expense benefits
  group health insurance plans, 344, 346, 347
  individual health insurance plans, 252, 254, 261
Medical expense policies
  preexisting conditions, 271
  waiting periods, 270
Minor beneficiaries
  releases from, 113
  special laws, 113
Minors, 75
  statutes regarding, 76
Misrepresentation, material, 84, 87, 172
Misstatement of age, policy provision, 181
Modes
  premium payment, 93, 130
  settlement, 118
"Modified life" policies, 191
Money purchase plans, 355
Mortality
  bills of, 13
  factor of premium calculation, 59
  increasing rate of, 47, 49
  patterns of, 47
  tables, 13, 47, 60
Mortality rate, increasing, 49
  industrial life insurance, 242
Mutual Benefit Life Insurance Company, 67
Mutual Life Insurance Company of New York, 67

N

NAIC Advertising Code, 283
NAIC Model Group Life Insurance Bill, 317
"Necessaries," 76
Net amount at risk, 31
Net level annual premium, 63
Net single premium, 61
  computation of, 62

New England Mutual Life Insurance Company, 67
New York Life Insurance and Trust Company, The, 66
Noncancellable health insurance policies, 251, 274
Noncontributory group life insurance plans, 317
Nonforfeiture benefits, 33, 68, 71, 144
  cash surrender, 144
Nonforfeiture laws, 71, 144
Nonmedical business, 95
Nonparticipating policies, 138

O

Occupation, 196
  policy provision concerning, 281
Offer
  acceptance of, 77
  rejection of, 78
Offer and acceptance, 77
  if initial premium unpaid, 101
  if no receipt given, 101
  in life insurance, 100
  under premium receipts, 101
Offeree, 77
Offeror, 77
Old age, problems of, 3
Option to surrender, 243
Optional modes; *see* Options, settlement
Optional policy provisions, health, 281
Optionally renewable health insurance policies, 273
Options
  automatic, 149
  dividend, 93, 138
  nonforfeiture, 144
  settlement, 118
    agreements, 126
    assignees, trustees, executors, election by, 158
    election of, 119
    fixed-amount, 123
    fixed-period, 122
    interest option, 120
    life income, 124, 125
    requirements, 119
    short-term survivorship problem, 177, 179, 180
Ordinary life insurance
  definition, 20
  policy; *see* Whole life policies
Other insurance, policy provision, 282
Ownership
  incidents of, 186
  family life policy, 231
  life insurance for children, 222
Ownership rights, 152, 186
  transfer of, 153, 158, 159

P

Paid-up benefits, 146
Paid-up privilege, dividends, 143
Partial disability, 257
Participating policies, 137
Partnerships, 91
Pascal, Blaise, 11
Pay-as-you-go insurance, 57
Pay-as-you-go premium, 52
Payees, supplementary contracts, 184
Payor benefit, 225
Penn Mutual Life Insurance Company, 67
Pennsylvania Company for Insurance on Lives and Granting Annuities, The, 66
Percentage participation
  group health plans, 348
  individual health plans, 270
Period certain annuities, 290
Permanent group life insurance plans, 334
Plan, change of, 160, 161
Policy forms, 104
Policy loans, 165
  automatic premium, 132, 136
  benefit to policyowners, 165
  under extended term insurance, 147
  interest on, 133, 134
  repayment of, 134, 136
  request, 133
Policy provisions
  assignment, 154
  change-of-plan, 161
  dividends, 138
  entire contract, 105
  grace period, 132
  ownership, 152
  policy loan, 135
  premium payment, 130
  reinstatement, 162
  required, 132
Policy reserve
  amount of, 69
  computation of, 70
  operation of, 70
  prospective method of computation, 70
  retrospective method of computation, 70
Policyowners' dividends, 137
Power-to-appoint, 110
Prediction of loss, 10
Preexisting conditions, 271
Premium loan, 132, 136
Premium payment, modes of, 93, 130
Premium rates, industrial life insurance, 241
Premium receipts
  approval type, 103
  binding, 103

Premium receipts—*Cont.*
  conditional, 98, 102, 103
  insurability type, 102
Premiums
  computation of, 12, 59
  gross, 64
  group life insurance, 324
  initial, 98
  level, 19, 50, 57, 58
  modes of payment, 130
  net single, 61
  when payable, 130
  requirements for, 59
Prepaid hospital plans, 253
Presbyterian Ministers' Fund, the, 66
Present value, 62
Presumption of death, 168
Primary beneficiary, 110
Private annuities, 287
Probability, 11
Probability of death, 18, 47
Promise, assent to, 77
Proof, burden of, 171
Proposed insured, 97

Q–R

Qualified retirement plans, 353
Rate manual, 90
Rated policies, 100
Receipts; *see* Premium receipts
Recording method, beneficiary changes, 116
Reduced paid-up insurance, 33, 146
Regular medical expense benefits, group, 344, 347
Regulation of life insurance, beginning of, 67
Reinstatement, 161
  contestability after, 174
  family life policy, 232
  health insurance, 279
  policy provision, 162
Relation of earnings to insurance, 282
Release, of minor, 113
Renewal, automatic, 26
Renewal premium, 130
Renewal privilege, term life insurance, 23
Renewal right, health insurance, 273
Repayment, policy loans, 134, 136
Required policy provisions, health insurance
  change of beneficiary, 279
  claim provisions, 280
  grace period, 278
  reinstatement, 279
  time limit on defenses, 280
Required policy provisions, life, 132
Rescission, rules of, 84, 173
Reserve, legal, 68, 69

Reserve, policy; *see* Policy reserve
Reserves, group life, 328
Retirement annuities, 299
Retirement income contract, 301, 303
Retirement plans, 352
  "qualified" plans, 353
    allocated and unallocated funding, 357
    assumed benefit plans, 355
    combination plans, 360
    contributory and noncontributory plans, 356
    defined benefit plans, 355
    deposit administration plans, 359
    funding of, 356
    insured and noninsured, 358
    money purchase, 355
    prototype and master plans, 355
    tax advantages of, 353
    trusteed, 357
    vesting under, 354
  for self-employed individuals, 361
Revocable beneficiary, 111, 112
Riders
  added benefits by, 194
  limitation of coverage by, 194
  term life insurance by, 205
Risk
  definition, 8
  and insurance, 8
  life insurance, 17
  possibility and, 8
  pure, 9
  reduction of, 10
  speculative, 9
Risk appraisal, 94, 99
  employee group life insurance, 318
  family life policy, 231
  health insurance, 264
    factors of insurability, 266
    issue limits, 268
    occupation, 266
    participation limits, 268
    sources of information, 265
Risk appraiser, 99
Risk selection, 100
Risks not assumed, 169
  under the accidental death benefit, 171
  suicide, 170
  under the waiver-of-premium benefit, 198

S

Saving
  investment element, 31
  through life insurance, 44
Selection process; *see* Risk appraisal
Settlement
  death claims, 181

Settlement—*Cont.*
  one sum, 182
  option agreements, 126, 182
  optional modes of, 105, 118
  provisions, industrial life insurance, 245
  section of policy, 105
Short- or intermediate-term policies, 28
Short-term survivorship problem, 177, 179, 180
Simpson, Thomas, 65
Single-premium annuity, 289
Single-premium policy, 35
Society for Equitable Assurance on Lives and Survivorships, The, 65
Sole proprietorships, 91
Special policies for family needs, 211
Spendthrift trust provision, 125
Spouse's interest exclusion, 187
Standard premium rates, 99
State Mutual Life Assurance Company, 67
Statistics, life insurance, 13
Statutes, validity of contract, 79
Straight life annuity, 289
Straight life policy; *see* Whole life policy
Substantial compliance rule, 176
Suicide
  "burden of proof," 171
  clause, 170
  in family life policy, 233
Supplementary contracts, 182
Surgical expense group policy, 344, 346
Surgical schedule, illustrative, 262
Surrender values, 31, 33, 71, 144
Survivorship annuity, 293
Survivorship benefit, annuities, 296

T

Taxation of annuity income, 311
Taxation of matured endowment, 188
Taxes
  death, 185
  federal estate tax, 186
  "incidents of ownership," 186
  life insurance benefits, 185
Tax-sheltered annuities, 309
Teachers Insurance and Annuity Association, 306
Term life insurance
  "buy term and invest the difference," 43
  compared with endowment, 38
  convertible plans, 41
  definition, 22
  earliest policy, 22
  extended term, 33, 147
  for family needs, 40, 212
  fire insurance and, 22
  for mortgage protection, 40

Term life insurance—*Cont.*
  provided by riders, 205
  uses of, 39
Term life insurance policies
  classifications, 27
  conversion privilege, 25
  decreasing, 29
  increasing, 29
  level, 28
  longer terms, 28
  renewal privilege, 23
  short or intermediate, 28
Term-to-life-expectancy policies, 28
Time limit on defenses, 280
Total disability
  definition, 195
  waiting period, 197
Transfer-of-ownership by endorsement, 153, 158, 159
"Triple indemnity," 202

U

Uncertainty death and, 17
Unexplained absence, 168
Underwriter; *see* Risk appraiser
Underwriters, origin of name, 6
Unearned premium reserve, group life insurance, 328
Uniform Simultaneous Death Act, the, 178
Unilateral contract, 78, 82
Unincorporated business, 91

V

Value, cash; *see* Cash surrender value
Value, human life, 3
Variable annuity, 304
  accumulation period, 307
  accumulation unit, 307
  annuity units, 308
  definition, 306
  operation of, 307
  pay-out period, 308
Vested interest, irrevocable beneficiary, 112
Vesting under pension plan, 354
Void and voidable contracts, 75

W–Y

Waiting period
  group life insurance, 319
  hospital expense plans, 270
  waiver-of-premium disability, 197
Waiver-of-premium-disability benefit, 132, 194
  age limits, 198
  in annual premium deferred annuities, 300
  in disability income policies, 257

Waiver-of-premium-disability
   benefit—*Cont.*
   provisions relating to claims, 199
   risks not assumed, 198
   in term policies, 200
Waiver-of-premium-disability claims, 199
Whole life insurance, 29
   for retirement needs, 43
Whole life policies
   with adjusted amounts of insurance, 192
   compared with endowment, 36

Whole life policies—*Cont.*
   continuous-premium, 29
   graduated-premium, 191
   investment element, 31
   joint, 235
   limited-payment, 29, 33, 35
   modified life policies, 191
   special, 190
   uses of, 39
   varying premium rates, 190
Wright, Elizur, 67, 71
Yearly-renewable term policies, 28